TOO RICH

TOO RICH

The High Life and Tragic Death of King Farouk

William Stadiem

Carroll & Graf Publishers, Inc.
New York

First Carroll & Graf edition 1991

Carroll & Graf Publishers, Inc.
260 Fifth Avenue
New York, NY 10001

Library of Congress Cataloging-in-Publication Data

Stadiem, William.
    Too rich : the high life and tragic death of King Farouk / by
William Stadiem.
        p.   cm.
    includes bibliographical references and index.
    ISBN 0-88184-629-5
    1. Faruk I, King of Egypt, 1920–1965.   2. Egypt—Kings and
rulers—Biography.   I. Title.
DT107.82.S74   1991
962.05′2′092—dc20
[B]   91-12564
                                                                          CIP

Permission to reprint portions of Sir Miles Lampson's The Killearn
Diaries *was kindly granted by Sidgwick & Jackson.*

Permission was kindly granted by Sir Edward Ford to reprint excerpts
from his diaries.

Manufactured in the United States of America

CONTENTS

FOREWORD

I embarked on this project with the belief that King Farouk had a greater historical significance than merely that of being the last king who really lived like one. As the end of the monarchy in Egypt, Farouk stood at a terribly important juncture between the Middle East's imperial-colonial past and its revolutionary future. The press had not been kind to Farouk; the erstwhile storybook boy-king had fallen far from grace. I was fascinated by the sheer angle of this fall, as well as its effects not only on Farouk himself, but also on an Arab world that had looked upon him as its leader and its hope. As the embodiment of a millennial tradition of pharaohs and sultans, khedives and kings, how did Farouk, who had it all, lose it all? And how did his losing it all change the Middle East?

Researching this biography was a challenge. Farouk kept no diaries. He rarely, if ever, wrote a letter. He had no Boswell; his closest friend was a largely nonverbal palace electrician. His other immediate retainers, his Albanian bodyguards, his Nubian manservants, his Levantine "kitchen cabinet," were all dead. None left behind any memoirs. During Farouk's reign, the Egyptian press was tightly constrained by considerations of lèse majesté, while external reportage on Farouk was straitjacketed by the security exigencies of World War II. After the war, what coverage there was on Farouk focused on what is now called "life-style" and was of the yellowest hue. Any internal government files on Farouk that may exist in Egypt have proved inaccessible. Aside from rather spotty American and British diplomatic reports, King Farouk left virtually no paper trail, neither during his rule, nor in exile. Attempts to penetrate the Washington archival bureaucracy via the Freedom of Information Act were frustrating exercises of dubious freedom and scant information.

The alternative was oral sources; however, finding people who actually *knew* Farouk was frequently a transcontinental wild-goose chase. Farouk was one of those household names that no one knew anything about. The continuum of confusion ran from King Tut to King Saud to Adnan Khashoggi to Yasir Arafat. Most people associated Farouk with being fat, rich, and somehow awful. Although one wasn't at all sure why, Farouk's awfulness was associated with the amalgam of richness, fatness, and Arabness. The highly prejudicial image, whose roots went back to the Crusades, was that of a present day infidel, a Kuwaiti oil sheikh/arms dealer on a wild binge in Mayfair. "Why do you want to know about *him*?" was the inevitable response. In Egypt, there was rarely a response at all. There Farouk had become a footnote to history, an unwanted reminder of an incongruously sumptuous regal yore, a nonperson. To Egyptians in Egypt, Farouk was a dirty word.

These knee-jerk replies of contempt, disgust, or arrogant ignorance always came from people who had never known Farouk, directly or indirectly. Tracking down others who had come face-to-face with the man was a near-Holmesian endeavor, an adventure that took me across the globe. It was worth the effort. The diaspora Egyptians of the vanished Old Order were a fascinating lot, a singular, endangered-species aristocracy that will surely vanish with their generation. They told me their stories, wonderful stories, as did the mistresses who were now princesses and opera stars and novelists, and the rich men who were now poor, and the poor who were now rich. Their Farouk and the tabloid Farouk were altogether different creatures. The stereotype was shattered, and out of the ogre emerged a real man, a real king. In the end I had a story and a world and a Farouk I frankly never expected.

William Stadiem
Santa Monica, 1991

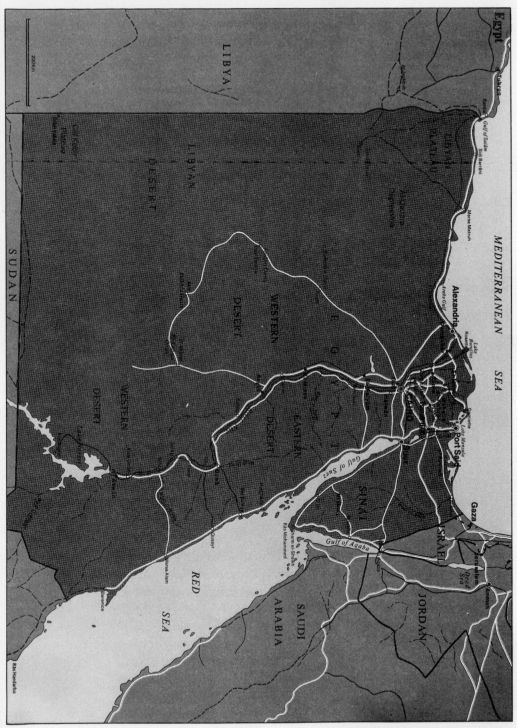

Printed with permission of APA Publications (HK) Ltd.

Map of Modern Day Egypt

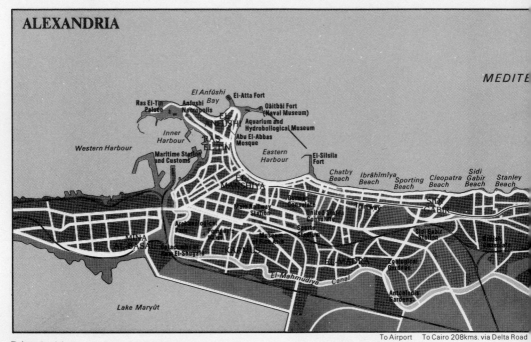

ALEXANDRIA

MEDITE

El Anfûshi
Bay
El-Atta Fort
Ras El-Tin   Anfushi   Qâitbâi Fort
Palace   Necropolis   (Naval Museum)
                          Aquarium and
                          Hydrobiological Museum
Inner   Abu El-Abbas
Harbour   Mosque
EL
ANFUSHI
RAS
EL-TIN
Western Harbour   Eastern   El-Silsila
                               Harbour   Fort
Maritime Station
and Customs
                                          Chatby   Ibrâhimîya Sporting Cleopatra Sidi
EL   Beach   Beach   Beach   Beach   Gabir Stanley
MANSHIYA   Beach   Beach
                        German
                        Consulate
                        United States
Main Railway   Consulate
Station   Tramway   Sidi
Archaeological   Sports   GABIR
Museum   Stadium   Sidi Gabir
Ptolemy   Station
Column
MINA   Museum
EL-BASAL   of Fine Arts
        Pompey's   EL-MAZRA
        Pillar KARMUS
Ras El-Shugale   Zoological
                                                     Gardens
                El-Mahmudiya   Canal
                                              Antoniadis
                                              Gardens
Lake Maryût

To Airport   To Cairo 208kms. via Delta Road

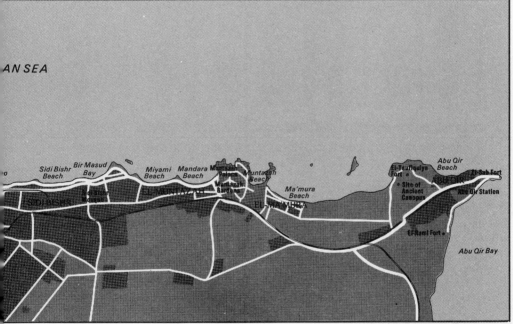

AN SEA

Sidi Bishr Beach

Bir Masud Bay

Miyami Beach

Mandara Beach

Muntazah Palace

Muntazah Beach

El-Mandarh Mosque

SIDI BISHR

EL-MUNTAZAH

Muntazah Gardens

Ma'mura Beach

EL-MA'MURA

El-Tawfiqiya Fort

Abu Qir Beach

El-Sab Fort

ABU QIR

Site of Ancient Canopus

Abu Qir Station

El-Raml Fort

Abu Qir Bay

To Rosetta (Rashid) 57 kms. from Alexandria

Map of Alexandria

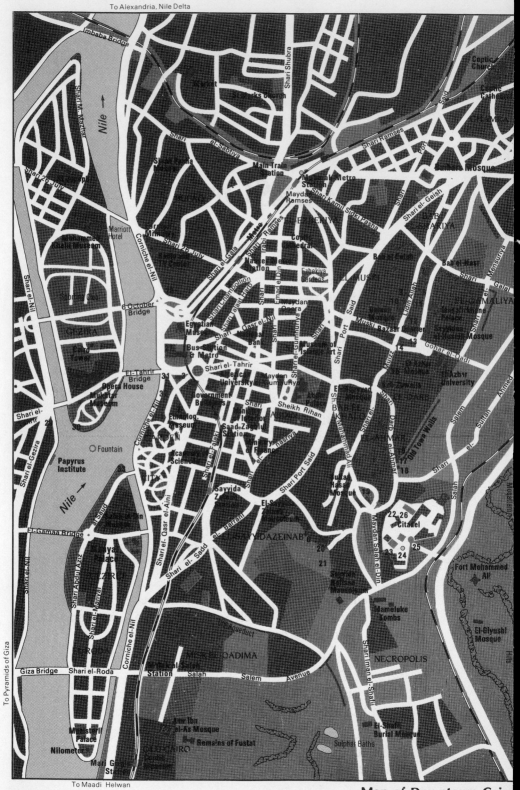

To Alexandria, Nile Delta

Imbaba Bridge

Nile →

Shari M. Mazhar

Coptic Church

Coptic Cathedral

Shari Shubra

Karkat

St. Marks Church

Shari el-Sabtiya

Shari Ramses

Shari Port

Main Train Station

Shari Kamil Sidki Pasha

Mahata Metro Station

Maydan Ramses

Shari el-Geish

Shari Galy

BABA DARIYA

Shari Bur el-July

Shari el-Galaa

Maspero

Shari Ramses

Marriott Hotel

Corniche el-Nil

Shari 26 July

Ahmed el-Din

Bab el-Fetuh

Bab el-Kasr

Mensuriya

Mohammed Khalil Museum

Minon

Shari Champollion

Shari Talaat Harb

Coptic Cathedral

Ezbekiya Gardens

EL MUSKI

Said

EL-GAMALIYA

Nasr el-Plaza

Maydan Opera

Muski Bazaar Unior

Ildin Allah

Sidna el-Hussine Palace

Saydoua el-Hussein Mosque

Egyptian Museum

Shari Qasr el

Bani

Shari Gumhuriya

Museum of Islamic art

Shari Port Said

Gohar el-Oadi

6 October Bridge

GEZIRA

Cairo Tower

Bus Station & Metro

Shari el-Tahrir

Maydan Gumhuriya

El Azhar Mosque

El Azhar University

El-Tahrir Bridge

Opera House Mukhtar Museum

University Maydan

Sheikh Rihan

EL DARB

Shari el-Nil

Government Buildings

Shari

Shari el-Khaimamagh

Shari Sultan Ahmed

Ethnolog Museum

Saad Zaghiul Station

AL-MAR

Old Town Walls

Academy of Science

Ministry of Finance

Maydan nasriya

Shari el-Falak

Shari Port Said

Sayyida Zeinab

Sultan Hasan Mosque

Shari el-Gezira

Fountain

Papyrus Institute

Nile →

Shari el-Manyal

El-Sayyida Zeinab Mausoleum

SAYYIDAZEINAB

Maydan Salah el-Din

Citadel 22 26

25

El-Gamaa Bridge

Manyal Palace

Shari el-Qasr el-Aini

Shari el-Sadd el-Barrani

20

21

23 24

Fort Mohammed Ali

Shari Abdel Aziz

ZIR

Shari el-Roda

Corniche el-Nil

Sayyida Ragkas Mausoleum

Mameluke Tombs

Shari Iman el-Shafii

NECROPOLIS

El-Glyushi Mosque

Giza Bridge

Shari el-Roda

MASR EL-QADIMA Station

Aqueduct

Salah Salem Avenue

Hills

Ministry Palace

Nilometer

Mari Gir Station

Amr Ibn el-As Mosque

Remains of Fustat

OLD CAIRO

Sulphat Baths

El-Shafii Burial Mosque

To Maadi Helwan

To Pyramids of Giza

Map of Downtown Cairo

PERSONAE

Abboud, Mohammed. Scottish-trained engineer who became a multimillionaire industrialist, the richest man in Egypt after Farouk.

Acheson, Dean. American secretary of state who refused to allow aid to Farouk during the coup that deposed him.

Aga Khan. Spiritual leader of the Ismaili Muslims, famous for his temporal wealth and racing stables. Part of Farouk beau monde in pre-Nasser Egypt and postwar Europe.

Ali, Mohammed. Greco-Turkish founder of Farouk's dynasty and the father of modern Egypt.

Ali, Prince Mohammed. Anglophile uncle of Farouk and heir apparent to the throne of Egypt. Detested his nephew.

Andraous, Elias. Farouk's economic adviser. The only honest man in the king's Levantine kitchen cabinet.

Auchinleck, General Sir Claude. British commander in chief of the Middle East during World War II. Known as "the Auk."

Banna, Hassan el. The "Supreme Guide," ascetic leader of the radical fundamentalist Muslim Brotherhood, the society instrumental in burning down Cairo on Black Saturday in 1952. Assassinated, allegedly at Farouk's order.

Baring, Sir Evelyn, Lord Cromer. Hated fin de siècle British overlord of Egypt. Dean of white-man's-burden school of Middle East diplomacy, instilled Anglophobia in Egyptians of all classes. Known as "Over-baring."

Berrier, Annie. French chanteuse discovered by Farouk at the Scarabee Club in Cairo whom he vainly attempted to promote into international star with record "Chanson du Nil."

Caffery, Jefferson. Louisiana-born American ambassador to Egypt during the coup that toppled Farouk. Farouk unwisely trusted that Caffery and America would preserve his monarchy as a bulwark against his Communist-inspired opponents.

Campbell, Sir Ronald. British ambassador to Egypt after Sir Miles Lampson.

Capece Minutolo, Irma. Farouk's "official" mistress during his dolce vita exile, a teenage Neapolitan convent student whom Farouk transformed into an opera star.

Carioca, Tahia. Famous Egyptian belly dancer with whom Farouk was romantically linked.

Cattawi. Prominent Cairo Jewish family that was an integral part of Farouk's royal circle.

Chermside, Anne. English governess to Farouk's daughters.

Churchill, Sir Winston. Prime minister of England. Farouk picked his pocket.

Cohen, Lilianne. Poor teenage Alexandrian Jewess whom Farouk groomed into glamorous Cairo singing sensation at the Auberge des Pyramides.

Coward, Noël. British playwright who had a feud with Farouk during World War II.

D'Emelio, Carlo. "The lawyer of kings and the king of lawyers." Farouk's general counsel in Rome.

Douglas, Sir William Sholto. British air marshal during World War II who led the pro-Farouk Anglo contingent in Cairo and was censured by the British ambassador for his friendship with the king.

Dulles, John Foster. American secretary of state whose antimonarchist stance backfired on him with Nasser.

Eden, Sir Anthony, Lord Avon. British foreign secretary, later prime minister, who had a long history of antipathy to Farouk and a short history of utter detestation of Nasser.

Elwes, Simon. British playboy portrait-painter who allegedly had an affair with his subject Queen Farida.

Eugénie, Empress. Empress of France and guest of honor/mistress of Khedive Ismail at opening of Suez Canal.

Fadia, Princess. Youngest daughter of Farouk.

Faika, Princess. Third, most intellectual sister of Farouk.

Faiza, Princess. "Party princess," most social of Farouk's sisters.

Farida, Queen. Née Safinaz Zulficar. Elegant first wife of King Farouk, who was incorrectly selected for him by his mother, Queen Nazli, for Farida's putative "manageability."

Farouk, King. King of Egypt.

Fathia, Princess. Farouk's youngest sister, banished from Egypt for her romance with a commoner, who later murdered her.

Fawzia, Princess. Most beautiful, oldest sister of Farouk, first wife of the shah of Iran.

Fawzia, Princess. Middle daughter of Farouk, named after his favorite sister.

Ferial, Princess. Eldest daughter of Farouk.

Fields, Gracie. English music hall star, Farouk's first hostess in exile at her Capri resort.

Ford, Sir Edward. Etonian-Oxonian private tutor to Farouk, endlessly thwarted in his efforts to turn Farouk into a perfect English gentleman.

Frederica. Princess of Greece whom Farouk unsuccessfully tried to seduce.

Fuad, Prince Ahmed. Son of Farouk, briefly king of Egypt until monarchy abolished.

Fuad, King. King of Egypt, martinet father of Farouk.

Galhan, Edmond. Fountain pen distributor who became immensely rich as Farouk's (defective) arms procurer in 1948 war with Israel.

Gamal, Samia. Egyptian belly dancer romantically linked with Farouk.

Gatti, Annamaria. Italian hairdresser, Farouk's final date the night of his death.

George VI, King. King of England while Farouk was king of Egypt.

Ghali, Riad. Husband and killer of Farouk's sister Fathia, swain of Farouk's mother, Nazli.

Gordon, General Charles. Also known as "Chinese" Gordon, murdered at Khartoum.

Guinle, Irene. Legendarily stunning Alexandrian Jewess, first mistress of Farouk.

Guinness, Sir Walter Edward, Lord Moyne. British minister of state in Cairo, assassinated by Zionist extremists in 1944.

Hachem, Zaki. Harvard-trained fiancée of Narriman Sadek. She jilted him to marry Farouk.

Halim, Prince Abbas. Dashing Egyptian flying ace and a contender for Farouk's throne, interned by British during World War II for his German sympathies.

Hassanein, Ahmed Mohammed. Farouk's beloved personal tutor, renowned Egyptian explorer, and secret lover of Farouk's widowed mother.

Hilmi, Abbas. Khedive of Egypt deposed by the British on the eve of World War I for his German sympathies.

Hitler, Adolf. German führer who courted young Farouk by giving him a custom Mercedes convertible.

Hohenlohe, Princess Patricia "Honeychile." Georgia-born radio star on *Bob Hope Show* who was one of Farouk's girlfriends. She later married an Austrian prince.

Hussaini, Haj Amin el. Mufti of Jerusalem. Aristocratic, fanatic pro-Nazi Muslim spiritual leader of Jerusalem who helped maneuver Farouk into 1948 war against Israel.

Hutton, Barbara. Woolworth heiress who gave Farouk a $50,000 vase he mistook for a chamber pot.

Ismail. Ambitious khedive of Egypt who built the Suez Canal and bankrupted his country, leading to its century-long occupation by the British.

Khorshied, Itmad. Mistress of Salah Nasir, director of Egypt's General Intelligence Bureau. Wrote a book about the GIB's alleged murder of Farouk in Rome.

Kirk, Alexander. Dandyish American minister in Cairo during World War II.

Lampson, Jacqueline Castellani, Lady Killearn. Young wife of Ambassador Sir Miles Lampson. Her father was Mussolini's medical chief of staff.

Lampson, Sir Miles Wedderburn, Lord Killearn. Giant old-school imperialist British ambassador to Egypt and Farouk's archnemesis.

Maher, Ahmed. Prime minister, brother of Ali Maher, former nationalist extremist who was himself assassinated.

Maher, Ali. Farouk's favorite prime minister, brother of Ahmed Maher, interned during World War II for German sympathies.

Masri, General Aziz el. Farouk's boyhood military tutor who turned on his former pupil and became mentor to revolutionaries Nasser and Sadat.

Montgomery, General Sir Bernard. Victor over Rommel at El Alamein, led postwar British troop withdrawal from Cairo and Alexandria to the canal zone.

Mosseri, Helene. Cairo Jewish high society grande dame who introduced Farouk to potential mistresses.

Nahas, Moustapha. Opportunistic, corrupt pro-British prime minister of Egypt, leader of the Wafd party and longtime adversary of Farouk. Later switched to become king's man.

Nakib, Dr. Adham el. Alexandria doctor who turned the roof of his hospital into Farouk's *garçonnière*. His son became Queen Narriman's second husband.

Narriman. Queen of Egypt. Cinderella-story second child bride of Farouk's. Bore him his only son, left him after he was deposed.

Nasir, Salah. Head of Egyptian General Intelligence Bureau, allegedly masterminded murder of Farouk in Rome.

Nasser, Gamal Abdel. President of Egypt. Leader of the "Free Officers" and architect of the revolution that toppled Farouk.

Naylor, Ina. Stern English governess of Farouk.

Nazli. Queen of Egypt. Wife of Fuad, mother of Farouk. Sequestered in harem by traditionalist Fuad, she became a "liberated" woman after his death.

Neguib, General Mohammed. 1948 Israeli war hero figurehead, first president of Egypt, ousted by Nasser power play.

Nokrashi, Mahmoud Fahmy. Prime minister, former nationalist extremist, like Ahmed Maher, himself assassinated by the Muslim Brotherhood.

Obeid, Makram. Ambitious Wafd party rival of Prime Minister Nahas. Published *Black Book* outlining corruptions of Nahas and family.

Onassis, Aristotle. Greek tycoon whose insult to Farouk killed the sale of the casino at Monte Carlo.

Orloff, Pierre. White Russian geologist husband of Farouk's daughter Fadia, not approved of by Farouk.

Osman, Amin. Anglophile Wafd party leader assassinated by the Muslim Brotherhood.

Pahlevi, Mohammed Reza. Shah of Iran, first husband of Farouk's sister Fawzia.

Rainier, Prince. Ruler of Monaco who gave his close friend Farouk citizenship in exile.

Rommel, Field Marshal Erwin. Nazi leader who almost conquered Egypt.

Roosevelt, Franklin D. U.S. president who held great hopes for Farouk as leader of the Middle East.

Roosevelt, Kermit. CIA operative who gave aid and comfort to the anti-Farouk Free Officers while posing as Farouk's supporter.

Rostum, Abdul. Farouk's chief Albanian bodyguard.

Russell, Sir Thomas. Arabist English commandant of the Cairo police.

Sadat, Anwar el. President of Egypt after Nasser. Imprisoned by British for pro-Nazi activities, member of the Free Officers, revolutionary leader.

Sadek, Assila. Ambitious mother of Narriman. Called by Farouk "the worst woman in the world."

Seif ed-Din, Prince Ahmed. Brother of Princess Shivekiar who tried to murder King Fuad.

Serag-ed-Din, Fuad. "Strongman" of the Wafd party involved in the Black Saturday Cairo riots.

Sergeant, Lucy. Irish midwife at birth of Farouk.

Sharif, Omar. Lebanese-Egyptian movie star whose family hosted all-night gambling sessions for Farouk.

Sherine, Ismail. Second husband of Farouk's sister Fawzia. Nicknamed "Pretty Boy." His appointment as minister of war outraged the Free Officers; was one of the triggers of revolution.

Shivekiar, Princess. Machiavellian first wife of Farouk's father, King Fuad. Her brother tried to murder Fuad; she tried to alienate Farouk from his mother and his wife.

Sidky, Ismail. Prime minister under both Fuad and Farouk, architect of nationalism.

Simaika, Victor. Polo-playing, big-game-hunting aristocratic Cairo Coptic playboy; amatory rival of Farouk.

Sirry, Hussein. Prime minister. Farouk's uncle by marriage to Farida.

Sjoberg, Gerda. Swedish nanny to the young Farouk. Sjoberg kept a revealing diary of palace life.

Skelton, Barbara. Beautiful English novelist married to Cyril Connelly and George Weidenfeld. Farouk's second mistress (after Irene Guinle) during World War II. They continued their affair into his exile.

Stack, Sir Lee. British commander of Egyptian Army whose 1924 assassination was charged to later prime ministers Ahmed Maher and Mahmoud Fahmy Nokrashy, who themselves were also assassinated.

Stevenson, Sir Ralph. British ambassador to Egypt when Farouk was deposed.

Thabet, Karim. Farouk's Lebanese-Egyptian press secretary and most despised member of his kitchen cabinet.

Toussoun, Princess Fatma. Wife of Farouk's cousin, had longtime crush on Farouk.

Truman, Harry S. President of United States when Farouk was deposed.

Valle, Pietro della. Farouk's barber and palace intimate.

Verrucci, Ernesto. Leader of Egypt's "palace Italians." King Fuad's chief architect and chief procurer.

Victor Emmanuel III. King of Italy to whom Farouk gave a home in his post–World War II exile.

Wavell, General Sir Archibald. British commander in chief, Middle East, during World War II, took Sir Miles Lampson's dream job as viceroy of India.

Windsor, Edward, duke of. Friend of Farouk's during schoolboy days in England.

Wissa, Gertie. Leader of Coptic high society in Egypt.

Yussri, Wahid. Dashing sportsman son of Princess Shivekiar who was longtime companion of Queen Farida and object of Farouk's intense jealousy.

Zaghlul, Saad. Firebrand father of Egyptian nationalism.

Zulficar, Youssef. Jurist father of Queen Farida, whom Farouk made a pasha and ambassador to Persia as the quid pro quo for his daughter's hand.

TOO RICH

THE END

I

THE END

There were a lot of mad dogs roaming around the 110-degree blast furnace that was Cairo, but the summer of 1952 was one time when the Englishmen knew to stay inside. The anti-British riots earlier that year had turned the glittering Nile metropolis that had become a Middle Eastern fusion of imperial Rome, fin de siècle Paris, and Edwardian London into something more closely resembling post-Sherman Atlanta. The previous January 26 was known as Black Saturday. On that day, at his vast Abdine Palace, King Farouk was leading six hundred honored dignitaries down a gastronomic gauntlet from caviar to quail to île flotant to celebrate the birth of his son and heir to the throne of Egypt, Prince Fuad. Abdine was a 550-room jewel set in slums, a Buckingham Palace in Cheapside rather than St. James's, and in these slums a mob of thousands of radical student nationalists, Communists, and religious fundamentalists was massing to extirpate imperialism, and particularly British imperialism, from their country.

By the end of the bloody, blackened day, most of the foreign institutions that had given Cairo its international glamour, that had made it Sybaris on the Nile, had been burned down. The rioters destroyed Shepheard's Hotel, the legendary arabesque caravanserai, with its Long Bar and its gin slings and "suffering bastards" that had cooled everyone from Stanley of Livingston to General "Chinese" Gordon of Khartoum to Lawrence of Arabia to Fairbanks and Pickford of Hollywood. They torched Groppi's, which was Cairo's Fouquet's, and Cicurel, which was its Harrods, and Madame Badia's, which was its Regine's, and the Turf Club, which was its Boodles. By July, Cairo, which for the past century had bloomed as one endless European pleasure garden, had become as pleasure-less and lifeless as the foreboding Mameluke tombs in the City of

the Dead. Consequently, King Farouk was more relieved than ever
before to pack his two hundred trunks, assemble his valets and
barbers and doctors and tailors and chambermaids and chauffeurs
and procurers and lead the official government summer exodus to
Alexandria, where everything was quite a bit cooler.

From July to October, ever since the time of Farouk's grandfather Khedive Ismail, who built the Suez Canal and "Europeanized"
Egypt, Alexandria became the country's summer capital. The government operated out of two grand palaces on the Mediterranean.
The "official" palace was the Italianate Ras-el-Tin, overlooking the
site of the Pharos lighthouse and the library that had made Alexandria the greatest center of learning of the ancient world. By now,
scholarship was of minor consequence. After Farouk, cotton, Egyptian cotton, was king. Money and power were what mattered in this
Cannes-like necklace of verdant rainbow-hued villas and brilliant
white Victorian resort hotels strung along the twelve-mile corniche
overlooking the cobalt sea. And no one had more money and more
power than the young king who luxuriated in Montazah, the other,
"party" palace at the far end of the corniche from stately Ras-el-
Tin.

An edifice that was built to be wild, Montazah was a red-brick
and white-sandstone Florentine fantasy palazzo, five stories of
sweeping, columned verandas surmounted by a ten-story vertigo-
inducing Tuscan bell tower, in turn topped by a Hieronymus Boschian nightmare of gargoyles and sinisterly contorted lightning
rods. The visual cacophony of the palace was counterpointed by the
serenity of the gardens, hundreds of acres of jacaranda and oleander
and hollyhocks protected by a cordon of dramatically windswept
pine trees. A herd of a hundred gazelles roamed free in what had to
be one of the great seduction spots of the planet. With the waves of
the Mediterranean crashing on all sides, Farouk had his choice of
courting the current object of his oft-fleeting affections at a hilltop
Palladian temple, a Nantucket lighthouse, a Roman nymphaeum, a
London bridge, or a *From Here to Eternity* surfing beach.

But King Farouk wasn't courting right now. He had a new seventeen-year-old wife and a new son, and, more important, an explosive
country to defuse and rule. Despite the near impossibility of the
task, Farouk felt he had the situation under control. He thought he
was doing a good job. After all, just months before he had made the
cover of *Time,* with the pyramids and the sphinx in the background,

and was lauded as the great white hope of the Middle East. "When a fellah needs a friend" was the punnish cover subtitle. Inside, *Time* called Farouk "the locomotive" for his bottomless gusto and joie de vivre. He wasn't castigated for his three-month European bachelor party—the most expensive moveable feast in history—in which Farouk and his entourage of yes-men and starlets and harlots and Rollses and yachts "did" the grande luxe hotels, restaurants, and casinos of the Continent, from Biarritz to St. Moritz, or for his four-month honeymoon, in which he repeated his bachelor grand tour to share it with his new bride. It may have been decadent, *Time* conceded, but it had panache. The world was entering the Eisenhower era of prosperity, of conspicuous consumption, of la dolce vita, and Farouk was the world's highest liver. Even his girth became part of his myth. A mere sixteen years before he was a tall, slim, devastatingly handsome Prince Charming who became the fairy-tale boy-king of the land of the pharaohs. That such a male beauty could become bloated, bald, and bestial was not now regarded as a fall from grace. Farouk was still the king, every inch the king, and kings could do as they pleased. Decadence was the royal prerogative.

Despite the January riots, Farouk felt nearly invincible, more in control of Egypt than ever before. This was because Black Saturday was directed not against the king but against the British; the king wanted the British out of Egypt as much as any young nationalist-peasant-firebrand or firestarter. The British had been promising to leave Egypt since 1882, when they commenced their "temporary" occupation to stabilize a country bankrupted by Farouk's profligately visionary grandfather, the khedive Ismail, who built the Suez Canal and the grand boulevards and grand palaces that transformed Cairo and Alexandria from medieval Arab backwaters into glorious European-style metropolises. But the British guarded the canal, its lifeline to India and its empire and the cotton that was the grist for its Lancashire mills, as jealously as the khedive's Nubian eunuchs guarded the royal harem. Thus the English turned Egypt into a "veiled protectorate," which was an imperialist euphemism for "colony." They built their Pall Mall men's clubs and played polo and cricket at their Gezira Sporting Club and kept the Egyptians out, even the richest and most social ones. The only words of Arabic most of them knew were *walad* and *koura,* which meant "boy" and "balls." Farouk despised the English, whose arrogant wog-bashing imperialism was personified in the six-foot-five-inch

Etonian-Oxonian old-boy white-man's-burden long-term ambassador, Sir Miles Lampson, later Lord Killearn. Lampson patronized Farouk terribly, called him "the boy." When, during World War II, Farouk refused to appoint the prime minister of Lampson's choice, Lampson ringed Abdine Palace with British tanks and forced the boy at gunpoint to accede to the British will. It was the most humiliating incident both of Farouk's young life and of Egypt's in the twentieth century.

Only after World War II, Lampson's reassignment to Asia, and the commencement of the sun's crepuscular descent on the British Empire did the English troops begin their retreat out of the cities and into the canal zone. Black Saturday, it was hoped, would keep them *in terrorem* and lead to their disappearance from Egypt altogether. But Farouk was very clever here. Although he privately applauded the results of Black Saturday, outwardly he extended to the British his deepest condolences for their charred clubs and charred bodies. Let the British blame the Communist agitators. Let them blame the religious fanatics. But don't let them blame the Palace for their troubles. The British still needed Egypt, its cotton, and its canal, and they desperately needed a friend. Let it be me, Farouk laughed to himself, and it was. George VI invested Farouk as an honorary general in the British Army, a distinction held by no other reigning sovereign. It made Farouk certain that if the anti-imperialist push ever came to antiroyalist shove, one crown could rely on the other. After all, the British still had a huge army in Suez, one that could quell any Egyptian unrest if necessary, and Farouk was not above taking advantage of his old enemies.

Farouk's other allies, he assumed, were the Americans. England's postwar economic doldrums having rendered it fiscally incapable of maintaining its century-old Pax Britannica, whereby England shouldered the burden of keeping the world at peace, the United States had stepped into the Cold War breach as the world's democratic Big Brother. America was particularly interested in the Middle East because of oil and because of Israel and because of the rapacious eyes of Moscow on these volatile, oppressed-peasant-intensive countries so ripe for revolution. Farouk, as would befit a king, was as warm to the Communists as the American Legion post in Peoria would be to Alger Hiss. In fact, Farouk's hatred of communism was as rampant as that of J. Edgar Hoover's or Joseph McCarthy's. He didn't even want the Russians to have an embassy

in Cairo, but he was forced to by Sir Miles Lampson. "Good God,"
the British ambassador told "the boy," "the Russians are our allies!" Farouk was certain the Russians were funding and fomenting
the Muslim Brotherhood, promoting revolution under the cover of
religion, and were the main inspiration behind Black Saturday.

With its starving peasant multitudes and grossly unequal division
of wealth, Egypt had all the right stuff for communism. But it didn't
have the inclination. Farouk understood the country he ruled was
one of the most loyal, peaceful, and accepting nations on earth. He
had five thousand years of obedience on his side. Farouk's subjects
were the descendants of the masses that worshiped the pharaoh as
God and built the pyramids and Karnak and Luxor and the Valley
of the Kings under the most backbreaking conditions. He was their
king. He was an institution. As the repository of the most ancient
tradition of monarchy on earth, Farouk was Egypt's—and the Middle East's—bulwark against a Communist revolt of the masses.

The new American ambassador to Egypt, Jefferson Caffery, was
the dean of the diplomatic corps, having previously headed the embassies in Rio and Paris. Caffery was a Louisianan, a courtly, drawl-
ing Southern-plantation aristocrat, whom King Farouk figured
would be as at home in the cotton fields of the Nile delta as in those
of the Mississippi delta. Caffery had his blacks; Farouk had his
fellaheen. They were fellow travelers. Besides, who else would the
Americans support if they didn't support the king?

The student revolutionaries who burned Cairo down on Black
Saturday were heavily influenced by the Communists. The various
political leaders in the country—the ones who hadn't been elimi-
nated in a tidal wave of assassinations in the last few years—were
widely splintered, and most were suspected of major corruption in
one form or another. Finally, there were the Free Officers. This was
a small radical cell within the Egyptian Army that had not gotten
over their ignominious defeat by Israel in the 1948 war and were
blaming King Farouk for their misfortunes, claiming that he sold
them down the Red Sea by war profiteering from defective arms
that caused the Goliath that was Egypt to lose to the slingshot
Davids across the Sinai. It was true that the palace purchasing
agent, a former fountain pen importer, had acquired a large cache
of World War II Italian weapons that often misfired under battle
conditions and played a part in Egypt's military rout. While the
agent did subsequently become a rich man, there is no evidence that

Farouk himself made any gain from Egypt's loss. Nonetheless, the Free Officers led by Gamal Abdel Nasser and Anwar el Sadat, who had met as young cadets at the Royal Military Academy, used Farouk as their galvanizing scapegoat.

Farouk wasn't worried about these gadflies because he knew that their wartime Nazi sympathies would instantly poison the British and the Americans against them. The old Arab proverb "The enemy of my enemy is my friend" notwithstanding, it was totally unacceptable for these virulently anti-British officers to have been pro-Nazi. The British had imprisoned Sadat for nearly three years during the war for his role as a Nazi secret agent, and Nasser helped support Sadat's family while his comrade was behind bars. The chief mentor of Nasser and Sadat was an overt Naziphile, General Aziz el Masri, who had accompanied the young Farouk to school in England as his military tutor but had been dismissed by Farouk's father when el Masri reported that Farouk had been cutting his classes to attend tutorials of a different sort at a posh Mayfair brothel. As wartime chief of the Egyptian general staff, el Masri had not only passed British secrets to the Germans, but was planning to defect to Berlin. Sadat was a principal in engineering el Masri's flight to the Reich, but the traitorous general's plane crashed, and he spent the rest of the war in Egyptian hospitals and jails.

After the war, when the enemy of Nasser and Sadat's enemy Britain became Russia rather than Germany, the Egyptians found it very simple to make the switch, and much of the Free Officers' rhetoric, published on anonymous mimeo sheets that were leafleted around the country, had Communist overtones. Farouk may not have been a saint, and he may not have been a statesman of Churchill or Roosevelt caliber. But he was very young and getting better and, as he saw it, the least of all possible evils in the very imperfect world that he ruled.

So Farouk lay back and smelled the jasmine and honeysuckle and luxuriated in the soft breezes from the Mediterranean. He played with his new son and, less frequently, with his three daughters from his prior marriage to the exquisite ex–Queen Farida, whom, like his new wife, Narriman, he had married when she was sixteen but, unlike Narriman, was sleek, beautiful, of patrician stock, cultured, and altogether queenly. All Egypt wept in 1948 when Farouk repudiated Farida by saying "I divorce you. I divorce you. I divorce you," according to Koranic law. Few could understand how Farouk

could walk away from this storybook romance for his endless succession of mistresses that ran the distaff spectrum from princesses to
novelists to movie stars to belly dancers to showgirls to b-girls.
Even fewer could understand why Farouk, with his embarrassment
of feminine riches to choose from, would settle on the chubby
dumpling of a teenager he had met at the shop of the royal jeweler
while she and her then-fiancé were shopping for a wedding ring. For
the decidedly bourgeoise Narriman, Farouk's romantic interest was
like winning the lottery. Was Farouk marrying her to prove he had
the popular touch, to endear himself to the masses? Or was he
playing Pygmalion? Before their marriage he had sent Narriman to
Rome for a year of polish—culture, languages, etiquette—to re-
make her in the royal mold. Maybe Farouk had actually fallen in
love. Narriman gave him the one thing Farida hadn't—a male heir,
which assured the continuation of his dynasty.

Succession guaranteed, Farouk, for the first time in his life, became a family man. At Montazah, he gathered Narriman and the
children for swimming outings at the beach of Sidi Bisr, for fishing
trips on one of his yachts and screenings of the latest films he had
sent from Hollywood, Cecil B. De Mille's *The Greatest Show on
Earth,* and *High Noon,* in which Farouk was quite taken with the
young female star, Grace Kelly.

Farouk remained an insomniac. Sometimes, while the Palace
slept, he would rouse his oldest and best friend, and now most
trusted aide, the Italian Antonio Pulli, former electrician at Abdine
Palace who had repaired Farouk's toy trains when he was a child,
and, together, take one of his over two hundred cars for a fast drive.
This July Farouk was in a Cadillac state of mind. He would descend
to the royal garage and pick one of his new red Cadillac convertibles and roar off down the corniche into the city. Farouk had a
law enacted that only Palace cars could be painted red, to prevent
any police confusion by—and interference with—his grand-prix
style of motoring. Farouk's first nocturnal destination was usually
the ornate Royal Automobile Club, which was anything but the
AAA. There, under the crystal chandeliers of one of the *salles
privées,* he would play a few hands of baccarat or chemin de fer with
the Bentley and Daimler owners who were Alexandria's foreign
plutocracy, a Greco-Jewish-Levantine elite to whom he might lose a
quick few thousand dollars and then carry on to his final night spot,
the Mossat Hospital. It wasn't to get his blood pressure tested. The

king had had the top floor of the hospital converted into an elabo-rate penthouse *garçonnière,* the ultimate bachelor pad in Egypt, with a full staff of beautiful nurses and at least one Grace Kelly look-alike, to minister to royal inflammations. Yet he would always be back at Montazah to greet the day with one of his lavish English hunt breakfasts shared with his wife and beloved, long-awaited son.

Despite these occasional midnight runs, at thirty-two, the boy-king seemed to be growing up. For the first time in his pampered life he had started taking some responsibility for his actions and was trying to live up to his name, which in Arabic meant "one who distinguishes right from wrong." To begin with, he had gone on a diet. During the R months he imported planeloads of oysters from Denmark and embarked upon a regime of bivalves that would allow him his protein without the fat but with the added kick of the mollusks' reputed aphrodisiacal qualities, in which he put stock. He still might have his dozen eggs for breakfast, but he had them poached, not fried, and instead of buttery croissants he ate dry toast. His gymnasium-size marble bathrooms in his palaces, famous for their multiheaded showers and pre-Jacuzzi water-jet bathtubs decorated with naked slave-girl mosaics that added an aquatic chapter to the Kama Sutra, had been refitted with vibrating belts, treadmills, and other state-of-the-art reducing machines. Every morning Farouk's Nubian and Sudanese manservants and Circas-sian chambermaids vigorously massaged his body to take off pounds and equally vigorously massaged his scalp with potions dating to the pharaohs to add on strands.

While trying to improve his body, Farouk was also working on his mind, or at least his peace of mind. To that end, he had finally severed all relations with his mother, Queen Nazli, who had dressed him as a little girl when he was a little boy, sequestered him in the harem without a single contemporary male friend until his father sent him to military school in England at fifteen, and had done everything in her power to keep him helplessly dependent on her. Nazli had even hand-picked Farida as Farouk's wife, because she felt she could control her. But she couldn't, and neither could Fa-rouk. Farida had affairs with other men that, given Egypt's man-as-god double standard, pained the king much more than the king's affairs pained the queen. Farouk was betrayed not only by his wife, but also by his mother, who had her own affair with Farouk's chief tutor, the supposedly above reproach Ahmed Mohammed Hassanein, a revered scholar-soldier-explorer who was Egypt's answer to Lawrence of Arabia. But Queen Nazli's dalliances did not stop with Hassanein. She began another dalliance with a handsome, much younger minor diplomatic officer and Coptic Christian named Riad Ghali whom she married off to her daughter, Farouk's baby sister, at the Fairmont Hotel in San Francisco. The entire ménage went to live in Beverly Hills, where both mother and daughter converted from Islam to Catholicism. Shocked and humiliated by the scandal and sacrilege, Farouk, in effect, excommunicated the two women, confiscating their extensive lands and banning them from Egypt forever. Yet Farouk was not oblivious to other family ties. He saved his most beautiful and eldest sister, Fawzia, who had been bartered into a joyless dynastic alliance with the shah of Iran, by arranging her divorce, bringing her back to Egypt, and helping her plight a new troth with a dashing young Muslim officer whom Farouk appointed as his minister of war.

Stabilizing his government was even more difficult than stabilizing his family. In the six months after Black Saturday, Farouk had changed cabinets and prime ministers four times, settling finally on his friend, millionaire industrialist and statesman Hussein Sirry, with a mandate of democratic reforms that would reduce the spiraling cost of living, improve the sorry lot of the fellaheen and thereby take the edge off the hungry dissatisfaction that made them prey to Communist and other agitators. Israel remained a problem that had to be resolved, and over which Farouk was torn. Some of his best gambling friends were Jewish, as were his very favorite mistresses. Jews were among the pillars of Egypt's economy. Many were social lions as well; Queen Nazli's chief lady-in-waiting had been Jewish, as were a large number of the rich cotton brokers and factory owners who composed the pasha class. On the other hand, Farouk had in 1946 brought Egypt into the Arab League, which was dedicated to the maintenance of Palestine as an Arab country. This alliance was odd in that Egypt was not really an "Arab" country in the east-of-Suez mold of Syria or Yemen or Iraq, and Farouk's own ancestry wasn't Arab at all, but Greco-Turkish-Albanian on his father's side and French-Egyptian on his mother's. Egypt was rich and European and cosmopolitan, everything the other Arab League countries were not. All they had in common was language and religion. Nevertheless, because of Egypt's social hegemony, because of its "civilization," it stood at the head of the league, whose headquarters were

established in a great Cairo palace. Thus in one fell swoop Farouk
acquired, in effect, an empire of his own and greatly magnified his
international stature. The only catch in this social contract was that
he would have to become the Arab League's military champion
against Israel, a role that had backfired disastrously in 1948. Now,
in 1952, Farouk prayed and played for time to beg the imponderable
question of Israel until he could at least put his own house in order.

But not too much order. As long as Egypt maintained its chaotic
disequilibrium of Communists, Nazis, nationalists, royalists, Muslim Brothers, Zionists, Brits, and Yanks, Farouk believed he would
never be in danger of losing his throne. Besides, the concept of
monarchy was so entrenched in Egypt that Farouk couldn't imagine
his country without a king. In pharaonic times the king was considered a god, and commonly referred to as Great God. Whether the
king was popular or unpopular was of zero consequence; gods were
gods, and mortals didn't talk back. The Babylonian, Assyrian, Mac-
edonian, and Ptolemiac dynasties that followed the pharaohs maintained the same godlike traditions of the monarchy. Although by
the time the Muslims overran the country in the seventh century
A.D., the king-as-god concept had faded, Farouk knew he could
coast on this entrenched deifying monarchical tradition.

There were only two groups in the country who weren't awe-
struck and cultbound by this age-old sweep of royalty, as much an
immutable part of Egypt as the pyramids or the sphinx. One was
the disaffected Free Officers of Nasser and Sadat. The other was the
American CIA. From its birth as a nation, America had never been
the sweetheart of monarchy. Kings were simply autocrats to have
democratic revolutions against and were always to be regarded with
extreme suspicion. With the supercession of Pax Britannica with the
Truman Doctrine, America was understandably disturbed by the
multi-ring circus of the Middle East that it had assumed the task of
mastering. How could American logic prevail in a largely illogical
situation? Enter the CIA in the person of Teddy Roosevelt's swash-
buckling grandson Kermit, whose basic instincts were to storm the
pyramids the way his illustrious grandfather had stormed San Juan
Hill. Roosevelt had befriended Farouk at the king's lowest ebb during World War II, when British Ambassador Lampson basically
pistol-whipped him into acceding to Anglo orders. Roosevelt
pumped up Farouk that better days lay ahead after the war, when

the British would leave and Farouk would reign over a "free Egypt."

When Roosevelt returned to Cairo early in 1952 as the CIA's man on the spot, Farouk initially accorded a warm welcome to this member of an American royal family. Now, however, Roosevelt had a particular agenda, i.e., to make the Middle East safe for American democracy and ensure that the oil pipeline that fueled the American economy would never run dry. In matters of oil, Roosevelt and the CIA were most prescient in foreseeing the shortages of the 1970s; they didn't want the Russians, who also needed the commodity, to get the upper hand in the desert sands. America had to have, if not hegemony, at least harmony, with the Arab nations, and, Egypt, being the most civilized and prestigious of the lot, was the American linchpin.

In matters of Farouk, however, Roosevelt and the CIA woefully overestimated how malleable the young king would be. Roosevelt would whisper in his ear. Farouk would nod graciously. Then he would go and do something altogether different from Roosevelt's sage recommendations. Farouk was not about to let Roosevelt become another Miles Lampson: too polite to say no, the king was too independent, too proud of his own position to say yes. Farouk's chesslike four changes of prime minister exasperated Roosevelt, who was angling for a stability he saw would never occur on his terms with Farouk.

Roosevelt was even more exasperated by Farouk's refusal to dismiss his kitchen cabinet—a group of hyphenated Egyptians, predominantly non-Muslim, who were representative neither of the country nor of Kermit Roosevelt's ambitions for it. The leader among the inner circle was the Italian electrician Antonio Pulli, known as "the stork" because he could fall asleep standing on one leg; given Farouk's raging insomnia, Pulli had to learn to grab some shut-eye whenever and wherever he could. Another trusted Italian was Pietro della Valle, the king's barber. Farouk's chief economic adviser was Elias Andraous, a Greek widely implicated in questionable land schemes, while the royal chief of procurement (supplies, not women) was a Lebanese, Edmond Galhan, the fountain pen importer and alleged bagman in the Israel war-arms scandal. The "evil genius," the man most hated by the popular press, was a member of the press himself. Karim Thabet, a Lebanese who had the looks of Quasimodo but the cunning of Machiavelli, had been the son of the owner of the Cairo daily *Al Mokhattam*. His printed paeans and encomia to the young Farouk had won Thabet the post of the royal minister of information. Thabet got much more information than he gave, and, as an insider trader, got very rich in the process. In Roosevelt's mind, the whole lot should have gone, but Farouk was loyal to his friends and turned a blind eye to their possible transgressions. In the end, Roosevelt's exasperation led him into the arms of the Free Officers.

Although their disappointments resulting from Egypt's ignominious defeat in 1948 by the new and allegedly "weakling" State of Israel was the proximate cause of the Free Officers' pique, their long winter of discontent actually began as far back as 1929. King Fuad, in westernizing his army, had decided to send his officers to England for advanced training. Unfortunately, just as Fuad's son, Farouk, was rejected by Eton for lacking the proper academic background, Fuad's officers were rejected by Aldershot, the staff college, for having even lower scholastic standards. Many were barely literate. From 1929, then, the Egyptian Army recruited college graduates into its officer corps, in addition to opening up the Royal Military Academy to bright fellaheen like Sadat (his father was a farmer) and lower middle class types like Nasser (his father was a postman). As these meritocratic sorts rose through the ranks of the military, they rankled that they could go only so far because the top positions were held by the ill-educated Old Guard who resented this smart-ass new echelon and blocked their promotions.

The personification of the young officers' resentment was Farouk's commander in chief, General Ferik Haidar, nicknamed "the jailer" because he had prepared for the army not at the Royal Military Academy, but by wardening a frontier prison. Haidar and several of the other most despised old-boy generals were forced into retirement in a series of reforms initiated in 1950 to quiet public unrest about the 1948 arms question, and the young officers rejoiced. The party, alas, was short-lived. Farouk, always the loyalist, quietly reappointed all the generals to their old posts. The Free Officers came out of the closet with their protest and put up their man, graying, pipe-smoking war hero General Mohammed Neguib, the only soldier over forty any of them could trust, against the supposed shoo-in, Haidarite General Sirri Amer, in the 1952 elections for president of the Cairo Officers Club. "The Army Say NO to Farouk" was their campaign slogan, printed on flyers passed out all over the country. The election was small but symbolic, pitting the "people" against the "Palace." Shockingly, Neguib won by a landslide. Farouk invalidated the results. Because an assassination squad led by Nasser had fired fourteen shots at General Amer on the eve of the election but missed, Farouk saw the entire proceedings not as a democratic process or even a popularity contest but as a reign of terror. Consequently, he declared the elections null and void. Now the stakes had really gone up. The Free Officers were getting too free. Pamphlets were one thing, bullets another. Farouk assembled his advisers in the idyllic groves of Montazah to discuss how to defuse this time bomb. The king didn't feel pressed. He figured he had until October to come up with a plan. No one did anything in Egypt in the summer, particularly start a revolution. It was simply too hot.

Farouk's fatal error may well have been underestimating the thermal capacity of the fellaheen. Baking in their Cairo tenements, Nasser and Sadat listened over and over to what became the Free Officers' theme song, Rimsky-Korsakov's *Scheherazade,* and worked themselves up into a heatstroke of paranoia. They became convinced that Farouk was going to have them all assassinated imminently. They decided they would have to get him first. But how? He was the king, he controlled the entire army of Egypt, and the Free Officers group totaled at most three hundred while the politburo, the brain trust, numbered the grand total of—fourteen. Rimsky-Korsakov hardly seemed enough to spur them to the task. Wagner and a tureen of cocaine might have been more appropriate to this insanely hopeless mission.

The Free Officers' only bright spot was the promise of American aid. Kermit Roosevelt had had secret meetings with several of the men of the Nasser-Sadat would-be junta, and Nazi sympathies and Russian symphonies notwithstanding, Roosevelt liked them and conveyed his impressions to Truman's secretary of state, Dean Acheson. Here were young, educated military men America *could* control, Roosevelt briefed his boss. Important in Roosevelt's analysis was his sense that Israel ranked quite low on the Nasser-Sadat hate list, well behind Farouk, the Old-Guard generals, the non-Egyptian local plutocracy, and the British, in that order. With the Free Officers in control, America could pursue its pro-Israel Mideast policy without a blitz of interference from Cairo. In 1952, Nasser, who would go on in later years to become the leader of the Arab world, wasn't an Arabist at all. He hadn't visited a single Arab country. It wasn't Palestine that mattered so much to the Free Officers; it was the way they lost it, and Farouk, not Israel, was the target of their animus. What Roosevelt offered the Free Officers, though, was not tanks and jets and nuclear missiles. All he offered was an act of omission: if their Alice-in-Wonderland coup should somehow work, America would not enter the fray to save the king. It wasn't a grand gesture, yet it was an essential one that lent a certain legitimacy to an otherwise dubious enterprise.

Farouk, of course, had no idea of America's passive complicity. He wouldn't. It wasn't an act of state. It was a state of mind. Farouk was too rambunctious and unpredictable for Yankee tastes, for the American mentality that was best reflected in the famous Holiday Inn ad campaign: "The Best Surprise Is No Surprise." On July 20, Farouk had gone on one of his moonlight gambling runs from Montazah to the Royal Automobile Club. There he was pulled away from the tables by an urgent phone call from Prime Minister Hussein Sirry. Farouk had spies everywhere. The machinations of the Free Officers had been detected. Sirry warned Farouk some sort of attempted coup was imminent and gave the king two options. One was to coopt the Free Officers' one elder statesman, General Neguib, by naming him to Farouk's cabinet as minister of war. The other was to arrest Neguib along with the other plotting Free Officers.

With the roulette wheels spinning in the background and with Alexandria's European beau monde noisily placing their bets, Farouk asked for a rundown on the identities of his adversaries. At the end of the list, he simply laughed. A bunch of pimps, he dismissed the lot and went back to his game of chemin de fer. The next morning he also dismissed Prime Minister Sirry and appointed as his new minister of war the young man he had married to his sister Princess Fawzia to replace the shah, Colonel Ismail Sherine, whose nickname was "Pretty Boy" and who had no record of distinguished service except to his brother-in-law. Then Farouk adjourned to the beach at Montazah and went swimming. The sweet life of summertime Alexandria had lulled Farouk into the deepest sense of well-being and omnipotence.

The announcement of the appointment of the thirty-year-old Sherine reached Nasser in Cairo on July 22 and kicked him into overdrive. Believing that a purge of his little cell of revolutionaries was about to occur, Nasser declared that it was now or never for said revolution. Eight of the Free Officers assembled and made a final plan of attack. Their first step would be to capture the sleeping headquarters of the army's general staff in Cairo at a zero hour of one the next morning. The second was to capture Farouk, 125 miles away in Alexandria. They came up with a password, *nasr,* Arabic for "victory," and a slogan "Resolution and Boldness," and decided that only ninety of the three hundred Free Officers were trustworthy enough to let in on the plans for the coup. Nasser, who was the primary architect of the proposed takeover, had one tangible criterion for trustworthiness, sobriety. Only nondrinkers would participate in what was hoped would be a glorious revolution. With Farouk's spies all around, it was concluded that phones were easily tapped. The eight officers divided up the pool of rebels and spent the day contacting each in person and ordering them not to tell anyone of the plan, including and especially their wives.

What followed was a Keystone Kops comedy of errors. After the eight officers met, Nasser went straight to the home of Sadat to inform him that his task would be to cut all communication lines at the target staff headquarters. But Sadat wasn't in. He had taken his wife and daughter to a matinee at the movies. Nasser left a note under Sadat's door. Then Nasser went to the home of another Free Officer, who was in charge of a supply of weapons. He was at the movies too. Finally, Nasser was arrested by a motorcycle policeman who motioned Nasser's rickety black Austin to the curb. At first Nasser thought Farouk's spies had been particularly efficient. But what was troubling the cop was not the future of Egypt, only the fact that one of Nasser's brake lights was not working. Nasser promised to get it fixed and drove on to zero hour.

By seven that evening the spies had informed Farouk of the planned coup. At nine the king ordered the arrest of all the Free Officers. Two of the group who lived in Alexandria had already come to Montazah to betray Nasser and beg a royal pardon. In Cairo, a meeting was called for eleven P.M. of all senior army officers at staff headquarters. Thus by the time Nasser and another Free Officer arrived at the headquarters he planned to capture, the entire place was ringed by protective soldiers. The revolution seemed over before it had begun.

Driving around the Cairo suburb of Heliopolis, aimlessly trying to figure out what to do, Nasser and his comrade were suddenly surrounded by an army convoy. It seemed that arrest was certain, and it was. Nasser and his ally were held at gunpoint by a young lieutenant. But then a colonel came into sight, and Nasser broke into a huge smile. The man was one of the leading Free Officers, Colonel Yussef Sadek. Sadek had taken over this entire heavily armed and armored convoy and was barreling toward staff headquarters for the takeover he assumed was for twelve o'clock. If he had gotten the one o'clock zero hour correct, he would have been too late. The generals would have adjourned and sent the hounds out for the Free Officers. As it turned out, the convoy charged headquarters, killed two guards and wounded two more, and captured twenty of the most powerful Old-Guard generals in the country. Nasser's men seized the switchboard and began ordering the staff officers and troop commanders to report immediately to headquarters, whereupon they were captured and locked away. The Free Officers took their command, and the Egyptian Army soldiers, well trained in obedience to their superiors, simply took the orders that were given to them by the Nasser headmen. By one-thirty A.M., July 24, Nasser was sitting at the chief of staff's desk, smoking a fat cigar à la King Farouk. Cairo, sweltering, sleeping Cairo, was all his.

At four-thirty that morning, Princess Faiza, Farouk's most ebullient sister, was on a sailing party on a yacht in the Alexandria harbor. Faiza was famous for her parties, which often lasted several days. One of them saw all her guests dressing up in Napoleonic soldiers' uniforms, getting on horseback, and restaging the Battle of the Pyramids, *at* the pyramids, while a movie crew filmed the entire de Mille-ian extravaganza. Among Faiza's companions on the yacht was the American Robert Simpson, the young personal secretary of Ambassador Jefferson Caffery. It was a dead hour, but the harbor was buzzing with naval warships getting up steam. Odd, they thought. Even odder was the fact that all the lights in Montazah Palace were ablaze, and not just the ones in Farouk's master suite. Both Faiza and Simpson had the rudest possible awakenings when they called, respectively, brother and boss. Egypt was under siege.

Caffery, of course, was not surprised. Farouk was. When his valet first told Farouk of "unusual troop movements" in Cairo, the king had dismissed the report as insignificant. But now, in the middle of the night, a time that was usually devoted to card playing or doing the night shift on the Starlite Roof at Mossat Hospital, Farouk was dialing for dollars, or pounds, or whatever he could get. He spoke to

Caffery, who was also summering in Alexandria, as well as to the British ambassador, calling in his chips, saying if they wanted to save him, his dynasty, and Egypt as they knew it, they would have to call out their troops to restore order. Otherwise, he warned them, Egypt would eventually become a Communist sphere of influence.

The Americans had already made their decision. No appeal would work. The British ambassador called Prime Minister Sir Anthony Eden in London and sought orders. Eden hemmed and hawed. The king might have made Farouk an honorary general, but honors were all that England had left to give at this point. Hard pressed enough on their own sceptered isle, the English were on their way out of Africa. A joke Farouk had once made over cards proved prophetic. He had bid four kings and was called on it. When he laid down his hand, all he showed were three. Where was the fourth king, his fellow gamblers asked annoyedly. *I* am the fourth, Farouk roared with glee, and swept up the pot. Then he added that soon there would be only five kings in the world, the kings of clubs, hearts, diamonds, and spades, and the king of England. The age of monarchy was drawing to an end. But Farouk couldn't believe the curtain would be tumbling down so quickly. Aside from the obvious exigencies of Suez, surely England had other sentimental and financial ties to Egypt. Wasn't there a fellowship of royalty? Where were the old school ties? Certainly not to a bunch of pimps, of peasant crypto-Nazi, proto-Communist soldiers. England was quick to send tanks to Abdine to protect its interests in 1942. Where was it now?

While England waffled on its course of action, Farouk kept pressing Caffery to alter his course of avoidance. At the same time, the Free Officers made their first demand on Farouk, that he appoint as prime minister Ali Maher, now a very old elder statesman who, before he had been imprisoned as still another Nazi sympathizer during the war, had served both Farouk's father, King Fuad, and Farouk himself on various occasions in this highest post in government. Farouk thus thought things might not be so bleak. Ali Maher was the king's man. Perhaps reason and royalty would prevail, Farouk hoped.

Wrong! In England, Prime Minister Anthony Eden was on the hotline to Washington and President Truman and Secretary of State Acheson. Since Truman wasn't about to change course and help Farouk, Eden finally concluded that England's current frailties rendered him impotent to do anything other than follow suit. In Cairo, the British chargé d'affaires met with General Neguib and gave him the good news that England would not interfere with the coup. Now that staff headquarters had been captured, and the army was theirs, the Free Officers had accomplished the impossible. Now it was time to sharpen the long knives and get the king.

On July 24, Ali Maher came to Alexandria to meet with Farouk. He presented Farouk with a four-page letter from General Neguib with the Free Officers' further demands for reform, chiefly that Farouk dismiss his kitchen cabinet posthaste and appoint General Neguib as commander in chief of the armed forces. Farouk readily acceded, insisting only that he retain his best friend, Pulli, and his chief valet, Mohammed Hassan el Suliemani. But drunk with their new power, the Free Officers wanted far more than mere reforms. They wanted blood. Nasser dispatched two armored columns to Alexandria, one via the delta, the other by desert, to block any escape on Farouk's part.

Farouk saw that he wasn't even going to have the chance to fight for his throne. Instead, he would have to fight for his life. Before dawn on July 25, he rounded up Queen Narriman, Prince Fuad, and his English nanny, Anne Chermside, trundled them into the backseat of his red bulletproof Mercedes, and took the wheel himself. Riding shotgun, literally, with a submachine gun on his knee, was Farouk's personal pilot and aide-de-camp. Farouk planned to drive from sitting-duck Montazah to the more impregnable Ras-el-Tin for what would be either his last stand or his great escape from the land of the pharaohs. In a second Mercedes were Antonio Pulli, Farouk's three daughters, and their French nanny, Simone Tabouret.

Wary of the imminent arrival of Nasser's army units, Farouk raced at eighty miles an hour on a zigzag course down the bougainvillea-lined corniche and back streets, which were completely deserted because of the military curfew that had been ordered. He sent his daughters on a separate route. Both cars arrived safely at the grand palace, which was being guarded by several warships of the Egyptian Navy, still loyal to the king. Also loyal was Farouk's proud Sudanese Guard, an elite corps of desert warriors that was the fiercest contingent in the entire Egyptian Army. All in all, a force of over eight hundred men set up machine guns, barricaded the windows of the palace, and took their positions to save the king.

Farouk tried to engineer his getaway. He sent his pilot to the

nearby Almaza airfield to prepare one of his thirteen private planes
for a flight from Egypt. But Nasser's army had already seized the
field; all planes were grounded. If not by air, what if by sea? The
problem there was that the getaway boat, the great royal yacht
Mahroussa, in which Farouk's grandfather, the khedive Ismail, had
sailed into exile in Italy in 1879, was in drydock. The new batteries
that ran the ship's newly installed electrical system were still onshore being charged, and the army was guarding the yacht with
very jealous eyes. Farouk was too proud again to ask the British for
help. He'd rather go down fighting on his own than let them humili-
ate him one more time. He did keep talking to Jefferson Caffery,
and kept invoking the officers' Nazi past and Communist future.
How could America, the bane of both movements, allow Egypt to
fall to such an element? But Caffery proved to be nothing but sanc-
timonious. Why didn't Farouk get rid of his "unworthy advisers"
when we told him? he rebuked the king in his dispatches to Washington. Why did he wait to turn to me until it was too late? No,
Farouk had been a naughty boy. He hadn't listened to daddy. Now
he must be punished.

To kill or not to kill, that was the question the Free Officers
debated among themselves. They could execute Farouk right away,
without a trial. Or they could ship him out of Egypt. The trial
option was quickly dismissed; it would give Farouk too much time
to mobilize international support, and the Free Officers were well
enough aware of their own multiple Achilles' heels to invite rea-
soned public scrutiny. The Free Officers' chief mentor, General el
Masri, was all for the bloody termination of his former pupil. "His
head only interests me after it has fallen," he exhorted Nasser and
company. "You must kill and kill and kill. You must slay thousands
in order to purge the country." Nasser, in a rare instance, disagreed
with his idol. The bloodbath el Masri was urging, the purge of the
ruling elite, could result in a hemorrhage that might never clot.
Nasser wanted to run a country. He didn't want a civil war. And he
didn't want to make Farouk a martyr by killing him. A vote was
taken among the Free Officers. By one vote Farouk's life was
spared. "History will sentence him to death," Nasser assured them.

By late morning on the twenty-fifth, Nasser's troops finally arrived at Ras-el-Tin, and a Bren-gun shootout began. Several attacking soldiers were killed by the Sudanese Guard. The Nasserites took
cover in the Ras-el-Tin stables, where they killed Farouk's daughter

Princess Ferial's white Arab pony by stabbing it between the eyes. They also killed three pet dogs belonging to the little princesses. Farouk, a crack shot and game hunter who himself held the Swiss Marksman's International Certificate, stood on the balcony and brought down at least four of the attacking troops, while Queen Narriman stayed in the harem with Fuad and mimicked the boom-boom-boom and the *zeee-eee* of shells to keep the baby prince smiling while the bodies fell outside. In the harbor, Farouk's naval commander requested permission to begin shelling, but the king decided the navy was no match for the army commanding the Alexandria harbor forts. Such a battle would be suicide, Farouk announced, and called Caffery one more time, asking America this time not for Egypt but for his survival. This time Caffery, pressed by Princess Faiza's close friend Robert Simpson, finally gave in. A cease-fire at Ras-el-Tin was agreed. Simpson, in a car bearing the American flag, drove through the gates to guarantee the royal family's safe conduct until the Palace and the junta could come to final terms.

The next morning, July 26, Ali Maher arrived at Ras-el-Tin with an abdication ultimatum drafted by Sadat and signed by General Neguib:

> In view of your misrule, your violations of the Constitution, your contempt for the will of the nation, which has gone so far that no citizen can any longer feel his life, property, or dignity to be safe; and because, under your protection, traitors and swindlers are allowed to amass scandalous fortunes by wasting public monies while the people are dying of privation and hunger; and since these abuses were aggravated during the war in Palestine which gave rise to an abominable traffic in arms and munitions, the Army, which represents the strength of the people, has authorized me to demand that your Majesty abdicate in favor of the heir to the throne, His Highness Ahmed Fuad, on this day, Saturday, 26 July 1952, and that you leave the country on the same day before six o'clock. In the event of a rejection of this ultimatum, you will be held responsible for the consequences."
>
> (Signed) Mohammed Neguib

Farouk joked with Ali Maher, whom he had known all his life, about selling out to the Free Officers and asked him what his quid pro quo was going to be. Ali Maher did not joke back. Farouk sighed and reread the document, then agreed to abdicate on several conditions, chief of which was that he be able to bring Antonio Pulli, who was in his mid-sixties, out of Egypt with him, that he sail on and keep the royal yacht *Mahroussa,* that he take his priceless stamp and coin collections with him, and that his lands in Egypt, and those of his sisters, not be nationalized but be administered on their behalf. Ali Maher left Ras-el-Tin and called Nasser with Farouk's deal points. Nasser rejected every one except a guarantee not to kill the king and to give him a twenty-one-gun salute as he sailed away on the *Mahroussa,* which would drop him off in Naples, just as it had Khedive Ismail three quarters of a century before when the British deposed him. The yacht would then be returned to Alexandria.

At twelve-thirty, an Egyptian Supreme Court justice arrived with the instrument of abdication. Jefferson Caffery had also reached Ras-el-Tin to make sure Farouk signed and left in peace. The abdication signature took place in the sunlit marble main hall of the palace. With its soaring columns and elaborate friezes, it resembled the Roman Forum; Farouk must have felt like Julius Caesar on the ides of March. The two-sentence document was written in Arabic and began with the royal we:

> We, Farouk the First, whereas we have always sought the happiness and welfare of our people, and sincerely wish to spare them the difficulties which have arisen in this critical time, We therefore conform to the will of the people. . . .

Farouk read it and nearly wept. Humble pie indeed. He scrawled his signature, which was so illegible that he had to sign it again.

That afternoon Farouk packed. For his entire family there were sixty-six pieces of luggage, in some of which were hidden jewelry, gold, and priceless objects, still only a minute fraction of the treasures that had been in Farouk's estate. The oddest possessions that were being taken were numerous crates of champagne and Scotch, especially since Farouk's one major concession to being a devout Muslim was that he did not drink liquor. Of course, the Free Officers, who wanted to believe the very worst about the king, were convinced that his teetotaling was just a sham. The boxes of spirits, they laughed, were evidence of their correctness and Farouk's hypocrisy. In this instance, Farouk had the last laugh. The liquor crates were packed with gold ingots and represented the bulk of the fortune Farouk was able to get out of Egypt with him.

After packing, the king bathed one last time in his sunken tub and dressed for his final farewell. He chose his white admiral of the fleet uniform, with full regalia, out of respect to the navy that had stayed loyal to him. Then he assembled with Narriman, Fuad, and his daughters in the bejeweled, inlaid throne room of Ras-el-Tin to say good-bye to his sisters Fawzia and Faiza, who had gotten dispensations to see their brother one last time. By five-thirty, Ali Maher and Jefferson Caffery joined the royal party. Farouk made a major point of asking his young daughters whether they were coming with him to Italy, and leaving their mother Farida behind, of their own free will. Each stepped forward and declared that she was. Farida was conspicuous in her absence at this farewell party, as were most of Farouk's kitchen cabinet, laying low in dread of the prospective ramifications of their guilt by association.

At five forty-five, Farouk led his family down the grand marble staircase into the courtyard of the palace. There, amid the palms and the flowers and crying doves, the Sudanese Guard paid him their final salute, tears running down their dark, still-impassive faces. The Egyptian national anthem was struck up by the royal band, as the Nile green Egyptian crescent flag was slowly lowered, folded, and presented to the king. Farouk gave his warmest, saddest embrace to his man Friday, Antonio Pulli. How Farouk would miss him. Farouk gave a departing cheek kiss, in his mind the kiss of death, to Ali Maher and Jefferson Caffery, who would soon be taking all the credit for having saved the king's life.

As Farouk walked up the gangway, Narriman walked behind him while nanny Chermside cradled the new king in her arms. Farouk was in a daze. How could everything have fallen apart so precipitously? How could England have betrayed him? Even worse, how could America? How could they have been so stupid? Couldn't they foresee a Communist *deluge*? He cursed the weather, the enervating desert heat that had dichotomized the capital for the summer and created the torpid power vacuum that had allowed the Free Officers their dusty window of opportunity. He also cursed the gentility of his subjects and the blind obedience of his soldiers, their unquestioning loyalty to whoever gave them orders. The centuries of dogged docility to pharaohs and emperors and sultans and caliphs and kings, of building their pyramids and temples and tombs and mosques may have made the masses of Egypt temperamentally incapable of revolting against Farouk. By the same token, they were also temperamentally incapable of revolting *for* him. Maybe they were all victims of the heat. Maybe Farouk was a victim of hubris.

A moment after six o'clock, Egypt's new ruler, General Neguib, roared up to the quay in an army jeep. His driver, not knowing his way around the palace grounds, had taken a wrong turn. Neguib made his way to Farouk, who was on the bridge of the yacht, and saluted him. Farouk saluted back. Neither knew what to say. Neguib broke the ice, calling him "effendi," which was like "sir," but certainly not "your majesty." Then the general told the ex-king that he was the only Egyptian officer who had submitted his resignation in 1942 in protest of Sir Miles Lampson's act of imperial aggression at Abdine Palace, telling Farouk of how loyal to the throne he used to be.

Farouk was polite. He told Neguib he would have waited for him at the quay, but since the terms of his abdication stressed his departure at six o'clock, Farouk was merely trying to be punctual. Farouk asked Neguib to take good care of the Egyptian Army, which, he reminded Neguib, his great-grandfather had created. Farouk closed by warning Neguib that he faced a monumental task. "It isn't easy to govern Egypt, you know."

Before he departed, Neguib asked Farouk not to blame him for the coup. He started to refer to "the others—the fanatical ones," then held his tongue. Tears filling his eyes, he bowed and kissed Farouk's hand. Then he turned and left the yacht, which cast off its moorings. As the twenty-one guns boomed their tribute from an adjacent naval frigate, the *Malik Farouk,* the *Mahroussa* set sail away from the Mediterranean palace, the Quirinale-by-the-sea that the original dynast Mohammed Ali had built, and past where the Pharos lighthouse had stood and the library of libraries and the greatest civilization the world had ever known, the land of Tutankhamen and Ramses and Alexander the Great and Ptolemy and Cleopatra . . . and Farouk. It was all over now. In a few days, the same press that had put Farouk on the cover of *Time* would be dancing on his living grave. The "locomotive" had been derailed, and the blood on the tracks would provide an endless feast for the fourth estate. The last king to really live like one had left his throne. The institution of monarchy would never be the same.

Nor would Egypt and the Middle East. Soon the purges would

start and the long knives be drawn. The foreigners would flee and the elaborate "Western" civilization of the Mohammed Ali dynasty would crumble. The glamour would go, and the money would go, and Cairo would deteriorate beyond belief, from the London and Paris and Rome of the Nile to a Tijuana with antiquities. More important, the siren call of Moscow would drown out the muezzin call of the minarets. Egypt was ripe for revolution, but hardly the democratic one Truman and Acheson and soon Eisenhower and Dulles would have liked. Yes, Eisenhower was a military man, and so were Neguib and Nasser and Sadat. But the similarities ended, as did the goals and values, with the uniform. These were ruthless times, and Nasser, the guiding light behind the coup, was the most ruthless of men. For all his excesses and frivolities, King Farouk, all 250 pounds of him, gave the powder-keg Arab world a sense of gravity. Without him the ballast was gone. America and England had placed their bets against Farouk; these bets were self-fulfilling prophecies. Yet if what they were looking for in what replaced him was control and predictability, they couldn't have been more grievously wrong.

II

MISTRESSES

Aside from Nero, Caligula, and Vlad the Impaler, few monarchs in history have endured a worse public image than Farouk of Egypt. The tabloids' wildest dreams were realized in Farouk, who raised the eyebrows of the entire world. Gargantuan gastronome, ruthless seducer, profligate gambler, war profiteer, Nazi ally, museum level kleptomaniac, imperial wastrel, these were ways the press described him. If there were seven deadly sins, Farouk would always find an eighth. Here was a man who ate a dozen eggs for breakfast and forty quail for lunch. He invoked the *droit du roi* over the most beautiful wives and daughters of his subjects and inspired himself to such conquests with the world's most elaborate pornography collection. Whether it was a stunning woman or a priceless art treasure, he took whatever he wanted; he even pickpocketed Winston Churchill's watch. Small wonder, then, that MI5 hated him. The CIA hated him too. All of which could make one stop and wonder. Could Farouk be all *that* bad?

That bellwether of fifties American values, *Life* magazine, provided a quick take on the slough of loathing into which Farouk was dispatched. The date was August 18, 1952, barely a month after Farouk had been deposed by the coup d'etat of the Free Officers, secretly aided and abetted, as would be learned in the cynical sixties, by the CIA. At the time, however, *Life* and its confreres in the fourth estate hailed the coup as a blow for democracy. On the left page of *Life* was a piece "Well Loved King;" subheaded "Grateful Norway gives hardy old Haakon VII a memorable party on his 80th birthday." On the right, "Unmissed Prince: King Farouk puts on a bathing suit while Egyptians make haste to forget him." Sartorially, Farouk had made a dreadful move. While the venerable and imperially slim Norwegian monarch looked appropriately regal in a double-breasted suit, Farouk, in exile at a Capri resort, was anything but pharaonic, with his huge hairy paunch stretching his near-bikini bathing trunks to their outer limit. Clutching a fat cigar as he walked past a swimming pool, he wore white espadrilles, dark gold-rimmed glasses, and a most unfortunate canvas hat with its front brim rolled up, à la Art Carney in *The Honeymooners.* The only thing he fit into was the stereotype of the ogrish Hollywood producer. The image was reiterated by *Life* some months later in a feature entitled "When in Rome, or . . . Gossip Is a Girl's Best Friend" on an international group of five ravishing charmers (American, Swedish, Austrian, Belgian, and Danish) in varying states of dishabille, who were "being pushed into fame, not because of their theatrical talents, but because of their friendship for a well-known and tireless nightclub habitué." *Life* didn't even have to identify the night crawler by name. The world knew.

While Farouk was being shuffled off by the press into the seedy wings of the public's imagination, *Life* was lavishing the royal treatment on another Oriental potentate. Resplendent in a vest and blue blazer on the cover of the November 3, 1958, edition was the most dashing member of that year's Harvard senior class, the Aga Khan. Back in Cambridge after the ultimate junior year abroad ministering to his twenty million Muslim followers, Prince Karim, or "K" as his classmates called him, was shown in a host of very democratic activities: playing soccer, studying in his Leverett House dorm room next to a nondescript print "he bought for $20"; getting his own mail under a directory that ran the American class system from Cabot to Zimmerman; and straphanging on the MTA. Imagine King Farouk on a subway. Aside from Prince Karim's grandfather's (the late Aga Khan) schoolmarmish secretary, and despite Karim's father Aly Khan's reputation as a playboy that rivaled Farouk's (Aly had married Rita Hayworth), there wasn't a woman in the entire article. Nevertheless, *Life* felt compelled to address the distaff issue: "Of girls he maintains a rigid silence except for saying, 'I thank God for women.' "

The Henry Lucians had once given King Farouk the Aga Khan treatment. In 1938, as a six-foot, slim, incredibly and blondely handsome boy-king, he, too, was on the cover of *Time.* He was quoted in a speech as chief boy scout of Egypt: "Young men and young women of Egypt, it is our task to bring our bodies into subjugation to our wills." A few years later, when *Life* did an exclusive photo spread on the 550-room Abdine Palace, which it called "possibly the most magnificent royal palace in the world," the magazine described the cover-boy monarch as "the very model of a young Muslim gentleman." He was portrayed as a family man, with his delicately ravishing Queen Farida; as a sportsman, in white hunter's pith helmet, khakis, and a Mauser carbine, with the head of a rare ibex he had shot; and as a holy man, in fez and morning coat under the long and foreboding portrait of his father, King Fuad, in Abdine's hall of ancestors. In short, he seemed the perfect king, a public relations fantasy of royalty.

How could this ideal young man, who came from a dynastic tradition that treated his as much like a god as any man could be on earth lose *everything?* So what happened? Born in 1920, crowned and adored in 1936, deposed and despised in 1952, and dead in 1965, King Farouk, in his brief life of extremes, has to be one of the great curiosities of the twentieth century. The characters in his story are as extreme as he was: The father, King Fuad, the destitute aristocrat manipulated to the throne by his all-powerful yet forbidden Jewish mistress. The mother, Queen Nazli, who sexually liberated herself after being locked in the royal harem for sixteen years. Farouk's tutor, Ahmed Mohammed Hassanein, the Lawrence of Arabia of Egypt and the object of his mother's desires. Antonio Pulli, the Italian immigrant who repaired young Farouk's electric trains and became the king's best friend and chief procurer. Queen Farida, the most perfect girl in Egypt, the Jacqueline Bouvier of the Nile, hand picked by Nazli for her son because the older queen felt she could control the younger one, who turned out to be darker than anyone could know. Queen Narriman, the ultimate underdog, the commoner who won the national romantic sweepstakes to give the king an heir. Fawzia, Farouk's most stunning sister, whom he sold into bondage in an arranged dynastic marriage to the shah of Iran. Fathia, Farouk's baby sister, whom he banished from the kingdom, along with his mother, for being in love with the same man, who, in the most bizarre of all plot twists, ultimately murdered the sister. Sir Miles Lampson, the arrogant, omnipotent British ambassador and black knight of Farouk's life, whom Farouk vowed to vanquish at any cost. The two peasant firebrands, Nasser and Sadat, whose singular goal was to "get" the king. There are Churchill and Roosevelt, Stalin and Hitler, Eisenhower and Dulles, Prince Rainier and Princess Grace, the duke of Windsor, Barbara Hutton, Aly

Khan, and Porfirio Rubirosa. And, finally, as interesting as anyone in a saga in which sex is a highlight as well as a key, there are the mistresses.

Irma Capece Minutolo, the last and "official" mistress of King Farouk, had played her most recent role as an oversexed opera singer in Franco Zeffirelli's 1988 film *Young Toscanini.* The movie starred the former stunt boy and Francis *(The Outsiders)* Coppola discovery C. Thomas Howell as the eighteen-year-old maestro-to-be and Elizabeth Taylor as the aging diva who helps get Toscanini his first chance to conduct, in Rio de Janeiro. Irma played a member of a touring opera company who tries, unsuccessfully, to seduce Toscanini on the ship from Genoa to Brazil. Irma also sang in the film's *Aida,* opposite Taylor's slave, as the pharaoh's daughter. If Taylor was playing the Maria Callas of the time, Irma was playing the Irma, a well-known, if not celebrated, well-regarded, always-working Italian opera singer.

The gossip sheets of the fifties had described Irma as a cab driver's daughter, Miss Naples of 1953, a bit actress. Pictures of her beside Farouk in the Café de Paris on the Via Veneto revealed a slightly exaggerated fusion of the two pneumatic icons of the period, Sophia Loren and Anita Ekberg, fire and ice. The Italians even made jokes about her name, rechristening her "Irma Capace de Totalo" or "Irma, Capable of Anything." The image was a décolleté blond Gypsy, big eyes, big lips, big bosom, something out of a Fellini movie. The present-day reality was more like David Lean. Irma's apartment in a verdantly luxurious gated and guarded low-rise modern condo complex on the Via Valgardena, in a tony outskirt of Rome, was an exercise in good taste, as was Irma. Tall and statuesque with reddish hair and bright green eyes that, in fact, matched the color of the Egyptian flag, Irma, about fifty, wore a red silk dress that was very Via Condotti and vivaciously served Campari and soda in her sedate gray living room filled with modern paintings and pictures of opera and cinema colleagues such as Zeffirelli and Lina Wertmuller. She had just won the Maria Callas award for being the leading Italian female singer of the year, and was very proud of this. She was even prouder of her relationship with King Farouk.

Irma adored Farouk and the life they led. In a place of honor on her mantel were two smiling pictures of her and Farouk, one in the

Alps on skis, another, at the beach, in bathing suits. Both were of heroic proportions, though the heroism played better with Irma.

"The dolce vita died when he did," Irma said. But before recounting her royal romance, Irma insisted on exposing her own royal roots. Neapolitan cab driver? According to Irma, the Capece Minutolos were, along with the Caracciolos, one of the two great families of Naples, dating back to the 1100s and having given the country fifteen cardinals and an acting pope. Proudly displaying her family's genealogy chart and its coat of arms, Irma explained that her father, in the dislocation following World War II, found himself, not behind the wheel of a hack, but at the Lancia dealership in Naples. Her mother had been a fledgling opera singer who gave up her career to marry and raise Irma and her brother, who grew up to work at the U.S. embassy on the Via Veneto in Rome.

It was Irma's mother who led her, indirectly, into contact with Farouk by bringing her sixteen-year-old daughter to the Canzone del Mare, the Capri beach club owned by British music hall star Gracie Fields, where Farouk's ill-suited *Life* photo by the pool was taken. Actually Irma had met Farouk several years before when she had been chosen by the members of the Rowing Club of Naples as their flower girl to present a bouquet to the then-reigning Egyptian monarch when he was feted at a banquet at the club.

Thus there was a mutual sense of déjà vu when the exiled ruler spotted the now-ripe adolescent in a bikini diving into the Canzone pool. Emerging from the water, Irma locked eyes with Farouk, who lounged, wearing a white cotton terry-cloth robe emblazoned with the Egyptian royal crown, in a nearby chaise conversing with an important Neapolitan lawyer. Farouk rose, walked over to Irma, took off his dark glasses, stroked her reddish-blond hair, and complimented her on her form. The lawyer recognized her and reminded Farouk of the flowers she had presented to him at the Rowing Club. The next day Farouk returned the favor. He sent 150 roses to the hotel where Irma was staying with her mother.

Irma said she was smitten by Farouk on the spot, struck by the beauty of his blue-green eyes, which she described as "sphinxlike." Didn't his girth bother her? Not at all. She remembered him when she was thirteen and he was king. The girth, she felt, became him. It was part of his royalty. The baldness, the fatness, the glasses, all may have made him less of a boy. To Irma they made him more of a king. Although Farouk was a mere thirty-two himself, he seemed much older, much grander than his years.

The next night, a Miss Capri pageant was being held at the Canzone. Although Irma said it was unseemly for a soi-disant highborn Neapolitan to enter such a contest, her host in Capri, another highborn Neapolitan who happened to be on the jury, felt it would be fun and pushed Irma's mother into letting her daughter join the field of twenty contestants. Irma won. Farouk was in the first row.

Although Irma and her mother were supposed to stay in Capri for the entire month, the arrival of Farouk's flowers sent the mother packing herself and her daughter back to Naples. For Mrs. Capece Minutolo, no advance could have been more unwanted. After all, not only did Farouk have perhaps the world's worst reputation as a playboy, but he was still a married man. His second wife, Queen Narriman, with whom he had been initially smitten when she was sixteen (exactly as he had been with his first wife, Queen Farida), was living with him and their infant son, Fuad, and Farouk's three daughters by Farida, Ferial, Fawzia, and Fadia. Farouk's family had a fetish for F's. His father, Fuad, thought the letter brought good luck, hence his naming Farouk's four sisters Fawzia, Faiza, Faika, and Fathia. Irma's mother was not interested in her daughter becoming another F.

But the king was too recently unthroned to conceive of not having his royal way. He tracked down Irma's address in Naples and began sending huge bouquets of flowers every single day, bouquets which Irma's mother intercepted and promptly disposed of. He then started calling. Irma was not allowed to answer the phone. One day, however, her mother was in the garden and Irma picked up the buzzing receiver. It was the king. He wanted to know what Irma thought of the flowers. What flowers, she asked. Farouk got right to the point, in perfect Italian, in a strong, soft, utterly persuasive voice devoid of self-doubt. He told her he was in love with her, that she was his only ray of light in the dark night of his exile. He wanted her to become his third queen. What sixteen-year-old could resist?

But then Farouk disappeared. The flowers stopped. The phone didn't ring. The royal courtship was over before it began. In September Irma returned to her high school studies at the Escuola Principessa Maffalda with a glum determination. This was the ultimate heartbreaking schoolgirl crush, but her mother had made her so ashamed of it, Irma didn't dare tell her friends. Then, one day about a month later, the family driver who took Irma to and from school wasn't in his car waiting to take her home. His Alfa Romeo was there; the driver wasn't. Down the road from the school, Irma couldn't help but notice an emerald-green Rolls-Royce glinting in the sun. Then, from behind, a man in a dark suit who had the confidence-inspiring air of a banker came up to her and announced that he was King Farouk's secretary. Would she come with him?

Carrying her book bag, Irma followed the secretary down the palm- and bougainvillea-lined school driveway to the Rolls-Royce. An Egyptian crescent flag flew from the antenna. A coat of arms was embossed on the front door. The secretary opened the door with smoked windows. Inside, waiting in the backseat, was King Farouk, looking striking in a pinstripe suit.

He took off his glasses and peered at Irma with those hypnotic sphinxlike eyes. She was trembling. She had never even kissed a boy. What would she do with a king? Farouk reached over and stroked her hair. He adored that reddish-blond hair. Irma said she was worried about her driver. Farouk assured her the driver was taken care of, that he would take her home in fifteen minutes. Farouk again told her how much she meant to him, that he had fallen in love with her. Trembling, Irma repeated some of the calumny that she had heard from her mother, about all the women, the thousands of women. Farouk laughed in an all-knowing way that somehow made her feel better. The others meant nothing to him. Irma did. Come with me, he proposed to her. Come and be my third queen. He stroked her hair again. This time, though, Irma broke into tears and bolted from the Rolls. She ran up the hill to the Alfa Romeo. The driver was waiting. She offered a deal with him. If you say nothing, I'll say nothing. He nodded assent.

Two more weeks went by. Not a word from Farouk, who was living with his family in a great estate outside Rome in the Alban Hills. The town was called Grottaferrata, next to the summer palace of the popes at Castel Gandolfo. During a recess, the school janitor approached Irma and told her she had a call in his quarters. It was Farouk. He promised her that the next day she would be getting another bouquet of roses. Except in this bunch there would be one imitation flower. Find it, he instructed her, and examine it closely. Very closely. And then call me.

The following day a huge bunch of roses arrived at the janitor's room. Next to the clanging anvil chorus of pipes and boilers, Irma examined the delicate flowers. Finally she found the imitation. She opened the bulb and was left breathless. Inside was a huge ruby ring encrusted with diamonds. The poor janitor had never seen anything like this. Her hands shaking, Irma dialed Farouk's private number. After being passed through three functionaries, Farouk answered. She told him that he shouldn't have given her anything like this. Of course he should, Farouk laughed. But why me? Irma wondered. Why me? Because you're different, Farouk said. Because you're a child. Because you're so pure. Because I adore you. He asked her simply to think about him for one hour every day and promised to see her when he returned to Naples in two weeks.

Irma broke her one-hour pledge to Farouk. She thought about him twenty-four hours a day. She read through every tabloid, every *Oggi,* every *Gente,* for daily news of Italy's most famous exile. The nightclub escapades with the Swedish blondes and the Dutch red-heads gave Irma cause for despair, as did the existence of Farouk's wife. But Queen Narriman also fueled Irma's fantasies, and gave her hope. For Narriman was a commoner who had married the king. Like Irma, Narriman had been only sixteen, blond, volup-tuous, and, of course, virginal. Her royal wedding was straight out of the Arabian nights; her four-month royal honeymoon in Europe was probably the longest and most expensive in history, Farouk lavished his new bride with priceless jewels and priceless art and haute couture and haute cuisine, block-booked the crème of grand hotels, from the Danieli in Venice to the Carlton in Cannes to the Royal Monceau in Paris, dressed the entire honeymoon party of sixty on the royal yacht in identical blue blazers, white ducks, and yachting caps, and took them ashore in a fleet of Rolls-Royces. Life with King Farouk was an endless magic-carpet ride. Irma was dy-ing to take it. If it could happen to Narriman, it could happen to her. Narriman was a peasant. Irma was a Capece Minutolo.

The courtship continued with Farouk's return to Naples. Irma left school early and took a train to the seaside area of Posilipo, where she met the king in the private room of one of the great nautical restaurants there. As she ate spaghetti alla vongole veraci, Farouk stroked her hair, and nothing more. He gave her a letter to take home with her. Reading it was even more thrilling than receiv-ing the ruby in the fake rose. In the note he poured out his deepest sentiments. He signed it "Re Farouk." Irma read the one-page letter over and over. Yet, again, Farouk disappeared from her life. Perhaps her rival Narriman had won, Irma feared.

In March 1953, the newspapers broke the headlines that Narriman had left Farouk. The king made a public statement blaming Egyptian Premier Mohammed Neguib for breaking up "his happy marriage by using that most powerful of all weapons, the mother-in-law." Irma studied the pictures of Narriman in black ermine and dark glasses with her identically dressed mother, Assila Sadek, and her black poodle, Jou Jou, boarding a plane to Geneva. Narriman denigrated the marriage to reporters: "It was the will of Allah, and when Allah wills he places scales before our eyes and seals our ears to wise counsel." She vowed to go back to Cairo, revolution notwithstanding, get a divorce, and get custody of her son, Fuad, now fourteen months old and now nominally King Fuad, king of Egypt and the Sudan, since Neguib, Nasser and the generals, though having deposed Farouk, had not yet abolished the monarchy. Under Islamic law, a child was required to remain with its mother until age seven. To the generals King Fuad was the grand prize. They would use all the tricks in their arsenal to lure the nineteen-year-old Narriman back to Egypt, not least of which was *Mère* Sadek, who Farouk publicly described as "the most terrible woman in the world."

Within weeks of Narriman's departure for Switzerland and then Cairo, Irma got another phone call at the school janitor's. Now she knew she would be queen number three. Farouk was inviting her to come to live with him at Grottaferrata. To Irma, whose only intimacy with the playboy king had been to let him fondle her hair, it seemed tantamount to a proposal. To Irma's mother it seemed insane. As for her old-world father, the matter was never even presented to him as a possibility. Nevertheless, Mrs. Capece Minutolo came to see how lovesick her daughter was. She also may have realized that no matter how many cardinals or Knights of Malta there may have been in the family tree, there wasn't one white knight riding to the aid of the family today. She saw the diamond. She saw Farouk's letter. Although Farouk had declared on his arrival at Capri, "I am no longer a rich man," no one on earth believed him. His fortune in Egypt had been estimated at upwards of $50 million, one of the greatest of his day, in the Getty-Gulbenkian league, and it was widely suspected that a substantial part of it had been secreted offshore in Switzerland, in anticipation of *le déluge*.

For Mrs. Capece Minutolo, the contrast between the throne of
Egypt and the Lancia showroom had to be tantalizing.

When Irma's school let out in June, Irma's mother finally gave
in. Sounding like Narriman, she told Irma that if this was God's
will, let God's will be done. To that end she made up the excuse that
Irma was going off to Rome for the summer to a language school to
"improve her French." But *père* Capece Minutolo thought French
wasn't necessary. The backup plan then kicked in. Irma was going
to live for the summer with a religious order, the Sorelli di Sacro
Cuore, or Sisters of the Sacred Heart, in their convent near the
Spanish Steps. Religion played much better than French; father
yielded. The day of her departure, her father was working and
could not accompany Irma to the Naples train station, where she
was picked up by Farouk's Rolls-Royce and driven to Grottaferrata
to his fortresslike new home, the Villa Dusmet.

The Rolls passed the gate, manned by three guards with machine
guns, and drove through the parklike grounds up the hills of ter-
raced gardens to the forty-room, square red-stucco palazzo. At first
she was afraid to get out of the car because of three snarling watch-
dogs stalking the grounds—a mastiff, a Doberman, and a German
shepherd. But the hounds were held at bay by plainclothes Jacob,
Abdul, and Shaker, Farouk's bald and bullish Albanian bodyguards. One guard took Irma's small suitcase, packed with her
three best dresses and little more, and led her into the villa. The
entrance hallway was filled with suits of armor and Renaissance
paintings and medieval tapestries, nothing Egyptian at all. No
sphinxes. No King Tut treasures. But, then again, Farouk had been
unseated by a blitzkrieg overnight coup. He had had only hours to
leave the country, and was lucky to have escaped with his life. And
there he was, resplendent in a double-breasted suit at the top of the
grand marble staircase with his "best friend," a yipping little mutt
puppy named Ana, short for Anacapri, so named because he found
the stray dog on the dock when he disembarked from his great
yacht *Mahroussa* for the last time before General Neguib recalled it
to Egypt. He felt the dog and he were two displaced souls with a lot
in common. Ana became Irma's best friend, too, in a matter of days,
and Farouk would joke about which female he felt more jealous
about.

Farouk descended the staircase and kissed Irma's hand, slowly,
sensuously, but no more than that. He then showed her around the

villa, introducing her to his three daughters and their French governess, Mademoiselle Tabouret, and to little Fuad and his English governess, Miss Chermside. Irma, who was almost the same age as daughter Ferial, was slightly abashed at being there. What should she say? Nothing. Farouk went on to show Irma to her own wing of the villa. Her bedroom was modern, all art deco, but what really impressed her was her huge marble bathroom with its sunken bathtub, something out of a Rita Hayworth movie Irma had seen and mentioned to Farouk on their afternoon at Posilipo. Irma later learned that Farouk had had the bathroom reconstructed to the Hayworth film's specifications especially for her arrival. There was also a third governess, an older German woman whom Farouk had retained especially for Irma. In the weeks ahead the German, who had previously been employed by the English royal family, would work on Irma like a drill sergeant in etiquette school. Before his marriage to her, Farouk had sent Narriman to Rome to learn the social graces. Now he insisted on socializing Irma. She spent hours in the long halls of the villa in a gown and train with one book on her head and two books under each arm learning to walk and curtsy. Why? Because Farouk was going to present her to the courts of Europe as his third queen. She had to be prepared. He also brought in tutors for music and literature, as well as a riding instructor, and numerous top couturiers and furriers to dress Irma for her upcoming "debut." So much for the days. What about the nights? Farouk was a perfect gentleman, Irma insisted. He treated her like one of his daughters. Anticipating the inevitable skepticism that the playboy king would be running a sort of imperial fresh air fund for Neapolitan virgins, Irma laughed and insisted nothing happened sexually with Farouk for the longest time.

Although Farouk may have been preparing Irma for the Elysée Palace or El Escorial, where he actually took her was the Via Veneto. In 1953, the dolce vita that Fellini would immortalize in his 1959 film was already in high gear, and a cornerstone and founding father of that high and sweet life was King Farouk. The Via Veneto, a one-mile winding street that led from the gardens of the Villa Borghese down to the Bernini fountain of the Piazza Barberini, used to be a quiet suburban outpost until the 1950s. It was a common sight to see shepherds herding their flocks down the street, leading them across to the Via Appia Antica on the other side of Rome. The street which led to the Parioli district, which was the equivalent of Rome's Upper East Side, had one great hotel, the Moorish, domed Excelsior, one great palazzo, which housed the American embassy, and a few *latterias,* or milk bars, where wholesome horseback riders would stop for light refreshment after a brisk ride through the bridle paths of the Villa Borghese. There were no nightclubs, no paparazzi, no celebrities, no action.

Then Hollywood came to the Tiber. Cinecittà, or cinema city, the great Roman film studio built in the Mussolini era to produce Fascist epics, had by 1943 fallen into shambles and had been converted into a refugee camp. When the postwar Italian film industry began to revive, the prevailing style was the neorealism of De Sica's *Bicycle Thief* and Rossellini's *Open City,* films that eschewed the artifice of sound stages. Eventually, however, the Italian auteurs began returning to the studios, and Cinecittà came back to life. Six thousand miles away, the American moguls had a truffle hound's nose for a bargain. The epic cycle, which began with Mervyn Le Roy's *Quo Vadis* (in 1951) and would end with the Joseph Mankiewicz donnybook *Cleopatra* in 1963, was about to begin. Why not go to ancient Rome to film ancient Rome? Why not go to Cinecittà, where there were no unions, where the lira was anemic and the dollar was all-powerful, where grand illusions could be created at a steep discount from California prices, and where the parties, the women, and the food, things that mattered deeply to Hollywood moguls, were decidedly better than in Hollywood? And so they came.

The first big American production that showcased the advantages of Roman shooting was Henry King's 1949 *Prince of Foxes,* starring Orson Welles as Cesare Borgia and Tyrone Power as a Renaissance con man. When Rome burned, at least at Cinecittà, and Peter Ustinov fiddled as Nero, and *Quo Vadis,* which despite its nearly three-hour running time, became a huge hit in America, Rome became *the* cinematic hotspot, complete with its own branch of the William Morris Agency and a Yankee-style hamburger joint called the Nuovo Coloni, which flew Nathan's hot dogs in from Coney Island to provide nostalgic sustenance for the agents and their sometimes homesick stars.

King Farouk himself had done a cameo in one of these early offshore productions. Before he was deposed, on his fabled honeymoon with Narriman in 1951, he was lounging in the garden in the Cesare Augusto Hotel in Capri. Richard Brooks, the American director who went on to win an Oscar for *Elmer Gantry,* was trying to film a scene from a painting theft caper movie, *The Light Touch,* starring Stewart Granger and Pier Angeli, in the garden of the hotel. An assistant asked Farouk's chamberlain if the king would move so the scene could proceed. The chamberlain consulted the king, who took a deep puff of his Havana cigar, and refused. Then Brooks's assistant came up with a brainstorm. He introduced Pier Angeli to the chamberlain; she told him she was dying to meet the king. The chamberlain conveyed the message, but the king, instead of consenting to move, asked to be in the film. Brooks agreed; and Farouk was filmed, waving in the background. Afterward, Farouk asked what his extra's salary would be. When none was forthcoming, he tried to work it out in trade with Pier Angeli, but her mother was on location with her and kept her daughter away from the friendly monarch. *The Light Touch* also featured Truman Capote playing the concierge in the hotel. It was an utter failure at the box office.

The American film community turned the Via Veneto into their own Sunset Boulevard and the Excelsior into their Beverly Hills Hotel. And, one by one, the *latterias* became sidewalk cafés, and the *drogherias* (groceries) became nightclubs, and in 1953 King Farouk became their most celebrated habitué, holding night court with Irma as his queen of darkness. With his caravan of Rolls-Royces and Mercedes parked nearby, and the three armed Albanian guards and several Italian policemen standing at attention, Farouk and Irma would have a huge meal at a trattoria like the Piccolo Mondo, a Via Veneto grotto frequented by the film community, then would repair to the Café de Paris, a block-long sidewalk sittery, né *latteria,* on the "right" side of the "beach," as the Via Veneto came to be called. Farouk never drank alcohol, in the good Muslim way, imbibing instead seeming gallons of *aranciata,* a sweet fizzy Italian orangeade made with lots of sugar. Farouk intimates believe that it was the soft-drink sugar rather than the gargantuan meals that made the king as fat as he was. During these al fresco sit-ins, with waiters in attendance with portable plug-in telephones around their necks so patrons could call New York or Los Angeles, Farouk would entertain movie stars from Anna Magnani to Errol Flynn to Ava Gardner to Orson Welles, who tried, unsuccessfully, to get Farouk to back a modern-dress version of *Julius Caesar.* Other playboy millionaires, like Brazilian tycoon "Baby" Pignatari, would stop by, as would Italian aristocrat playboys like Count Dado Ruspoli, writers like Tennessee Williams and a host of other politicians, industrialists, p.r. men, society procurers. Everybody wanted to meet a real king.

There was, of course, always a spot at the table for a beautiful woman or two or three. Irma, nonetheless, stifled her jealousy. Farouk was charming enough for all comers; he never let her feel neglected. By two o'clock, Farouk and his ever-swelling entourage would leave the Café de Paris for one of the Via Veneto nightclubs —the Open Gate, the Jicky Club, the Pigalle, or Farouk's favorite, Bricktop's. Downstairs, on the "wrong" side of the street, West Virginia–born Ada Beatrice Queen Victoria Louisa Virginia Smith, who had come from bootleg Chicago speakeasies to Paris boîtes and, finally, to the Roman "beach," serenaded the likes of the duke and duchess of Windsor with "Miss Otis Regrets" and other Broadway tunes. The only time Farouk wasn't pleased here was when Bricktop sang "Go Down, Moses." One night Irma was washing her hands at Bricktop's and lost her ruby ring. An hour of hysteria later, a waiter returned the ring, and Farouk tipped him one hundred dollars. Small wonder the service staffs on the Via Veneto loved him. The entourage would usually get back to Grottaferrata at dawn, Farouk would hastily kiss Irma's hand good night, send her off to her wing, and not see her again until nine the next evening for another night on the town.

Although Irma kept writing her parents from Rome with fabricated tales of life in the convent, within a month of her arrival she was on the cover of every Italian scandal sheet, and her father was apoplectic. Farouk decided to go to Naples and face the family. Irma's father remained indignant. Why, he asked, didn't the king come to ask his permission to take Irma before he did so. Because, Farouk replied, you would have locked her in a nunnery forever. Mr. Capece Minutolo remained adamant. Irma was never welcome again at his house. She was still a minor and Farouk was responsible for her now. After that meeting, Irma didn't see her father for three years.

Who she did see were the crowned heads and beau monde of Europe. In 1954 King Farouk rented another huge villa outside of Lausanne, to house his children and from which to send them to Swiss schools, and he took Irma off on a grand tour that lasted a year and a half. They went from St. Moritz to Chamonix to Kitzbühel to Cortina, from Prince and Princess Hohenlohe, to

King of the Night • Farouk on the town with his bodyguards.

Brain Trust of the Revolution • Anwar Sadat and Gamal Abdel Nasser, who plotted the coup against Farouk.

Prince Charming • (top, left) Farouk on his first European grand tour, St. Moritz, 1937.

Principessa • (top, right) Irma Capece Minutolo, the "official" mistress of Farouk in exile.

Pygmalion and Galatea • Farouk at Irma's recital, helping her realize her dream of becoming an opera diva.

Baron and Baroness Von Thyssen, to the prince of Lichtenstein. They went shopping in Paris and Geneva, gambling in Biarritz and Monte Carlo. They stayed on Onassis's yacht and in Rainier's palace and the villas of Saudi princes. With the three Albanians, two Italian guards, two governesses, and two male secretaries, they traveled in a private wagon-lit, or in their caravan of the Rolls-Royce, two Mercedes, and a bus to carry their luggage, all painted Egyptian green. When they returned to Rome in 1956, Farouk bought an entire floor of a new apartment house for himself on the Via Archimede in Parioli, and rented an apartment for Irma on a different floor.

Yet for all their time together, Irma never felt she knew much about Farouk. On their travels they always kept separate suites. When they were back in Rome, she would see him only one or two nights a week, to go to the opera or diplomatic affairs or other official functions. He kept Irma busy with private music teachers. Her fantasy was to become an opera singer, and Farouk was intent on being her fairy godfather. Irma's mother had wanted to sing, too, but she gave up her dream to be married and have Irma. Irma practiced every day, both to become a star and by becoming one to vindicate herself, and her king, in the eyes of her parents. Farouk stopped taking her to the nightclubs. He never took her gambling. He never talked about politics with her. He never talked about his finances. He never took her to visit his family in Switzerland. He never told her of his plans. She was a teenager; her guileless innocence was what he seemed to cherish about her. She was too in awe of the king to ask any prying questions. Sometimes he would tell her of the glories of Egypt, of the palaces he had left behind, the art treasures, the jewels, the fleet of cars, the yachts, the desert hunting lodges, the animals he had shot and killed. Once, driving along the shoreline from Naples to Sorrento, he began to cry quietly. Later, he explained. The Italian corniche reminded him of the one of Alexandria he had left behind.

Farouk never talked about his sisters or his mother. He never talked about other women, but Irma knew there were many, just from reading the papers. Once she tried to question him about them, but Farouk brushed the query aside. There are certain things you won't be able to understand, he told her. He wanted her to remain a child, she was convinced, and accepted her enforced minority. Instead, they had fun. They skied. They watched private

screenings of films of Farouk's favorite movie stars—Jerry Lewis
and Esther Williams and John Wayne. He hated English stars, including the Beatles, when they erupted on the scene. It all began
with his stern English nanny, Farouk told Irma. He didn't tell her
about the stern English ambassador to Egypt who others said was
the key to his downfall, but, as Irma said, the king kept politics out
of their relationship. They listened to Frank Sinatra, Bing Crosby,
and Louis Armstrong records. Sometimes Farouk would play the
piano and Irma would sing. And, despite the other women, Irma
was convinced Farouk loved her above all. Once she and her governess impulsively took the Rolls to the beach at Anzio. Farouk had
half the Italian police in a dragnet for her. Another time a new,
handsome Italian guard exchanged smiles with Irma. Two days
later the guard disappeared. Farouk wanted Irma childish, he
wanted her innocent, and he wanted her *there,* even if he was not.
He was more jealous than Othello, Irma said.

But what about the sex? What was the ultimate playboy like in
bed? How kinky was he? What perversions had he dreamed up from
all the pornography? How miniature *was* the penis the world loved
to snicker and gossip about? The penis matter was the first thing
everyone always inquired about regarding Farouk. Not his land
policies, not social welfare for the fellaheen, not his stance on Israel,
but his penis. Was it really so little? How could the sex king have a
tiny organ? Was all the sex a bluff?

When asked what kind of lover the king was, Irma blushed. Perfectly normal, she said, lowering her eyes and evading the issue. Sex
wasn't that important to them. She was a child to him. They rode
on Vespas together. They played blindman's buff. They sang songs
to each other. She was his "official" mistress. If there were strange
things, devious acts, he saved them for the "others." She never saw
the king's pornography collection, but he did have a large locked
bookcase that she could never find a key for. There was one other
thing, she said, and blushed even redder. He had a pair of handcuffs
and sometimes locked her to a chair. But it was just a game. And
one more. He had a special chain that he wore on his fingers that he
would lock onto hers, Irma told me. Another game. Years later,
Irma was still protective of the great love of her life. Farouk and
Irma's story was not a tale of sex. It was a Pygmalion story about a
fallen king who raised a poor teenager out of the rubble of Naples

into the high life and royalty of Europe and onto the stage at La Scala.

Irma's proudest moment with Farouk was in April 1963 when Irma came home again to Naples to make her singing debut in the city's artistic circle. Wearing a diamond tiara and emerald necklace and two huge ruby bracelets that Farouk had taken back from Narriman when she left him, Irma was nearly derailed by a half-hour power blackout. But Farouk saved the day by bringing in candles from a nearby church. Irma performed for a large crowd that included her entire family who had by now forgiven her, with arias by Puccini and Verdi. At the end Farouk, in the front row, led the bravos with tears in his eyes, then rushed the stage with a huge bouquet of flowers, crowning the evening for his Fair Lady. If he could only see this, Irma mused, pointing at her Maria Callas award, her own eyes brimming with tears.

More tears came when Irma screened a videotape of a documentary about King Farouk that had been done recently by French telejournalist Frederic Mitterrand (nephew of ex–Premier François) for Antenne 2, a French channel. The most touching moment came at the end with newsreel footage of Farouk's funeral cortege through the streets of Rome in April 1965. Following directly behind the black hearse with its walnut coffin draped with the Egyptian crescent flag was his stricken thirteen-year-old son, Fuad, and right behind him, all in black mourning dresses, with veils, were Farouk's three daughters, his first queen, Farida, and Irma. Here, at his death, was the place she had waited for all her life with him. After thirteen years she had finally been accepted, for the world to see, as the "third queen." The crowd of hundreds that followed her, Irma pointed out, did not include the Rainiers and the Onassises, the Hohenlohes and the Von Thyssens, but mostly poor working people and their children, people that Farouk had been good to, bartenders and waiters and hungry people from the slums where he had often taken Irma on missions with money, food, and clothes to aid those in need. She pointed to a man in a wheelchair behind her in the newsreel, a man whose wheelchair Farouk had bought for him, who had beseeched "Dona Irma" to let him into the procession, and whom she obliged. These were the people who came to remember Farouk for the final time, not as a king, not as a playboy, not as an orgiast, but as a friend.

Here was a Farouk that was not expected. It was natural that the memories Irma wanted to bask in would be rose-tinted rather than vitriolic. But it was hardly the Farouk Gore Vidal remembered on the Via Veneto sucking the breast of a hysterical blond *putana* whose fat purse had been snatched by a thief on a motor scooter. Laughing at her plight, sucking her nipple, and giving her enough new money to make it all right for her.

Farouk's lawyer, Carlo d'Emilio, painted a similarly positive picture. Ninety, with a papal suite of offices overlooking the Tiber and the Castel Sant Angelo, d'Emilio was a tiny, elegant man with a full head of slicked-back hair and a natty striped shirt. He was known as "the lawyer of kings and the king of lawyers." He had represented the Italian royal family, King Zog of Albania, King Michael of Romania, *ad infinitum regium.*

Farouk had been kind to Italian King Vittorio Emmanuele when he went into exile in Egypt after World War II. When Farouk's crown was toppled, Italy returned the favor by offering him sanctuary. D'Emilio, counsel to the Italian House of Savoy, had met Farouk at Vittorio Emmanuele's funeral in Egypt in 1947. The day Farouk stepped off the *Mahroussa* in Naples in 1952, he contacted d'Emilio. They remained close until Farouk's death. D'Emilio recounted how Farouk was watching the Italian version of the American television show *Double or Nothing* when a young contestant took the big risk in an effort to pay for her ill mother's major surgery. She lost and began weeping on the air. Farouk called the station and gave the girl the three thousand dollars she would have won. D'Emilio was immensely fond of his former client. No horror stories from him.

The Via Veneto was clogged with tour buses and airline offices and stores selling knockoff Gucci bags to Japanese tourists shepherded by guides with colored flags. Aside from the ghosts of Anita and Marcello, there was nothing to see except the sidewalk cafés where the stars used to sit before the epic cycle ended and the trade unions got tough, *Cleopatra* gave way to spaghetti westerns, and the Hollywood expatriates moved on to the King's Road of swinging London. And, of course, King Farouk died. Now the paparazzi took tourist pictures. None of the Farouk era nightclubs remained in their original incarnation. There were a lot of shills promising dream girls and torrid floor shows and delivering overweight, weary b-girls and overpriced, watered-down champagne. A few of the restaurants remained, like the Piccolo Mondo, still serving delicious food, with vast antipasti cornucopias at the door and stunning platters of fritto misto and arragosta fra diavolo being rushed to the tables of rich Japanese by venerable waiters who, with big smiles, remembered Farouk as their favorite customer.

American survivors of the dolce vita still abounded, taking the sun and their Cinzanos at the Café de Paris: Dr. Frank Silvestri, doctor to the stars who treated Taylor and Burton and Power and Christian and Ekberg and Steele; Captain Norman Cohen, World War II flying ace who trained all the Alitalia pilots after the war; Charles Fernley Fawcett, "the mayor of the Via Veneto," in his seventies still a courtly Southern gentleman and glamorous soldier of fortune who had just gotten back from Afghanistan. They all remembered Farouk very fondly. They called him "Big Jim." They sat with him and drank champagne, on him, while he sipped orange soda. They kept their women from him, though, because he could charm women away from anyone, and he loved to do it. He could make any woman feel like a queen, these men concurred. After all, he wasn't just any fat roué. He was the king. Farouk loved people, they said. He loved a scene. And it didn't have to be a glamorous one. Even toward the end, when the dolce vita was winding down and Farouk was running out of money, he never gave up and went to sleep. He would take whatever girls he could find, and go to the railway station and sit in the all-night espresso bar, watching the demimonde and milk trains come and go. He knew the schedule by heart. But no one mentioned an orgy, a black mass, or white slavery. Nothing.

Another old friend of Farouk's was Filippo Moroni, an aging, dashing Via Condotti jeweler who held a court of his own at the Hotel d'Inghilterra during the cocktail hour, kissing and first-naming all the English and American dowagers passing through the lobby. Thirty years before, Moroni had been at his dentist's office where a young girl was hysterical over a wisdom tooth problem. While the nurses called the girl's father, Moroni calmed the child and cheered her up. The father finally arrived to find his daughter all smiles. The father was King Farouk. As a gesture of gratitude Farouk took Moroni into his moveable feast that ended only with his death. Farouk used Moroni to sell off some of his royal jewelry when times got hard, and to manufacture the hundreds of gold medals with his image that Farouk used to give away every year, like Rockefeller and his dimes. Moroni said that Farouk loved dives

and strip joints and hated the gloss of high society. He didn't like it
when he was king, he didn't like it afterward. All he really wanted
was to be normal, Moroni said, and got up to embrace another rich
visiting widow winded from a long day of shopping.

There was another jeweler, Giuseppe Petochi, at whose ancient
shop on the Piazza di Spagna Farouk used to shop at least twice a
month to buy engraved eighteen-karat-gold compacts for his current flames. On the Via Gregoriana there was Carlo Palazzi, haber-
dasher to the stars, in his elegant shop with its Renaissance ceilings
and modern metal sculpture. Palazzi, who had dressed everyone
from Charlie Chaplin to Clark Gable to Marlon Brando, got his
start at fabled shirtmaker Battistoni. He felt Farouk had the most
impeccable taste of any of his customers. Resplendent in his dark
gray suits, his delicate striped shirts, his watch chain, Farouk made
the young Palazzi more intimidated than anyone he waited on, including the duke of Windsor. He knew precisely what he wanted.
You couldn't "sell" him. And, above all, Palazzo said, a king was a
king.

Across the Tiber at the Piazza Cavour, there was Roman journalist Lello Bersani, who had accompanied Farouk on a trip to north-
ern Italy in the late fifties when the king decided that he needed to
look for a job in corporate public relations. It was a preposterous
pursuit, conceivable only by someone who had no idea of what a job
was. Bersani recounted Farouk's odyssey through the big businesses
in the Milan-Turin industrial belt. It was the first time a king had
ever sought employment. Bersani described Farouk's nervous excitement at the notion of actually *working,* his utter dejection when
every company turned him down flat. Bersani also accompanied
Farouk to the Cannes royal wedding of ex-King Simeon of Bulgaria,
not for his own pleasure, for he detested such events, but to introduce his daughter Fawzia to society. Bersani described Farouk as
just another nervous father wanting the best for his child, and when
the royal revelers gave Fawzia less than a royal welcome, Farouk
retreated to a corner armchair, took off his regalia, and quietly
wept.

Human, all too human. Everyone in Rome who had had any
personal contact with Farouk seemed immensely fond of him. It
was only those who had seen him from afar, or who had believed
the scandal sheets, who held him in disdain and contempt. Unlocat-
able was Annamaria Gatti, the blond twenty-two-year-old voluptu-

ary who was Farouk's companion the night he died. Farouk had picked her up himself (no bodyguards) in his white CD-plated Fiat 2300 (he had sold the Rolls-Royce) in her tenement flat on the Via Ostiense, a slum neighborhood on the poor side of the Tiber near the warehouses of Rome's public markets. They then drove out on the Via Aurilia Antica to a restaurant/roadhouse called the Ile de France for a midnight supper. Farouk devoured a dozen raw oysters with tabasco sauce, lobster thermidor, roast baby lamb, with roast potatoes, a creamy chestnut Monte Bianco, two oranges, two big bottles of Fiuggi water, and a Coca-Cola *digestif.* Then he lit one of his huge trademark Havana cigars, took a long drag, gasped for breath, clutched at his throat. At first the restaurant staff thought Farouk was acting out, playing one of the practical jokes for which he was famous. But then he collapsed at the table and didn't get up. A Red Cross ambulance was called. The king was taken to San Camillo Hospital, where rescue efforts failed. Farouk was pronounced dead at 2:08 A.M., March 18, 1965. In his possession were two American thousand-dollar bills, a wad of 10,000-lire notes, a gold pillbox for his blood pressure medicine, and a 6.35 Baretta in a holster.

Annamaria Gatti, whom Farouk had been seeing several times near the end of his life, would know the *real* Farouk, the decadent Farouk of great blondes and great legs of lamb. But Annamaria Gatti had disappeared. Her mother, who operated two beauty salons, had also vanished soon after Farouk's death, having sold the two shops. No autopsy was done, no inquest initiated. Farouk's own doctor, Dr. Luigi Donati, said that the king, who weighed over three hundred pounds at the time, had had a history of high blood pressure. The cause of death was attributed to a cerebral hemorrhage. There were no police files on the matter. Case closed.

Why did Farouk wear a gun? Because the only thing he was afraid of was assassination, Carlo d'Emilio said. Thirteen years after being deposed? Who would want to kill him? D'Emilio shrugged. It could have been lots of people, he added cryptically. But who? The celebrated lawyer of kings just shrugged again. When Irma Capece Minutolo was asked about Farouk's assassinophobia, she concurred. But she was vehement in insisting that Farouk's blood pressure had been the cause of his death. Only at the Society of Italians in Egypt was there a dissenting Roman voice. The society, housed in a *bella epoca* office building at the Porta Pia, leading to the Piazza della

Repubblica, shared space with the societies of Italians in Syria, Lebanon, Morocco, Arabia, and other Muslim countries. There were a lot of men in their late sixties and seventies padding about. On one wall of the Egyptian office was the Egyptian seal of the falcon and the flower. On the other was a painting of Christ on the cross.

The head of the society, Signor Zottich, was, like Farouk's chief of staff, Antonio Pulli, an Italian electrician, in charge of the power plants of the foreign embassies in Cairo. After talking about the pre-coup glory days, when Cairo and Alexandria were the crossroads of the world, Zottich stated very matter-of-factly that Farouk had indeed been killed, slowly poisoned to death by an Egyptian maid on employ by Nasser's secret service. It sounded like something out of James Bond, although the CIA had been accused of similar preposterous-sounding but actual attempts on the life of Fidel Castro, exploding cigars and the like. Why would Nasser kill Farouk? So the people of Egypt couldn't demand his return and overthrow Nasser, who wanted to leave nothing to chance. Several other old Egypt hands came in and repeatedly echoed Zottich's theory. Such speculation sounded like the work of idle minds and lurid imaginations unable to accept the obvious cause of Farouk's death as terminal excess. But where was all this excess? It wasn't to be found in Italy, where King Farouk could have won the noblest-Roman-of-them-all award. One would have to look elsewhere.

III

The ribbon of *autopista* that snaked between Malaga and Marbella on Spain's Costa del Sol evoked one of the lower loggias of Dante's inferno: the traffic jams of smoke-belching lorries, the screaming ambulance sirens racing to attend to a myriad car crashes, the shattered remains of which littered the shoulders, the skeletal abandoned high rises, silent testimony to the overestimation by rapacious developers of the allure of this erstwhile Mediterranean paradise. The roadside restaurants flew Union Jacks and flaunted large "bangers and mash" signs to lure in budget holidayers from Liverpool and Newcastle who had come to bask in the brutally unforgiving oven heat. The once-quaint fishing village of Marbella had acquired the ambience of the Persian Gulf, with establishments like the Fawzi-Baalbaak pastry shop, the Isfahani carpet emporium, the Banco Saudi Anglais setting the tone. There were a few bullfight billboards, but not as many as those the likes of JESUS VEX DETECTIVES. INTERNATIONAL PRESTIGE ON THE COSTA DEL SOL, which was also in Arabic, for the benefit of the countless jittery expatriate Levantines zooming past in red Ferraris. Across the Strait of Gibraltar Morocco was visible. But right here and right now, Lebanon, specifically Beirut of the good old days, was palpable. Glimmering white mosques and glistening white condominium complexes in Alhambra modern filled the barren mountainsides along the sea, while in the ersatz-Antibes harbor/shopping complex of Porto Banus, sleek kept blondes in string bikinis peacefully coexisted with fat veiled wives on the leviathan Saudi yachts.

Igor Cassini in Florence had indicated one of the keys to King Farouk could be found in this last resort. Cassini, brother of playboy designer Oleg, had been the Hearst newspaper chain's gossip columnist "Cholly Knickerbocker" during the years of Farouk's exile. Although his beat was the New York–Palm Beach café society circuit and not the Via Veneto, Cassini said that he knew someone who had had a torrid affair with Farouk. This could illuminate the king and his persona. The woman in question was Princess Honeychile Hohenlohe, a genuine American princess, whose brother-in-law Prince Alfonse Hohenlohe had founded the Marbella Club, the spectacular, more Tahitian-than-Andalusian resort hotel that had put the region on the gilded map of the jet set.

The "Casa Honey" was just about a mile down the beach from Porto Banus. The low-slung white cabana of a house could have easily been in the Malibu Colony, except for the pitted dirt approach road, the flock of chickens, and the fact the house hadn't had running water for the last several days. The princess, the maid said, was down the road taking a shower. When the princess, who for the last few years had written a society column for the Marbella Club magazine, finally arrived, she was stunning, tall, taut, blond, with a very short skirt and very long legs, the embodiment of *The Prince and the Showgirl*. Adnan Khashoggi, she was quick to say, had recently seen her and pinched her "sixty-nine-year-old ass, and he said it was hard as a rock." Age was no deterrent to Honey, who said she had just become a mother. The way she looked, if anyone could beat the clock, it was she. However, her maternity had actually come by her having adopted her young maid's out-of-wedlock daughter. She spoke in the slaky Southern drawl of her native Georgia, from whence country girl Patricia Wilder went out to conquer the world, first as Bob Hope's Dixie belle comic foil on his national radio show, then as the globetrotting wife of an Argentine beef baron, and finally as an Austrian princess whose husband, Prince Alexander, ran the Millionaire's Club, a precursor of his brother's Marbella Club, at the ancestral castle near Kitzbühel. She talked about her Hollywood romances with Clark Gable and Tyrone Power, both of whom she threw over for her riding teacher, and her flings with John F. Kennedy in the dank bomb shelters of World War II London. Several hours and a wine bottle later, she finally got to King Farouk.

Honeychile adored Farouk. In her lifetime of celebrated and charming bon vivants, he ranked close to the pinnacle. Unfortunately, before Honey could say what put him there, her dinner guests arrived from their off-premises ablutions. One was her former brother-in-law, a tall and extremely handsome, regimental-

stripe-shirted Argentine gentleman rancher. The other was a Nova
Scotian beauty pageant–type of German parentage who had just
divorced a British M.P. A midnight dinner was convened at another
Moorish fantasy condo complex called the Marbella Hill Club. This
arabesque wedding cake was owned by one of Honey's titled
friends, the count Bismarck. While a fado singer serenaded Honey
with melancholy love songs in Portuguese, she reminisced about
Farouk.

She shared two tidbits. One was that in Farouk's main office at
Abdine Palace in Cairo, he had two plaques on his desk that said
PATIENCE. The other was that Honey called Farouk "Bumblebee."
Why? "Bumblebees don't make honey," Honey roared. The subject
quickly shifted to all the ungrateful biographers Honey had aided,
then to cholesterol. Honey said her doctor had pegged hers at an
off-the-charts 360, a number she blamed on a recent extended visit
to the castle of Baron and Baroness von Thurn und Taxis, "where
they served nothing but cream sauces." Honey's 360 would have
sent anyone with any intimation of mortality off to the oat bran and
olive oil shelves. But not Honey. She began with foie gras, continued with a huge steak in a creamy sauce, and finished with a heart-
popping chocolate concoction also drowning in cream. At two-
thirty A.M., she aimed her Mercedes down to the *autopista* toward
Algeciras for more revelry at a down and dirty roadhouse with a
"Play It Again, Sam" pianist.

Honey's round of cocktails, weddings, luncheons with assorted
titled visitors, dinners with Sean Connery, siestas, showers, et cetera
rendered extended dialogue about Farouk or anything else completely futile. In between these *de rigueurs,* she did share a few
highlights of her romance with Farouk. Honeychile had come to
Egypt in 1949 with her Argentine husband on a polo expedition
with a glamorous entourage that included tobacco heiress Doris
Duke and her then husband Porfirio Rubirosa, who would go on to
marry Barbara Hutton. Because Honeychile's own marriage was on
the rocks, when she met Farouk at a Cairo club, she was willing to
accept his instantaneous blandishments, if only to pique her philandering consort. From palace balls to duck shoots, Farouk took
Honeychile everywhere in an Egypt at the peak of its glamour.
With Europe still in postwar ruin, Egypt was the place for the
international crowd to go on its endless holiday. In a sense, it was
the last real kingdom, where royalty proceeded unabashed, and no

royal was less abashed than Farouk. According to Honey, Farouk
was instantly smitten with her, and vice versa. Having recently divorced his first wife, Farida, he was certainly the most eligible king,
if not man, in the world. Honey said he had the most mellifluous
voice, the most perfect manners, the greatest sense of humor, that
she never ever thought of him as the porcine lecher that was the
party line of the yellow press.

What had started for Honeychile as a jealousy ploy ended up as a
full-fledged love affair. The Argentine went big game hunting in
India. Honeychile moved into Abdine Palace with the king.

"I could have been a queen, but I settled for being a princess,"
Honey said. Later on she qualified this. She couldn't have really
been a queen; she could have been a royal mistress. Farouk had
offered to set her up in her own palace overlooking the pyramids.
She would be his jewel of the Nile, the most beautifully kept woman
since Madame de Pompadour. He had already decided to marry
Narriman, who would give him the son he wanted above all else.

Honeychile stayed in touch with Farouk after his exile. He
brought Irma Capece Minutolo, whom he nicknamed "Bombola,"
to Honeychile's castle resort in Kitzbühel, where they hunted, rode
horses, and skied. Honeychile described a lavish party she gave in
Farouk's honor in Paris. Farouk walked out because he believed the
aristocratic Egyptian woman who took the seat next to him was a
spy for Nasser, who Farouk was convinced was out to kill him.
Recollecting her friend the Aga Khan's remark that "America will
cry bitter tears" over dumping Farouk for Nasser, Honeychile sub-
scribed to the theory that Nasser, and not overindulgence, was the
cause of Farouk's demise at the Ile de France. She believed that
Annamaria Gatti was the one who poisoned him.

With the ribald Honeychile, princess or not, one could feel little
compunction about asking lurid details about her *liaison dangereuse*
with Farouk. But she would constantly segue off into an anecdote
about another famous friend—Khashoggi, Imelda Marcos, George
Hamilton. Honey was the gossip equivalent of a great striptease
artist, with heavy emphasis on the tease, tantalizing, but never delivering. Alone for a moment away from the M.P.s and movie stars
and the Almanack de Gotha crowd, Honey was at last confronted
with the burning question about the royal organ. "I'm saving that
for my memoirs. I'm not *giving* that away," she said with a wink.

Several weeks and aesthetic light-years away from Marbella, a grand dinner was being held in one of the grandest apartments on Paris's Avenue Marceau. A long table of chic Champs-Elysées fashion moguls mixed with more somber heavy-industry types and their immensely decorative couturiered wives. Liveried Arab waiters served the pièce de résistance, a *loup de mer* flown in that morning from the waters off Lebanon. The host that had gone to such gastronomic lengths was Sheikh Khalil Al Khoury, the son of the former president of Lebanon when Farouk was king of Egypt. In many ways, the sheikh was quite Faroukian. The same age Farouk would have been had he lived, he was large and very rotund, as befits such an epicure. He had an eye for beauty, testimony to which were the wives and single women—a Russian actress who obliterated the Volga boatwoman stereotype, a *Paris-Match* reporter who could have been in the movies and in fact was the daughter of Olivia de Havilland. Khalil had a garrulous charm as immense as he was. That afternoon, the current premier of Lebanon, a dear friend of his, had been blown up. Despite his grief, as evinced by the way he twirled his emerald worry beads, he carried on with a delightful evening.

The sheikh told stories of how his father had sent him to Egypt to visit his contemporary, Farouk, in the late 1930s. The beginnings of what might have been a beautiful friendship were undermined, however, when Farouk took Khalil up in one of his air force bombers, flown by what Khalil decided was no mere air force functionary but a daredevil stunt pilot. Seeing the sphinx upside down was not Khalil's idea of high adventure. Practical-joker Farouk naturally loved it, or at least the mal d'air it caused his young guest, who developed a permanent aversion to flying. Over the roast partridge and chestnut puree course, Khalil lamented how spoiled Farouk was. Had he been more responsible, Khalil said, Nasser wouldn't have been able to take over and there might have been peace in the Middle East.

Lighter chat prevailed over the Havana cigars and rare eaux-de-vie, during which Khalil recalled another of Farouk's mistresses, whom he hadn't seen for years. "The most beautiful girl in Egypt," he mused. "An Alexandrian Jewess. Remarkable." A few puffs on the Havana later brought him her name. Irene Guinle. This was the same woman whom Gore Vidal had referred to as the most beautiful of the Farouk mistresses, women he called "chubby chasers," and who had also been extolled by David Slavitt, a highbrow Yale literature professor who had in the seventies written a novel with Farouk as the central figure. *The Killing of the King* was an ensemble caper piece about a melange of preppies, nymphos, movie hustlers, Hungarian con men, and the like who conspire to murder Farouk in dolce vita Italy. Not exactly a roman à clef, Slavitt had admitted, but his greatest source of verisimilitude for his Farouk was Irene Guinle, who then lived on Park Avenue. Unlisted in old New York *Social Register*s, *Palm Beach Life*s, *Beverly Hills Celebrity Society*s, and the like, wonder of technology, there she was, right in the Paris minitel.

"I was the love of Farouk's life." Thus categorically spoke Irene Guinle in her small garden studio apartment on the edge of the Bois de Boulogne. Petite, blond, perfectly coiffed, and wearing a Chanel suit, Irene's look was very soignée, very *seizième arrondissement*. On the other hand, her persona was much more autocratic English dowager; she exuded peremptory self-confidence. Perhaps a dash of bravado was there too. Irene, at seventy, was beyond surprise. She had been married five times, to an Egyptian, a trio of Englishmen, and a Brazilian. Three of the five had been very rich, one, Carlos Guinle, the richest man in Brazil. Regrettably, Irene had gotten little, at least materially, for all her beauty and all her conjugality. When Guinle died very suddenly and prematurely, his family used their immense leverage in the Brazil courts to invalidate his will. And in that macho country there was no automatic, legally required, "widow's share" of the inheritance. Hence Irene was forced to live on her wits, as a society interior designer in Rome, and now as a cosmetics consultant in Paris. In 1988 she was preparing to leave for a month in Kuwait to advise a start-up fragrance operation that was planning to bring Joy to the Persian Gulf. Her apartment was being turned into a co-op, at an unconscionably inflated price that only certain oil-slick Kuwaitis could then afford. She was going to have to move. Here was a woman who had lived at Abdine Palace in Cairo, at Sutton Place in England, in a mansion in Ipanema, on Park Avenue, and now she was old and scrambling to find a little studio in Montparnasse, if she was lucky. She wasn't exactly looking back in anger; but she did sense the irony of her predicament and she was weary of still having to hustle for work and shelter when she seemingly had had it made, time after time. Even without a royal endowment, she retained a royal air and a sense of entitlement—at least to male attention. Here was a woman who knew men. She claimed to know Farouk better than anyone else. She had met him when he was twenty-one and king and she was twenty-one and perfect. She had been his mistress for over two years; their lives kept intersecting thereafter for the rest of his life. She could describe the boy-king in full post-adolescent flower, when he was handsome and his sap was high. Irene was there at the high-water point of Farouk's reign, the glory days. Biographers' games of straight chronology could come later. Now it was time to jump ahead to what everyone wanted to know about: the sex. His mistress would provide a portrait of the monarch as a young seducer. One expected a torrid love story. One got something completely different.

Irene Guinle was Alexandrian, from an ancient Venetian Jewish trading family that had come to Egypt in the 1700s and prospered as cotton brokers. Irene spoke six languages; one wall of her apartment was brimming with books in all of them. Another wall contained a bar as well stocked as Harry's, evidence of frequent entertaining. A black and white photo above the fireplace showed a slinkier, sexier version of Grace Kelly. This was Irene at a white-tie gala with Aly Khan in Rome in what appeared to be the quintessence of Hollywood-on-the-Tiber fifties glamour. In the thirties, when Hollywood-on-the-Pacific was even more glamorous, Irving Thalberg's MGM globetrotting scouts had discovered the seventeen-year-old Irene in Egypt and offered her a fat contract to make pictures in California. "My mother wouldn't dream of it," Irene laughed. "She thought actresses were by definition whores." Instead, at seventeen her mother married her off to Loris Najjar, another well-born English-educated Alexandrian Jew of twenty-nine. Like MGM's man in Egypt, Najjar had spotted Irene at the Alexandria Sporting Club. "Frankly, I had a very good body," Irene said. "I did a lot of sports—swimming, riding, tennis. My most famous thing was that I had a terrific—not fat like the Americans like it—but a *very* good bosom."

Najjar was an unabashed anglophile who dressed in Savile Row suits, and when the war broke out, changed his name to Grant and joined the British Army. Even before the war, however, Najjar could not contain certain other English public school predilections. On his wedding night with the virgin Irene, at the Mena House Hotel overlooking the pyramids and which Winston Churchill would use as his Cairo digs, Najjar seemed to show little interest in her *belle poitrine*. Instead, he opened an attaché case and brought out a folding cane, a pair of high-heel black patent leather shoes, and black stockings. "Here I was, the healthiest, most sporty girl you could dream of. I got married without even powder on my face. I had never even flirted before, and here was my new husband wanting me to beat him to death. The next morning I got up early and hid behind the pyramids, but he eventually found me. I had no idea divorce could exist. I thought marriage was forever. I had to beat him until he bled, then scrape the high heels down his cuts, or else he would never come, and I had to do this three times a day. But Najjar kept telling me that 'everybody does it that way.' I started getting very sick, losing my hair, and finally after four and a half years I was able to get a divorce. So after that, you can imagine how relieved I was to meet Farouk."

Irene's first encounter with the king came in 1941, shortly after her divorce. With Rommel's Afrika Corps poised at the Libyan border in its inexorable move toward the grand Mideast prize, the Suez Canal, Alexandria was abuzz with calm-before-storm anxious gaiety, and British troops having their last tomorrow-we-die R&R flings. Irene had been most active in charity work. Because of her beauty, she appealed not only to lovers of things English like her ex-husband, but to the Anglos themselves. She was one of the most popular figures at the benefits that raised money for the war effort. She usually commanded the champagne bar, where a bottle of Mumm's went for one hundred Egyptian pounds and a kiss went for another hundred.

One of the biggest of all these fund-raising events was the Alexandria Red Cross ball. Helene Mosseri, the widow of a prominent Greek Jew, was a chief organizer of the ball. She asked Irene to man, not the champagne bar, but an orangeade bar. Orangeade? Irene was confused. Then Helene explained that King Farouk was coming, that his favorite drink was orangeade, and that Farouk had spotted Irene, knew she was a recent divorcee, and wanted to meet her. Court gossip at the time had it that Farouk and his queen, Farida, despite their storybook marriage and two daughters, were having their troubles and external temptations. Helene Mosseri was a very personal friend of Farouk's, so close that she had a royal hotline in her bedroom on which the insomniac king called her at all hours. Farouk made it clear he wanted to meet someone new. Helene suggested Irene.

"I wouldn't hear of it," snapped Irene, who had never met the king and, at the moment, didn't want to. "I was allergic to anyone pro-German." Ever since the British occupied Egypt in the late nineteenth century to "stabilize" the economy that the khedive Ismail had so overextended in building the Suez Canal and Europeanizing Cairo and Alexandria, the British had been regarded by the locals as nothing better than imperialist pigs. The European communities in the country liked the Anglo stability; the Egyptians loathed it. Thus with the Nazi war machine at the gates, many Egyptians saw Germany as their liberator from the British shackles. Farouk and his court were suspected by the British of having Axis leanings. Irene had a simpler explanation. "He was twenty-one and still a total child. He didn't know how to be a king. All he cared about was who would spoil him more, the English or the Germans. For his marriage to Farida, the English gave him a set of golf clubs. He never played golf in his life. The thing he adored most was cars, and the Germans gave him the most beautiful custom-made Mercedes roadster. Like a child, he preferred the best toy. Golf clubs! So this put the idea in his head about being able to kick the English out if the Germans won the war, and then being a *real* king."

According to Irene, Farouk was a virgin when he married Farida, "a commoner from a good family" who had been hand picked by Farouk's mother, Queen Nazli, who "didn't want to take orders from some princess" from Farouk's dynasty to whom the king might have otherwise been betrothed. Nazli had taken enough orders from Fuad. Farouk's father was a most suspicious man. He had, in effect, locked his vivacious queen up in the harems of his palaces until his death in 1936, which was Nazli's liberation. What Nazli didn't realize was that she was wedding her virgin son to what Irene called "a manhunter like you've never met. Farida was the first girl in Farouk's life. He was a total innocent. He never thought she would turn against him." When she did, Farouk began to look at the field, if not play it. Waiting in the wings was Princess Fatma Toussoun, the beautiful wife of Farouk's cousin, Prince Hassan Toussoun. The highborn princess had had a long-unrequited crush on Farouk, but she was too highborn for Nazli to have accepted her as a controllable daughter-in-law. Fatma had married her prince only after Farouk had wed Farida. Now Fatma, sensing a new opportunity, threw herself on Farouk. Because Fatma's husband stood below Farouk in the dynastic pyramid, he had no standing to prevent Farouk from taking his wife, if Farouk wanted her. No one in Egypt could question the king's pleasures, whatever they might be. "Fatma wanted Farouk to kick Farida out and make her queen of Egypt," Irene said. "After all, divorce is easy in Islam. All Farouk had to say is "I divorce you" three times, and it was over. So Farouk said to Fatma, okay, give me a son and I'll marry you. But if he had been all that serious, he wouldn't have come looking for me."

Unable to find Irene at the orangeade bar, Farouk cornered her at one of the gambling tables, where she was surrounded by a corps of British officers in uniforms, while society leaders served as croupiers. Irene realized something odd was going on when she started winning every time she bet. That night she was wearing a white muslin dress with embroidered red feathers (for the Red Cross) around the edge, and adorned with two huge real red feathers. The dress had come from Madame Bertin, Alexandria's top couturier. Irene sensed someone looking down this dress. She turned around and there was Farouk, in full summer khaki military regalia, beaming like a Cheshire cat. Attendants quickly brought a gilded throne for Farouk to sit on. He gave Irene the throne and sat beside her on a small chair. She quickly became the cynosure of the entire ball. Trays of gambling chips came for Irene to bet. After a huge win, Farouk told Irene how he had asked Helene Mosseri to station her at the orangeade bar. He invited her to come for a moonlight swim at Montazah. Irene thanked him, refused him, and left him at the roulette wheel.

Irene was on her way out the door when she ran into Sir Miles Lampson, the British ambassador. Lampson was the huge, intimidating ne plus ultra of imperial career diplomacy. He was contemptuous of Farouk, whom he referred to as "the boy." Farouk saw Lampson as the autocratic father figure any spoiled boy, not to mention a king, would detest. Lampson, in the months ahead, would prove to be the bête noir of Farouk's entire existence and a turning point in the young monarch's life. For the moment, however, Lampson deeply rued the golf clubs he had given to Farouk. He believed that Farouk was pro-Axis at a time when the British, on the defensive, could scarcely afford a fifth column. In Irene Guinle he saw one of his own. "Of course you must go swimming at the palace," Lampson insisted sotto voce on the veranda overlooking the twinkling lights of Alexandria. "You must."

"I didn't have the slightest interest in Farouk," Irene insisted. "I did it only because I hated the Germans. I did it because we had to win the war." Whatever she did, she played hard to get. The king's Rolls-Royce took Irene home to get her bathing suit. At two A.M. she arrived at the cupcake Italianate palace amid its romantic gardens along the sea. With its long beaches and crashing waves and jasmine scents, Montazah, under this full moon, probably was one of the great make-out spots on earth. But Farouk kept his regalia on and stood on the sand while Irene changed into her eye-popping white bathing suit and plunged into the warm sea. All Farouk did was watch. He didn't make a move. When Irene finished swimming and returned to the Palladian temple bathhouse to change, she left her sandals on the beach. Farouk dutifully went back for them and brought them to her, but that was it. He said good night, and the palace Rolls brought Irene home.

The next morning, at ten A.M., Farouk was on the line. "It's me," he said without saying his name.

"What should I call you?" Irene asked.

"What should I call *you?*" Farouk parried. "I think I'll call you Poochie."

"Then I'll call you Poochie too," Irene replied, as blasé as possible.

"When can I see you?" Farouk queried.

"You can't see me," Irene snapped. "I'm very busy and, besides, I hate people with beards."

Farouk had grown a beard not only as a symbol of Muslim piety but as a political gesture, encouraged by his advisers to coopt the rapidly growing fundamentalist paramilitary group, the Muslim Brotherhood. The brotherhood's twin aims were moral purification and Anglo extirpation. Only by purging the country of British influence could Egypt's Islamic culture flower once again. The movement, which had wide currency among student groups, also called for social justice and, as such, was potentially a major threat to the rich upper class of Egyptian pashas, who played polo and ate strawberries and cream with the English. These plutocrats supported the monarchy out of self-interest, while the fellaheen, the peasants, did so out of blind faith, just as their ancestors had since the time of the pharaohs. But now, for the first time in centuries, this blind faith was being reexamined. The Muslim Brotherhood was led by the charismatic Supreme Guide Hassan el Banna, an ex-headmaster who traveled the cities and countryside, from mosques to coffee-houses, in billowing white robes and a tasseled turban, preaching the Koran. The anti-British corollary to his gospel exalted young Farouk as not only king of Egypt, but also, positing that Egypt was the dominant force of the Arab world, as the caliph of all Islam. This was an even bigger ego boost for the young king than the Mercedes roadster. How *could* he embrace the British under such circumstances?

With Egyptians of all levels hostile to the English, the Italians at war against them, and even their French allies harboring extensive jealousies and antipathies, the only foreign community that the English could squarely count on were the Jews. Irene Guinle, consequently, had her task cut out for her. How could one woman, even the most beautiful one in the land, keep Farouk out of Hitler's rapacious clutch? "He was a child. I knew I could handle him," Irene said.

At first, although Farouk steadfastly refused to shave his beard, he kept calling Irene every day, several times a day, for over a month. "He was like a baby wanting a toy," Irene said. "The worse I treated him, the more he had to have it." After these endless entreaties from both Farouk and Ambassador Lampson, Irene finally relented and agreed to go on a real date with the king at Montazah Palace. "I wore a little black lace dress that was so complicated to undo that I knew he'd never get anywhere with it," Irene reflected. They partook of a ten-course dinner of oysters and pigeon and sea bass, cooked by a French chef and served by four Sudanese waiters, or suffragis, in the king's massive bedroom overlooking the moonlit sea. Farouk, as always wearing a military uniform, talked endlessly about Irene's family and her failed marriage. "He had spies all over the place. He was the nosiest person on earth. If you sneezed, he had to know about it," Irene said.

"You've done your homework," Irene complimented him on his research about her. "No mistakes." Then, after dinner was over, she said it was time to go.

"Don't you want to stay a bit more?" Farouk asked.

"And do what?"

"Excite me."

"I'd really like to go back home."

By twelve-thirty, a palace Cadillac had Irene back at her parents' home in Alexandria. Ten minutes later, Farouk was on the line.

American Princess • Prince Alexander Hohenlohe and his wife, Patricia "Honeychile" Wilder, the Georgia-born former star of the Bob Hope radio show and lover of Farouk.

Les Girls • Farouk and a contingent of distaff admirers at a 1941 party at Aldine Palace.

Popperfoto

Kingdom by the Sea • Montazeh Palace, on the beach at Alexandria, the scene of many of Farouk's moonlight seductions.

"His pleasure was the telephone." He had to see her again. They dated like this for another two months, with nothing happening. "Farouk," Irene said, laughing, "was *not* a Don Juan."

Irene eventually accepted Farouk's invitation to spend the entire weekend at Abdine Palace. Her parents had moved to their Cairo apartment at Suleiman Pasha Square for the winter season (they still kept their house in Alexandria). By that time she had ceased to worry about improper advances. "A man who has ideas doesn't wait *that* long," she said. "I was absolutely right. We spent a nice, quiet evening in his wing of the palace. His servants had opened my suitcase in his bedroom, but that didn't bother me. I never wore a nightgown. It was too hot. I asked him, do you mind if I sleep naked? And he said, not if you don't. He didn't wear anything either. So he kissed my cheek good night and we both slept naked in this bed, it was the biggest bed I've ever seen, without doing anything. The next morning we went to the indoor palace pool and we played in the pool, naked, like two little children on holiday. Sex didn't enter it at all. And, after my marriage, I was delighted it didn't."

He never did *anything?* "He wasn't interested in sex," Irene insisted. "He had no sexual appetite." What about fetishes? Surely there was something kinky about Farouk. "Perversity was beyond his wildest dreams. He liked to hold me like a child would hold a kitten. He'd hold my head in his arms and say what a lovely head, or he'd squeeze my feet and say what beautiful feet. And he'd kiss my cheek like he was licking an ice cream cone. But sex, never."

And the famous member that was the subject of such rife speculation? "To be honest, I never looked at it, I never touched it. I never thought about it. I was quite naive, especially after my marriage. Once I was with a girlfriend at the beach and a handsome beachboy came by and my friend said, 'Look at his parcel,' and I looked under his arms and didn't see any parcel. I had no idea what she was talking about."

Despite the absence of sexual fireworks, Farouk told Irene that he was in love with her. What about Fatma Toussoun, Irene chided him. Farouk told Irene that his cousin's wife, Fatma, had just given birth to his daughter, which mattered so little that Farouk sent Fatma a pearl necklace at the hospital and never even went to visit the little girl. Wasn't that proof enough what he thought of her? Meanwhile, the supposedly cuckolded cousin did nothing but smile and look the other way. In Farouk's dynasty, normal standards of behavior simply did not apply. The only rules of the game were those Farouk made up as he went along. Under such unconventional circumstances, there was no way Farouk could be expected to behave conventionally.

Farouk began taking Irene out in public. She became his "official" mistress. They went out to nightclubs like the Scarabee or the Kit Kat, which was supposedly full of spies, including the Hungarian showgirls. When they arrived the band would always strike up one of Farouk's favorite songs like "I Get a Kick out of You." Irene also began to introduce the king to her circle—the British circle. At first he wouldn't go. "Once when I was dressing to go to the Allied Ball, he got on his knees and held my legs and said, you're so beautiful, please don't go. I said, if you weren't so stupid, you'd go with me. He didn't go, but the next day he shaved his beard."

If Irene didn't have sex with Farouk, what *did* she have? "He was fascinated by the fact I was a Jewess. The only person Farouk ever listened to was his father, Fuad. Fuad was his oracle, and Fuad told him that the best women in the world were Jewish women, especially when they were cultured. The love of Fuad's life was Mrs. Suarez, a leader of the Jewish community in Cairo. Not only did they have a passionate affair for twenty years, but she pushed the English into making Fuad king, whom," according to the laws of succession, was not next in line. Earlier Suarez had been instrumental in arranging Fuad's first marriage to his nineteen-year-old cousin, Princess Shivekiar in 1896. That the princess was one of the richest women in Egypt was essential for Fuad, who was nearly bankrupt from huge gambling debts. Once Fuad had the princess's wealth, Mrs. Suarez steered it into investments with her Jewish industrialist friends, who turned one great fortune into an enormous one. Mrs. Suarez died of a heart attack at a ball while waltzing in Fuad's arms. Fuad never forgot her, and Farouk never forgot the great love of his father's life. He saw in Irene a chance to revel in his father's wisdom.

Farouk wanted to have the best of all possible worlds, as would befit a Muslim king who had everything, including a Jewish mistress. He would shave his beard, he would go to English tea parties. In return, he insisted that Irene convert to Islam. He gave her one of his rare gifts, a tiny bejeweled Koran, sent an Arabic teacher to her house every morning to give her Koran lessons, and gave her a new Arabic name, Fathia, the same as his youngest sister, which meant "all is open before you." Irene hated the lessons, hated to wake up every morning to a piety class, yet she went along with it.

Irene's reward was that she became the best-known young woman in Cairo. "I would wear a scarf not to be recognized," Irene remembered. "But even the little beggars in the street would recognize me and shout and salute me, 'Long live Irene.' Farouk took me to the incredible parties given by Princess Shivekiar (Farouk loved the princess because she always remembered his birthday). There were colored tents in this glorious park where she lived, with French, Italian, and Russian food, and pink champagne by the gallon, and three orchestras, and four hundred guests, the Four Hundred of Egypt. And they would stand on chairs to look at me when we arrived, saying after the war, that will be the next queen of Egypt."

Irene was popular with everyone except her mother, who forced her out of her family's apartment into one of her own. This was fine for Irene, who had never gotten along with her mother and had not forgiven her for having pushed her into the S & M marriage with Loris Najjar. "If I had married the king of England, my mother would have found something wrong with it. I didn't go with Farouk because I wanted to be queen of Egypt. I just wanted to be free of my mother." Irene's mother used to make the king of Egypt wait in the street whenever he came in one of his Rollses or Bugattis to pick up Irene. She would never invite him upstairs. "My mother said that the moment the Germans took Egypt, Irene Najjar would be the first woman to be hanged at Mohammed Ali Square."

Did Irene ever meet the *real* queen of Egypt? "Never. Farida never went to balls, only showed her face on state occasions." Nor did Irene ever run into Farida or her daughters at the palaces. "Abdine had five hundred rooms. The women were in the *haremlik.* I was with Farouk in the *salamlik.*" And what did they do? "We played Ali Baba games in the palaces, walking down these rococo corridors in the middle of the night completely nude, opening secret doors into rooms containing the most fabulous jewels. Farouk was the most ignorant donkey you ever came across. He loved having these treasures but he didn't really know what they were. He would open one drawer with millions worth of diamonds, another with emeralds, another with rubies, but he'd close them right away be-

cause he thought I might take something. Then we would go down
to the royal garage and he would press buttons, and doors would
open and he would show me all of his cars. There were dozens, and
all in red. Nobody else in Egypt except the king could have a red
car. He had a law passed for that, and on some of his cars he'd have
these horns that made animal sounds, like a dog barking, or a dog
screeching as it was being run over. We'd drive out to the pyramids
in the middle of the night to look at "his" pyramids and "his"
sphinx, but he had no real interest in history or antiquities. They
were just more toys. The thing he loved most was to play in the pool
naked. He always wore this huge emerald ring. And one time we
were lathering each other up with soap in the pool, and I grabbed
the ring and said it's mine now, and he jumped out of the pool
thinking I would take his ring. He was so mean. He told me he
wanted me to wear a different dress every night he saw me. I said,
fine, buy them for me. Farouk laughed that big, big laugh. Never.
'Your father's rich enough,' he'd say. We never talked politics, just
gossip about people, just rubbish. He made me tell him funny jokes,
like the one about the Jewish woman who was in bed with her
husband, Solomon, who couldn't sleep. Solomon explains, 'I'm worried. I don't have the money to pay Jacob tomorrow! So the wife
goes to the window, opens it, and starts yelling across the street,
'Jacob, wake up. Wake up. Solomon can't pay you tomorrow.' Then
the wife goes back to Solomon and says 'Go to sleep. Now *he's*
going to be up all night.' Farouk loved that one."

"Farouk never wrote a letter, never read a paper, never listened
to music. His idea of culture was movies. He never even played
cards until I made the mistake of buying him a 'shoe' and teaching
him how to play chemin de fer. He got hooked on that. Farouk was
an insomniac. He had three telephones by his bed, which he would
use to ring up his so-called friends at three in the morning and
invite them to come over to the palace to play cards. No one could
refuse the king. He got the biggest kick from having important
people bow and say 'your majesty.' But not me. I never called him
majesty once in my life.

"The best part were the breakfasts, served by the suffragis in the
bedroom on silver trolleys with the most beautiful china and porcelain and crystal. Neither of us ate a thing. We sent it all back to the
kitchen. Farouk never ate lunch either. This was before he got fat;
he was quite handsome at twenty-one. The thing he liked best was

macaroni and cheese. He never touched bread. He only ordered it in restaurants to make bread balls to flip at the fancy people coming in and watch how they'd act when he hit the mark. How he roared with that laugh.

"He had three hundred people working for him at Abdine; he called them 'the little people of the palace.' He'd reward the one who gave him the best gossip of the day. 'Good for you, my boy,' Farouk would say. 'You're a friend of the king. Next time you do even better for me.' The poor man would leave, and Farouk would laugh again. 'Dogs' he'd call them! He was a wonderful driver and a wonderful shot. Driving and shooting, and yachting, these were his only hobbies. I'd arrange these glorious hunting weekends at his palaces at Inchass and the Fayoum. I'd invite all my English friends.

"People were terrified when he'd invite himself to their homes. He never sent anyone flowers; he never gave house gifts. When he did come, people put away their special things because the next morning a truck would come from the palace to collect anything he fancied. In Egypt, if you say you admire something, the polite response is 'help yourself.' Farouk took that literally. If he wanted something, he went after it, the way he went after me."

What, then, did Irene like about a man with neither sexual nor intellectual interests? "I didn't like anything." I *had* to be with him. I *had* to keep him away from the Germans." Despite Irene's intervention, British Ambassador Sir Miles Lampson was not about to leave anything to either chance or romance. In early February 1942, at a fever pitch of pro-German student demonstrations, the pro-British Egyptian prime minister resigned. Lampson wanted to be sure that the successor was *his* choice and not Farouk's. As early as 1940, Lampson, who wore long gray frock coats and gay polka-dotted bow ties and whom Farouk ridiculed in Arabic as "Gamoose (water buffalo) Pasha," had seriously discussed with London the option of deposing "the boy." When Farouk kept hedging in appointing Lampson's man, Moustapha Nahas, the popular leader of the Wafd political party, as prime minister, Lampson took action in one of the most high-handed acts of British imperialism toward a country that was not even a British colony. He surrounded Abdine Palace with a phalanx of British tanks, shot the locks off the palace gates, led an armed contingent up the grand staircase, burst into Farouk's study, accused the king of various and sundry treacheries, and presented him with an Instrument of Abdication. At first Farouk demurred because the instrument was shoddily drafted on torn British embassy notepaper. Then, playing for time, he confounded Lampson by agreeing to accede to the prime ministerial choice of "the Schoolmaster," as Farouk also lampooned Lampson.

The humiliating incident was a terrible shock to the system, not only of Farouk but of all of Egypt and only stirred the venom of anti-British fervor. While the British leaders were once grudgingly welcomed at Egyptian high society functions, now they were boycotted. But not by Irene. She was also being pursued at the time by Winston Churchill's son Randolph, who had come to Egypt in 1940 as a young officer in an elite commando force that included Evelyn Waugh. Randolph called Farouk "the dirty pig." Farouk was oblivious to Randolph, and unimpressed by Sir Winston, whom Farouk yawningly regarded as "another fat Englishman."

Still, Irene was convinced that Farouk had pilfered the gold cigarette case Winston had given Randolph for his twenty-first birthday and Randolph had in turn given her. "When Farouk asked to see it, being a very special gift, I said, 'Never, you kleptomaniac, I'll never see it again.' And he said, 'King's honor.' Like a fool I trusted him and I never saw it again until it turned up here in Paris at the Cartier Exhibition at the Grand Palais, long after the Free Officers had Sotheby's auction off Farouk's vast palace collections in one of the largest sales in history in 1954.

The Abdine affair, according to Irene, "wounded Farouk in the deepest part of his soul. As his mother, Nazli, said, 'If only Lampson had arrived with a box of chocolates instead of tanks.' I told Farouk it was a good lesson for him. 'This only happened because you were on the wrong side. You're better off with the English.'"

Irene continued to be Farouk's official mistress for over two years, mostly sleeping nude together, playing water games in the palace pool, and gossiping. "Farouk had no complex about anything, except that he was so sure of himself, it became a complex. He was very clean, with impeccable manners, except that he loved to burp all the time to annoy people. He always slept naked. He never snored. He was incredibly lazy. He never even went for walks. When we would go into the palace gardens, supposedly for a walk, he would sit on a bench and watch me walk. In his mind, not having to do a thing was what being a king was all about. He had no real passion for music or culture; he never read. He did like his dog,

a huge *German* wolfhound. He had a mania for the color green—
his sheets, his dressing gown, his slippers all in that Egyptian royal
green—and he had F's emblazoned on everything. He was never
sick. He adored his bathrooms, which were the biggest and most
elaborate I've ever seen, and he did bathe himself, though he enjoyed having his servants put his shoes on. He wanted them to be at
his feet.

"The other thing about being king was that he owed nothing to
anyone. Once, when tires were being rationed, I asked him to get
two tires for my father's car. Farouk pressed the remote control that
opened all the palace garage doors and flashed his countless autos,
then laughed and gave me nothing. Once my brother had pneumonia, and there was no penicillin, and the only way I was able to get
any through him was to threaten to tell the world that the king of
Egypt could have saved a life and didn't.

"Farouk would talk to me until five in the morning on the phone.
About what? Nothing. He'd ask about gossip, what are you doing
tomorrow, who's giving a party, who lost at cards, who was there,
what did they wear. He wasn't stupid, but he wasn't educated, and
he was totally happy that way. He was the king. He was robustly
healthy. He was very gay. Everything made him laugh. He thought
he was very clever by teasing people and proving he was so powerful that no one could resist him. He was totally sure of himself."

And what about the issue of sex? "One day Farouk told me: 'You
must get fatter.' Well, I couldn't get fat. I ran, I swam, I did gymnastics. I weighed forty-seven kilos then. My waist was the size of
my head. For Orientals, a woman who is thin is usually poor. I was
worried Farouk had 'ideas' when he wanted to fatten me up. But he
didn't. He was just teasing me."

By the end of 1943, the German menace in North Africa had
been repelled. The urgency of Irene's romantic mission had dissipated, and Irene was hanging on out of inertia rather than exigency.
The end came at a duck-shoot at the Fayoum that Irene had arranged for Humphrey Butler, whom she described as "the bastard
son of the king of England." There was a beautiful English secretary whom Humphrey had brought as his date to Farouk's hunting
lodge at the marshy desert oasis south of Cairo. At least Irene
thought the secretary was Butler's date, until that evening when she
saw Butler drinking alone at the bar. Irene went up the stairs to
Farouk's bedroom. The door was locked. Irene began pounding at

the door. When Farouk finally opened the door, Irene saw the English girl in the giant *lit conjugal.* "I hope you're comfortable in my bed," Irene said, and returned to the bar to get drunk on brandy with Butler. Irene decided to sleep in the room Butler was sharing with a British general. Farouk, later that night, came looking for Irene. Butler intercepted the king, explained that Irene was ill. "I have the right medicine for her," Farouk deadpanned.

Irene was unable to sleep. She was convinced the romantic Englishwoman had been planted on the weekend by Karim Thabet, Farouk's unctuous, treacherous (and pro-German, Irene insisted, calling him "the monster") press adviser, who wanted to use the Anglo beauty to terminate Farouk's obsession with Irene. The following morning, Irene seemed to have turned the other cheek. She had the servants cook an elaborate breakfast, with the high table prepared *à trois*: Farouk, Irene, and the Englishwoman. While Irene was putting on the charm, none of the other guests realized that the servants had been ordered to pack up the Englishwoman's bags into a royal car. Just as another round of croissants was being brought out, Irene turned to her would-be rival and said, "Isn't it a pity you don't have time to finish? You've just been called back to Cairo." And the suffragis hustled the interloper off into the car and into the desert.

"What have you done?" Farouk fumed. "She's an incredible woman. She's fantastic."

That was the coup de grâce. Irene refused to speak to Farouk for the rest of the day, then returned early to Cairo and hid out at the home of Helene Mosseri. "You'll be queen of Egypt," Farouk cried frantically as she departed. "You'll have my son." Farouk, through his spies, found Irene at Helene Mosseri's. She then went to stay in Humphrey Butler's suite at Shepheard's Hotel. Farouk, like a bloodhound, found her there as well and burst into the grand main dining room in khaki military shorts, weeping. "Oh, your majesty, you must have caught a cold," Humphrey Butler intervened, trying to allow Farouk to retain a shred of dignity.

"Although at the beginning I couldn't have cared less about Farouk, I had come to like him," Irene conceded. "He was charming, like a naughty child you couldn't help liking. So I did like him. I never loved him, though, and at the end I lost my patience." Irene went back to Alexandria to stay with her prominent Jewish friends, the Lambrosos. There she met and was taken with a twenty-three-year-old British officer named Percival "Val" Bailey, at a party given by a British admiral. During their courtship, Farouk followed them everywhere, unseen but not unfelt. If they were at a nightclub and went dancing, they would return to their table to find one of Farouk's trademark pith helmets and walking sticks in Val's chair. Irene saw her romance with Val as an escape from Egypt and her notoriety as mistress of the king. The marriage would bring with it a British passport and the exit visa she knew Farouk would forever block if she were to remain an Egyptian citizen. A month and a half after they met, Irene and Val were married in the Anglican Church of Alexandria.

Irene began making plans to move to England, to Sutton Place, the stately home of Val's aunt, the duchess of Sutherland, and later the estate of J. Paul Getty. Before she could depart, Irene was visited by Antonio Pulli. "Farouk loved only one man, and that was Pulli, and he loved only one woman, and I'm sorry to say it was me." Pulli came to visit Irene. "He said, 'Madame Irene, he's dying. He's been in bed six days straight. He doesn't eat. He doesn't go to Parliament. He doesn't meet with his ministers. Please see him. Just once more before you go.' " Irene returned to Abdine. She found Farouk in his huge bed. She told him she was married and leaving him for England and forever. "And then he stood up and went into a rage and said, 'If you leave, you'll never set foot on Egyptian soil again. You'll never have a visa. You'll be blacklisted. And as for me, I will declare war on the Jews. I'll lose my hair. I'll lose my eyesight. I'll only go to whores, and I'll spend the rest of my life gambling.' " I said, "My dear, no one can stop you from committing suicide.' And I left, not believing a word he said. And for the first time, the only time in his entire life, he was telling the absolute truth."

IV

People danced to one of the four rumba bands, which had been
instructed to play from breakfast onward throughout the
weekend. Soon after midnight the guests were told to appear
on the palace roof in their sleeping attire, as it was now a
dressing-gown party. Melinda did not have one, so she took
the sheet from her bed. Pink champagne was served, and she
was complimented on the originality of her costume. The
King, in a white kimono, crept under the mosquito netting
and, settling back on the cushions, sentimentally held her
hand, while Miss Bella (a belly dancer) shed all her clothing,
exposing her shorn pubic hair.

"It's the custom here," Yoyo said, holding up his arms for
inspection. "We shave everything."

As Miss Bella wobbled her stomach, Melinda took puffs
from his cigar.

Suddenly he rose, saying, "It's time for my partouze."

Picking out the prettiest girls on the roof, he had them shepherded to his suite.

Back in her room, the King was seated on the edge of the
bed reading *Vogue*.

"It's an old number," he said, "and not a good one at that.
It wasn't the partouze I'd hoped for, because you weren't in it.
What's the matter? You look upset. Come across and I'll give
you a pick-me-up."

Stifling her tears, Melinda followed him into his private
apartment and, curling up on the bed, sipped champagne while
he showed her his stamp collection. "I thought these would
cheer you up," he said, pleased at her interest, as, leaning
against the gold netting with tropical butterflies fluting the
edges, she slowly turned the pages of an album containing
photographs of the Queen. Later he produced a pack of cards
and they played gin rummy. She won every time.

"You're a little minx." He began to get peevish. "What kind of *confiture* does a chick call for when it's just been hatched? It's a riddle."

"I've no idea. I give up."

"Ma me laid." The King roared aloud, very pleased with himself. "What is black and white and red all over? Come on. That's an easy one."

"I can't guess that one either."

"A newspaper," he chuckled. "Ha! Ha! Now I beat you." Melinda was bemused after drinking so many glasses of champagne. Her head spun and a buzzing sound filled her ears. The King pulled the salmon-pink cord with its tasselled end out of his dressing gown pocket and caressing his long, curly whiskers, glanced cautiously round at the bed. "I would give anything for a spot of flagellation right now. Just bend over. It won't hurt."

"I must go," she protested, but sank dizzily down as he gently eased her back on the counterpane. "It looks well against your flesh." He tapped her lightly with the tassel. The cord made a dull, thudding plop when it met her skin and her whole body tingled. As the blows rained harder, his breath fanned her neck and at each stroke a cool current of air passed over her back. Tensely she awaited each thud with a forlorn feeling which was not unpleasant. His heavy breathing increased. "It's coming faster," he bellowed, until with a prodigious roar he gave a final lash and somersaulted across the bed to the floor. "I did enjoy that. Will you let me do it again sometime?"

This is a passage from *A Young Girl's Touch,* a roman à clef written in 1952 by Barbara Skelton, who was postwar-England's leading literary femme fatale, its whore of Mensa, and incidentally, "the little English secretary" who was the proximate cause of Irene Guinle's schism with King Farouk on that lost weekend in the Fayoum oasis in 1943. Barbara, the daughter of a Foreign Office civil servant and a music hall showgirl, "a Gaiety Girl," was married to famous British author Cyril Connolly *(The Unquiet Grave,* editor of *Horizon* magazine) then divorced him to marry Connolly's famous British publisher George Weidenfeld. Connolly's divorce proceedings cited Weidenfeld as corespondent. But Barbara had second thoughts about her first husband. When Weidenfeld divorced Barbara in 1956, he cited Connolly as corespondent, in what was turning out to be a Brit-lit version of a French bedroom farce. One of London's prominent "lost girls," or independent adventuresses who later found herself as a successful novelist, Barbara was romantically entwined with a heady list of inspirators: poet Peter Quennell, critic Kenneth Tynan, film producer John Sutro, *Harper's* and *New York Review of Books* editor Robert Silvers, *New Yorker* cartoonist Charles Addams, *News of the World* heir and biology professor Derek Jackson, publishing heir Alastair Hamilton (son of Hamish), and *Nouvel Observateur* columnist and ex of Françoise Sagan, Bernard Frank. And, of course, King Farouk. King Farouk?! Who, according to Irene Guinle, never read a book, was devoid of any intellectual curiosity. How did he fit into Barbara's pantheon of literary lovers?

Choisy le Roi is a former royal village slightly east of Paris that made the celebrity maps when Roberto Rossellini and Ingrid Bergman made it their secluded love nest during their scandalous postwar affair. Little that is royal or romantic remains of the town, a twenty-minute train ride from Nôtre Dame, other than the picturesque château housing the *mairie,* the maple-and-elm-shaded park, overshadowed by looming white tenements housing North African laborers, the scent of the rosebushes overpowered by the wafting stench of Tunisian *merguez* sausages grilling in the local snackeries.

Barbara Skelton, now in her seventies, kept her Paris pied-à-RER (the speedy Paris commuter train) in a simple, well-maintained apartment house across from a municipal park, the same building where her last lover, Bernard Frank, lived with his young wife and daughter, for whom the erstwhile femme fatale, who never had children of her own, now baby-sat. Time had taken little toll on Barbara's legendary lithe, catlike beauty. She wore a red sweater, gray slacks whose color matched that of her pageboy, Chinese kung fu slippers, and no makeup. Yet she was a knockout, very reminiscent of Katharine Hepburn. "That's no compliment," she snapped in her smart, vinegary English accent. "I always thought she was totally devoid of sex appeal. Farouk loved Katharine Hepburn movies. He made me sit and watch them with him in the palace screening room, just the two of us, and he kept telling me how much I looked like her. I'm sure he did it just to annoy me." Despite having modeled for Schiaparelli and despite her legions of high-toned male admirers, Barbara (like other naturally effortless beauties) never thought she was particularly good-looking. "I have a bun face and

no eyes whatsoever. It wasn't my face that they went for, so it must
have been my personality." Salty and barbed and extremely knowing and witty, Barbara was definitely a woman who would be impossible to flatter or slip anything by, a hardcase indeed, and, by the
same token, a real challenge.

A passage from her first volume of memoirs, *Tears Before Bedtime,* gave a good idea of the fast world she came from and the
skeptical way in which she regarded it, and the basis for why she
thought that the showgirl rather than the know-girl like herself was
the true model for the femme fatale.

> Schiap's model girls were very mixed. There was one pig-
> faced American, Sally, very tall and chic; a Danish beauty
> married to Adrian Conan Doyle, who kept a cobra that they
> fed on live rabbits; and a Russian, Luba. But the most beautiful
> girl was a Norwegian called Gerda, who had been a Ziegfeld
> Follies showgirl. Blond and blue-eyed like my mother, they
> had similar values in life. One was that you should marry for
> money, though neither of them was tough enough to attain her
> ambition.

Barbara insisted on watching the Paris news on her huge television before lunch. She rhapsodized about the rugged Sam Shepard
look-alike newscaster, in his BCBG (Bon Chic Bon Genre—which
is the French equivalent of preppy) green tweed sport coat and rep
tie, go on about the Prix Goncourt as the main story of the day the
way some *Entertainment Tonight* reporter would rattle on about the
Oscars. She railed about how the second volume of her memoirs,
Weep No More, was not in the London bookstores to coincide with
the rave reviews from the British critics. And then she served a
magnificent boeuf eu daube that was worthy of a peasant grandmother in the Auvergne and a total surprise from an ultra cosmopolitan Bloomsbury femme fatale.

Then she turned to Farouk. Barbara remembered the first time
she saw him was in 1936, when she was taking the *Viceroy of India*
to visit her uncle Dudley, a general in charge of British medical
services in India. When the *Viceroy* docked in Marseilles, the incredibly handsome sixteen-year-old Farouk, whose father had just
died, boarded the ship amid great pomp and ceremony. One night,
on the Mediterranean leg of the journey to Suez, a drunk woman
created a scandal in the first class saloon by trying to drag Farouk

onto the floor into a fox-trot. Barbara's most vivid image was the flotilla of hundreds of candlelit feluccas, looking like fireflies, and thousands of fellaheen who turned out to greet the boy-king when the *Viceroy* arrived at night in Alexandria. Farouk departed the ship on a long red carpet on the gangplank, and the huge celebration of the king's arrival continued until dawn.

Six years later, Barbara was back in wartime Egypt as a cipher clerk in the Foreign Office. Her sponsor was the diplomat Donald Maclean, who would later become famous, with fellow Oxford classmates Guy Burgess and Kim Philby, as a Russian spy. She met Farouk at the Auberge des Pyramides, Cairo's top nightclub, when the king was shooting bread balls and peanuts at the stuffy black-tie revelers who came to drink champagne and watch the floor show of Paris Lido–level showgirls, magicians, animal acts, and French chanteuses. Barbara caught Farouk's eye, and the next day the equerry who had invited her to sit at the king's table brought her a written invitation for the Fayoum weekend. She remembered traveling there on the "Continental Clipper," a *Spruce Goose* supertrailer that was nearly fifty feet long and weighed nearly eight tons. Farouk had purchased this land yacht that resembled a giant centipede through his American purchasing agent, Armand Hammer, as a mobile palace with which to escape Cairo if Rommel ever beat the British and entered the city, the king's alleged pro-German leanings notwithstanding. Hammer had bought Farouk everything from Fabergé eggs in Russia to magic tricks on Broadway, but the Clipper, Hammer recalled in his memoirs, was the most outlandish folly of all. Of course, it didn't work. The tires blew out in the desert heat; the electrical system shortcircuited; the glasses and rare vintages from the bar went flying at every small turn. Barbara described how Farouk brought a trumpet on the trip not only to summon his guests to the hunt in the morning but also to call reveille for aid whenever the Clipper broke down and the shortwave radio failed. She also recalled the long columns of fellaheen lined up along the highway "kowtowing and clapping" as the highway monster alternately roared and sputtered its way through the endless desert.

Barbara remembered Irene Guinle only vaguely as a "fabulous beauty." She acknowledged taking Irene's place as Farouk's "official" mistress in 1943, seeing him usually once a week for the next several months. Barbara said what endeared him to her at the beginning involved some cheap fish-shaped earrings that she had bought in the *mouski* (bazaar) that Farouk had taken from her at the Fayoum. He said he was going to give her a surprise. A week later, under her pillow, she found a jewel box. She opened it to find the fish had been copied in gold with emerald eyes. Farouk was not only a king; he was a good fairy.

"I was nicknamed Kiwi, after the famous boot black, as I always had a shiny face," she wrote in *Tears Before Bedtime*. "Sometimes we'd dine in the Abdine Palace and afterwards watched movies or swim in the vast Palace swimming pool. Farouk always drove me back to the Villa Moskatelle (her rooming house) and, as we passed through the Palace gates, I had to duck so as not to be seen by the dozing nightwatchmen. In spite of the rather dull sycophantic people surrounding the King, I must confess I was never bored. I was always treated with great courtesy. . . ."

"Swam," Barbara admitted to me, blushing like a convent schoolgirl, was a euphemism. Sometimes Barbara did swim while Farouk lounged in the water. Usually, however, Barbara and Farouk would play underwater erotic games in the royal piscine. "He loved that more than anything else. Otherwise, he had little interest in sex. We'd hold hands and cuddle when we were watching those Hepburn movies, but there was no real seduction. He was my type, though, totally my type. Farouk had a very regal bearing, totally sure of himself, but part of that was that he expected a woman to do *everything* for him. He was something of a hermaphrodite, really more woman than man. He wasn't a good lover at all, though he did kiss rather nicely (contrary to Irene Guinle's experience). The sex was quick. He got a very quick erection. He lay on his back and I got on top of him. It gave me no pleasure whatsoever."

Barbara described how Farouk's pubic and underarm areas were shaven, as in her à clef novel, and talked about his small penis. "It was tiny, but it did get hard, and he adored having it sucked. You know, he made jokes about absolutely everything, about his starting to get fat and losing his hair, about the British treating him so shabbily, but he never, ever joked about the size of his penis. Never."

Again, contrary to Irene Guinle's experience, or lack thereof, Barbara did have a physical relationship with Farouk, albeit not a particularly inspiring one. "We rarely had sex more than twice a day, once in the pool and once before bedtime, usually after spanking me. I liked his spanking me. I guess he liked the notion of subduing this back-talking vixen," Barbara said, laughing. "That excited him. I did whatever he said. You see, I'm very passive," she confessed. "I never asked for sex or made an aggressive move in my life. The man *always* had to make the first move. I always wanted to be more pushy, more like those masculine American girls. Even when I was married, I would never ask Cyril for sex. Besides, he was resistant. He said it 'depleted his brain cells.' I didn't say anything, but I did get cross. Weidenfeld was the opposite. He wanted it eight times a day. Farouk didn't have me there for sex. He had me there because he thought I was amusing."

Although Barbara felt that Farouk was "a complete philistine," she found him amusing as well. "He was very adolescent. He didn't have the stuff to be a great king, he was too childish. But he never lost his temper, he was incredibly sweet, with a good sense of humor. He wasn't a grand passion, but I was bored to death with all the British officers I knew in Cairo. Life in the palace with Farouk was not boring."

She described a slice of this life in *A Young Girl's Touch,* which, she said, was a very true mirror of her actual experiences, and whose passages are nearly identical to those in her real-life diaries covering the same events, such as her flogging by Farouk, *viz;* "I am deadly tired and ache all over from a flogging of last night on the steps of the Royal Palace. I would have preferred a splayed cane, but instead had to suffer a dressing gown cord which created a gentle thudding sound over an interminable period."

> King Yoyo (as she called Farouk) was expecting a large bunch of letters and the latest American magazines with pin-up covers, which were soon brought to him on a tray with a rock-crystal goblet of fresh fruit juice. Dismissing the two armed guards who slept at the foot of his bed, he lovingly turned each page, now and then moistening his forefinger with a broad wet tongue. After a cursory glance through the pile of begging letters that came to him from cranks all over the world, he stepped into a bubble bath prepared by a black masseur who, after scenting and soaping the hairy thighs, tickled him in his itchy spots with a gilt-handled backscratcher shaped at the tip in the likeness of a female hand with pointed, ruby, enamel nails. Wrapped in a silk toga, he seated himself before

an amber glass while one Nubian tweaked his toes, another massaged his scalp with an aromatic hair grower, as the court barber slapped his balloon cheeks with a warm towel and tweaked his imperial moustaches with a pair of curling tongs.

"Has that little minx had her breakfast?"

The barber knew at once to whom he referred.

"Send someone to tidy her room. I bet it's in a pickle."

After gargling with a sweet mouthwash he sprayed his shaven armpits with Chanel and gathering up a breakfast tray strode along the passage. . . .

Surveying the disorder which the servants had not had time to clear, he remarked on the shabbiness of her underwear and said, "We must get you fixed up soon." Presenting her with a bright green bathrobe, he kissed the top of her head. "You're my little cabbage who needs looking after and I'm the one to do it."

Following her about the room, he noted the dust that had gathered on the furniture and ordered the servant to remove it.

When she was dressed they set off on a tour. He led her first to the ancestral wing; lining the stone cloisters were family effigies and lifesize portraits reminiscent of Yoyo himself; those that did not have the aristocratic waxed moustaches were bearded and black. In an adjoining hall he showed her his cherished collection of apostle spoons.

"These are almost complete," he said.

At the royal armory he took her arm. "It takes six slaves to keep this place shipshape with the polishing alone. We're nearly out of Brasso. I get it direct from your country when there's shipping space. Feel the point of this." He jabbed a lance into her right calf and beamed.

In the painted tiled chamber adjoining were mother-of-pearl chests crammed with carefully-dated, neatly arranged labels that had been steamed off innumerable bottles, from mixed ketchups to soft fuzzy drinks.

"A lifetime's work. The memories they hold for me!"

A further wing was filled with one show case after another which he unlocked for her benefit, as with sincere admiration she praised his hoard of matchboxes, mossers, whistles, alarm clocks and glass eyes, all minutely indexed.

"As you can see, I am a serious collector. *Touche pas,*" he warned, seeing Melinda [Barbara] flicking through a catalogue exhibiting the spare parts of a Mercedes. "I know what you women are like with your hot, lipsticky fingers."

"You are a heavy smoker," she said, after seeing the fifth case of pipes.

Before the stacks of wine lists and book jackets she congratulated him on being such an assiduous reader.

"I can honestly say," he boasted, "that I've never read a book in my life. . . ."

Back in his private chambers he opened the built-in cupboards and pointed out the rows of white suits, in linen, silk, shantung and sharkskin.

"I really prefer ducks," he confided, "but wait till you see the special get-ups."

Passing hundreds of pairs of newly polished shoes in their trees as being of no consequence, he showed his silken underwear and, entering another room, stood entranced in front of a long line of costumes protected by pink satin slips, which ranged from the uniform of a Salvation Army general to a Watusi chief's headdress of Kolobus fur.

"There's any dress you'd like to mention. Have you seen anything to beat it?"

Never, she had to admit, while her face reflected great pleasure.

Barbara went on about Farouk and the dressing up for dinner as Antony and Cleopatra, and his ministers coming in costume as Churchill, Roosevelt, and Stalin. She talked about Farouk's daily checkup by his private doctor, his cleanliness fetish, with his mega-bathrooms, with footbaths and sitz baths and bidets and futuristic showers, the way he would smash plates at state dinners if they had a smudge or a crack ("He was obsessed with germs"), the ceremonial way his orangeade was corked and chilled, as if it were the finest champagne.

"Farouk seemed to prefer rather simple food," Barbara wrote in *Tears Before Bedtime.*

"He was very fond of chicken carcasses, claiming the parson's nose (rear end) to be the best part of the bird. He loved oysters and fruit, and wherever we went, there were large platters of muscat grapes, figs, and mangoes from his own plantation, and those delicious rose-pink watermelons with huge black pips that taste so good when eaten iced with fresh goat's cheese."

She talked about his kleptomania, the way he would practice eminent domain and requisition crystal chandeliers and grand pianos and priceless art from the homes of the subjects who had the fortune, or misfortune, as it were, to have the king as their guest.

Barbara's life was completely dichotomized. By day, a mild-mannered cipher clerk dressing in proper bureaucratic garb, living in a little hostel. By night, a sexpot, dressing in haute couture the king insisted she wear "to fix herself up" for assorted balls, operas, polo matches, horse races. After a while, Farouk even set her up in a villa overlooking the Gezira Sporting Club in the British-dominated section of Cairo called Zamalek, with a fully equipped bathroom for the king's many ablutions as well as a direct "hotline" to Abdine Palace.

Eventually, the British decided that their cipher clerk was getting too close to Farouk for their own comfort. "After all, I was in a sensitive position, and they were convinced Farouk was setting me up just to get information from me. What they never could understand was that Farouk couldn't have cared less. The only communications to England that mattered to him were his telexes ordering silk neckties from Hawes and Curtis. There was absolutely nothing political about him then," Barbara said. "In the end, though, the British simply wouldn't have it. They decided to ship me out."

The king did not weep when Barbara left to go to work as a cipherine in Athens. His cavalier behavior actually annoyed Barbara. Farouk's going-away presents to her consisted of a roast chicken from the Auberge des Pyramides and an opossum foot warmer. He had allowed, in fact encouraged, her to run up a huge bill with Cairo's leading Italian dressmaker, which he, ungallantly, made no gesture toward paying, leaving Barbara no alternative but to stiff her creditor. "Farouk was staggeringly cheap," she said. "Or maybe he just hated gold diggers, and this was another of his jokes."

Barbara didn't hear again from Farouk until 1950, and had never thought she would. At the time she was engaged to Cyril Connolly, and her "lost girl" days seemed to be over. Then Farouk called her. He was on his famous three-month European summer bachelor party. Every day his conspicuous consumption antics made front-page headlines, so much so that the two prostitutes who lived below Barbara's flat in London's trollop-intensive Shepherd's Market in Mayfair had crossed the Channel to Deauville to become camp followers in the king's ever-swelling entourage. Farouk had divorced Farida in 1948 and was engaged to Narriman Sadek. This was, supposedly, his last fling. And since Barbara, too, was getting married, she thought that perhaps she should have a last fling as well.

Oddly enough, Barbara said, Cyril Connolly encouraged her to take the trip. "He thought I could get money from Farouk to pay for our honeymoon." She laughed. "He had no idea how tight this king was." Barbara met Farouk's entourage at La Baule in Brittany, where they had taken several floors of the Hermitage Hotel. There were two dozen official guests, including Farouk's doctor and barber, bodyguards, and innumerable hangers-on who followed Farouk's odyssey down the casinos of France's Atlantic Coast all the way to Biarritz. Farouk passed out berets to all of the entourage, to gallicize his Egyptians for the journey.

"Farouk was fatter than I could have ever imagined, like a stuffed animal. And now he had this passion for gambling, which I never really noticed in Egypt. He called me 'my mascot.' I don't think I was there for sex as much as for being a good luck charm. I did sleep with him. In each hotel we went to he had a special huge bed installed for him, and he always was joking about partouzes and all the whores that he had used, but I think it was all talk. One big show. We never had another girl with us. We'd have sex, maybe once a day, if that. We didn't have a pool to get him excited. He'd have me get on top and that was it, and I can't remember a thing about it. He was the king. He expected service. He'd lie on his back like a beached whale and I'd come to him. Mostly he liked to cuddle.

"As I said, the sex wasn't the thing. It was the gambling. I'd sit beside him as his mascot and he'd give me a pile of chips to play roulette with. I stored as many of them away as I could, as I always lost. He'd play sometimes until dawn, and the casino would always stay open for him, and whenever we came in or went out there was always a big crowd of people yelling, *'Vive le roi! Vive le roi!'* You know how the French love royalty.

"Cyril turned out to be more jealous than I first thought. He got an assignment from the *Daily Mail* to do a piece on Farouk and came over to La Baule but Farouk wouldn't give him an interview. Farouk hated journalists. Hated them. I tried to explain that Cyril was a *real* writer and not one of *those* journalists. Farouk wouldn't hear it. Cyril got his own black beret and followed us anyhow. I rode in Farouk's big car, a Cadillac convertible, I think, and a bus followed the fleet of cars, carrying all the luggage. Farouk always drove. He loved to drive. He was an excellent driver.

"On the way we'd stop at famous starred Michelin restaurants that would open up at odd hours to make meals for the king. His men would collect the oddest things at these places, steaming labels off wine bottles and the like, and they would send them back to Egypt. When we got to Biarritz, we stayed at the Palais hotel. We took at least two whole floors. Farouk never really talked about Narriman. I guess he wanted someone of the people who could give him a son, but I couldn't figure out why he chose someone who seemed so ordinary. Really, our trip was all on the surface. He never talked family or politics or anything. Only joking, eating, gambling, shopping. One night he asked to see these lovely eternity rings I had had for years and years. I never got them back. I'm sure he took them and had them woven into Narriman's famous be-jeweled wedding dress. As consolation he called the man from the Boucheron store and had him bring me a gold cigarette holder and this vulgar clip that he pinned to my evening dresses. It was like a Scout's merit badge. After Biarritz Farouk and his group kept on to Cannes, and Cyril and I went to the Dordogne. I was glad to get away, especially from the press. I had become the 'mystery woman.' Back in London Farouk had sent Cyril a box of Egyptian mangoes, maybe as a consolation prize for not giving him an interview. I stayed in touch with Farouk. He always called me Kiwi; he sent me a huge basket of exotic plants when I married Cyril. I finally was able to introduce the two of them in Rome. Cyril was terribly ex-cited, but the two had absolutely nothing to say to each other. Farouk did pay for the lunch.

"Another time he invited me to spend a week with him at the Villa Dusmet when he had gone into exile. It was a funereal, dead, gloomy place. His children weren't there, not even any staff. Just some bodyguards and his girlfriend Irma. It was like a haunted house. Irma was very lush and beautiful. But Farouk left us both alone in that big house while he went into Rome every night. Maybe he left me home so he didn't have to pay my liquor bills. In any case, I began getting terribly claustrophobic, being a prisoner in the country. So one night I went into Rome by myself. I ended up going into this nightclub off the Via Veneto and who do I run into but Farouk with a table of whores. He thought it was hilarious. I always knew I wasn't his type at all, but for some odd reason he liked me, and I always liked him."

V

DYNASTY

Having gotten the sex at least somewhat out of the way, it is time to get to know Farouk as a person. The mistresses were, as mistresses tend to be, great fun. But Farouk definitely compartmentalized his life. He had an Oriental potentate's harem view of women, keeping them in their place, dedicating them to his whims. He didn't let them in on the big picture, whatever that was. To find out, one had to start at the beginning, and to do that, one went directly to the end.

The broad, leafy, and majestic Avenue Foch, Paris's most expensive address, had been dubbed by local wags the Suez Canal because the Jews lived on one side and the Arabs on the other. Aside from the occasional servant in a djellaba taking the afghans and wolfhounds for a walk under the spreading chestnut trees on the vast, parklike median, the untutored eye would probably be unable to tell the difference. The avenue was largely lifeless, except for the allées crowded with double-parked black Mercedes limos bearing men of affairs, and double-parked red BMW convertibles bearing women of affairs, deluxe motorized prostitutes offering five hundred dollars' worth of fantasy, a brief joyride away in a *hôtel de vingt minutes,* or, weather permitting, al fresco in a sylvan glade in the nearby Bois de Boulogne.

Ironically, it was the so-called Jewish side of the avenue that was the home of the once, last, and probably unlikely future king of Egypt, thirty-nine-year-old Farouk Fuad, the only son of King Farouk. The initials on the imposing 1920 limestone building buzzer read "F.F." Upstairs was a penthouse apartment that was one of the grandest in the city. A three-story-tall sun-drenched living room with a walnut-paneled library in the upstairs gallery overlooked the Eiffel Tower looming above the millionaire's row of flats on the

"Arab" side of this Gold Coast. Inside the regal room were the illustrious ancestors: a huge portrait of Mohammed Ali, the warrior founder of the dynasty; the khedive Ismail; a black marble bust of King Fuad; a photo of King Farouk in the desert tent of King Abdul Aziz of Saudi Arabia; and two portraits of Farouk, one in full regalia at sixteen, when he had just become the boy-king, and another in full regalia at twenty-eight, when he was getting fat and bald. There was an Egyptian flag, velvet sofas in Egyptian green, a marble obelisk, a replica of the centerpiece of the Place de la Concorde, mounted scimitars, scenes of the Nile painted by Fuad's stepmother ex-Queen Farida. There were autographed photographs of other kings—Hassan of Morocco, Hussein of Jordan, and of Saudi princes. This was indeed the apartment of a king. But it was the end of the line.

Prince Fuad, as he is now known, has a career in high-level public relations for international companies that want to do business in the Arab world, where his contacts are of great value. It is the kind of work Farouk in his exile tried to find but couldn't. Fuad was born on January 16, 1952. When his father was deposed in July 1952, his abdication was in favor of the baby prince, who then became King Fuad II. From this accession, Fuad was a king in exile, for Farouk took the baby with him to Italy, not only for the child's safety but also as a gambling chip in the game of nations that was being played out. Fuad's reign was short-lived. On June 18, 1953, the Revolutionary Command Council abolished the monarchy altogether and declared Egypt a republic. The dynasty, which was begun by Mohammed Ali in 1805, by revolting against his Turkish commanders, was officially over.

"My father received two special telegrams when he was deposed in 1952," Prince Fuad said in his imperial salon. "One was from his mother, my grandmother, Queen Nazli in California." They hadn't spoken at all since 1948, when Farouk banished her and his youngest sister, Fathia, from Egypt over Fathia's love affair with and marriage to Riad Ghali, a Copt and minor diplomatic functionary who had first been Nazli's lover. In her wire Nazli wished Farouk luck and safety. "The other was from King Abdul Aziz, begging my father to come and live in Saudi Arabia, and promising him that he would be back on the throne in six months. But my father stayed in Italy. He never saw his mother or Egypt again. As long as he lived, though, there was always talk about his coming back. I'm sure that's why they killed him."

Fuad was convinced that his father was assassinated by an over-eager Egyptian secret service wanting to please its big boss, President Nasser. "Perhaps it was not Nasser's death order. Perhaps Nasser looked the other way. In any event, in 1965, Nasser was worried." Fuad cited reports in the Arabic press. One Egyptian secret service man admitted that his main task was to spy on Farouk in Rome. Another was that two Egyptian secret service officials were in the kitchen of the Ile de France restaurant the day Farouk died. The mistress of Salah Nasr, the sinister head of the Egyptian secret service, had written her memoirs in 1988, outlining how Farouk had been given a special "poison pill." "The family didn't ask for an autopsy when my father died," Fuad said. "We were all too shocked. I was only thirteen. Poisoning never occurred to me."

Fuad, who has never been back to Egypt, proudly displayed an invitation to a function at the Egyptian embassy in Paris. "A few years ago, they wouldn't recognize me. Now there's a lot of revisionist thinking and talk of the Age of Farouk as being a sort of golden age. Now they see that he was a good friend of America, he was anti-Communist, he was for free enterprise—everything that Nasser was not. Given the terrible mess Egypt became, my father looks brilliant in hindsight."

Fuad looked more like a scholar than a ruler, with his glasses, his pale skin, his thinning hair, his serious demeanor. Only his Armani tweed jacket, his Charvet striped shirt, and his Dior belt suggested an Avenue Foch provenance rather than a library at the Sorbonne. There was only a whisper of a resemblance to his father. More of the arrondissement was Fuad's wife, Princess Fadila, a chic, raven-tressed beauty with piercing eyes, who was often on French best-dressed lists. She had gained a bit of weight since her marriage in 1977 at the royal palace in Monaco, in which Prince Rainier and Princess Grace were the couple's witnesses at the Muslim service. The weight probably would have appealed to King Farouk, whose taste in his Rome days was distinctly toward Junoesque. Born Dominique France Picard to an Alsatian Jewish family, she was introduced to Fuad by her brother, who was his classmate at the Le Rosey School in Switzerland. Le Rosey is the most exclusive of boarding schools. Its alumni include the shah of Iran, Fuad's uncle by marriage; Prince Rainier, Fuad's unofficial guardian; and Richard Helms, former head of the CIA, without whose intervention Fuad might have been on the throne of Egypt today. When Fuad married Dominique, she took his religion and a new name, Fadila, respecting both Fuad I and Farouk's prediliction and superstition regarding the letter F.

Fuad and Fadila were joined by the royal children. The eldest, Mohammed Ali, was a strapping blond, curly-haired seven-year-old who kicked a soccer ball through the Egyptian antiquities. Too strapping for his parents, who said they were trying to put him on a diet to avoid the dynastic propensity to portliness. However, given the superb, buttery *tarte tatin* the princess had put out for an afternoon snack, it would be an uphill battle. Ali's sister, Fawzia, named after her aunt and great-aunt, was nine, blond, delicate, and charming. She kissed her parents on both cheeks and curtsied. The baby brother, Fakr-el-Din, was only three; he had already acquired a taste for both the *tarte tatin* and video games.

As the end of his line, Fuad felt a great pride in, as well as responsibility for, preserving his father's memory. He had an amazing collection of photography, not only of Farouk's glory days— going to the coronation of King Edward with the young duke of Windsor, shooting gazelle in the desert with Farida, striding through the columns of Luxor, holding court to Roosevelt and Churchill, but also other days, good and bad, family days and lonely days. The most amusing snapshot was of Farouk in exile on the shores of Lake Geneva, wearing a Davy Crockett coonskin cap.

Fuad was a gentle, philosophical man who seemed to bear no rancor toward the slings and arrows history had shot at his father. His greatest regret seems to have not known Farouk better. Farouk was in Rome and Fuad and his half sisters were in their Swiss schools. Family reunions occurred only a few times each year, and then only for a few hours a day, because Farouk always slept late into the afternoon.

"My father wanted me to be elegant. He always chose my clothes for me. Once he saw me wearing false-jeweled cuff links. He was so upset that he took off his own diamond and emerald cuff links with the F's on them and traded with me. He wore my fake cuff links," Fuad said.

Fuad remembered his father taking him out for chocolate sundaes. He remembered the giant stuffed tiger and the remote-control

The Romantic Englishwoman • Author and literary *Femme Fatale*, Barbara Skelton, who had a wartime affair with Farouk.

Party Favors • Farouk throwing breadballs at his favorite Cairo nightclub, the Auberge des Pyramides.

AKHBAR EL YOM Publishing House (Cairo)

A Pair of Kings • The final two monarchs of Egypt, Farouk and his son, Fuad.

Associated Press

Sherman tank Farouk gave him as birthday presents. He remembered walking behind his father's cortege in Rome when he died. "My father thought Rome was unsafe for his children. There were too many Egyptian secret service around. That's why he kept us in Switzerland. I would come down on the train with his Albanian bodyguard, Abdul Rostum; he was a lovely man, completely illiterate, completely loyal. I stayed in the guest room in Parioli. My father loved Rome so much that he knowingly risked his life by staying there. He didn't care about the secret police. He wanted to go out, to enjoy himself. He was a brave man.

"As a boy I wanted to be a doctor," Fuad said, "but my father discouraged me. In fact, he was very displeased. He wanted me to be kingly, even if I couldn't be king. He wanted me to go into public service, not into one of the bourgeois professions. He was very insistent that I get along with my half sisters, even though they had a French nanny and I had a British one. He got me a British nanny to prove he wasn't prejudiced against *all* things English," Fuad said, smiling. "He *was* glad that Miles Lampson's career went to the dogs. Lampson was the one person he really hated," Fuad said, taking a very subtle satisfaction that Lampson, after the war, was replaced as British ambassador and was denied his ultimate career goal of viceroy of India, the pinnacle of British imperial diplomacy. It was Lampson's arrogance that destroyed any chance the British had to salvage their reputation with the Egyptians. It also gave Farouk a cause, and a chance to become a great leader. How he lost that chance was the tragedy of his life.

Fuad had a deep need to try to understand his father and his fall. To do so, it is essential to keep in mind the impossible dynastic acts Farouk had to follow. The line of succession from pharaoh to Farouk was a five-thousand-year zigzag course which for most of its most recent centuries was downhill all the way. How could Farouk, or any ruler, compare to the legends who had gone before him—Tutankhamen, Ramses, Ptolemy, Cleopatra, Saladin, Mohammed Ali? Yet rather than cringe in the long shadows of these illustrious predecessors, Farouk began his reign by basking in them. Farouk was Egypt's golden boy. The country looked to him to bring it into the future, and, at the same time, back to a past whose glories could not be surpassed by any other civilization. If Farouk's subjects wanted him to accomplish any one task, the choice was simple: Get the British out of Egypt. That was Farouk's real mandate, to break the yoke of imperialism that had been Egypt's scourge since the dog days of the Assyrians in the seventh century B.C. If Farouk could do that, and only that, he could join the pantheon, and more. So hated were the British that if Farouk could somehow drive them away, he would be a messiah.

Egypt's endless history of foreign domination—by Assyrians, Babylonians, Persians, Macedonians, Greeks, Romans, Arabs, Turks, French, and last but most hated, British—was not without its high points. Egypt has been a tale of three magnificent cities—Thebes, Alexandria, and Cairo. Cairo came first, or at least its predecessory environs of Memphis, which was the capital of the pharaonic Old Kingdom. Thebes, with its great temples of Luxor and Karnak and its death Valley of the Kings, was capital of the Middle and New Kingdoms. Alexandria in its day as the seat of the Ptolemaic dynasties was the capital of the intellectual world and one of the greatest cities on earth. Its day lasted for over six centuries, from its foundation by Alexander the Great, who came from Macedon to conquer Egypt from the Persians in 332 B.C., and its development by Alexander's successor, General, then satrap, then King Ptolemy.

With its famous lighthouse, library, and medical school, Ptolemaic Alexandria was the crown jewel of the Mediterranean, a Greek city-state at the mouth of the Nile that would have impressed Plato and Aristotle. Euclid of geometry, Aristarchus of astronomy, Archimedes of the screw, Eratosthenes, who first measured the earth, and Erasistratus, who first posited the connected between sexual difficulties and nervous breakdowns, all worked and studied at the Mouseion, or shrine to the muses, the forerunner of modern universities. There were more Jews in Alexandria than anywhere other than Jerusalem, and the city was the leader in validating Christianity on a philosophical basis and serving as the metropolitan midwife in delivering the new religion into the Roman world. At the same time, Christianity echoed, if not borrowed, the symbols of the spirituality of ancient Egypt: the resurrection of Osiris as the sun god, the mother goddess Isis with her son Horus, the looped-cross ankh, the symbol of life.

The last of the Ptolemies was Cleopatra, who became queen at seventeen, married two of her brothers, had earth-shaking affairs with Julius Caesar and Marc Antony, and died at thirty-nine by asp bite, all in the name of power. With Cleopatra and her power went

Alexandria, which fell to Octavian and became the second city of the Roman Empire. In A.D. 45, according to Coptic (Egyptian Christian) tradition, Christianity was introduced into Alexandria by St. Mark, whose first convert was a Jewish shoemaker. Despite the efforts of the generally unholy Roman emperors to compel the worship of no god other than themselves, God, bolstered by Osiris tradition, eventually prevailed. Paradoxically, the rise of Christianity marked the decline of Alexandria. When Emperor Constantine moved the Roman capital to the shores of the Bosphorous, religious dissension between the Byzantine Christians and the Coptic Christians turned Alexandria into a theological battleground that tore the city apart and made it easy prey for the Muslim Arabs who conquered the city with little effort in 641.

The Arabs were not responsible for burning the great library; that barbarity was the work of the Christians. In fact, the Arab invaders tolerated the Copts and made them the tax collectors of the realm. They also respected Alexandria and its grand traditions. But the city was already of the past and fast fading. If the Greeks and Romans looked to the sea, the Arabs looked to the desert. When the victorious Arab leader General Amr wrote to the caliph in Arabia: "I have taken a city of which I can only say that it contains 4000 palaces, 4000 baths, 400 theatres, 1200 greengrocers and 40,000 Jews," the caliph responded by rewarding the bearer of Amr's message with a spartan meal of bread and oil and dates. The Arabs didn't care about this great city with its great culture and its great harbor. They didn't even care when the Venetians stole the body of St. Mark from Alexandria, hiding it in a barrel of pickled pork to deter the curiosity of Muslim harbor officials. The Arabs were in every way indifferent to maritime Alexandria. They wanted a desert capital. To that end, they went back to the beginnings of Egypt and founded a new city near the ancient one of Memphis, on the site of the Roman fortress called Babylon, and called it Fustat, which quickly grew. Al-Qahirah was the name of one of Fustat's early subdivisions, which eventually took on the name of the burgeoning city itself: Cairo.

It was the Cairo of the fifteenth century, and not Baghdad, that was the actual setting for *The Arabian Nights.* As it is written there: "He who hath not seen Cairo hath not seen the world. Her soil is gold; her Nile is a marvel; her women are like the black-eyed virgins of Paradise; her houses are palaces; and her air is soft, as sweet-smelling as aloeswood, rejoicing the heart." The Arabs called Cairo "Mother of the World." Yet as this was written, Cairo had already seen better days and would soon see worse.

Cairo's high-water mark occurred in the eleventh century, when it became a sophisticated metropolis of half a million people living in five-story buildings that had running water and an advanced sewer system, at a time when London and Paris were still mired in the medieval. But all the sophistication was obliterated by a series of seven low Niles that began in 1066, the year of the Norman Conquest of England. Famine spread, and Cairenes became cannibals, looting the palaces and libraries. Compounding Egypt's precarious position was the commencement of the Crusades, which were motivated not only by missionary zeal but also by greed for the treasures of the East.

Enter Salah-ed-Din, or Saladin, a Kurdish general who captured Jerusalem, held Richard the Lionhearted at Acre, and became the scourge of the Crusaders. The greatest warrior of a warrior age, Saladin built Egypt into an empire that extended all the way to Damascus and Aleppo. Saladin's successors, facing the onslaught of Genghis Khan and his Mongol hordes, reinforced their army and guaranteed its loyalty by conscripting an elite force of slave warriors known as Mamelukes, from the Caucasus Mountains. The Circassians, as the people from this forbidding region above the Black Sea were called, were renowned for their fierceness as men, their beauty as women. The tallest and fairest of all Caucasians, the Circassians were the prototype of the Master Race, more Aryan than the true Aryans farther to the east in the Hindu Kush.

As soldiers, the Circassian Mamelukes lived up to, and beyond, their genetic reputation. In short time, these slaves became masters, murdering the Egyptian sultan in 1250, seizing control of the country, and defeating the Mongol invaders as well as the crusaders, expelling them from their footholds along the Palestine coast. The Mamelukes thereby became the heroes of the Islamic world. The system by which they perpetuated their power was a military slave oligarchy. Young Circassian boys would be impressed as slaves and brought to Egypt, where they would be converted to Islam and rigorously basic-trained as soldiers. Once inculcated with religion and militarism, they would be set free and placed in the private army of one of the Mameluke nobles, or emirs. The pre-eminent emir was designated sultan, whose power was checked by his need for the private armies of his fellow nobles in the wars against outside invaders. To prevent any "softness" in these armies, sons of warriors were never allowed to pursue military careers or succeed their fathers in power. Instead, new slaves from the Caucasus were continually being brought to Egypt.

The most powerful of all the Mameluke sultans, Mohammed An-Nasir, was the rare exception to this strict policy against nepotism. Stepping into a power vacuum created by the unanticipated death of his sultan father and the stalemate among the emirs in deciding who among them should succeed to the top position in Cairo, An-Nasir took the throne at nine but was treated worse than any slave to make sure he was unable to exercise real authority. The emirs' discipline backfired. An-Nasir escaped the palace in his early twenties, fled to Syria, raised his own army, returned to Cairo, and murdered each of his father's emir rivals, consolidating all authority in himself. Not wanting to be dependent on the private armies, the bellicose An-Nasir then became a great peacemaker and kept Egypt out of war. He devoted himself to culture and the arts and built many of Cairo's finest mosques and palaces, turning the city into an Arabian Nights fantasy.

Too much of this culture proved fatal to Egypt. Because An-Nasir had the Mamelukes stop fighting, the Egyptian military ceased to be the world's supreme fighting machine. After Sultan An-Nasir's death, the country fell apart, its demise accelerated by the outbreak of the Black Death and the invasions of Tamerlaine. Meanwhile, the Mamelukes refused to adapt to the changing world of war. They had been trained as a cavalry force and refused to fight by any other method. The use of gunpowder was more than newfangled; it was for sissies. Real men used swords. The Ottoman Turks, who became the major rivals of the Mamelukes, weren't proud. In 1516, the Turkish cannons decimated the Egyptian horse soldiers, and the Ottoman Sultan, Selim the Grim, became the master of Egypt. Cairo became a vassal to Constantinople, Egypt an Ottoman province. While Europe was thriving in the splendors of the Renaissance, Egypt was mired in a dark age. New routes to Asia bypassed Egypt altogether, and the voyages of Columbus and his successors proved that the sea, not the sands, was the high road to the future.

The counterpoint to Europe's galloping modernity was a burgeoning love affair with the past, and no past was more romantic than that of Egypt's. It is not surprising that the rise in power of monarchs like Le Roi Soleil would engender a fascination with and vogue for the original sun kings, the pharaohs. When Louis XIV died, he ordered that his body be embalmed and mummified. Also deeply intrigued by the Middle East was Napoleon Bonaparte, who saw himself not only in the Valley of the Kings but also in the tradition of Alexander the Great. In 1798 he brought a huge force to Egypt, landing at Alexandria and proceeding up the Nile Valley to defeat the enervated Mamelukes at the Battle of the Pyramids.

The Egypt Napoleon found was little more than a second-rate Turkish colony filled with sand-buried antiquities, one of which was the Rosetta Stone, which was discovered by one of Napoleon's officers and took twenty years to be deciphered. Napoleon did not have long to dwell on his disappointments with the country. The British expelled him from Egypt in the Battle of Aboukir in 1801. The British themselves departed, though hardly for good, in 1803, leaving the country to their then-allies, the Turks.

Because the Turks themselves were weak and had a hard time controlling their Mameluke subjects, a new power vacuum followed this European military exodus. Into it slipped the illustrious founder of King's Farouk's dynasty. To dispel the widely held notion that Farouk was an "Arab," it should be stressed here that his dynasty was in no way Arab whatsoever. Mohammed Ali was, if anything, a Greek, but there were other European strains in his makeup. Born in 1769 in the Aegean port city of Cavalla, in the border region between Macedonia and what is now Turkey, Mohammed Ali was an ambitious orphan brought up by a French tobacco merchant. He strategically married the daughter of the mayor of Cavalla and quickly rose through the ranks of the Ottoman military. He arrived in Egypt in the wake of the British departure and became second in command of the mercenary Albanian wing of the Ottoman occupation army that was trying to create a fragile peace in the disrupted country.

Peace under the Ottomans was impossible. The reason the Egyptians endured the rule of the Mamelukes as long as they did was that they thought the Mamelukes would preserve the status quo and protect them from foreign invasion. Napoleon's brief conquest undermined this assumption and demonstrated how anemic the Mamelukes actually were. The new Ottoman would-be peacekeepers made the French expeditionary forces seem as polite as the Vatican Guard. These soldiers raped women at will, took whatever fancied them under the excuse that they were merely compensating themselves because their officers had not. At the same time, both the Ottomans and the Mamelukes assessed the population with onerous taxes for which they saw no benefit. Two Ottoman governors in a row were assassinated.

Sensing that the Ottoman horse he had ridden into Egypt was a losing one, Mohammed Ali adopted the role of a neutral peacemaker and reformulated his Albanian mercenaries as a high-minded, above-the-fray police force. At the same time, he sidled up to the Mameluke leaders, or beys, who soon took an upper hand, albeit an unsteady one, against the Ottomans. By 1805, the spiritual leader of Cairo, the rector of Al Azhar University, the Oxford of Islam, declared the Ottoman governor of Egypt deposed and proclaimed Mohammed Ali the new governor of Egypt. In Istanbul, the Ottoman sultan was too deep in his own problems to cavil with this local coup. The Ottoman Empire, reeling from a disastrous war with Russia, whereby it lost the Crimea, would soon be mocked by the czar as the "sick man of Europe." Egypt could only make it sicker. Mohammed Ali softened the blow by making a large show of his loyalty to the Sublime Porte, as Constantinople was known. It was all show.

Consolidating his power, Mohammed Ali used the Mameluke armies to repel the invasion of a new British expeditionary force at Rosetta in 1807. The severed heads of hundreds of British seamen were then speared on stakes to decorate the streets of Cairo, testament to the country's continuing medievality. The testament continued in 1811, when Mohammed Ali invited 470 of his Mameluke allies to the ancient citadel overlooking Cairo to celebrate the investiture of his son Toussoun as a military commander. The governor's guests proved to be a captive audience. After coffee, he gave a signal. The gates of the fortress slammed shut. All 470 Mamelukes were massacred, thus ending with poetic barbarity their seven-century reign of terror. Egypt could rejoice that their foreign occupiers were finally gone. Free at last. Even though Mohammed Ali himself was as un-Egyptian as anyone, the local population viewed him as one of them. He was their liberator.

Soon Egypt saw how foreign, though not malevolently or imperially so, Mohammed Ali really was. Under his rule, feudalism immediately gave way to modernity. Instead of continuing to emulate Saladin, the most famous warrior-sultan of Egypt's Islamic past,

Mohammed Ali Pasha (his new title, Turkish for "lord") took Napoleon as his role model and set the tone for his dynasty by looking to Europe for inspiration. The white-maned, white-bearded Mohammed Ali, whose portraits resemble a cross between Ali Baba and Santa Claus smoking a hookah, did not share the Arab's aquaphobia. He set about building up a navy and a merchant marine and did his all to encourage international commerce by revitalizing Alexandria, which had shrunk to a ghost port of barely five thousand inhabitants. He initiated the growth of the long staple cotton that would soon create an entire class of millionaires in Egypt. He also imported silkworms and mulberry trees from Syria and cashmere goats from India, and built factories to manufacture the silk and wool, as well as rifles, gunpowder, and other basic defense items that Egypt had formerly imported.

Soon Mohammed Ali went on the offensive. He conscripted the fellaheen into the top standing army in the Middle East, then recruited French officers, out of work after the fall of Napoleon, to lead it. One of them, Colonel Joseph Sève, converted to Islam, renamed himself Suleiman Pasha, and was a direct antecedent of King Farouk's mother, Queen Nazli. Sève and his fellow Europeans became the nucleus of an international society, at first centered in Alexandria, that would flourish and give Egypt its cosmopolitan character in the century ahead.

Despite all the foreigners in his midst, Mohammed Ali was nonetheless a very Oriental potentate. He never learned any of the languages of the Western Europeans he imported. He had a huge harem, and reputedly fathered over one hundred sons and even more daughters. He dressed in flowing Turkish robes, ate without silverware, reclining on carpets, had a staff of soothsayers, believed in genies, was terrified of the evil eye, and was not above beheading or otherwise torturing his enemies in very "Oriental" ways. In short, he lived like his "master," the Ottoman sultan. Soon Mohammed Ali decided that their positions should be reversed.

Mohammed Ali's forces conquered much of the Hejaz—what is today Saudi Arabia—as well as the Sudan, from whence flowed the Nile. Even though conscription for these campaigns was highly unpopular, using nationals for the army was Mohammed Ali's first move in giving Egypt back to the Egyptians. Leading this campaign of Egyptianization, as well as Mohammed Ali's armies, was his eldest son, Ibrahim. At sixteen, Ibrahim had been sent to Constantinople as a sort of hostage to ensure his father's continued fidelity to the Sublime Porte. His year on the Bosphorous turned Ibrahim into a rabid Ottoman-hater and a proud nationalist fond of saying that the hot sun of Egypt had baked him into an Egyptian. While son was promoting native Egyptians to the officer ranks of the army for the first time since the pharaohs, father was likewise integrating native Egyptians into the government and civil service.

Mohammed Ali continued to look abroad, attacking Greece and finally making his big move in conquering Syria and declaring war on his nominal overload, the Ottoman sultan. Egypt's increasing power made the European leaders highly nervous. Newspapers in London and Paris cooked up a true yellow press campaign of a new holy war, with Muslims slaughtering Christians. It took an entente of England, France, and Russia to put an end to Mohammed Ali's dreams of empire. The entente was led by the British lord Palmerston, who was deeply worried that Egypt would use up for itself all the long staple cotton so prized by everyone from the shirtmakers of Jermyn Street to the factories in Lancashire. British industry survived by its exports, making "white shirts for brown men," and Palmerston couldn't (and wouldn't) risk competing with the factories of Mohammed Ali. In 1839 Mohammed Ali's invading armies were a day's march away from Constantinople when Palmerston and company got in bed with the Ottoman sultan. The mighty British fleet, which had sunk the Egyptian Navy off Greece as an early warning sign in 1827, now anchored in the sea, guns raised, across from Mohammed Ali's new and grand Ras-el-Tin Palace in Alexandria. The British admiral, Sir Charles Napier, came ashore to give the pasha this ultimatum: "If your highness will not listen to my unofficial appeal to you against the folly of further resistance, it only remains for me to bombard you, and by God I will bombard you and plant my bombs in the middle of this room where you are sitting." It was clear to Mohammed Ali that his imperial days were over. Egypt never forgave the British for it.

Conceding his unqualified allegiance to the Ottoman sultan, Mohammed Ali was forced to abandon his navy, to replace his Egyptian officers with Ottoman ones, and drastically to reduce the size of his army. Unable to expand Egypt outwardly, Mohammed Ali spent the rest of his life modernizing his adopted country. He built hospitals staffed with French-trained doctors, drained swamps, created universities and government presses, and even banned Cairo's famous dancing prostitutes, exiling them to Upper Egypt so that the sensibilities of European visitors would not be violated.

Mohammed Ali, for all his nascent nationalism and humiliation, at the hand of Europe, was anything but xenophobic. Although perhaps his greatest accomplishment was in giving the Egyptian fellah a sense of self-esteem for "beating" the hated Ottoman overlords, at the same time the great pasha never turned his back on Europe. Rather, he embraced it, especially France, importing French experts and exporting his son Ismail to Paris, where he would see the creation of the *grands boulevards* out of the medieval slums and thereby get his own inspiration for the transformation of Cairo in Paris's imperial image.

E. M. Forster wrote that the real reason Mohammed Ali admired European civilization was "because it made people aggressive and gave them guns," but he had no sense of its finer aspects, and his "reforms" were mainly veneer to impress travelers. Then again, Forster was British, and the British, whether journalists or statesmen, have tended to regard modern Egypt with a jaundiced eye. Mohammed Ali, as well as most of his successors, returned an equally unforgiving stare. The one country the pasha detested was Britain, the architect of the demise of his own foreign ambitions. After Britain forced Mohammed Ali to accept nominal Ottoman vassalage in 1841, it also forced him to lift the trade embargoes that protected his infant industries. British goods immediately flooded into Egypt, while Egypt was once again reduced from being a manufacturer to being a supplier of raw materials chiefly to Britain.

On the autocratic side of his progressive ledger, Mohammed Ali confiscated all the country's privately held land, making himself, in one fell swoop, the richest man in Egypt. He created his own new elite by distributing this land among his family, retainers, rural government administrators, and tax collectors. At the low end of the social pyramid, while Mohammed Ali may have given pride to the fellaheen, he also broke their backs. His system of corvée, forced labor, definitely provided Egypt with a modern infrastructure. The cost was in lives. When the Suez Canal was built under the corvée, over 100,000 fellaheen died in the project.

Socially, Mohammed Ali lived better than any king in Europe since Louis XIV. His Shoubra Palace on the Nile in Cairo was a marble-pavilioned pleasure dome worthy of Kublai Khan, with crocodile fountains and naked-nymph frescoes and a harem of hundreds of women cavorting in real life for the pasha's delectation. Certain pleasures of the East were worth preserving. When Mohammed Ali died at eighty in 1849, he had magically remade his kingdom from a feudal backwater into a modern land that the great powers of Europe could not help but covet.

Mohammed Ali's son Said expanded his father's internationalism by granting Ferdinand de Lesseps a charter to build the Suez Canal, hence the honorarium of the name of the new city, Port Said, at the entrance to the isthmus. De Lesseps, an ambitious French consul at Alexandria and cousin of Empress Eugénie, had befriended Said when he was a boy. Mohammed Ali, worried that his son was prone to corpulence, had placed him on a very restrictive diet. Ali, who himself had never learned to read before he was forty and found this no impediment, was blithely unconcerned with his son's academics. He was, however, obsessed with Said's weight. Frenchman de Lesseps took pity on the deprived boy and invited him to the consulate for secret feasts of macaroni. Years later, Said signed de Lesseps's charter without even trying to read it, retaining for Egypt a mere sixth of the prospective profits from the venture, the vast majority going to the foreign promoters.

In 1869, when the canal opened, Said had died and been succeeded by his nephew Ismail. Ismail had taken the new title of khedive (which meant "viceroy") of the sultan of the Ottoman Empire. Such fealty was polite but illusory; aside from wearing the fez and stambouline, the long, collarless frock coat that was the costume of the Ottoman rulers, as a sign of respect to Constantinople, Ismail was an absolute monarch.

The bearded, bullish, heavy-lidded, green-eyed Ismail was Farouk's grandfather. In his extravagances, he was also Farouk's inspiration. The khedive's education in Vienna and Paris, his perfect French, and his warm welcome as a young man in the courts of the "Continent" (and not the dark one) resulted in his determination to make Egypt part of Europe. To that end, once he became ruler in 1863, he began rebuilding central Cairo in the monumental Parisian grand boulevard style of Baron Haussmann. He completed the vast royal palaces of Ras-el-Tin in Alexandria and Abdine and Koubbeh in Cairo in the Italianate style. He built an opera house in Cairo specifically for the opening of the canal. Verdi was composing *Aida* for the event. The cotton blockades of the Civil War in America had created a worldwide shortage that had made Ismail an enormous windfall. He used it to build railways, telegraph lines, irrigation canals, hospitals, and universities to lure the Europeans. To further cosset them and prevent them from feeling too alienated, he perpetuated a system known as the Capitulations, under which foreigners in Egypt paid no taxes, were not subject to any Egyptian laws, and would be tried only in their own courts, the "mixed courts," as the complex foreign judiciary that was set up came to be called.

The Suez Canal inaugural was probably the party of the century. The French imperial yacht, the *Aigle* (bearing Empress Eugénie, Ismail's alleged mistress), led the sixty-eight-ship procession. Following behind were Emperor Franz Joseph of Austria, Crown Prince Friedrich Wilhelm of Prussia, and Prince Henry of the Netherlands, as well as thousands of other European royals and plutocrats who came to mix with the Ottoman nabils, African chieftains, and Indian maharajas at the balls and pageants and trips up the Nile and around the pyramids and to the opera (Verdi was late with *Aida,* so they did *Rigoletto* instead) and, in general, to see how "Western" Egypt had become. They stayed at the Arabian Nights Gezira Palace, which Ismail built especially to lodge them for the event and which has now been converted into the Cairo Marriott.

Lest his zeal to please the Europeans brand Ismail a turncoat wog, a sort of Egyptian Stepin Fetchit, it must be noted that he still retained certain Oriental potentatisms—he impatiently had his treacherous finance minister, whose mother had been the khedive's wet nurse, strangled when the poisoned coffee didn't work—and he always outdid the Europeans at their own pretensions. He ordered up elaborate French banquets of classic *après moi le déluge* dishes such as lièvre à la royale, served on priceless Sèvres china and diamond-studded crystal, washed down with champagne and Chateau d'Yquem, with the extra "Oriental" fillips and frissons of the guests being waited on by Nubians in turbans and livery, whirling dervishes supplying the entertainment, and dwarfs and eunuchs in the wings providing the intrigue. Visitors to the khedive's palaces slept on solid silver beds, under silk mosquito netting, sat on gilded Empire furniture under Gobelin tapestries, walked on Italian marble, and shat in solid gold toilets. The experience compared favorably to Versailles and Windsor. Commencing a distaff tradition that came into full (de)flower under Farouk, Ismail kept innumerable European mistresses, often presented to him as "palace guests" by his continental friends. Some of the women were granted business concessions and became quite prosperous.

Many of the khedive's ministers and palace officials were European themselves, some having previously served such ill-fated masters as Napoleon III and Maximilian of Mexico. They found Cairo a safe harbor, as did a large number of Confederate officers who became mercenaries for Ismail, as also did the famous British General Charles "Chinese" Gordon, so called for his heroics in the capture of Peking and the suppression of the Tai-ping rebellion. Gordon served Ismail as his governor of the Sudan, where he was later killed and decapitated in the violent native uprising at Khartoum in 1885 that precipitated the even more violent British reprisal under Lord Kitchener at Omdurman in 1898.

The only problem with Ismail's dazzling westernizations was that they bankrupted him. Better at high hospitality than high finance, Ismail found himself saddled with Shylockian rates of interest. In a deal masterminded by Prime Minister Disraeli for Queen Victoria, Ismail sold off a huge controlling block of Suez Canal stock to the British for four million pounds, a mere fourth of its original value. By 1879, the national debt was at a back-breaking one hundred million pounds. The European lenders, led by the Rothschilds, got nervous. All his assimilation notwithstanding, Ismail was not "one of the club." He was a potential deadbeat; he had to go. The British and the French set up as their hatchet man the Ottoman sultan, backing him up and providing him with a power he had long before lost. They had the sultan send a telegram to his vassal, addressed to the "ex-khedive of Egypt." Ismail was now back to being a pasha. His son, Tewfik, the sultan informed him, was the new khedive. Ismail was well aware of the Anglo-French long knives behind the Sublime Porte. He saluted his son as his new master and, four days later, sailed from Alexandria to Naples on the royal yacht *Mahroussa,* the same ship that would take his grandson, Farouk, and his great-grandson, Fuad, into a similar Italian exile three quarters of a century later.

Ismail died in Constantinople in 1895, having grown fat and depressed about never getting to see his transformed Egypt again. His cosmopolitan legacy remained. At the time of his exile, over 100,000 Europeans were living in Egypt. More arrived for the winter season, for Ismail had placed the country on the grand tour map as the ultimate holiday destination. Aside from all the history and

the Capitulations to lure the foreigners, there were Anglican and
Catholic churches, synagogues, Pall Mall exclusive men's clubs, La
Scala–level opera, Rue de la Paix–quality shopping, and to Europeans who hated the cold and the damp, the Mediterranean breezes of
Alexandria and the desert warmth of Cairo. These were irresistible
attractions, as were the prospects of making a killing in the nascent,
protected economy.

Soon, unfortunately, there was trouble in paradise. Khedive
Tewfik was shy and parochial and altogether different from his father; at the time of his accession at age twenty-seven, he had never
left the country. One of the most notable accomplishments of his
regime was the abolition of flogging as a punishment for the fellaheen. Nevertheless, it was too late for gratitude; the peasants were
about to bite the hand that had beaten them. Colonel Ahmed Arabi
was a fellah from the Nile delta town of Zagazig who had risen to
become a high-ranking officer in the Egyptian Army. Now he
wanted to use his position to help those from whose lowly ranks he
had risen. Arabi led a movement against Tewfik and his Mohammed Ali dynasty, whom Arabi characterized as Turkish overlords,
as well as against the European debt-mongers. "Egypt for the Egyptians" was his slogan, one that threw Tewfik and the British into
each other's arms. Arabi led a series of nationalist demonstrations,
surrounding Abdine Palace with thousands of armed troops, chant-
ing, "We are not slaves." Tewfik's response was a petulant, lame
one: "I am the khedive and I do whatever I like." In 1882, Arabi's
demonstrations had mutated into a threatened full-scale insurrection. Tewfik called for help. Intervening to protect the Suez Canal,
the naval lifeline of the empire, Britain sent its fleet into the Alexandria harbor. The boats raised their guns, inciting a huge riot among
the Arabi followers, in which over fifty Europeans were murdered.
Afterward the British began a bombardment that continued for
over ten and a half hours, and destroyed much of the European-
looking city. Then the British landed, defeated Arabi's forces in the
desert at Tel il Kebir, and exiled the fellah firebrand to Ceylon.
Although the British declared that they had arrived only to "rees-
tablish order" and promised an immediate departure, they remained in Egypt until 1956.

The new, official British presence, known as the "veiled protectorate," was epitomized by their consul general Sir Evelyn Baring,
an aristocrat of the famous Baring brothers banking family, a major

in the Royal Artillery and a career diplomat with service across the empire from the Indies to India. His nickname was "Overbaring." The Egyptians called him "The Lord." The French, the Germans, the Russians, and the Turks began getting annoyed at the British presence, demanding to know when the British were going to get out. As soon as the debt is paid off and the khedive's authority has been reestablished, the British assured their fellow colonialists. Baring's first order of business was indeed to pay off the national debt. But the British still didn't leave, owing to the series of crises in the Sudan that cost the life of Chinese Gordon. Meanwhile, Khedive Tewfik died in 1892 and was succeeded by his eldest son, Abbas Hilmi, who was cut more in the mold of his grandfather, Ismail. Educated in Europe, the reddish-haired, brown-eyed, portly young khedive had Ismail's perfect, continental manners. He was so worldly, he even had a pet bulldog, although traditional Muslims, perceiving such pets as unclean, were offended. Whatever Abbas did, Sir Evelyn Baring was not impressed and gave Abbas the stern-headmaster treatment, his justification being totally racist, in the oldest, British imperial sense: one had to treat "Orientals" firmly, anything southeast of the Danube constituting the Orient.

Baring's imperialist partner in Egypt was Lord Herbert Kitchener, the sirdar, or commander in chief, of the Egyptian Army. In 1898, Kitchener avenged Chinese Gordon with a smashing victory at Omdurman, his twenty thousand men defeating the sixty thousand of the khalifa Abdullah. The result was that the Sudan, which had formerly been conquered by Egypt, now became the Anglo-Egyptian Sudan, flying both flags. Any hopes of Egyptian nationalists that the British would be out of this part of Africa were extinguished. The Mohammed Ali dynasty, by seeking British aid to maintain its hegemony, had been hoist on its own petard.

On a social as well as commercial basis, Egypt continued to draw business as well as tourism. The stability provided by the British was a magnet. Posh resort hotels were built, like the Winter Palace at Luxor, the Cataract at Aswan, a new addition to the 1841-founded Shepheard's Hotel in Cairo. The Gezira Sporting Club was founded in Zamalek for the polo-golf-tennis sporting life of the British plutocracy and bureaucracy. Native Egyptians were excluded, as was the ruling "Turkish" aristocracy. This Egyptian exclusion act was supposedly the brainstorm of the xenophobic Lord Kitchener. The question was, whose country was this anyhow? Abbas Hilmi seemed to know the answer. Rather than beat the British, he basically ignored them, concentrating on augmenting his personal fortune, erecting an ersatz Italian palazzo as his summer palace at Montazah and another mansion on the Bosphorus. Many members of the Mohammed Ali dynasty had married Ottoman royalty. With all his relations there, the khedive felt Constantinople was a second home, and in some ways more inviting to him than an Egypt where he was treated with condescension by the British on one hand and resentment by the native Egyptians on the other. In Cairo, Abbas settled for comfort and privilege, surveying from his royal carriages preceded by his liveried running footmen a gilded cage of an empire in which he was more a vassal than a prince.

When World War I broke out in 1914, Khedive Abbas Hilmi was in Constantinople visiting the Turkish sultan, Mehmed V, a gentle man who was so gentle that there was a movement afoot in the dwindling Ottoman Empire to have Abbas Hilmi replace Mehmed and be designated caliph. Whatever Abbas's Ottoman ambitions, his Anglo antipathies were well understood, and when Turkey threw in its wartime lot with the Germans, Britain invoked guilt by association, even though Egypt had in no way entered the war and had declared itself neutral. Britain at last saw an opportunity to declare the country a full-scale British protectorate. Its Foreign Office statement continued: "The suzerainty of Turkey is thus terminated and His Majesty's Government will adopt all measures necessary for the Defence of Egypt and protect its inhabitants and interests." Britain immediately deposed Abbas Hilmi as a vassal of the Turkish sultan, thereby an ally of the Germans and an enemy of the British Empire, and replaced him with his uncle, Hussein Kemal, the second son of Khedive Ismail. The British gave Hussein the new title of sultan of Egypt, which was, of course, belied by the ubiquity of the wartime British presence. Under the guise of "defending" the Nile and the Suez Canal, Britain used the country under Egyptian commander in chief Lord Edmund Allenby as the launching pad for its campaigns in Palestine and at Gallipoli. Egypt may have been free of the Turks, but in fact it was less free of England than ever before.

When the new sultan died in 1917 after overeating at a banquet at Abdine Palace, an unexpected opening occurred regarding his successor. The British first chose Hussein Kemal's sportsman son, Prince Kemal-el-Din, but Kemal refused. He said he preferred to have his time free to hunt big game in Africa, then added, "I have the best wife and the best horse in the world. Why should I want anything more?" Actually, Kemal was pro-German. Feeling that Germany would win the war, he did not want to be a puppet of the losing side. The British then gave the nod to Hussein's brother, the twelfth and youngest child of the khedive Ismail, Ahmed Fuad, who spoke even less Arabic than Lord Cromer.

Fuad was only eleven when he left Egypt in his father's forced exile to Italy. There the family were guests of King Umberto, who installed them in his Villa la Favorita in Naples. The young Fuad was educated at schools in Geneva and at the Italian Military Academy in Turin. After graduation, Fuad became an artillery lieutenant in the Italian Army. He was based in Rome and developed a deep passion for that city, all things Italian, and, above all, gourmandizing and gambling, which he imparted to his son, Farouk. Family ties then secured him the post as aide-de-camp of the Ottoman sultan in Vienna, and finally resulted in his return in 1895, at age twenty-eight, to Egypt to be aide-de-camp to his nephew but sovereign (because of the scattered secession), the khedive Abbas Hilmi. Fuad at the time was destitute. Despite Fuad's habits of a sybaritic prince, his nephew gave him the wages of only a functionary. He ran up tabs all over Cairo, with the porters of all *the* men's clubs, at the Long Bar at Shepheard's Hotel, and with service people from haberdashers to harlots. His only way out of the red was by strategic conjugality. The chief object of his affections was the rich and prominent Mrs. Suarez. But she was off limits, first because she was married and unwilling to get a divorce, and, second, because she was Jewish. The next best solution for Fuad, then, was to plight his troth to his heiress cousin, the nineteen-year-old Princess Shivekiar.

Shivekiar's grandfather and Fuad's uncle, Prince Ahmed Fahmi, was the older brother of Khedive Ismail, and would have been khedive himself had he not died in a railway accident. Prince Ahmed's son, Ahmed, had three children, Shivekiar and two brothers, Mohammed Abrahim and Ahmed Seif ed-Din, with the latter of whom Shivekiar was widely rumored to have had an incestuous affair in the pink palace where they grew up across from the British Residency on the banks of the Nile. The rumors did nothing to deter the fiscally strapped Fuad. He married the weak-chinned, high-spirited Shivekiar in 1896. Nine months later they had a son, Ismail, who died after another nine months. That was the end of

Shivekiar's childbearing as well as any illusion of romance in this marriage of opportunism. Fuad, invoking the precepts of the Sublime Porte that a woman's place was in the harem, locked his wife in the palace he had inherited and resumed his secret affair with Mrs. Suarez.

While at the palace, Fuad spent his time looking for dust and dirt the servants may have missed, smothering any imagined odor by spraying with cologne from a solid gold atomizer he constantly carried with him. Fuad's fetish for cleanliness was said to have come from an incident as a boy, when a pail of garbage was accidentally thrown all over him, or it may have simply been his fastidious Italian military training. The army regimen may have also accounted for his waking up at six every morning to do a drill of exercises, always in front of a mirror. What Fuad's narcissism stemmed from was not instantly apparent. Squat, portly, jowly, and sporting an upturned twirled mustache, Fuad compensated for his natural limitations by being a dapper dresser in very British pinstripes, a pocket square, spats, and a cane, as well as his de rigueur fez. Savile Row meets Al Azhar. The "Oriental" side of Fuad came out not only in his intense sexism but also in his mysticism. His most trusted confidant after Mrs. Suarez was his Indian fortune-teller, who promised him that one day he would be king. The mystic also told him that the letter *F* was his good luck symbol, hence the names of his children to come and the profusion of F's on everything Fuad owned, from carriages to dishes to furniture to hairbrushes.

While keeping his wife in purdah, Fuad had no compunction squandering her fortune, especially gambling at cards. Then one day in 1898, his luck ran out. Fuad was at his favorite haunt and Cairo's most exclusive preserve, the Mohammed Ali Club, when Shivekiar's allegedly amorous younger brother, Prince Seif ed-Din, incensed at the shabby, high-handed treatment his sister was getting from this fortune hunter, burst into the club, ran up the stairs, cornered Fuad in the Silence Room, and shot him three times, in the leg, in the chest, and in the throat.

As the assassin prince sauntered nonchalantly down the grand staircase, pashas and diplomats dived for cover behind the plush leather couches and Fuad lay bleeding to death. The prince was soon arrested by British officers. Doctors rushed to the club, where they concluded they had no choice but to operate on the spot. Fuad,

The Source • Mohammed Ali, the founder of Farouk's dynasty.   Imperial War Museum

Ship of Jewels • The *Mahroussa*, Egypt's royal yacht, which carried the Khedive Ismail into Italian exile in 1879, and did the same with Farouk in 1952.

Patrimony • King Fuad, Farouk's father.

still conscious, screamed refusal when they tried to knock him out with chloroform. Among his many paranoias was anesthetics. The doctors took the bullets from his chest and leg. However, the one in his throat was so delicately close to an artery they decided not to risk removing it. While the surgery was going on, the half-delirious but always superstitious Fuad spotted a nightingale on the window ledge outside. He told himself: If it sings three times, I will live. The bird sang three times. Fuad finally lost consciousness. He did live, albeit with a bullet in his throat which caused a laryngeal spasm that resulted in an occasional and uncontrollable doglike bark. The yelping was quite a shock to anyone who wasn't prepared for it, but the protocol was to ignore it completely. Once Fuad became king, he took revenge on all those who looked askance or at all on his infirmity. Anyone who raised even the slightest eyebrow at the bark was immediately and irrevocably stricken from the palace guest lists.

As for the revenge on Seif ed-Din, Lord Cromer ordered a trial, if only to prove that the Egyptian royals were not immune to prosecution, that they had no license to kill. One famous, typically English colonial snippet of the testimony was that of the arresting officer describing his capture of the prince: "I saw the nigger standing at the top of the marble steps and closed with him and overpowered him." The court sentenced the prince to five years hard labor at the quarries where the stones for the pyramids had been dug, during which time he wrote a series of death threats against the khedive and other fellow dynasts. Lord Cromer decided Seif ed-Din was insane and sent him off to England, to a genteel madhouse in Tunbridge Wells in Kent.

Soon after Fuad recovered from his shooting, he divorced his cousin. Shivekiar went on to marry four more times, the last time in 1927. One of her sons, Wahid Yussri, was reputedly the lover and, later, secret husband of Farouk's wife, Queen Farida, a romance whose cupid was said to have been Shivekiar herself, as one way of wreaking revenge on the line of Fuad. Another was her taking Farouk under her wing, giving wild parties for him, encouraging his womanizing and gambling and general debauchery and thereby keeping him from his kingly duties. If this was revenge, Farouk loved every minute of it. Shivekiar's New Year's Eve parties were annual exercises in glamorous excess that neither Farouk nor anyone else who was anyone in Egypt would ever dare to miss.

After his divorce, Fuad, ever mindful of the royal prophecy of his Indian seer, devoted himself to appearing "kingly." The royal road to high visibility was paved with charity. Fuad was the president of the new international and secular Egyptian University in Cairo. He was the main sponsor of the Red Crescent, Egypt's Red Cross, the head of the Royal Geographical Society, and, most appropriately for the cleanliness fetishist that he was, the founder of the Museum of Hygiene. He was also the patron of the intrepid young explorer Ahmed Mohammed Hassanein, fresh out of Oxford. Fuad sent a Hassanein-led expedition to the uncharted reaches of the Libyan desert, which won Hassanein the gold medal of the Royal Geographical Society. Like Shivekiar, Hassanein would also figure in the life of Fuad's son. Fuad appointed him Farouk's chief tutor. What Fuad did not figure was that Hassanein would also become involved in a romantic tutorial with Fuad's second wife and Farouk's mother, Queen Nazli.

Fuad was desperate to become king of something. Because he was not in the direct line of succession (not that it necessarily mattered, given the vagaries of British domination), but also because he knew how fickle the British were, Fuad put himself in the running to be named king of Albania, then also part of the Ottoman Empire, of which Fuad considered himself in good standing. He was, alas, passed over. Luckily, the British smiled on him and believing that his bark was far worse than any bite he might have, appointed him their sultan.

Sultan Fuad's first order of business, unpleasant as it might have seemed to him, was to find a new wife. It wasn't kingly to be single, less so to be divorced, and far less so to have Jewish and Italian mistresses. Furthermore, it was essential that a ruler should have an heir. So the fifty-year-old Fuad went looking for someone eligible. After Shivekiar, he had had enough of princesses. He had already used her capital and Mrs. Suarez's investment advice to make himself rich; money now was no object. He wanted someone queenly, beautiful, docile, and fertile.

He found her at the theater, a tall, regal young woman with dark, sultry eyes that promised an excitement that her stately bearing did not. Fuad started asking about her. He found out her identity from Lady Graham, wife of the first secretary of the British Residency, as the embassy was known in protectorate days. Her name was Nazli Sabry. She was the daughter of the minister of agriculture. She was nineteen. Although not of dynastic stock, she was as *haute* as a *bourgeoise* could be in Egypt. She was descended from the French mercenary officer hero, Suleiman Pasha, who had married the daughter of Sherif Pasha, three-time Egyptian prime minister. Educated in Paris, Nazli spoke French as perfectly as the cosmopolitan Fuad. Fuad made his proposition, if not proposal, to Nazli's father through Lady Graham. Nazli turned him down flat. He was too old for her. Believing that no commoner, however highly placed, could say no to the sultan, Fuad persisted in his courtship, insisting that Nazli at least meet him face-to-face. She finally did, at Lady Graham's, and Fuad apparently was irresistible. They were married, without fanfare, in a small palace wedding on May 24, 1919.

The next order of business was to get an heir. At the beginning, Fuad cosseted his new wife, indulging her every desire, such as getting her special combs from Paris. It wasn't so much love, however, as superstition. Fuad had to have a boy. He didn't want to do anything to upset the stars. He even began praying, promising Allah that he would stop gambling and drinking if his wife gave him a son. In the end, a nightingale like the one that "saved" his life at the Mohammed Ali Club years before provided the good omen. The bird perched on Fuad's palace bedroom window. Fuad declared that if the bird sang three times, Nazli would birth a boy. The bird sang three times. Farouk, of course, beginning with the talismanic *F,* the "one who knows right from wrong," was born at Abdine Palace February 11, 1920, or Guimada I, 1338, on the Arab calendar, which dates time from the death of the Prophet.

There were nasty rumors. Because there had been a closed-door marriage ceremony, gossip had it that Nazli had already borne the child *before* Fuad married her, and secreted it in the palace until its official "birth." Had the baby been a girl, Nazli would have been discarded. The same rumors resurfaced thirty-two years later when Narriman gave birth to Farouk's son. Farouk's line to his mistresses, "Give me a son and I'll marry you," may thus have stemmed from his father. Gossip notwithstanding, the formal arrival of Farouk was celebrated throughout Egypt. Fuad gave the palace obstetrician a bonus of a thousand pounds in gold. He ordered an additional ten thousand pounds in gold distributed to the poor and another eight hundred for the mosques in Cairo. Throughout Cairo and Alexandria, delta and desert, lambs were slaughtered and roasted for celebratory feasts, cannon fired all through the night, and the faithful called to prayer for the newborn prince, whom, in April, Lord Allenby formally recognized as "the lawful heir to the Sultanate." Fuad's continued dynasty was thus assured. The eyes of the world were on the little prince who would become the final pharaoh.

VI

THE BOY-KING

Of all the princes on earth, few have been more spoiled and more insulated from the realities of life around them than the young Farouk. One of those realities was his mother, Sultana Nazli. Sultan Fuad also tried to insulate Nazli from the hard duties of motherhood from the very start by surrounding his heir with surrogates—English midwives, governesses, and nannies. Fuad even had a special, fecund peasant girl imported from a legendary milk-and-honey area of Turkey noted for producing hale, hearty, and handsome long-livers to breastfeed the baby mogul.

In the first decade of Farouk's life, Fuad made Nazli a breeding machine, producing the four *F* daughters, one after another. In return for her efforts, Fuad kept Nazli a virtual prisoner in the harem, or women's wing, of Abdine, which he had redecorated with F's on everything. Overseen by Fuad's eunuch in chief, a tremendous Ethiopian named Rizah Aga, five smaller eunuchs from Nubia, dressed more like prime ministers than palace watchmen, in morning coats, striped pants, and red fezzes, guarded the never-photographed harem, keeping it locked from nine P.M. to four A.M. Nazli, who had been quite the girl-about-town before her marriage, was now reduced to a kind of Egyptian Anne Boleyn in the Tower of London. Aside from an occasional opera opening, when Nazli would be glimpsed behind a latticed screen, a royal wedding, or funeral, when she would be glimpsed behind the veil (which was required by law for all Egyptian women in public until 1927), Nazli never left the harem. Her ladies-in-waiting were her chief link with the outside world. Madame Cattawi, an aquiline, Amazonian Sephardic Jewess who was far more royal than even Nazli herself was the head lady-in-waiting, and was also a close friend of Fuad's Jewish mistress, Mrs. Suarez. Their positions in palace life is evidence of the high importance of the Egyptian Jews who were prominent in cotton and banking, and the country's absence of anti-Semitism, at least among the upper crust. One of the tragedies of the Middle East is the diaspora of this Jewish elite to Europe and America (but not Israel) after the fall of Farouk in 1952.

Another of Nazli's ladies-in-waiting, whose title was an honor and whose duty was to be part of Nazli's entourage at state functions, was Zeinab Zulficar, the wife of a judge on the Mixed Court of Appeals in Alexandria, whose daughter Safinaz would eventually become Farouk's Queen Farida. But that was after Fuad had died. While he reigned, he would allow no such palace intrigues as matchmaking, or anything else that would have softened his iron grip over his son and heir. Knowing Nazli was intelligent, ambitious, and capable of such swipes at control, Fuad preempted Nazli's own maternal imperatives, making all decisions about Farouk's upbringing by himself and implementing them through his instrument, the governess Ina Naylor, whom Farouk called Ninzy, and whom he always ran to kiss first when given the choice between governess and mother. "Why don't you kiss me?" Nazli exasperatedly once asked the boy. "Because you wear too much rouge," the prince retorted, and cuddled up in the protective arms of his governess. Nazli was, in effect, under a sort of house arrest for the next sixteen years; she was allowed to visit her son only an hour or so a day. Fuad monitored all her phone calls, his eavesdropping occasionally exposed by his involuntary "bark." Nazli's resentment grew exponentially. It would explode into an obsession with control even greater than Fuad's the instant the ruler died.

Meanwhile, having taken total authority over his palaces, Fuad set out to do the same over his country. This was somewhat more problematic. His chief early nemesis was a fellah leader who had taken up the mantle of Egyptian nationalism that Ahmed Arabi had first worn. Saad Zaghlul was a peasant wunderkind who was a leader of his class at Al Azhar, a judge at twenty-four, and at fifty the head of a delegation that was planning to go to London in 1918, at the close of World War I, to demand that the protectorate be dissolved and Egypt be made independent. London's curt refusal to receive Zaghlul fanned the flames of unrest far more than a courteous runaround would have done. The Egyptian word for delegation, *wafd,* became the name of the new nationalist party that would develop into the most powerful force in Egyptian politics. Mob violence erupted. Seven British subjects were murdered on a train. The rabble-rousing, ascetic-looking Zaghlul was arrested and deported to Malta. In time, Lord Allenby brought Zaghlul back to quell the unrest, and over the next few years an uneasy volley of proposals and counterproposals regarding the British presence Ping-Ponged between Cairo and London.

Sultan Fuad didn't like being a British puppet. However, he knew Zaghlul, who saw himself in the George Washington, father-of-his-country mold, was no friend of the palaces. Oddly enough, Fuad's wife, Nazli, whose own mother had died when she was young, had gotten close to Zaghlul's wife, Sofia. Their relationship was nearly that of a surrogate mother and her "daughter." That proximity was perhaps the inspiration for the isolation of Nazli in the harem. Sofia Zaghlul was never allowed to visit. No fifth columns would be tolerated. If he had to choose, Fuad would take the British over the fellaheen anytime. Better a puppet than a nothing.

The wily Fuad saw the volatile situation with Zaghlul as a way to get even more power for himself. To that end, Fuad picked his own delegation to send to London, specifically excluding Zaghlul. When Zaghlul reacted, predictably, by exhorting the masses to protest by besieging, among other venues, Abdine Palace, the British reacted, also predictably, by again arresting and deporting Zaghlul, this time to the Seychelles. Having finally had enough themselves, the British, in 1922, the same year Howard Carter discovered the tomb of Tutankhamen in the Valley of the Kings, finally terminated the protectorate status and recognized Egypt as "an independent sovereign state," withdrew the state of martial law that had been in effect since the outbreak of World War I in 1914, and upped Fuad's status from sultan to king. His was a nominally constitutional monarchy that gave him the power to dissolve Parliament, order new elections, and appoint forty percent of the Senate. Under Lord Allenby, the British troops would remain to protect the security of British "communications" and other foreign interests in Egypt and the Sudan; nevertheless, Fuad had scored major points in popularity by organizing the perception that he, not Zaghlul or anyone else, was the man who finally won "independence" for Egypt.

Zaghlul seemingly had nine lives. He may have been in the Seychelles; the Society of Vengeance which he directed from his exile kept the bullets flying in his honor until he was again allowed to return. He was elected prime minister in 1924, on a platform to get the British out, troops and all. Following Zaghlul's landslide, a series of British officials were shot in broad daylight, culminating in the assassination in 1924 of Sir Lee Stack, the British sirdar, or commander in chief, of the Egyptian Army and governor general of the Sudan, in front of the Ministry of Education in Cairo. That rain of bullets proved to be a final volley and a last straw. Zaghlul, ailing at sixty-four, didn't have the stamina to remain on the barricades; the British were too proud and arrogant to be intimidated out of the country, and certainly not with the Suez Canal and their cotton supplies at risk.

Zaghlul resigned, succeeded by another cagey delta peasant, Moustapha Nahas, who had accompanied him in exile to the Seychelles. Having paid for his legal education by working as a telegraph operator, Nahas was a homely man. He had a camel's face, and eyes which went in opposite directions, "one on Upper Egypt and one on Lower," as locals joked. Nahas had the popular touch and might have caused Fuad a new case of "Zaghlulitis" had not another violent specter of his past come back to haunt the king.

In 1925, Fuad's would-be assassin, Shivekiar's brother Prince Seif ed-Din, escaped from his asylum in Tunbridge Wells and made his way to Constantinople, from which he launched a legal assault on Fuad to recover the vast fortune that had been confiscated by the state on the prince's internment and now was being administered by Fuad as king, thereby increasing his already staggering royal fortune. It leaked out that the chief behind-the-scenes legal wizard for the mad prince was none other than Nahas, and that the legal fees he was receiving were over one hundred thousand pounds. Nahas had to bow to the outrage of the "people" who had until then identified with him. He resigned as prime minister. Fuad had vanquished his opponent through the inside information gleaned from the network of spies that Farouk would inherit and exploit. From Shepheard's hall porters to newspaper reporters, from British intelligence officers to bribed Wafd functionaries, and especially from Sudanese and Nubian suffragis of every major home—organized by Fuad's own chief butler—Fuad had eyes and ears everywhere in the country. Knowledge proved to be power. By 1928, Zaghlul was dead. With Nahas on the sidelines and the British thrilled to have a friend in the palace rather than an enemy in the streets, Fuad was the undisputed king of Egypt, able to rule his country as autocratically as he did his family.

The one exception to Fuad's all-British-Isles nursery staff for his young prince was a Swedish auxiliary nanny named Gerda Sjoberg, whose diaries, serialized in Swedish newspapers when Farouk was deposed in 1952, give a rare peephole view of palace life in Egypt in the 1920s.

Gerda remembered being driven from the Ramleh Station in Alexandria to Ras-el-Tin by King Fuad's chief physician, a Dr. Shahin, the only noneunuch allowed in the harem. She briefly met Fuad, whom she described as a thick man who resembled a fat eagle and who spoke to her in French, and separately, Queen Nazli, who also spoke to her in French and looked like some beautiful Parisienne one might encounter at Maxim's or on the Rue de la Paix. The young Farouk, then four, spoke perfect English. When he was introduced to Gerda, he threw his arms around her and said, "I'm very glad to see you. You're my madame, aren't you?"

A typical day for Farouk began at eight, when a small band awoke him by playing the Egyptian national anthem outside his window. A Nubian servant then came into his chambers, drew the prince's bath, and laid out his clothes. After his ablutions, Gerda would help Farouk dress, then sit with him while he had his tea and toast with butter and marmalade. After breakfast, his chief man-servant, Mohammed, wearing a red embroidered robe, entered the chamber, kissed the ground, then kissed Farouk's hand. Mohammed led Farouk into the palace gardens, carrying an umbrella to shade the prince from the burning summer sun and moving as the sun moved. For the hour from ten until eleven Farouk was required to simply sit in the garden to learn patience, while Gerda told him a story or the band played for him. That completed, he would do fifteen minutes of calisthenics or stretching. At eleven, Gerda would wash Farouk's hands and brush his hair for the first of the prince's two daily visits to his mother in her apartment in the harem. After an hour with Nazli, Farouk would be taken from the harem to the palace dining hall, where he would sit alone at a table resplendent with flowers and gleaming silver and be served a lunch by two Nubians in Nile green robes and white gloves that usually consisted of roast chicken, green beans, chocolate cake, and grapes. Lunch would be followed by Gerda's undressing the prince, who proceeded to a two-hour nap.

At four-thirty Farouk was up again and more formally dressed in a green silk suit with a white collar and cuff links. He would have tea in the palace with his princess sisters and play in the gardens until seven, when he was summoned again to Nazli for a half-hour visit to the harem. Gerda would take him back to his chambers, where the Nubians would assist him in his nightly bath and Gerda would tell him a story that put him to sleep. Farouk was fascinated by Gerda's young nephew, Jan, in Sweden. Farouk put Jan's photograph next to his bed and made him his imaginary "best friend." King Fuad wouldn't allow him any real ones.

Gerda's impression of Queen Nazli was that she was bored to death. Alone with her servants and eunuchs, except for her brief and formal visits from her children, she was not even allowed into the garden and almost never saw her husband. All she did all day was change clothes in her enormous wardrobe. Her big event of the summer was the move from formal Ras-el-Tin to the vacation palace of Montazah. Although the two were only miles apart along the Mediterranean corniche, preparations for the departure required three days of packing and unpacking. What passed for a crisis occurred when one of Nazli's favorite hats was lost. It was discovered packed in a chamber pot.

On the day of the transfer, Nazli dressed in yellow chiffon, Farouk in a navy blue silk suit and a red tarboosh. Farouk had a formal audience with his father, who remained at Ras-el-Tin conducting the affairs of state. The farewell was as portentous as if father and son would never see each other again. Nazli and Farouk proceeded down a red carpet to a caravan of waiting cars, past hundreds of saluting officers. Farouk loved the fanfare as well as the brief trip along the sea, which was his only exposure to the real world. All through the journey, Nazli was required to wear a veil and was guarded by her eunuchs as though a war were going on. Gerda described Montazah as an Eden of rare flowers, gazelles, and birds from the Sudan surrounded by a high wall and three hundred gardeners doing nothing but watering all day long. For the royal family summer life was equally monotonous. The only excitement would be when King Fuad would visit and have a tantrum over some minor shortcoming of one of the servants, such as if Farouk's shoes were not stored on the proper shelf. Farouk spent most of his play time tossing about his pet kitten and smashing rare vases. He loved to throw things.

The next major excitement of the year was the return to Cairo for the fall season in October. Fuad and Nazli left on separate his and hers royal trains. Prince Farouk had his own private railway car in Nazli's train. He was less fascinated by all the red carpets, saluting troops, and flying banners than in pressing his face to the train window and seeing the fellaheen plowing the fields of cotton, rice, and sugar cane behind blindfolded water buffalo in the Nile delta, the bedouins on camels in the desert, the poor villagers in their mud huts who came out to pay homage to the baby prince. At every whistle stop along the way, where the stations were festooned with flags and packed with subjects, Farouk would be led out onto the train platform for a salute and a rousing cheer.

The Ramses Station in Cairo was a botanical garden of flowers for the royal arrival. Though Nazli was covered in a veil and shielded by her chief eunuch's black parasol, Gerda could see that she was dripping in jewelry and wanted nothing more in her life than to show it off. Everyone bowed to the ground as Nazli, then Farouk, marched down the red carpet. A large band played the national anthem; the royals entered the waiting horse-drawn carriages, and the parade through the endless crowds of Cairo to Abdine Palace began. Fuad's carriage, a copy of a seventeenth-century French *carrosse*—with gold wheels and pulled by eight white horses draped in red and gold—led the procession, surrounded by twenty guards in imperial livery riding white horses. Following Fuad was the carriage of the prime minister, pulled by six black horses. Everyone else had four horses. The parade lasted for hours and ended in the front court of Abdine, paved with red brick that gave the impression of an immense red carpet. In all, it was a fusion of ancien régime and *1001 Nights.*

On her own nights off, Gerda was grateful to get out of the palace and into the souks. She adored ancient Cairo, with its pungent perfumes of garlic and coffee. She would climb to the top of the minaret of the Ibn Touloun Mosque and watch the sunset over the other mosques and the palaces and the pyramids. Then she would go alone to the grand hotels, Shepheard's and the Savoy and the Continental, and observe the sheikhs and pashas ogling the rich Western women tourists dressed in clingy chemises and ropes of pearls dancing the Charleston, while their own wives were locked in their respective harems.

In Cairo, the royal family's time was divided between the official Abdine Palace and the rural weekend palace, Koubbeh, in suburban Heliopolis. Again Gerda recalled the hectic pomp and ceremony of each moving day, with Fuad racing about with Nazli's diamond tiara under his arm, Nazli rummaging among her thousand and one dresses, deciding which to take and wear in front of her mirror for no one except her eunuchs to see, and the Nubian servants working and sweating so that their curly hair turned straight. Amid the blooming acacias of the Koubbeh gardens, little Farouk loved to go out on rowboats in the man-made lakes and canals. Gerda evoked the dislocations of Ramadan, when no food, no perfume, and no smoking were allowed from the daylight hours from six to six and the servants were lazier, and Fuad angrier, than usual. Fuad, who loved to eat, passed a law allowing an exemption from fasting by buying food for twenty poor people for one month. Nobody in the palace ever seemed to go hungry, least of all the enormous 250-pound nurses hired to breastfeed Farouk's baby sisters.

"The truth doesn't exist in Egypt," Gerda wrote in her diaries. "Breaking promises is normal. Farouk is already perfect at this. He loves to lie. But it's amazing Farouk is as good as he is, given his mother." Gerda grew to hate Nazli, who called her *"chérie."* Nazli devoted herself to subterfuges to get out of the harem. Sulking constantly, Nazli feigned several nervous breakdowns for many months to convince Fuad to allow her to go to Europe for a "health cure." Sailing on the royal yacht, where Fuad had walls built to create a floating harem, Nazli was bombarded by cables warning her not to be photographed without a veil, and exhorting her to go easy on her hats and Isadora Duncan scarves.

While Nazli was away, Gerda went to an exorcism where a camel covered with jewels had its throat slit. The guests rushed to the dying camel with gold cups to collect the spurting blood, then painted their faces with the blood and danced around the dead beast of burden. In another vestige of the Old East, Gerda also met Farouk's grandmother, the eighty-three-year-old widow of Khedive Ismail, who wore a henna wig, painted her eyelids dark red, wore a huge watch on a belt around her stomach, and had only one arm. A former palace harem slave, she had been caught stealing and her arm chopped off as punishment. When Ismail saw her, he was dumbstruck by her beauty and made her one of his four legal wives. He had two hundred others, not to mention his foreign pursuits, the most famous of whom was the French empress Eugénie. Ismail's most famous courtship gift to her was a solid gold chamber pot with an emerald in the shape of an eye embedded in the dead center of the bottom. "My eye is always on you," the khedive told the empress.

Gerda did her best to keep Farouk in line by stressing the good example of his dream friend, Jan, to whom Farouk wrote letters and sent cotton seeds to see if they would grow under Sweden's midnight sun. Eventually, Gerda went back to Scandinavia. All her responsibilities devolved upon Farouk's governess "Ninzy." A Girl Guide, field-hockey-sturdy widow of a doctor in Yorkshire, Mrs. Ina Naylor was imported from England by Fuad to take up the task of prince-rearing left off by Gerda Sjoberg and commenced by Farouk's beloved midwife, Lucy Sergeant.

Miss Sergeant had sung Farouk Gaelic cradle songs and told him old Irish nursery rhymes, and he remembered her birthday with a telegram every year until he died. Mrs. Naylor, on the other hand, sang no songs. She was a martinet in the strictest British tradition. In a series of memoirs Farouk penned in 1952 following his abdication, he romanticized the stiff-upper-lip drill-sergeant toughness and shed some light on who was the boss in the palace.

> "My mother asked me to remove my jacket, as I looked hot. The nurse protested sternly that I would be sure to catch cold, but I was only too glad to remove my jacket upon my mother's invitation, and at once I did so.
>
> "Mrs. Naylor, who seemed to find difficulty in understanding that the Egyptian climate is considerably hotter than in England, made no further comment, but the next time my sisters and I went to visit Mother, she dressed us with exacting care in thick woolen undergarments that almost completely covered us.
>
> " 'Now,' she said severely, 'if any of you removes your coats this time, you will see what will happen when we return to the nursery, for I will teach you obedience. It does not matter who invites you to disobey me—Her Majesty or anybody.'
>
> "Of course, when Mother invited us again to remove our coats, my sisters were afraid to do so. But I removed mine. And when we returned to the nursery that afternoon I was punished."

When he wasn't bundled up in scratchy woolens, Farouk was dressed up like a girl, in white cotton blouses with big bows, shorts, black patent Mary Jane shoes with white cotton socks. His round, soft features and long, over-the-ear blond, wavy hair added to the feminine effect, as did his isolation from other boys. As Mrs. Naylor wrote: "Quite the most striking fact about his early life is this: that until he came to England for the first time six months before his father died, he had never spent an hour alone in the company of a boy. His only playmates had been his four sisters. His devotion for his sisters has saved him from the loneliness of a boy who has spent his life in a palace alone."

The sisters, in order of age, were Fawzia, whom Farouk called Wuzzy, Faiza, Faika, and Fathia, whom he called Atty. The sisters called Farouk Luky, an appellation deriving from the baby Atty's gurgling mispronunciation of her big brother's name, and one that stuck.

The royal children divided their time among four palaces. There was the main residence, Abdine, in Cairo, the khedive Ismail's Italianate behemoth considered the richest palace in the world, famous for its alabaster Byzantine hall with its life-size mosaics of naked dancing girls, its Suez Canal salon with its giant Canaletto-style painting commemorating the grand opening ceremonies, its five-hundred-seat gilded theater, and two-hundred-car garage. On the far side of Cairo was the four-hundred-room Koubbeh Palace, also built by Khedive Ismail. This area of Cairo, about ten miles away from the Abdine Palace, was known as Heliopolis, and in ancient days had been the seat of worship of Ra, the sun god. Later, legend had it that Mary and Jesus sought refuge here after fleeing from Bethlehem. Fuad considered Koubbeh Palace his own refuge. Koubbeh's forbiddingly high, six-mile perimeter wall surrounded seventy acres of vast pleasure gardens, lakes and pools, horses and camels, as well as a private railway station. Fuad preferred the residential Koubbeh, his "country" palace, to the more formal Abdine, and this was the principal locus of Farouk's childhood during Egypt's "winter" season from October to May. During the summer, the entire government moved to Alexandria, where affairs of state were conducted at Ras-el-Tin at which the royal yacht *Mahroussa* docked. Affairs of other sorts transpired at Montazah, with its little schoolhouse on the beach that Fuad had built so his son could get his lessons with a sea view.

Fuad was fond of saying, "It is nothing to be a prince, but it is something to be useful." Accordingly, he planned his son's education with great care. This education began when Farouk was five. The regimen he had followed under Gerda Sjoberg was now increased in rigor. He would be awakened earlier, at six A.M., which was when Fuad arose to do his exercises. His tutorials would start after breakfast, at nine, until lunch at one, after which he would ride his horses, Sammy and Silvertail, swim, or learn to scale palm trees under the tutelage of his French gymnastics instructor. But studies came first, at least theoretically. It was very important to Fuad, who didn't speak Arabic, that Farouk, who had a facility with languages, master the one of the people he was being groomed to rule.

Aside from languages, Farouk hated studying. Notebooks found at Abdine after 1952 bore some telling remarks from his tutors. "Improve your bad handwriting and pay attention to the cleanliness of your notebook," one wrote. It is regrettable that you do not know the history of your ancestors," chided another to the prince, who may have known little about his own dynasty and even less about his country—Farouk never even visited the pyramids, a mere twelve miles from Abdine, until he became king. Most of the tutors were not above sycophancy. "Excellent. A brilliant future awaits you in the world of literature" was the encomium on one short essay that contained seven spelling errors and the sentence, "My father had a lot of ministers and I have a cat."

Fuad was always self-conscious about his own less-than-ramrod physique and his family's propensity to obesity. He went on two-day fasts, eating nothing but fruit. He put his own son on an even stricter diet, not only to make Farouk slim but to assert culinary authority over Nazli, who had a mother's concern that her baby was hungrily wasting away. A war of the larder broke out, with Nazli smuggling cream cakes and other high-fat, high-sugar confections to Farouk and Mrs. Naylor seizing them and throwing them into the trash. Poor Farouk was so ravenous from all the temptation that on occasion he ate his cat's dinners to supplement his own.

Farouk's chief hobbies were fishing in the sea at Montazah, taking pictures with the elaborate Kodak equipment his father had bought him, and driving around the serpentine roads of the palace grounds. Farouk was car crazy. There is a picture of him at six driving an electric model T, dressed in a fez and an ermine-trimmed velvet coat. At eleven, Fuad gave him his first real motor car, an Austin Seven. Soon afterward, the king of Italy presented him with a custom Fiat. At fifteen, Fuad gave Farouk a racing Morris.

Despite the lavish cars, Fuad kept Farouk on an allowance that was as strict as his diet. Still, he was an incipient philanthropist; out of the five pounds he received each month, he gave two of them to a poor family that worked at the palace, and another two to help poor children of palace servants to buy books for their own studies. "He was the very essence of kindness and loyalty to friends and servants," Mrs. Naylor wrote. "While riding one day, he lost a diamond tiepin, and some months later one of the stable employees was arrested when trying to sell it. Farouk pleaded in vain that the man should be pardoned. His father decided that an example must be made of him. Never again did Farouk wear any jewel when riding. He said it was wrong to run the risk of putting temptation in the way of poor people."

Farouk also stuck up for his Ninzy. When the famous portrait painter Laszlo came to Abdine to do the official Palace likeness of the prince, Laszlo asked the then nine-year-old to sign his autograph book. Farouk said he wanted Mrs. Naylor to sign as well. Laszlo demurred. He wanted only royal signatures. Farouk demurred also. If Ninzy couldn't sign, Farouk couldn't sign. Laszlo relented. Underneath Mrs. Naylor's lone noncrowned autograph in his collection, the snobby painter added, "Present at all sittings for Prince Farouk's portrait: autographed by special request of HRH."

Farouk had a definite affinity for palace servants, who were divided into two camps: English and Italian. In the former, there were Mrs. Naylor; Fuad's chief chauffeur; his motorcycle outriders; his aide-de-camp, Colonel Castle-Smith; and his pharmacist, Titterington, whom Farouk called Titters. Titters was the official food taster for the wary king and his son. Among the Italians were Ernesto Verrucci, who was Italophile Fuad's chief architect as well as beard for his mistresses, Pietro della Valle, the palace barber, and Antonio Pulli, who became the boy's only real male friend. Farouk loved to make excuses to evade his tutors and hide out and hang out with Pulli and the Italians in the palace shops and garages. From them he learned about jokes and he learned about women.

First, the jokes. One April Fool's Day, Farouk asked his father to pose for a photograph. The king obliged, but instead of a flash, out of the trick camera popped a three-foot coiled green snake. For once, the somber monarch laughed. Farouk liked to free quail from the traps so carefully laid by the Montazah gamekeepers. He took an air rifle and shot out all the ground floor windows of a wing at Koubbeh. He teased his sterner tutors and gym masters with threats of reprisal against them "when he was king." When Queen Nazli was entertaining Queen Marie of Romania in the harem, Farouk asked the Balkan sovereign if she would like to see his two horses. When she replied in the affirmative, Farouk obliged her quite literally. He brought Sammy and Silvertail up the grand staircase of Koubbeh into the harem salon. The two queens were not amused.

Normally, Queen Nazli would do anything to spend time with her son. Nazli would sometimes smuggle Farouk from his chambers in Abdine's Belgian wing (so called because its first guest was the king of Belgium) through the chambermaids' chambers to the queen's wing, to sit with her and her own soothsayer over a boiling cauldron. As superstitious as her husband, Nazli didn't merely dabble in the occult, she dwelled in it. Sending donations to each mosque in the city on the eve of the birth of each of her children, always wanting a son, the queen was chided by Nanny Naylor: "Majesty, you cannot bribe God." Nazli's bedroom, where her séances were held, must have exerted a special spell over the adolescing Farouk. On the wall above Nazli's gold-framed, silk-curtained, queen-size bed was a life-size, very realistic erotic painting of a blond-tressed naked nymph lying seductively on her own queen-size bed. Nazli's adjacent drawing room contained more life-size nudes, provocative tableaux from some of the racier tales of the Arabian Nights, involving fornication, sodomy, and bestiality, all in the name of high art. Whether a visit to Nazli's sanctorum was more provocative than one to Fuad's, where his chief Circassian serving girl slept on a mattress on a rare Chinese carpet at the foot of the royal bed every night and five other Turkish beauties were right outside in the marble corridor to attend to the monarch's every whim, is a matter of conjecture. Whichever, Farouk's earliest views of women as creatures of caprice and domination, combined with the backroom war and whore stories of Antonio Pulli and his Italian cronies, undoubtedly colored Farouk's later relations with the opposite sex.

When Farouk was twelve, in 1932, he made his first public appearance, taking Fuad's place at a Royal Air Force show at the airport in Heliopolis. In 1933, he became the chief scout of Egypt. By then, adolescent acne aside, he had sprouted up to become an incredibly handsome, fair-haired young prince in the duke-of-Windsor mold, a head taller than his father. The fellaheen loved him. In fact, against the rabble, Farouk was his father's unexpected secret weapon. With Nahas discredited in the Seif ed-Din lawsuit, the mantle of the mob passed to Hassan el Banna, the fanatic fundamentalist founder of the Muslim Brotherhood. An Islamic bluestocking who had previously established the Society for the Prevention of Sin, el Banna believed that Egypt had become a moral cesspool because it had looked to the West instead of to the Koran. In spite of his palatial roots, his diamond tiepins and his English sports cars, Prince Farouk prayed to Mecca five times a day on his priceless prayer rug. He washed his hands, his feet, his hair according to Muslim tradition. He spoke the caliph's Arabic. He gave his allowance to the poor. In all, he was King Fuad's rebuttal to Hassan el Banna, the great blond hope of Islam. If Egyptians wanted a white knight, a young savior, Farouk was the one. The Egyptians called him "the honest good shepherd." The world press called him "Prince Charming."

The arrival in Egypt of diplomat Miles Lampson as British high commissioner, having previously served as minister to China, marked a watershed in Prince Farouk's life. Lampson, who was to become Farouk's worst nemesis, had the brilliant idea that "the boy" be sent to Eton to get an education befitting a monarch-to-be. But the future king was rejected, flat out. He didn't have any Latin and Greek, which were required. He failed the Eton entrance exams. This put the lie to the high marks Farouk's tutors had showered upon him. In truth, aside from languages, he knew almost nothing. It was embarrassing indeed to Egypt, and to the royal family, to have their standard bearer turned down. Farouk had to be redeemed. But no one wanted to risk trying Harrow or Winchester or another famous public school, for the results would probably be the same. For a while, Fuad had fixated on one school he knew would take Farouk, his old alma mater, the Turin Military Academy.

But the clouds of war were gathering. In 1935, Mussolini's Italy invaded Ethiopia. Suddenly, the Suez Canal was placed in a new and very real jeopardy. High Commissioner Lampson couldn't have the young Farouk in the West Point of his prospective enemy. If it were going to be a military academy, it had to be a British one. Fuad and Lampson finally settled on the Royal Military Academy at Woolwich. It didn't have quite the cachet of Sandhurst, but it did have a noble Egyptian tradition. Sir Evelyn Baring, Lord Cromer, had gone there. So had Chinese Gordon. The only one who was opposed to the choice was Queen Nazli, who didn't think her boy was ready to leave home. As usual, Nazli's opposition had no weight whatsoever. In late October 1935, Farouk and a twenty-man blue-chip entourage sailed for England on the British cruiser *Devonshire.* On the gangplank, the sheltered prince fought back the tears and held up two fingers, for the two years he was going away—to become a man.

The royal educational mission settled in to Kenry House, a stately home in Kingston Hall, Surrey, near the "Shop," as the academy at Woolwich was called. Kenry had formerly served as the residence of Prince Chichibu of Japan. It was a huge, sprawling place on twenty-nine acres of manicured grounds, surrounded by British policemen. Farouk wasn't being directly admitted to Woolwich. Instead, he would be an extramural student, taking occasional classes to prepare himself for the school's exam so that eventually he could be admitted as a full-time cadet. No student ever had the wherewithal to be so prepared. With Farouk were his chief tutor; his military tutor; his own professor of Arabic; a British officer who was his fencing and combat tutor; a squash tutor; his private doctor, without whom no true gentleman, and certainly no prince, should ever have left home; and a complement of cooks, valets, and other servants.

"It was a good, hard life at Woolwich," Farouk wrote in his memoirs sixteen years later, either disingenuously or out of a nostalgia for the way he would have liked to be in his English reveries. "And I was sorry I did not have longer there. I scrambled awake at reveille and took my cold shower and pulled on the skin-tight uniform trousers over legs that were still wet (for there was no time in those morning parade rushes to dry oneself properly). I have known what it was to stub out one's furtive cigarette when the sergeant's footsteps could be heard around the corner. My mother had been afraid that I would be exposed to Western bad habits, particularly the immoderate use of alcohol, but my father said, 'Farouk has plenty of inherited common sense and I am sure he will be all right.' "

In reality, Farouk never woke up at the "Shop." Instead, he woke up to a warm bath in Kenry House and was driven to Woolwich in a Rolls-Royce, usually only two afternoons a week. The first time Farouk sat for his entrance exam, he failed, causing his father great consternation back in Cairo. Fuad called his two chief tutors to task. Both were capable of rising to it. His academic tutor was the Anglophile explorer Ahmed Mohammed Hassanein, whose desert expeditions Fuad had underwritten. Farouk's military tutor was the General Aziz el-Masri. A Circassian Young Turk who had been a revolutionary officer for the Germans in World War I and had gone on to head the Cairo police academy, el-Masri was as anti-British as Hassanein, a star fencer at Oxford, was pro. Although el-Masri had been instrumental with Kemal Ataturk in leading the revolt against the Ottoman sultan that had turned Turkey into a constitutional monarchy, King Fuad somehow trusted the loyalty of this former radical.

Where they did part ways was over Farouk's educational progress, or lack thereof. Even after Farouk failed his exams, Hassanein sent reports back to Fuad that the prince was shaping up brilliantly. El-Masri's reports were completely different. He said that Farouk expected that all the test answers be given to him. Further, instead of going dutifully to the "Shop," Farouk was off in a different direction. El-Masri imparted that the would-be student prince was being driven into nearby London to shop, to drink, even to visit a fancy bordello in the heart of Mayfair. It was easier for Fuad to believe the wholesome and hopeful accounts of Hassanein than the bleak notes of el-Masri. Further, Mrs. Naylor was appalled at the fierce little general's lack of couth; she insisted to Fuad that he had no place whatsoever in a diplomatic mission to civilized England. In the end, el-Masri agreed and resigned.

Farouk's own later account of his "Shop" days mirrors the accepted "official" report:

> I was a frightful dud at mathematics and could find little patience with the subject. What really did interest me was science, and I used to take my classroom textbooks home with me to read for pleasure, so that I was soon months ahead of the rest of the class.
>
> When I came to England as a student, I spent much of my pocket money browsing among the secondhand bookshops, and although it has also been said that I had a bright red sports car with which I used to terrify the inhabitants of Woolwich, this was not true. I would have loved such a car, but all I had was a bicycle, and I used to get lifts into London from a friendly lorry driver in Woolwich, who took me in twice a week.

Farouk went on to reminisce about his five A.M. runs in the pea-soup fog and how he learned to box. He wrote about his friendship with the young duke of Windsor, who took him to weekend rugby and soccer matches. In return, Farouk took credit for teaching the duke the latest British Army slang, which he learned from his boxing-tutor sergeant. That he dined at Buckingham Palace, or marched with other kings in the funeral procession of King George V to Westminster Abbey held far less retrospective allure for Farouk than the rough and ready pursuits of the "Shop." The only problem was, the memories were not founded in fact.

Even the apologist Hassanein privately admitted that most of Farouk's time was spent sleeping late and shopping, which endeared him to the townspeople, particularly the merchants, who called him "Prince Freddy." In London, he spent a fortune on Bond Street for jewels and antiques for his family, and he loved visiting the Pall Mall clubs. The jokester prince also enjoyed humiliating his tutor. At one club, lounging by the fireplace with a group of members, he beckoned Hassanein, who was standing outside the room. When the explorer arrived, Farouk handed him the butt of his cigarette to dispose. "My manservant," Farouk gleefully told his companions.

The prince's British idyll ended abruptly six months after he arrived, on April 29, 1936, when his father died at age sixty-nine, of a heart attack precipitated by gangrene in the ill-lodged bullet wound in his throat.

In accordance with the Muslim ritual of an immediate burial, Fuad was interred the next day at El Rifaii, the immense royal mosque of the Mohammed Ali dynasty. Seven live bulls were herded into the square outside the mosque as the six-thousand-strong procession of princes, diplomats, holy men, and soldiers marched through Cairo to Fuad's final resting place. When they arrived at the mosque, the bulls' throats were slashed, following tradition, with blood spurting all over the coffin and the dignitaries.

While these sacrificial rites were occurring in Egypt, Farouk remained in England, preparing to go home. Now king of Egypt, Farouk, who had never sat again for the Woolwich entrance exam, left Surrey without ever having been admitted to the "Shop." He first went to Buckingham Palace, wearing a black suit enlivened by a red fez. There he visited his friend the duke of Windsor, now King Edward VIII, who would abdicate later that year to marry Mrs. Simpson. The English king offered the Egyptian king a British de-

stroyer to take Farouk back to Egypt. Farouk said it wasn't necessary, and proceeded to Victoria Station where he, Hassanein, and
his entourage were seen off by Sir Anthony Eden, the duke of Kent,
and by the Egyptian ambassador to Britain. At Dover, Farouk was
serenaded by a bagpipe honor guard of Scottish highlanders as he
boarded the French ship *Côte d'Azur,* and was escorted across the
English Channel by two British warships, *Scout* and *Scimitar.* He
took another special train on to Marseilles, stopping in Paris at the
Gare de Lyon for a condolence call by the president of France.
There were more salutes at Marseilles when he boarded the Penin-
sular and Orient liner *Viceroy of India* for Alexandria, the journey
on which Barbara Skelton first saw the striking young man whose
mistress she would become.

On the dark early morning of May 6, when the *Viceroy* docked in
Alexandria, the port was, as Barbara Skelton remembered so viv-
idly, lit up for a festival. The mourning for Fuad had been transformed into a welcome celebration for Farouk. The flags that had
been at half mast for Fuad's death now were raised to full mast. The
British fleet fired off twenty-one-gun salutes, and Farouk left the
Viceroy of India for the *Mahroussa,* which took him across the
Alexandria harbor to the dock at Ras-el-Tin as the royal band
played the national anthem. The new king was greeted by the soon-
to-be-revealed-as-treacherous Prime Minister Ali Maher, who rode
with Farouk in an open Rolls-Royce down the corniche to the
Ramleh Station, where a special train would take them to Cairo.
The route was jammed with thousands of well-wishers, troops, police, and firemen, united in saluting their new ruler and showering
him with rose petals from balconies. "Long live the king of the
Nile!" "Long live the king of Egypt and the Sudan!"

Hundreds of thousands of fellaheen lined the tracks in the delta
to see King Farouk. Cairo was a festival of flags and banners greet-
ing the young monarch. Farouk left the train and went down the
red carpet to be received by High Commissioner Miles Lampson
and the entire Cairo diplomatic corps. Farouk then entered another
waiting Rolls-Royce, which took him through the teeming, cheering
city to the foot of the citadel and the El Rifaii Mosque. He knelt
and prayed at the alabaster tomb of his father and then emerged to
the accolades of thousands of white-turbaned, white-robed theological students from Al Azhar University, many of them members of
the Muslim Brotherhood. All of them were squarely in the corner of

Beach Boy • Young Farouk on the Mediterranean at Montazeh with his favorite sister, Princess Fawzia.

In the Driver's Seat • With his three sisters, Fawzia, Faika, and Faiza, Farouk tools around at eleven in his first of hundreds of cars.

Golden Gloves • Farouk toughening up at fifteen, at the Royal Military Academy, Woolwich, England, 1935.

The New King • Farouk, accompanied by his Oxford-trained tutor, Ahmed Mohammed Hassanein, returns to Egypt to assume his throne, 1936.

the king, who was even praised by the normally staidly circumspect London *Times:* "The dignified but modest bearing of His Majesty created an excellent impression." After El Rifaii, Farouk went on to Abdine to join his mother and sisters. The huge square in front of the palace was filled with an endless procession of Boy Scouts and Girl Guides. The chief scout of Egypt was now its king. The country was in ecstasy.

Farouk made his first speech the very next day from the balcony of Abdine:

> It was the will of Allah that I be deprived of a last meeting with my father. I start a new life which I embrace firmly and with goodwill. I promise that I will dedicate this life to your service and to the continuous efforts for your prosperity. With my own eyes I have seen your love and attachment and I say to you that I intend to maintain this solidarity for the sake of our dear Egypt. I believe that the greatness of a king is in the greatness of his people. I want to bring reforms and in this Allah will help me.

Part of the reason Egypt was so eager to embrace Farouk was that the people were relieved and thrilled to have seen the last of Fuad. As the *New York Times* reported the day of Fuad's funeral:

> In view of the fact that Egypt was officially mourning today the death of King Fuad, the entire country was retaining a surprisingly normal atmosphere, with everyone going about his business as usual.
> Except for the sight of flags at half-staff and a picture of King Fuad draped in black, there was little to indicate that the country's ruler had died only yesterday.

If Fuad had made himself the strongest and richest man in the country, he had also made himself the most detested. He had personally acquired one seventh of all the arable land in Egypt by the creative use of eminent domain. If Fuad fancied delta land, he would ask the reluctant owner to name his price. If he said a thousand pounds a feddan (an Egyptian acre), Fuad would pronounce it too high, call in a royal appraiser who would value the land at, say, ninety pounds a feddan. Fuad would then pay the flabbergasted owner one hundred pounds a feddan and declare what a sport he was. If the owner refused, Fuad would manage to render the land of no value by officially relocating the irrigation channels of the Nile. In short, a Fuad offer could not be refused.

Fuad, who prided himself on his foreign roots, referred to his subjects as "these Egyptians," or even less politely in French, "*ces crétins.*" He was the Scrooge of Egypt. His conniving miserliness was not confined to his own class. General Mohammed Neguib, who led the coup against Farouk in 1952, remembered him in his revolutionary memoir, *Egypt's Destiny.*

> Before he ascended the throne, Fuad had been an impover-ished playboy who owed money to everyone. Once he became King, however, he devoted himself to saving as much money as he could. He never spent a piastre if he could possibly avoid it. He gave nothing to charity, except on formal occasions, and . . . once ordered the flogging of a Royal Guard who had picked some dates from one of the palm trees in the Garden of Bustan Palace. In 1925, to save money, Fuad even abolished the free rations that had long been one of the perquisites of the officers of the Royal Guards.

All this meanness had its rewards. Farouk inherited a fortune estimated to be as much as one hundred million dollars, invested in Europe as well as in Egypt, control of nearly seventy-five thousand acres of the most fertile soil on earth, two hundred cars, five pal-aces, two yachts, numerous hunting lodges and royal rest houses from the Mediterranean to the Sudan, a private train, an air force at his disposal. Yet because of his perfect manners, his terrific good looks, his seeming humility, and his apparent piousness, the Egyp-tians didn't begrudge him a piastre or a feddan. From the age of the pharaohs, the country had a millennial tradition of venerating its rulers who bathed in asses' milk while its workers toiled in camel dung. Blind faith and acceptance was a way of life. Yet no pharaoh, no Mameluke, no khedive ever began a reign with such unquestion-ing, enthusiastic goodwill as King Farouk.

And none was as unprepared to rule. Here was a completely sheltered, virtually uneducated sixteen-year-old, expected to fill the spats of his wily, politically astute father in a loaded tug-of-war between nationalism, imperialism, constitutionalism, and monar-chy. Because of his innocence, every faction viewed Farouk as a manipulable instrument of its own designs. No sooner had Fuad died than new elections were held in which the Wafd, or nationalist party, won over eighty percent of the seats in the Parliament's lower house, the Chamber of Deputies. Fuad's old nemesis, Nahas, was restored to his former glory as prime minister. Prince Seif ed-Din's legal pork barrel scandal was forgotten. The new king was thus faced with a powerful Egyptian adversary who would continue to haunt him through his reign, as would his English adversary, Miles Lampson. And even within the royal family, intrigues were afoot. Prince Mohammed Ali, Farouk's uncle, Fuad's oldest living male relative and heir to the throne should anything happen to Farouk, was not without his ambitions. His every suggestion for the new king's well-being was therefore heavily screened for hidden agendas. Finally, there were Hitler and Mussolini to take into account, both with rapacious big eyes on the Suez Canal.

Under the circumstances, everyone agreed that the very best course of action was to get Farouk out of Egypt and back to England to get on with his education. According to Muslim law, he would not attain his majority until he was eighteen, and the two-year breathing space would provide a welcome opportunity for him to mature and for Egypt to better prepare for his ascendancy. Unfortunately, Queen Nazli would not allow her son out of her sight now that she had him back. She immediately fired Mrs. Naylor and imported her own English governess, Mrs. Broadbent, to raise her son and her daughters according to her wishes. After all, she *was* the queen.

A three-man Regency Council was established to guide Farouk's destiny and that of Egypt until he reached eighteen. It was a delicate balance between the interests of the dynasty, the wishes of Fuad, and the needs of Nazli. Representing the dynasty—and the English—was their heir presumptive, Prince Mohammed Ali. The grandson of Khedive Ismail and son of Khedive Tewfik was a pro-British world-class horse breeder and art collector. His banyan-shaded Manyal Palace on Roda Island in the Nile was a virtual museum of some of the greatest treasures of the Ottoman Empire. Delicately aquiline and white-bearded, the prince, who dressed like an Edwardian dandy but always wore his tarboosh at a rakish angle, reminded everyone that he was not just another clubman. As the leading proponent for the young king's English education, the prince was thwarted on the Regency Council by Nazli's Francophile brother, Cherif Sabry, who was then undersecretary of state for foreign affairs. Rounding out the council was Fuad's man, Abdul-Aziz Izzet, a charming, monocled diplomat who had spent three years in London as Egyptian minister to the Court of St. James's and was married to Fuad's niece. Izzet was an Anglophile, too, but he was determined to honor Fuad's dying wish to prevent his cousin Prince Mohammed Ali from doing anything to usurp the throne from his son. Izzet kept the faith and voted with Sabry to keep Farouk out of England and on the scene in Egypt.

Into this Egyptian standoff strode the imposing figure of Miles Lampson, who came up with what he considered a brilliant, Solomonic, or perhaps Suleimanic, compromise. If they couldn't bring Farouk to England, why not bring England to Farouk? The England Lampson envisaged would be embodied in a tutor sent out to civilize and, by definition, Anglicize this unruly "Oriental" potentate.

The brainstorm came when Lampson was in London in the summer of 1936 for the negotiations of the new Anglo-Egyptian treaty, one which, incidentally, would "demote" Lampson from high commissioner to ambassador and abolish the Mixed Courts, subjecting foreigners to Egyptian law for the first time since the Capitulations were instituted in the nineteenth century. Although most of the new treaty points were cosmetic, Lampson, who had the most grandiose imperial notions, resented any diminution in his august stature. He didn't like the idea of kowtowing to a teenage king. With the proper English education, Lampson was sure Farouk would be inculcated with the appropriate set of values. "The boy" would learn respect. Lampson went to his own old school, Eton College, to visit the headmaster. He wasn't asking Eton to reconsider and accept Farouk. He wanted the headmaster to find him the perfect tutor to send to Egypt.

Edward Ford, now Sir Edward, at eighty, was still ramrod stiff as a Grenadier Guard, which he was, and alert as an Eton schoolboy, which he also was, at his Regency home on one of the Little Venice canals near Regent's Park in London. Sir Edward, who was only twenty-six when he tutored Farouk, went on to a distinguished career as a barrister in the Middle Temple and then as private secretary to Queen Elizabeth, for which he was knighted. Sir Edward had many fondly ironic reminiscences of his year with Farouk, which, despite great expectations, turned out to be something of an academic farce as well as a preceptorial version of *Waiting for Godot.*

Ford had come down to London from New College, Oxford, in 1934 and was trying to "earn a little pocket money" while deciding whether to become a barrister or a schoolmaster. To do so, he went off to Canada and took a series of jobs tutoring young boys, which convinced him to choose the bar over the classroom. He passed his bar exams the summer of 1936, and was serving in the supplemental reserve of the Grenadier Guards when he was called to appear at the Foreign Office. "I was worried I might have given away some state secret," Ford said. "But instead I met this enormous man, Miles Lampson, who said he wanted me to go out and teach Farouk. He wanted to give him something of what he might have got had he gone to Eton. 'You're not really expected to produce a scholar,' he told me. 'Just teach him to behave as you'd expect a decent English boy of his age to behave.' It was a question of manners, not losing one's temper. It would have been easiest to have sent Farouk to Eton and treat him exactly like the other boys, but, you see, you *couldn't* treat Farouk like the other boys."

Accepting Lampson's offer, Ford proceeded to Marseilles, where he took a ship via Malta to Alexandria. At the dock he was met by Fuad's and then Farouk's aide-de-camp, Colonel Omar Fathi who took him not to Montazah Palace, as Ford had expected, but to the Summer Palace Hotel at the nearby beach resort of Sidi Bishr. "We have to ease you in," Ford was told. He waited and waited for two weeks at the hotel before he was finally taken to the palace. "Farouk had inherited his father's court," Ford explained, "and they wanted their jobs to continue. They weren't going to risk anything by overstepping the mark, which led to a lot of sycophancy on their part, I'm afraid. If I had had the cooperation and goodwill of the court, things might have been easier. Fuad couldn't have died at a worse time."

When Ford finally met the king, Farouk immediately insisted they take a swim together. Ford was impressed by Farouk's good looks, courtesy, and perfect manners, despite the fact that Ford was convinced that from the start "Farouk thought that fundamentally I was a Foreign Office spy." When Ford finally began his lessons, which were to last an hour each day, Farouk would use his every wile to avoid them. "I wanted to use a big canvas, have him read H. G. Wells's *History of the World,* Van Loon, that sort of thing.

And it was very important that he learn to speak well, both impromptu and to orate properly. I chose bits from the *Oxford Book of English Prose* and sent him to the far end of the room so I could see how much I could hear. He quite liked playing at that. He was not bad company at all. But he was totally incapable of concentration." No sooner would a tutorial commence than Farouk would buzz for a servant to bring in orangeade. Or he would insist on showing "Mr. Ford," as he called his young tutor, some of his family treasures. Or he would insist on taking Ford for a very fast drive in one of his eight red sports cars. "He had this American love of just 'going for a drive.' He didn't care what he saw." Driving was the joy in itself. Even when Ford tried to arrange a nonacademic activity like a horseback ride in the desert or a game of tennis, Farouk would never commit himself. "I'll let you know," he would always promise Ford, and never did. "He had no idea how to deal with anyone his own age; he didn't know anyone," Ford explained. "He was half a private schoolboy of nine or ten, and half a sophisticated young man of twenty-three, able to sit next to a great man like Lord Rutherford [a distinguished chemist] and impress him a great deal, usually by bluffing. He did have a very good eye, a royal eye. In England, he was able to spot the most valuable rare book in the Trinity College library at Cambridge. It may have been pure luck. But it impressed everyone. And he spoke wonderful English and Arabic."

Ford's abortive lessons dwindled to a maximum of two a week. As a result, he had a great deal of leisure time in Alexandria. "I led quite a part-time life with him. I spent a lot of time at the Grenadier Reserve barracks in Alexandria. I rode horses on the grant plantations. I got a beach bungalow, very nice it was, at Sidi Bishr, and a Sudanese servant, Ali, who looked after me. I had a splendid time."

Ford never did anything outside the palace with the young king. "Farouk wasn't desperately interested in girls at the time. He never went out to the nightclubs until years later. I did, though. I'll never forget all the beautiful dancers. They came from Lebanon and all over Europe. It was a wonderful life," Ford reflected.

While Ford was leading the life of a desert squire, the new king was learning how to exercise his prerogative. He requested from the Regency Council that a new railway station for the royal train be built at Montazah to replace the rickety royal siding there. He had

Ernesto Verrucci draw up an elaborate design. But the council said no. The royal train was used only twice a year, to deposit the royal family at Montazah at the beginning of the season and to take it back to Cairo at the end. A new station, it concluded, was a pointless extravagance. Farouk was incensed. He personally assembled a demolition convoy, brought it to the old station, and tore it down. The council, faced with a fait accompli, yielded to the king's designs. Otherwise, Farouk had no involvement in the governing of his country. Until he reached eighteen, he was content to remain a figurehead. But a figurehead needs adoration, and to that end, the Regency Council decided to get the king out of his palaces and out among his subjects.

Ford got a chance to see the rest of Egypt in January 1937, when Hassanein invited him to join Farouk's month-long royal tour of Upper Egypt on his yacht up the Nile. It was the first time Farouk would have seen the country he ruled and the antiquities that had captured the dreams of the world. The trip also marked the "coming out" of Queen Nazli and her daughters, whom Fuad had confined to the harem. There were no tutorials, but Ford kept a diary that provided unusual insight into the quotidian life of Farouk and his circle and the way it was perceived by the British "overlords."

Leaving from the Cairo Turf Club, Ford was driven to Helwan, or Helwan-les-Bains, as local pundits called the garden resort on the Nile, for the embarkation. Leading the flotilla was the royal yacht, the *Kassed el Kheir,* carrying Farouk, Queen Nazli, his sisters, and the chief dignitaries, followed by four paddle steamers and motor launches. One of the steamers was occupied solely by the royal bodyguard. Another had much of the Egyptian cabinet, while still another was a Noah's Ark of cows and water buffalo for milk. Following the boats up the Nile was an even larger fleet of cars, led by the king's scarlet Rolls-Royce, his red Packard, and a caravan of red Cadillacs. These autos were to take the king and his court to tour the villages and the sights at dockings en route.

Here are some of Ford's notes on the passengers of the yacht. As for the titles of pasha, bey, and effendi, they correspond in descending order roughly with the British lord, knight, and esquire. Or, as Ford put it, "A pasha may perhaps be defined as a person who looks important, a bey thinks himself important, an effendi hopes to be important." Basically, pasha and bey were titles conferred by the

king. Effendi was a polite way of addressing members of the learned
professions.

> The Prince Mohammed Ali wears his tarboosh on one side
> at a rakish angle, has silvery side-whiskers, a white moustache,
> and generally has an air of Turkish distinction, that practically
> no Egyptian can boast. Aziz Izzet looks, and is, a courtly
> Turkish gentleman with European manners and a touch of
> nobility about him. He might be found any day in a London
> Club and taken for an old-established member. Cherif Pasha is
> said to have a sturdy common-sense: he does not look distin-
> guished and resembles his sister the Queen in having a row of
> large protruding upper teeth.
>
> The next wave of cheering heralded the arrival of the Queen,
> accompanied by the four Princesses, all dressed alike in white
> turned-back hats and grey tweed coats and white stockings. I
> had been in Egypt five months and never yet seen Her Majesty.
> The top part of her face is pretty, but her teeth are very ugly,
> and (like the other women there) although veiled below the
> nose, she was far too highly colored with rouge.
>
> His co-professor, Ahmed Bey Youssef; Mourad Mohsen Pa-
> sha, Keeper of the Privy Purse; Hassaneln Pasha, Comptroller
> of the Household; the King's physician, a common-looking
> little fat man, but genial enough, Dr. Kafrawi by name; and
> Omar Fathi Bey, the chief A.D.C. Their minds are filled with
> few thoughts except those of preferment, and the main, if not
> the sole, preoccupation of these Court officials is that they shall
> not do, nor seem to do, anything which could possibly offend
> His Majesty. Few of them have much work to do, and still
> fewer have any recreation or hobby. They are very courteous,
> at least to those who have any chance of being useful to them.
> The sycophancy that is the order of every day is repugnant to a
> European: but with them it is almost a necessity. This accounts
> for the loathsome familiarity of the King's personal servants.

Ford's two favorites were Nazli's brother, the former governor of
Alexandria, Hussein Sabry, and Hassanein, Ford's fellow Oxonian:

> [Sabry] is young looking, though he must be a good fifty, is
> sprucely dressed, intelligent and amusing. Many stories of his
> amours are current—and he certainly supports a beautiful mis-
> tress somewhere in Roumania. He is known to be, or to have
> been, enormously in debt, from which King Fuad is supposed
> to have partially saved him . . . he is altogether what one

might expect of a well educated Turk who has French blood in him. He wore a high-necked, rather feminine dark green jumper and a canvas coloured light shooting shirt. The whiff of rather expensive scent, or hair-oil, was unmistakable. . . .

When we passed a crowd of shouting fellaheen on the banks, he said, "And if you gave them a piastre each, they would come and shout for someone else tomorrow"—a significant remark. . . .

As for Hassanein:

I sit next to him for most meals and his reminiscences of Oxford are a delight to me. He has a quick wit, great courtesy, an interest in all subjects, and is a quite unusual type of Egyptian. Slim, sharply featured, with a sallow colour and grey hair brushed straight back from a high forehead, he has an unmistakably Bedouin look. There is said to be Scottish blood in his ancestry, and this makes him fairer than most Egyptians. He has keen, penetrating eyes, never looks sleepy, and has an air of refinement that the coarse looking Egyptian type entirely lacks. He has never had political inclinations, and, though he is a firm believer in Egypt's right to govern herself and a fervid Moslem, he is quite without that aggressive conceit which marks other ambitious men in this country. Although his culture and his intellect are occidental, his mentality and nature are of the east. He has an eastern courtesy, and, in conversation, an eastern way of leading you off the path you have selected by a sympathetic evasiveness.

Although Ford and Farouk were on the same boat, Farouk evaded Ford as successfully as he did at the palace. Ford never gave him one lesson. "I am never asked to do anything!" he lamented. Nor was he invited to the nightly film screenings on the yacht's "royal deck." After a while, Ford grew insulted that "His Majesty" stopped even bidding him good morning. He had become a nonperson. He didn't fare much better with Nazli. When introduced to her by Hassanein, "she appeared to pay little attention to me except to give me her hand. She then immediately turned to the pasha and asked, 'Is the king ready?' as if impatient of waiting longer. I shook hands also with three of the princesses, who smiled charmingly, and with the three *dames d'honneur,* who shook hands formally."

The trip was an endless party, with each village turning out in full regalia to fete the new king. The sheikhs and *mudirs* (governors) of the various provinces, resplendent in redingotes or djellabas, competed to outdo each other in hospitality, staging camel races, stick boxing, gymnastics, concerts and banquets, duck shoots and animal sacrifices for Farouk, all immortalized by the king's retinue of photographers. Over a thousand stills were taken, and twenty-five thousand feet of motion pictures with the king's state-of-the-art Cine-Kodak sound camera. The narcissism boggled Ford as a "record of unrivaled stardom, of which Greta Garbo might well be envious."

Aside from the king's monumental self-absorption, Ford also found fault with His Majesty's whims. One "rather thoughtless and unnecessary caprice for a boy of 16 3/4" was Farouk's desire to have a single tap for hot and cold running water in his stateroom. Perhaps it was because Ford was a sturdy Englishman, used to cold baths in the pea-soup weather of Eton, that he seemed so indignant. "This may be easy enough to do at short notice in a palace at Cairo, but in a boat on the Nile late at night, it is not so quickly done." Adding injury to insult, the new rigging leaked through the royal deck into Ford's cabin. The January freeze on the Nile and the damp chambers may have evoked schoolday memories for the young old boy.

Ford found the royal family rather hypochondriacal. Aside from two royal barbers who shaved the king every other day and had been appointed by Fuad to do so since Farouk sprouted his first whisker at thirteen, there were three doctors, and a pharmacist, and two medical assistants on board. Ford noted "so many chests of medicines, lotions, creams, restoratives, prescriptions, bottles, pastes, etc., that it is practically impossible to walk round the decks."

Ford was not amused by the general apathy about the splendors of ancient Egypt the group was seeing. All everyone did was "smoke innumerable cigarettes, drink coffee, and chat among themselves. . . . I had never thought to pass my time in the company of such closed minds—and in such high places. I hope it will not sound snobbish if I say that 'middle class' is almost the most fitting epithet for it. I find in it no trace of nobility either of thought or of behavior: no trace of these good qualities which ought to distinguish the rulers from the ruled, no trace of the mental and spiritual makeup of a cultivated European."

Ford, who learned that in Egypt it was disrespectful to have one's legs crossed in front of the king, felt, on one hand, that the fealty was excessive, and on the other, resented the "excessive familiarity" of the king's Nubian and Sudanese servants, who grew obese stuffing themselves on the royal leftovers and who were always slapping Ford on the back in a "jolly good fellow" mode.

Getting back to Farouk, Ford finally got a chance to sit with him at a lunch on the yacht:

> His Majesty came to lunch today. He was cheerful and friendly: I sat on his left. He is not easy to talk to, as he is apt to interrupt any continued speech to interpose jokes of doubtful value. He likes also to make an "impression" rather than to talk naturally. He is at his best chaffing or talking lightly on current things, but he does not evince much personal interest in the people to whom he talks. I commented on the palm branches twisted into arches, which the villagers had erected in his honour on the bank. He said it was like "Palm Sunday," and then asked if I had ever heard of "Ice Cream Sundae!" I said "no" at first, though he laughed heartily and, having soon seen the joke, if it was so, I told him that it was so bad that I couldn't be expected to expect that of him. Towards the end of the meal, in boyish mood, he made Mourad Mohsen Pasha, who was sitting on his right, turn away from him on some pretext, and then picked the handkerchief out of his pocket. This was followed by his harsh, almost vulgar, laugh—in which the Pasha and others joined, at the success of his boyish prank. For myself, I hardly thought his conduct in the large dining room in the presence of servants and the household was fitting to the dignity of a king making a triumphal tour of his provinces. But the flatterers showed no signs of protest.

Nevertheless, there was one encounter between Farouk and a "local saint," an old man in flowing white robes with a flowing white beard, which impressed Ford. The saint recited the opening of the Koran, then raised his arms to heaven to bring down a benediction upon the boy-king. Farouk then embraced the saint and shook his old hand in a self-confident yet humble way that made the crowds cheer. "His Majesty had played his part with a simplicity and dignity, which was wholly charming, and it must have made a big impression on the people there."

At the end of the month-long tour at Aswan, where tarboosh

yielded to turban and North Africa gave way to black Africa, after
Farouk had toured the Valley of the Kings and seen the tomb of
Tutankhamen, the royal entourage boarded the gleaming white
royal train back to Cairo. Despite Ford's many misgivings, the trip
had been a huge success. The king had touched his subjects; he had
given money to the poor of every village; the entire country, which
had been celebrating one long party the length of his journey, now
adored him. *"Vive le Roi"* had become the cry of January. Still,
Ford remained critical and shared his anxieties about the king's
deficiencies with Hassanein.

> I had frankly told the King some ways in which I thought
> he was failing. (The chief grievance was his unpunctuality. I
> also urged the folly of trying to bluff, to create a bubble reputa-
> tion which sooner or later must burst. His Majesty did not like
> my saying these things, told me he would not have allowed me
> to say them if he had known me less well, and denied strongly
> that he had ever bluffed.) Hassanein seemed to approve what I
> had said, though he suggested that it was no good talking like
> that to His Majesty now. His Majesty *was* King, and must be
> coaxed and wheedled: one must appeal to his pride, to his good
> sense, rather than reprove or admonish him. The pasha had
> sometimes had to do so, but he had now found "a more excel-
> lent way." The pasha himself was insecure of his position: he
> thought it likely that His Majesty would reject one who had
> had to act, so to speak, as his schoolmaster, especially when
> the inevitable intrigues started. The King, he told me, was very
> elusive, and often could not be found even in the palace. He
> receives most of his information and gossip, even on political
> matters, from his Berberine servants. He was no longer a boy,
> and had become a King. And he had the idea that a King must
> be perfect: therefore he must not be "found out." That is why
> he must have the reputation of doing everything [perfectly].
> His people expected that. No one must be allowed to prick the
> bubble.

Ford's greatest hope was to get Farouk out of what he saw as the
sycophantic, philistine miasma of palace Egypt onto the playing
fields, if not of Eton, at least of some English institution. It was a
frightfully bad nonposition to be a popular sovereign with no position, no powers, and nothing really to do. Ford prayed that once
Farouk was in England on his new upcoming royal tour of the

Continent, he could be persuaded to stay. Ford even talked to his old warden at New College about letting Farouk in for the winter term. The warden grudgingly agreed to the summer term. In the meantime, Ford planned a road trip that he and Farouk would take, *à deux,* across Europe from Athens to London. "I told him that he has one year left to enjoy himself, that he was going to be in a gold-trimmed straitjacket for the rest of his life." We would take a grand tour whose main point was *not* to be grand, to see the world as an ordinary boy, not a head of state. Then at Oxford, he would make a lot of friends. His studies wouldn't matter. They wouldn't have worked him too hard. The Japanese crown prince was at Magdalen, and that worked really well. So I put this all to him, rather enthusiastic, and what did he say? 'I'll think about it.'

"The sum total of my efforts to get Farouk a term at Oxford was to get him to spend *one afternoon* at Oxford," he said. "And our trip, for the two of us, came off *totally* different from the way I envisioned it."

Farouk left for Europe from Port Said on the *Viceroy of India* in April 1937, with his mother, sisters, Hassanein, and a traveling party of thirty-two others, seven tons of luggage, and over 250 bags. On the ship Farouk lived in the captain's quarters, but preferred wandering around the second and third class decks. In the first class saloon, a near-international incident took place when a drunk English metal dealer tried to drag Queen Nazli out on the dance floor. Hassanein, who was escorting Nazli, informed the bounder that he was in the presence of the queen of Egypt, to which the Englishman replied, "What the hell difference does that make?" He continued to hound Nazli until the captain intervened and sent the loud metal man to his cabin. Ford, in his diary of the trip, fretted that the contretemps "threatened to prejudice the queen forever against Englishmen."

In St. Moritz, Farouk never bothered to put on his beautiful new skis and go down the slopes. Instead, he preferred ice skating on one foot, and, even more, snowballing, which "was the only winter sport he indulged in to any extent," Ford wrote. "And this was done indiscriminately, at the Pasha, at his Berberine servants, at the Swiss Minister, the maître d'hotel, and any girls in the party—particularly on any expeditions which he undertook by car, by train or sleigh." Otherwise, Farouk would sleep late, sometimes until four P.M., then go shopping for medals, watches, and cuckoo clocks in the village, followed always by his private detective and cinematographer, or play the slot machines in his St. Moritz hotel, the Suvretta House.

Ford railed at being excluded from the king's high table, instead being dumped "with the accountants and masters of ceremonies," while everyone else starved for two hours or more past the appointed mealtime until Farouk finally showed up. After dinner, in the bar, over orangeade, the king spent hours throwing "little puff balls" at any girls he fancied and wanted to dance with. "Unfortunately," Ford wrote in his diary, "until I introduced to him two Swedish countesses, he showed poor taste in his choice, picking on a Hungarian Jewess of little distinction and obscure attraction (to the fury of some very Nazi Germans who were there!). This, and his friendships with another German Jew of about seventy, a coal merchant named Daniell, who lives in London, and with a middle-class Northumbrian businessman, led to a good deal of rather silly gossip in the hotel. He picked them up impetuously, probably playing at the gambling machine, where they clustered round him, while naturally the more gentlemanly people waited to be asked before being presented to him."

Queen Nazli was involved in her own adventures, drinking champagne and kicking up her heels in the hotel bar late at night after the press had left. She even danced with Ford, whom she had disdained on the boat. At one point she turned to Ford and confessed to him that she had never had any great affection for her late husband, Fuad. "When I married I just made babies," she told him. She was the mother of his children; passion never entered the social contract. Then she hit him with the zinger: "Mr. Ford, do you think I shall ever know the love of a man?" "I hope so," Ford replied, and retreated quickly to his room. The real answer to Nazli's question was Hassanein, who, Ford noted, "behaved like her spaniel, and followed to heel wherever she went." Their not-so-secret romance dated from this excursion.

Meanwhile, although, as Ford wrote "the Queen much resented the King's choice of friends, she herself got implicated with a worse adventuress, with a so-called French title, whose reputation was mainly for not paying her bills." Nazli had terrible sinus trouble but refused to go to Zurich to consult with a famous sinus expert. Instead, she used the French countess's "little man" in St. Moritz to get "ray treatments." The party next went by train of chartered wagon-lits on to Geneva for Nazli to go shopping. She ordered a fur coat and had everyone wait several days for it to be finished. Except for an expedition to the Jungfrau, Farouk killed the time shopping as well, for medals and coins, "indiscriminately by weight," Ford wrote. The hotel lobby was packed with antiques dealers hoping to sell something to the king. Chafing at the bit to get to England, Ford was hard pressed to restrain himself when Nazli delayed their departure another three days because she had found a hairdresser and a dentist in Zurich to whom she wanted to send her daughters.

To fill this void, the Swiss minister to Egypt was enlisted as Farouk's tour guide for a full program of events, chocolate factories and the like, but nearly lost his patience as he saw them one by one postponed, canceled, shortened, or altered. At the Swiss Cavalry School, where Farouk was forty minutes late, the band got even by holding him at attention by playing the Egyptian national anthem five times in succession. When a Communist paper in Geneva took Farouk to task for his lateness and for his riches compared to the poverty of the fellaheen, Farouk, for once, was not amused. He had Hassanein protest to the Swiss government for lèse majesté. Otherwise, wrote Ford, the king "kept himself to his rooms in the hotels. There he sorted his medals and coins, ate chocolates, fed at his own times, and was generally inaccessible to his staff. Only the doctor was invited in, only Hassanein had the right to enter."

More lèse majesté occurred when the royal party disembarked, belatedly, in England. Ford wrote:

> Their arrival in England was chiefly marked by the capriciousness of the Queen. Anxious to make her first appearance on the English stage a success, she took great pains to look smart, chic and European, and scanned all the press cuttings on the following day to see whether she had produced the effect she had strived for, and dispelled any ideas of a dusky oriental dressed in flowing robes and heavily veiled. Nobody apparently has the duty, or the courage, to sort such papers and to keep things offensive from royal eyes: and it was not long before she came across a cutting from the Daily Express headed "Queen Unveiled Reveals Lipstick," and continuing to say that Egyptians gathered at Victoria were surprised when, for the first time, they saw the face of the Queen which had been hidden from their eyes in Egypt. "A murmur of astonishment went up as she stepped from the train, dressed in a chic black coat of

obviously Parisian cut and with a Mayfairish hat sitting back over exquisitely curled red hair . . . etc." The article spoke of the skilful use of cosmetics on her face etc. and was clearly just a "hot" version of the prosaic news that Queen Nazli had arrived in England. However, the Queen showed that she had the same reaction to newspaper criticism as the King (if criticism it was). She was furiously angry and physically ill. She announced she was leaving England, she despatched Hassanein with protests to Buckingham Palace, the Foreign Office, the Egyptian Embassy and Lord Beaverbrook; and at the end of these various calls, she accused him of being party to this "outrageous attack" upon her because he had failed to beard the editor in his private house, and even threatened to dismiss him.

While Nazli was fuming, Ford was showing Farouk around London. Together, they went to the Mint, Buckingham Palace, Scotland Yard, to a criminal trial at the Old Bailey, and to the Law Courts. Farouk was so fascinated by the turning of the wheels of British justice that he asked to sit on the bench with the periwigged judge, who let him. He and Sir Edward attended several military presentations, a naval review, a Trooping of the Colour, and a tattoo, and two stately home weekends, the first with the Pembrokes at Wilton, the second with the Buccleuchs at Boughton, where the idea was for Farouk to meet teenage English noblemen. At first, Nazli, who wasn't initially invited, didn't want Farouk to go. She suspected a plot "that Hassanein was conspiring to estrange the king from her," as Ford said. Finally, the hosts relented and invited the Egyptian queen. Once there, Ford wrote, "her charm undoubtedly gained admirers and she in no way interfered with the King's pleasure."

Ford pointed out that while Nazli's influence over her son was perhaps greater than that of anyone else, in fact, on an absolute scale, it was "quite remote." As for the outings:

> The Wilton weekend was an undoubted success, for he [Farouk] impressed the older people there with his gaiety and spontaneity, but it was noticeable that he did not feel really at ease with his male contemporaries. At Boughton, where Mr. and Mrs. [Anthony] Eden were themselves guests, he behaved most inconsiderately in deciding to bathe [swim] some 12 miles away at 8 o'clock in the evening. Dinner for the whole party, including the Foreign Secretary, was put off for an hour and a

half, and a good deal of trouble caused to his host and hostess. He did little at Boughton to make anyone want to have him as their guest again.

Ford then had his brief moment of triumph, taking Farouk on a road trip to visit Oxford and Cambridge. Again, Queen Nazli refused to let Farouk go without her. Also again the king was usually late. One time, however, Farouk was on time, but his entourage let him down. Nazli didn't like car trips and insisted on a train, whose schedule did not allow a timely arrival. On the train to Cambridge, Ford described the scene:

> I could have wished that the Prince Regent [Mohammed Ali] and the Rector of Al Azhar had been there to see the Queen hatless in a thin printed cotton frock with short sleeves stretched at full length on the seat of a first-class railway carriage, locked in with the King's English tutor. Perhaps I should have been less amused, had I known (but I was not told) that at 5.45 the Vice-Chancellor (in bands, cap and gown) was standing at the gate of his College ready to welcome the King of Egypt to Cambridge. Thus robed and thus ready he stood for one and three-quarter hours, till 7.30, when the King drove up. The comedy, or tragedy, derived its point from the fact that for once the King *had* arrived in Cambridge on time but he had no Hassanein, no me, and no conception of what had delayed us or that the Queen was following him.

The king had left early with his servants and his detectives, but, on arriving without his advisers, he had no idea of what protocol to follow. Instead of proceeding alone to the gown, he went to the town, and spent the day buying puppies. Despite Farouk's tardiness, Ford was very impressed at Farouk's ability to finesse these situations.

> Nobody could show greater ability to pretend that nothing untoward had occurred than the King. However late, he would enter smiling, engage with men as formidable as Lord Rutherford in easy, friendly conversation, and I believe that the Vice-Chancellor completely forgot the inconveniences and difficulties in the presence of so much youthful charm and acumen. The King . . . left the impression behind of a precociously intelligent young man. It was amusing to hear him pretend here . . . that he had actually been at Woolwich. On being

shown an undergraduate's rooms, he said, "Ha, very comfortable, nothing like the bare rooms we lived in at Woolwich."

After Cambridge, Farouk went to Stratford-on-Avon to see the play *Cymbeline*. He bluffed that he had seen it, and continued bluffing at Oxford, where he charmed everyone. Everyone except Ford, who was increasingly distressed by Farouk's "careless indifference to his mother" and "his association with his servants." As for the latter, Farouk explained it simply to Hassanein. He preferred hanging around with his detective and his valets because *"they* don't nag at me." Still, Ford was appalled. "It was a repellent sight to see him slapping his Italian valets on the back, or to find them meekly submitting to having their tongues painted with black ink by him before going in Fancy Dress to a Servants' Ball in Kingston." Ford compared Farouk's self-aggrandizing tall tales of himself as a "man of the world" to those of Baron Munchausen, finding him least credible with young men of his own age, who saw through the king's charades, and with true experts in a field, such as a fingerprint expert from Scotland Yard with whom Farouk tried, in vain, to play Sherlock Holmes.

In early May, Farouk and company went to Paris. Having not been invited to participate in an official capacity at the coronation ceremonies of King George VI, who had succeeded Farouk's friend, the duke of Windsor, he and Nazli, who was particularly sensitive to being left out by the English, decided a continental departure would allow them to save face. Ford was left hanging, as he had been for the past year, as to what his future with the king would be. He wasn't sure whether he would be called to France, or called back to Egypt as a tutor, or returned to the Inns of Court to get on with his career as an English barrister. He did have one last audience with Nazli before she crossed the Channel, during which she evinced no concern about Ford's professional future but a great deal about her son's romantic one. She was most agitated that, as she told Ford, "that beastly Verrucci" was trying to get hold of the king and become in so many words the royal pimp. "The queen is being hard pressed, she told me, to provide a mistress or mistresses, for the king. I suggested to her that he would do better to take a lot of exercise now until he is a little older, when she had much better help him to chose a good queen. At the moment, the king is only just beginning to appreciate female charm. I see only harm in forcing it, and the possibilities of difficulties and scandals."

As it turned out, Ford never saw Farouk again until years later, after the war, in St. Moritz, when Farouk teased him directly about being a Foreign Office spy. In 1937, though, Farouk stayed in France and avoided his tutor. Eventually, the once-admired Hassanein, whom Ford now reevaluated as "serpentine," called Ford to Vichy, where Farouk and Nazli were taking the waters. Ford thought he was finally being included in the royal moveable feast. He was wrong. He was being sent for to be let go. At Vichy, Hassanein bade Ford the king's good-bye and presented Ford with a gold cigarette case. Smarting from being "chucked" so unceremoniously, Ford wrote Farouk a thank-you note, coupled with a stiff valedictory in which he exhorted the teenage king to lead a more orderly life and to be punctual, for everyone's sake. "It was slightly avuncular, a little bit pompous," Ford admitted, "but I was determined not to go without having said that." And off he did go, to a distinguished career at the Middle Temple and ultimately Buckingham Palace. Ford's frustrations with Farouk still rankled him. Here was a man unaccustomed to failure.

Ford brought out the report he wrote to Ambassador Lampson, which closed thus: "If I have done anything to introduce King Farouk to a country and people to whom he is allied, and to encourage friendship between them, perhaps I shall not have failed as miserably as, when I consider the hopes with which a year ago I sailed for Egypt, I cannot help thinking I have." Ford apologized profusely for the "naiveté" and the "sententiousness" of his diary entries. He was only twenty-six himself, and a stranger in the strangest of milieus. Today, he would have been far more tolerant. "I should have realized the mission was damned from the start," he reflected. "We had controlled Egypt so long, it was difficult for us to understand they no longer did what we told them."

VII

THE NEMESIS

Just as the young Farouk could not imagine a world in which he would not become king of Egypt, the young Miles Lampson could not imagine one in which he would not become viceroy of India. India was the crown jewel of the British Empire, and viceroy was the plum in the cornucopia of glamorously far-flung positions that made up the Foreign Office. At first glance, one might have guessed that Lampson's sights would have been set on 10 Downing Street rather than the Residency in Delhi. But prime minister was a political post and an often messy one. At six foot five and 250 pounds, Miles Lampson stood head and shoulders above any fray. His background and his breeding matched his majestic stature. He was born to carry the white man's burden.

Foreign service was Lampson's destiny, and he embraced it with jolly-good gusto. Coming of age in a world where Britannia still ruled the waves, Lampson took the missionary position that he was the savior of the heathen colonial world that he would bestride like the colossus he was. He never expected any interference with his ascendancy to the lofty heights of the British Empire. More important, he never expected to go *mano a mano* with King Farouk. What followed was a ten-year grudge match between the boy-king and the king's man that turned out to be a donnybrook not only for the two combatants but for Egypt, England, and the empire as well.

The complete Establishmentarian, Sir Miles Wedderburn Lampson actually had a revolutionary background. His paternal great-great-grandfather and namesake was one of George Washington's generals. The American Lampsons settled in New Haven, but Sir Miles's grandfather, having made one business fortune in the States, moved to England to make another, and retired to stately hominess as a baronet in Surrey. The English Lampsons married well; Sir

Mother's Boy • Farouk and his worldly mother, Queen Nazli, in St. Moritz in 1937.

Popperfoto

High Hat • Sir Miles Lampson, the arch imperialist British ambassador to Egypt, buttonholing Wafa politician, Makram Ebeid.

AKHBAR EL YOM Publishing House (Cairo)

English Gent • Farouk in London with the "right sort" of companions Sir Miles Lampson wanted for him.

Miles's mother was the daughter of a Member of Parliament, and instilled in her son the notion—and the duty—of public service. Born in 1880, little Miles himself had the most privileged of youths, divided between a town house on Pont Street in Mayfair and an estate on the moors of Killearn, in Scotland. He went on to Eton but saw no need to go further, and married the very blue-blooded Rachel Phipps, who was not only one of the New York "400" who fit into Mrs. Astor's Fifth Avenue ballroom but also a descendant of the white linen–mint julep Mississippi cotton plantation aristocracy.

In 1903 Lampson joined the Foreign Office as the first step in his envisioned glorious passage to India. His career unfolded perfectly according to plan, with increasingly important positions in Sofia, Vladivostok, Tokyo, and Peking, where his title was Her Majesty's Envoy Extraordinary and Minister Plenipotentiary to China. Lampson had become one of the darlings of the foreign service. A telegram to him from the foreign secretary Sir Austen Chamberlain, said it all: "Bravo Lampson, a Man." In 1933 Lampson was given Cairo, one of Britain's most important diplomatic posts, on a par with Washington and Moscow because of Egypt's essentiality as the fulcrum of the Middle East, the home of the Suez Canal, and the gateway to India, the Far East, and the oil of the Persian Gulf. Miles Lampson's new title was High Commissioner of Egypt and the Sudan. He was following some very large footsteps, those of Lord Cromer and Lord Kitchener, but, then again, Miles Lampson had giant feet.

In December 1933, Lampson sailed from Shanghai, stopping at the Happy Valley Cemetery in Hong Kong to pay final respects at the grave of his wife, Rachel, who had died three years before. Then the widower diplomat, accompanied by his two daughters and their governess, received a full honor guard salute and, escorted out of the Kowloon harbor by two British destroyers, set sail for his new position. Their ship, the S.S. *Ranchi,* stopped at the eastern outposts of the British Empire—Singapore, Penang, Colombo, Bombay, and Aden, where further salutes were given to the new high commissioner by the Grenadier Guards and by Scottish Fusiliers. The Lampsons finally reached Suez on an un-Egyptian bitterly cold January 7, 1934. There was more pomp and ceremony and a private train that took the family on to Cairo and the sprawling Residency whose green lawns and hedgerows and croquet courses and stone lions were an oasis of anglophilia on the banks of the Nile. *Honi soit qui mal y pense.*

Lampson was entranced by Egypt. He did a quick grand air tour of the country and was dazzled not only by the pharaonic antiquities of the Nile valley but by the more obscure Greek and Roman temples half buried in deserts near the Lybian border and the ancient Christian monasteries capping fierce granite peaks near Mount Sinai and the Red Sea. He was fascinated by the sheikhs and the monks and the gullah-gullah magicians and dancing dervishes and the snake charmers who all coexisted in this eternal landscape. Not only did Lampson adore the country. In the beginning, he even liked the ruling dynasty. He described King Fuad as a "good fellow, far shrewder than he gives one the impression of being." As for Prince Farouk, then fourteen, Lampson was even more impressed. "He struck me as refreshingly unspoilt," he wrote in his diaries. "Very big for his age and very simple in his enjoyment of elementary jokes. His English is extremely good. I think he owes much to his English nanny, Mrs. Naylor. . . . I was frankly impressed by him—a nice honest lad, I should say."

Lampson settled into the sweet life as England's "big man in Cairo." In addition to his normal diplomatic duties, he entertained foreign notables at garden parties, played golf and rowed sculls at the Gezira Sporting Club, developed a racing stable, studied Arabic, learned to fly, would dance Viennese waltzes and French gavottes at white-tie galas at Shepheard's or the Semiramis until three A.M., then would be up at five to go duck hunting in the Fayoum. Work hard, play hard, such was life in the imperial elite. But the social whirl proved lonely at the top. Lampson longed for his late wife. He needed a companion, a perfect hostess other than his daughters, who were forced to fill the role. At fifty-four, the big man found his little dream girl in the seventeen-year-old barely five-feet-tall Jacqueline Castellani, one of London's debs of the year.

Jacqueline Castellani was the daughter of the renowned Harley Street physician Sir Aldo Castellani. Jacqueline had been born in Ceylon, where her father, who was Italian, headed the British government clinic for tropical diseases, making numerous major contributions to the field, for which he was knighted. Jackie Castellani's glittering girlhood was well spent not only in Colombo and London, but also in Rome, where she was "adopted" on school holidays by the childless British ambassador there, who was one of her father's closest friends. A great dancer and a great flirt, Jackie was London's girl-most-likely. Her porcelain-doll beauty, her exotic and sophisticated background, and her game-for-anything vivacity made her the teen queen of the tea and crumpets set. In the spring of 1934, Jackie recuperated from the endless comings and goings of her coming out by taking a trip to Egypt with deb pal Betty Lampson, Sir Miles's niece. They stayed at the Nile Residency, and sparks were ignited, so much so that Jackie prolonged her stay until it was time for Sir Miles to take his late summer leave back in England. In what was literally a May-December romance, they wed in London shortly before Christmas before a huge pride of royals from all over the empire and the world.

Back in Egypt, Sir Miles's new family ties soon proved to be something of a sticky wicket. In 1935, the bad boy bully of Europe, Benito Mussolini, sent his planes and tanks against an Ethiopia whose arms were chiefly bows and arrows. Because Jackie's father, Sir Aldo, was the physician of the Italian royal family, he acceded to a request from Rome to become the chief doctor of the Italian Army, particularly in view of the tropical ailments the soldiers were facing in Africa. Sir Aldo stopped in Cairo en route to the war zone to visit his daughter and new son-in-law, who insisted that Sir Aldo's visit be incognito. Sir Miles kept Sir Aldo out of the spotlight, taking him on long drives out to the pyramids. Lampson hardly fancied the notion of being dragged into a war, albeit indirectly, on account of family ties. Yet he did understand the call of duty and its discontents. He wrote in his diary about Sir Aldo's troubled mind:

> He is terribly afraid that Mussolini is going to try and rope him in. As he explained to me, they have no experts in tropical medicine in Italy. . . . This upsets all his arrangements and engagements in America, England and elsewhere, and the poor man is in a great stew about it. But as he said rather pathetically, if you do happen to be an Italian, it doesn't pay to run counter to what Mussolini asks of you.

The year 1935 was terrible for democracy. While Mussolini was playing great white hunter against the Ethiopians, it was springtime for Hitler, who, with the death of von Hindenberg, had seized the presidency of Germany, renamed himself führer, and began his blood purges. Lampson had more than a sixth sense that the two dictators had their eyes on his prize of Egypt. He was also well aware of imperial Cairo's ties to imperial Rome, ever since the khedive Ismail went into an exile—an exile inflicted upon him by the British—in Italy as the guest of the House of Savoy. King Fuad, who had sailed into exile with his father, Ismail, had forgotten neither the Italian hospitality nor the British high-handedness. Italian was his first language, Italy his first love. His palace was packed with Italian retainers, so much so that Lampson was already worried about their influence on the impressionable Prince Farouk. Given his sheltered existence, these barbers, valets, and electricians were his primary male role models. Considering the looming presence of Il Duce in Ethiopia, Lampson saw he had the double challenge of weaning Egypt away from Italy, and Farouk, as heir to the throne, away from the Italians.

To these twin ends, Lampson arranged to create a grand illusion of English benevolence, generosity, and respect. He would send Egypt to the League of Nations; he would send Farouk to Woolwich. The Anglo-Egyptian Treaty of Friendship and Cooperation of 1936 was Lampson's diplomatic triumph. Forming an odd-bedfellow alliance with the great camel trader of Egyptian politics, populist firebrand and on-and-off Prime Minister Moustapha Nahas, Lampson orchestrated a campaign of Mussolinophobia. Palace proclivities notwithstanding, Egypt stood a real danger of being annexed by the rapacious dictator into his new, unholy Roman Empire. Except for the food, the British Empire was much more civilized, and Lampson wasn't really asking Egypt to be a colony, or even the veiled protectorate it had been since Khedive Ismail's deposal in 1879. Not at all. In fact, Lampson would even throw "independence" into the package. He wouldn't be high commissioner anymore. He would be the most respectful ambassador. He even agreed to the abolition of the Capitulations and the Mixed Courts, the symbol of foreign domination, extraterritoriality, and privilege in Egypt. All Egypt had to agree to was to guarantee that Egypt would side with Britain in the event of hostilities and to allow Britain to station up to ten thousand troops and four hundred pilots in the canal zone. British troops would thus leave Cairo and Alexandria and would return "to protect Egypt" only if there were a war.

As events had it, Lampson was much more prescient about the world situation than the Egyptians, who eagerly rushed to sign the treaty and start celebrating their independence day. The Egyptian

Parliament ratified the document by a landslide 202 votes for, and only eleven against, in what was, in some ways, a popularity contest between Lampson and Mussolini. It turned out to be the high-water mark for England; the next twenty years would be straight downhill. It is perhaps symbolic that when Anthony Eden, then secretary of state for foreign affairs, gave a celebratory luncheon for the Egyptian treaty delegation in London, the featured culinary pièce de résistance of Yorkshire grouse was mistaken by many of the Egyptians as stringy old crow.

With the country for the moment in his pocket, Lampson turned his energies on Farouk. The wild card Lampson did not anticipate was the death of King Fuad in April 1936. Mourning the loss of the monarch, Lampson wrote: "Slippery customer though he was, he was an immense factor in the situation here and . . . we could always in the last resort get him to act in any particular line that we wished." Fuad was particularly efficacious to the British as a buffer against the various and sundry warring Egyptian political parties. Farouk, however, frankly stumped Lampson, who didn't expect to have . . . "a young immature King on our hands. I frankly don't know quite how that problem is going to be handled." Lampson had thought Farouk would have had at least several years in England to make him "one of us." Instead, Farouk had had a bare six months of anglicizing "civilization," much of which involved shopping and brothel- and club-hopping.

Farouk became Lampson's first order of business after the funeral of King Fuad, during the long march of which Lampson developed blisters on his feet, was set upon by hysterical, shrieking peasant women mourners, and nearly had his frock coat and top hat splattered with the spurting blood from the slit jugular veins of the sacrificial oxen and buffalo at the entrance to the El Rifaii Mosque. Lampson was most impressed by the multi-gun salutes and air force maneuvers to welcome Farouk on his sad yet triumphant return from England to Egypt. Lampson was *not* impressed by some of the stories he heard from one of his palace "spies," Farouk's personal English royal pharmacist, Titterington, who got much of his gossip from Farouk's English governess, Mrs. Ina Naylor. Lampson wrote:

> The boy was quite above himself; running down the English
> Royal Family, and so on; King Edward had nothing to say; the
> Duke of Kent was only a girl; the Duke of Gloucester was

worth nothing, and so on. Furthermore, he had asked who was
now teaching his sisters music and, when he was told a certain
Mrs. Murray, said that had got to stop. As regards painting he
was told that another English woman was teaching them that.
According to Mrs. Naylor, he had said that he was not going
to have all this English influence round his sisters. All very
petty and rather tittle-tattle . . .

Armed with all this tittle-tattle, Lampson had his first meeting
with Farouk as king rather than as prince and still found him "a
very nice outspoken lad."

> It was an appalling task for him at his young age to have
> such heavy responsibilities thrust upon him. I did not wish in
> any sense to embarrass him, but as the destinies of his country
> were a matter of vital importance to us, I hoped he would
> realize that if at any time he was in real difficulty, or really
> puzzled, he would remember that we were honestly his friend
> and with no ulterior motives or axes of any sort to grind.

Lampson flattered the new king by comparing his situation to
that of young Queen Victoria. The queen had had the astute Lord
Melbourne to guide her. Sir Miles would be Farouk's Lord Melbourne. Farouk told the ambassador he intended to move ahead
very slowly and carefully, always keeping in mind his father's
motto, "Patience." Lampson told Farouk of his own family motto,
"D. W. O. F." which stood for "Don't Worry or Fuss." Farouk said
he preferred his own, as it was shorter. Lampson closed this first
royal audience by "rubbing in at one moment that he must beware
of Italian blandishments, but this I did very discreetly."
    Not wanting to abandon his project of anglicizing the young Fa-
rouk, which he felt was the best way to prevent the king's further
Italianization, Lampson tried to convince Queen Nazli to send her
son back to school in England. She wouldn't let him go. Lampson's
fallback position was to bring Eton to Farouk in the person of tutor
Edward Ford, to whom, as has been seen, Farouk gave the royal
runaround. Ford expressed his exasperation to Lampson, who had
hired him, and Lampson, also exasperated, decided to confront the
king and give him "a little lecture," as Lampson called it. "The
headmaster," which was one of the least pejorative of Farouk's
many nicknames for his self-imposed mentor and ultimate tormen-

tor, naturally understood how Farouk, like any normal blue-blooded boy of his age would prefer having a good time to studying. But, after all, he was a king and a king couldn't fritter away *all* his time "frivoling and enjoying himself."

Farouk assured Lampson he had made up a schedule and was grinding away at the books, making Lampson slightly abashed. The ambassador admitted he sounded "rather governessy," yet the "little lecture" turned out to be the first in a long series, with the recurrent sense of *déjà entendu*. At the end of each Mr. Chipsian chat, Farouk promised Lampson he would be "a better boy" and thus bamboozled Lampson just as adeptly as he had snaked Edward Ford. "King Farouk struck me as having come on a bit . . . and there is no doubt that he is intelligent and has excellent manners," Lampson wrote in his diary in December 1936.

With the treaty signed, Egypt in his pocket, and Farouk ostensibly immersed in his books, his English books, Lampson was able to get back to a more normal life. Much of what the embassy did was "receive" people; Jacqueline Lampson quickly became Cairo's Perle Mesta, giving state dinners and high teas and low bows to a gamut of guests that ran from British diplomats with names like H. St. John B. Philby and H.K.D. Gybbon Monypenny (perhaps an inspiration for Ian Fleming), to the famed French aviator Count Saint-Exupéry, who wrote *The Little Prince* and who was given R&R at the embassy after his plane crashed in the Egyptian desert and who was rescued from death by thirst by a tribe of bedouins, to Barbara Hutton, then the Countess Haugwitz Reventlow. Sir Miles was most impressed with "the richest woman in the world. She is also distinctly good to look upon; naturally excessively well-dressed and covered with the most marvelous jewels. Her husband . . . struck me as a pompous ass, terribly pleased with himself and full of his management of the financial side of his wife's affairs."

Despite the glamour of the Cairo "season," the world outside in 1937 was starting to burn. Haile Selassie had finally fled Addis Ababa, and Mussolini proclaimed his conquest complete. Ethiopia became the Fascist empire of Abyssinia. The Spanish Civil War had broken out. The Japanese invaded China, capturing Peking and Shanghai. In Russia, the Communist purges exiled Trotsky, who settled in Mexico. In America, President Roosevelt, fearing the worst, signed the Neutrality Act, while in England Neville Chamberlain became prime minister and would begin the policy of appeasing Hitler.

Nearby Palestine was also becoming a powder keg. The British Royal Commission's recommendation of a separate Jewish state provoked great consternation among Egyptian leaders. Prime Minister Nahas wanted Palestine as an independent Arab state, with religious freedom for Jews, but nothing more. He was oblivious to English foreign policy favoring a national home for the Jews. "This did not perturb Nahas in the least," Lampson wrote. "He maintained that the mandate was all wrong and that the only thing to do was to scrap it."

The father of Zionism, Dr. Chaim Weizmann, visited Lampson in Cairo and chided him about subscribing himself to Nahas's sentiments. Lampson sidestepped the issue. "The merits or demerits of partition were not my affair," Lampson wrote. "As regards Weizmann's threat that unless the Jews got what they wanted they might turn nasty, I said I hesitated to believe that the Jews would really do anything so foolish or so embarrassing to the British Government at this time of grave international issue." Lampson personally favored a truce that would beg the question for another decade, a quota system that would maintain what he called "the present racial proportion of the population."

Lampson was shuttling back and forth to London several times a year for briefings. He and Jacqueline visited the new king, George VI, who had succeeded his brother who himself had abdicated for Mrs. Simpson to become the duke of Windsor. At Buckingham Palace, the Lampsons joined the king and queen to see the new royal television set, while Princesses Elizabeth and Margaret climbed on the table, making and eating little mountains of sugar cubes. On more serious notes, Lampson met with Anthony Eden about Egypt's woeful unpreparedness, particularly in antiaircraft guns, in case of war, and with Prime Minister Chamberlain on Downing Street. Despite Chamberlain's severe attack of gout, he was very sanguine about his recent meetings with Mussolini and, optimist that he was, dissuaded Lampson from his antiaircraft-gun pitch by saying such preparedness "might choke off Mussolini's present overtures," notwithstanding Lampson's concern that "it would be fatal if the Egyptians got the impression that we were not taking the threat to their security sufficiently seriously." Lampson described to Chamberlain the big loophole in the treaty Lampson had masterminded, i.e., that Britain could bring in masses of troops in case of "an apprehended international emergency," but again Chamberlain, whose credo was "peace in our time," was in no mindset to consider ever invoking it.

Back in "independent" Egypt, on July 29, 1937, the seventeen-year-old Farouk attained his majority, which, according to the Islamic calendar, was eighteen lunar years from his birth. The Regency Council would be dissolved. Farouk would be on his own. It was coronation time. Farouk, his mother, and sisters ended their five-month grand tour of Europe on July 20 in Marseilles, from which they sailed to Alexandria on the Egyptian steamer *El Nil.* Farouk may have been understandably nervous. Until now, the most decisive act of leadership he had taken on in his entire life was piloting the electric locomotive of the Swiss Red Arrow Express from Geneva to Berne. The trainhands praised the young monarch as a hell of an engineer. Driving a train was, alas, slight preparation for driving a nation. Nevertheless, Farouk steeled himself to the task. At six feet, slim, and erect, he certainly looked the part. He would have to finesse the rest.

At the outset of his reign, Farouk's chief mode of shining through was to party his way over the rough patches of his monarchical shortcomings. The dazzling celebrations that marked his first years as king of Egypt captured the world's imagination and endowed the teenager with a certain grandeur and fairy-tale quality that cast a multihued smoke screen around the fact that he had absolutely no idea how to rule his enormously complex country. No boy of his age, except perhaps Alexander the Great, who conquered Persia at twenty-one, could possibly have been expected to rise to such an occasion. Yet who could notice the substance when the form was so entertaining.

Farouk's coronation outdid that of King George VI. From the moment he took the red carpet ashore to Alexandria, his countrymen, who were not possessed of an English-style reserve, went wild. Carbines went off in endless salutes, Egyptian Army aircraft swooped down in formation; the battleships of all nations in the Alexandria harbor boomed their big guns. In Cairo, the normal population of one million was tripled by the fellaheen arriving from all over the country, by reduced-fare Nile steamers, feluccas, cattle cars, ragged buses, camels, and donkeys. From many miles away the travelers could see the illuminated city, hear the pounding drums pumping up the dancing masses. Endless sides of mutton and beef were cooked on open spits in Cairo's parks and given out free. The entire metropolis, from the pyramids to the citadel, was a giant spectacle of fireworks, green crescent banners, and triumphal arches through which Farouk, whose handsome picture was festooned everywhere, would proceed en route from Abdine Palace to Parliament. For countless peasants, who had never before been outside their villages of mud huts and water wheels, the trip to monumental, modern Cairo was a visit to Oz.

At six A.M. on July 20, the cannons' roar at Abdine signaled the beginning of the march. Farouk, dashing indeed in his white field marshal's uniform and baton, set off with a green sash and a red tarboosh, got into his gilded coach pulled by horses and flanked by barefoot Sudanese runners in white flowing costumes, and starch stiff royal guards in red tarbooshes and white, blue, and gold uniforms, seeming cool as ice in the 104-degree heat. Farouk was supposed to be wearing the jeweled sword of Mohammed Ali, but it was somehow lost in the palace collections. Another suggested accoutrement, the solid gold headdress of that other boy-king, Tutankhamen, was too small to fit Farouk's very large, manly head. In a following scarlet Rolls-Royce rode Queen Nazli, shockingly modern by appearing only semi-veiled, and the four sister princesses, ages seven to sixteen, identically dressed as for an Alice in Wonderland tea party in big white hats, neat white dresses, and ankle socks. The marching bands played. The khaki cavalry on chestnut mares rode on. The long parade snaked through the city. Millions cheered.

The Chamber of Deputies, which was kept very cold by one of Egypt's first air-conditioning systems, was standing room only with British generals in regalia and Arab sheikhs in robes and European diplomats in formal dress, all paying their respects. Prime Minister Nahas, who had ridden to Parliament with Farouk in the gold coach, was dressed in top hat and morning coat, with his green badge of courage, the sash of the Order of the Nile. His introductory encomium to Farouk was, parenthetically, an ode to Ambassador Lampson, who towered above his Jackie in the first row of the dignitaries' gallery. Nahas gave Farouk credit for Egypt's independence, its membership in the League of Nations, the end of the Capitulations. Lampson couldn't help but smile. He knew the credit belonged to him.

Then Farouk ascended to the podium, took the oath of monarchy, and gave a brilliant and very democratic speech in Arabic that was music indeed to the millions of peasants who heard the address over loudspeakers in the Cairo streets as well as in the Nile villages that had been cabled up with electricity for this very occasion.

the king is the first servant of the country . . .
    the poor are not responsible for their poverty, but rather the wealthy. Give to the poor what they merit without their asking. A king is a good king when the poor of the land have the right to live, when the sick have the right to be healed, when the timid have the right to be tranquil, and when the ignorant have the right to learn . . .

Farouk's speech sounded like a declaration against the interests of his class. It also sounded like something his brilliant mentor, the poetic Hassanein, had composed for him. Lampson was dumbstruck. Here was a boy who never opened a book, whose Egyptian tutors gave him all the answers, who was a bluffer not a scholar, and yet here he was, as eloquent, as silver-tongued, as Disraeli.

    And if it is Allah's will to lay on my shoulders at such an early age the responsibility of kingship, I, on my part, appreciate the duties that will be mine, and I am prepared for all sacrifices in the cause of my duty . . . My noble people, I am proud of you and your loyalty, and am as confident in the future as I am in Allah. Let us work together. We shall succeed and be happy. Long live the fatherland!

Lampson didn't like the sound of "fatherland" either, especially in view of Farouk's and his dynasty's Italian proclivities, as well as the solicitousness being shown the young king by Berlin. "Fatherland" indeed! But Lampson wrote it off, for the moment, as a figure of speech, and to his own paranoia.

The celebrations continued for three more days, with balls and banquets at the palaces and mansions of the rich and titled across the city and more free food, fireworks, and music for the poor and displaced. Farouk donned a helmet, mounted a horse, and reviewed the army at the vast barracks and parade grounds at Abassieh. He donned robes and paid respects to Allah and to his noble ancestors at the El Rifaii Mosque. He donned his dinner jacket and partied with the beau monde until dawn, changed into uniform to greet the

Boy Scouts from his balcony at Abdine, and then put on a simple suit to drive through the slums of the city, distributing money to relief organizations for the poor. Farouk had something for everyone. An era of good feeling was upon Egypt.

When the coronation festivities subsided, Farouk took the royal train straight to Alexandria to bask in the beachy luxury of Montazah Palace and recuperate from his public relations coup. He arrived with his mother and sisters on August 5. It was supposed to be a quiet summer. It wasn't. By August 24, Farouk was on the front pages of the world press all over again. This time it was because the most eligible young man on earth had broken a world of hearts by having gotten engaged.

The very lucky girl was fifteen years old at the time. Her name was Safinaz Zulficar. She was from an important, if not royal, family of Turkish descent. Her father Youssef Zulficar was a judge on the Alexandria Mixed Courts of Appeal. Her mother, Zeinab, was one of Queen Nazli's ladies-in-waiting. In fact, mother and daughter had been part of the large party that had accompanied the Egyptian royal family on its recent skiing holiday in Switzerland. At the time, Farouk had paid absolutely no attention to Safinaz, who had left her lycée to join the grand tour. Queen Nazli, on the other hand, was smitten. Safinaz was a young woman in her own image, a petite, beautiful brunette upper bourgeoise who spoke perfect French and had perfect manners and yet was not of royal blood. She looked patrician even though she wasn't, and, to Nazli, that was her greatest asset. If there were going to be two queens in the family, Nazli wanted to be the first, and she certainly didn't want the second queen to be a princess as well. There were a number of genuine Ottoman princesses who had their eyes on Farouk, but Nazli, a well-born commoner who married up, always worried that their blood was better than her own. She could brook no competition. The petite, timid teenage daughter of her admiring lady-in-waiting could never give her anything less than total fealty. On this occasion, Farouk, who had not shown any great libidinous interest in the fairer sex, was as obedient as his mother expected him to be.

The courtship was almost nonexistent. Farouk drove his red Alfa Romeo convertible down the corniche from Montazah to the Zulficar villa, accompanied by his aide-de-camp, the taciturn Colonel Omar Fathi, who was one of the king's favorite driving companions, probably because he didn't complain about Farouk's daredevil

Grand-Prix maneuvers behind the wheel. At the villa one of the suffragis greeted the king at the door and told him the judge and his wife were away. Forget the parents, Farouk said. Get me Safinaz. The servant obliged and Farouk made his pitch, which had to be fairly dizzying to the fifteen-year-old Safinaz. He had to ask her father, she demurred.

Farouk said he would wait. Not so easy, Safinaz told him. Her father was on his way to Lebanon for two weeks. He had just left that day for Port Said, where he would board his ship for Beirut. Farouk took decisive, kingly action. He called the Alexandria chief of police, who was able to have the ship stopped before it left the port. Judge Zulficar was hustled off board and straight to Montazah, where Farouk was waiting with an offer. The judge wanted to refuse. He believed both Farouk and his daughter were too young, and they should postpone their nuptials for several years. Farouk—and Nazli—wouldn't hear it. They compromised on several months, and set a wedding date of January 20, 1938. The judge was overruled by the king. How could he dissent? For his concurrence, the very next day after their meeting Farouk raised the judge's title from bey to pasha and bestowed upon Mrs. Zulficar the Order of Kammala, which was the highest honor available to Egyptian women. The next week, for his fiancée's birthday, Farouk presented Safinaz with a check for $50,000 and a diamond ring worth at least as much. Young love could be blind; it could also be lucrative. Farouk also presented Safinaz with a new name that would perpetuate Farouk's father's fetish for F's. Safinaz was a Persian name that meant "pure rose." The new name, Farida, was Arabic for "the only one." The country began to get ready for another huge bash, the first Egyptian royal wedding since the time of the pharaohs. (Fuad had married Nazli before he became king.) Farida, after Nazli, would be only the second queen of Egypt since Cleopatra.

The betrothal further burnished Farouk's supremely popular image, so much so that twenty-two persons were crushed to death and another 140 severely injured when a cheering throng of eighty thousand surrounded the "official" summer palace of Ras-el-Tin in Alexandria in a show of loyalty and devotion to the new king. Farouk spent the next few days visiting the hospitals where the casualties were taken and meeting with his Cabinet to establish indemnities for the families of the deceased.

Back in Cairo for the fall season, Farouk, bolstered with self-confidence from all the adulation, made his first big political move in dismissing Prime Minister Nahas. Farouk never trusted the old revolutionary and Zaghlulite, seeing him as a natural enemy of the Palace. This perception was underscored when Nahas sought from Parliament the right to dismiss Farouk's Italian palace staff, led by Antonio Pulli. Since their salaries were paid by the state, Nahas felt the state, and not the king, should have the right to hire, fire, and set their salaries. Farouk was insulted by this attempted interference with his royal prerogative and, more important, with his best friends.

Then there was Nahas's bitter opposition to Farouk's chief of cabinet, Ali Maher, with whom he had once shared a law office at the turn of the century. The two men were diametric opposites, Nahas a peasant populist, Maher a dapper royalist. Maher had served King Fuad as prime minister while Farouk was in school in England and had developed a real taste for palace life. He was the Beau Brummell of Egyptian politics, wearing silk-tasseled tarbooshes, pearl stickpins, patent leather spats. Even though he dressed Savile Row, he hated the British and he hated Lampson and, as Farouk's chief political adviser, he was, in English eyes, as non grata as any persona in the country. This all threw Nahas into the arms of "Professor" Lampson. Farouk was thus as suspicious of his prime minister as Othello of Desdemona. Nahas had to go.

In Nahas's place, Farouk appointed as prime minister Mohammed Mahmoud, years before a Zaghlulite but a Balliol College–educated one who had become a close ally of King Fuad's. Nahas's ouster was distressing to Lampson, as was Mohammed Mahmoud's new cabinet, which included a number of pro-Italian ministers. Mussolini had recently increased his troops in neighboring Libya, while boldly announcing his ambitions to play a larger role in the Muslim and Arab world.

In view of Il Duce's disturbing proximity, Lampson decided it was high time for another "little lecture" to Farouk. "It will be fatal," Lampson wrote, "if the boy comes to think that he is invincible and can play any trick he likes. Personally I have always liked him and he certainly has a most remarkable intelligence and courage—one begins to fear almost too much of the latter." Meeting Farouk at Abdine Palace in December 1937, Lampson may have gone in thinking he was dealing with a "boy," but came out with a totally different impression.

"I found him rather baffling to deal with—in extraordinary good humour and apparently taking the whole thing rather flippantly whilst at times relapsing into a very 'kingly' attitude," Lampson wrote. He thought it was terribly high-handed of Farouk to have dismissed Nahas while his Wafd party still held a majority in Parliament.

> We must always remember that Egypt isn't England by a long manner of means . . . but my instinct remains clear that the whole business has been a great mistake. And as to the poor old Treaty I don't quite know where we stand, but there's this to be said, whatever Government now comes in and however much in a minority, they are bound to realize that they cannot afford to estrange the British Government. . . .

Finally, Lampson invoked a Latin phrase he had learned at Eton to describe Farouk's folly in dismissing Nahas and affronting Lampson and, thereby, England: *Quos deus vult perdere prius dementat,* which, translated, meant "Those God wishes to destroy, he first makes mad."

If Farouk was crazy, it was like a fox. In April 1938, in the first elections to be held that would test Farouk's new government, the king's men won in a landslide. Nahas and his Wafd were ignominiously trounced. Nahas's favorite slogan, "The king reigns; he does not rule," had been repudiated. Farouk, who had that magic popular touch, proved he could reign *and* rule. The Wafd may have been the party of the masses, but the masses preferred Farouk's parties. Farouk, with his grand gestures like buying shoes for twenty thousand barefoot fellaheen, made Lampson eat his words. If ever there was a majority king, Farouk was the man.

The king's greatest party was his wedding day, which was declared a national holiday and made his coronation look like a warm-up for this main event. Public transportation fares were slashed by seventy percent so that the millions of villagers who descended on Cairo in the dead heat of the previous July could return in the bracing cool of January. The public's good feelings were such that Cairo's pickpockets took an ad in one of the capital's daily newspapers declaring a moratorium on their "liftings" during the wedding festival. The broad avenues of the city were floodlit. Every main square was decorated with a huge royal crown studded with jewellike colored lights. On the Nile, a navy of feluccas and *dahabeheah*s (houseboats) were strung with pennants and candles.

The day before the wedding, Farouk gave continuous popelike audiences from his balcony at Abdine Palace to everyone from kindergarten groups who had sung songs written especially in honor of the nuptials to bedouins on prancing horses in from the desert to put on a show for their beloved monarch. In the mosques, Egypt was praying for Farouk. (Fourteen of the country's fifteen millions were Muslim; 800,000 were Coptic Christians, another 200,000 were Jews.) Egypt's religious leader, Sheikh Moustafa el Maraghi, the grand rector of Al Azhar University, gave an address praising Farouk's devotion to Islam as thousands of Al Azhar students cheered "Long live the pious king."

For all his piety, Farouk's wedding was, if not heathen, definitely modern. The ceremony itself, held in a drawing room of Koubbeh Palace, resembled a business closing much more than a love match. In fact, following Muslim tradition, the bride wasn't even part of the ceremony. Farida wasn't supposed to be there at all, but modern woman that she was, she watched Farouk and her father do the "deal" that plighted her troth from behind a *moucharabiya,* or wooden latticework screen, wearing a skimpy tulle veil that came up only to her nose and a Worth of Paris gown of silver lace over satin with an eight-yard train of shimmering silver lamé.

In the presence of Sheikh el Maraghi and three other holy men in purple robes and white turbans, King Farouk, in his black and gold field marshal's uniform, gave the morning-coated Judge Zulficar a check representing half of Farida's dowry. The other half was payable only in case of a divorce. Then the judge extended his right hand and pressed thumbs with the king. At the same time, Sheikh el Maraghi covered their hands with a green silk cloth.

"Do you agree to marry my daughter?" Zulficar asked the king.

"I accept her betrothal to myself from you, and take her under my care and bind myself to offer her my protection, and you who are present bear witness," Farouk said, then repeated the vow twice, according to Muslim law. Next the two men signed two copies of the calligraphy-on-parchment marriage contract, one of which was held by Ali Maher, as chief of the Royal Cabinet, the other to be filed in the archives of the Muslim religious courts. Then a white flag was raised over Koubbeh to signify that the deal was done and a 101-gun salute was fired for all Cairo to hear. The king and the judge retired to a grand salon to celebrate with an all-male entourage that included all the princes and *nabils* of the country, the Cabinet, and all the living former prime ministers of Egypt, including the hated Nahas. Sudanese waiters in livery served the traditional drink of rosewater and syrup and passed out gifts of golden boxes of chocolates, while cashmere shawls were presented to el Maraghi and the other ecclesiastics.

While the men were clubbing it up, Farida broke the Muslim interdiction against photography by posing for her portrait, *and* without her veil. The pictures of the new queen would soon hang in every shop window in Cairo as well as be reproduced as buttons and put on sale. As Joseph Levy, the local *New York Times* correspondent noted, underscoring Egypt's recent progress in the emancipation of women, "Queen Farida is a modern girl in every way, and he [Farouk] intends to let her live a modern life." Even though Farida's trousseau consisted of forty-five Paris gowns valued at $30,000, the new queen did make the one concession to tradition by eschewing makeup. The result was that she had the wholesome, fresh-scrubbed look of a Seven Sisters girl from Wellesley or Mt. Holyoke.

In time, Farouk awaited his new bride at the foot of the *Gone with the Wind*-like marble staircase, then escorted her out into the formal gardens as a band played the *Lohengrin* Wedding March and Farida's four nieces carried her long silver train. Waiting for the newlyweds at the palace lake was Queen Nazli. Farida bowed to Nazli and kissed her hand; Nazli kissed Farida and Farouk each on the cheek. They cut the wedding cake, which was large enough at twelve feet high and six feet around for a troupe of dervishes to jump out of. But they didn't. And the cake itself was not in the shape of a pyramid or sphinx but in that of a Palladian rotunda.

Back in the Koubbeh royal apartments, the wedding party surveyed the gifts from all nations. The French sent a Sèvres porcelain dinner service. The Greeks sent a bust of one of the Ptolemies who had ruled Egypt. The Turks sent a priceless diamond-encrusted gold jewel box. The Arabs sent a stable of Thoroughbred stallions. Mussolini sent an alabaster statue of the Emperor Diocletian. Hitler sent a custom-made Mercedes sports coupe. And King George of England sent a pair of Purdey shotguns and a set of golf clubs, which may have been wishful thinking on the English king's part, as the Egyptian king detested golf. The Cairo Jewish community presented Farouk with a casket bearing the Psalms of David printed on silver scrolls, while Egypt's Grand Rabbi opened a fund in honor of Farouk and Farida to feed hungry children. Farouk himself gave his queen a three-strand diamond necklace which he had seen at the Paris Exposition when he was there, as well as other jewels, the value of his largesse being estimated at $300,000 by an oohing and aahing press corps that responded to the entire affair as if Farida had won the grand prize on a quiz show.

In the streets Cairo was going wild with fireworks displays over the Nile and dancing in the streets to native musicians from across the land. Acrobats and magicians performed, and the pungently delicious scent of the hundred tons of lamb Farouk had donated to be barbecued to feed the poor whetted all appetites. The Royal Automobile Club gave a huge flower parade with floats designed as everything from hospitals to pyramids rolling through the sardine-packed multitudes in the streets between the two main palaces, Koubbeh and Abdine. The day after the wedding, Farouk mounted an Arab charger to review another parade, that of the Egyptian Army. The cavalry marched with their lances and green and red pennants. The Camel Corps rode on pure white ships of the desert. But the hit of the show was the modern equipment, not the picturesque—whippet tanks, antiaircraft guns, pontoons, heavy artillery, with Egyptian Air Force planes swooping down for low salutes. Downtown at the Rio Cinema a King Kong–size billboard of King Farouk was outlined with six thousand bulbs, while the Pharaonic Mail Line erected sixty-foot statues of Isis and Osiris and Horus pouring for Farouk and Farida the Wine of Happiness into the Cup of Life. Hundreds were injured, falling from balconies, crushed by trams, trampled by horses and camels, mangled in the post offices trying to buy commemorative stamps. It was a fusion of the Arabian Nights, the Valley of the Kings, the Pasadena Tournament of Roses, and Times Square, and when it was all over, days later, Farouk had captured the hearts of his country and the fantasies of the world.

For a while, even Lampson was won over. Thanking Lampson for the Purdey rifles (but not the golf clubs), Farouk joked about "the present political difficulties in France and the apparrent impasse in regard to finding a French government and laughingly observed that there were one or two spare governments in Egypt whom he would willingly lend to France." When Farouk found out that Lampson's own guns weren't Purdeys, he said, "Well, we must see about that—if you are good." Lampson enjoyed the king's sense of humor and left their meeting buoyed by his conclusion that Farouk was "essentially English in his outlook."

Farouk took Farida on a brief honeymoon at his country estate at Inchass, thirty-five miles outside of Cairo, where the king had his own private zoo, model farm, and futuristic ham radio communications center. Then it was back to Cairo to reign and rule, and, of course, to have one more giant celebration, this time for his eighteenth birthday on February 11. He and Farida seemed the most perfect couple. Unlike his father, who kept to Muslim tradition and sequestered Nazli in the harem, Farouk took Farida everywhere. He drove her in his car, he put her on postage stamps—how could the beautiful queen be a graven image, a subject of prohibition? They went to balls, to Shepheard's Hotel, to embassy cocktail parties. Farida was no back-street queen. Farouk, who surprised her with a different present—a jewel, a painting, a statue, a ring—every day of the first year of their marriage, was truly a teenager in love.

He even broke all traditions by bringing Queen Farida, along with Queen Nazli, who always insisted on—and got—equal time in the king's attentions, to the opening of Parliament in April, a Parliament without Moustapha Nahas and therefore one that represented Farouk's great political triumph, complementing his personal one. In his address, Farouk for once put himself totally behind England in applauding Prime Minister Neville Chamberlain's policy of friendship with Italy. The young king declared that an Anglo-Italian agreement would be "the surest guarantee of peace" in his time.

Lampson, loyal company man that he was, still wasn't so sure. An English dowager visiting Cairo brought disturbing reports from a stop in Rome that Lady Austen Chamberlain, the widow of the late foreign secretary and brother of Neville, had been giving high-toned aid and comfort to the Fascists.

> . . . giving large and sumptuous banquets, and that it is even now in the air that she should pay a sort of State visit to (Italian colony) Libya! . . . all this activity on the part of Lady Chamberlain is regarded in some quarters as rather pecu-

liar. I observed that I was surprised that she should be in a position to give these large banquets, as one knows that she was left extraordinarily hard-up by poor old Austen. I did not say so, but I suspect that brother Neville must have arranged this business.

When Lady Chamberlain herself visited Cairo, en route to Luxor and the Valley of the Kings, she assured Lampson that there was "no doubt whatsoever that the Italian people have no wish for any trouble with us." Her only worry was that the "British ambassador in Rome, Sir Eric Drummond, the Earl of Perth, "never sees Mussolini and spends all his time playing golf with certain local beauties. In fact, she was a trifle sniffy about it," Lampson noted.

For all his misgivings, Lampson nonetheless tried to be optimistic and not dismiss all Italians completely as the enemy. Yet. At a long lunch with Lady Chamberlain at Shepheard's Hotel, the lady introduced the ambassador to the Italian viceroy of the recently conquered Ethiopia, the Duke of Aosta, who impressed Lampson mightily as "a perfectly charming person. He is a magnificent fellow creature, 6 ft. 6½ inches tall and lithesomely built. We measured back to back and he beat me by a good one and a half inches. I liked the man immensely; in fact one felt one was talking to a very sympathetic companionable Englishman."

Lampson could only wish that all of Italy could be run by such aristocrats. Meanwhile, Mussolini's Fascist Black Shirt movement was proving most influential to the youth of Egypt. There were the Wafd Blue Shirts, encouraged by Nahas, who drilled like Hitler youth troops, saluting with a *Sieg heil!* slap on the chest. And there were the Royalist Green Shirts, encouraged by Ali Maher. The Green Shirts were also known as the Young Egypt Society and were able to shoot but not kill Nahas in a demonstration. In a tit-for-tat situation, a Syrian student, probably a Blue Shirt, took a wild shot at Farouk at an Alexandria beach in the summer of 1938. Farouk was secretly flattered that he was worthy of an assassination attempt. It made him feel that he had arrived as a politician. Outwardly, he made political capital of the situation, claiming he was saved by the miniature Koran he always carried in his breast pocket. Farouk the Pious. Farouk the Invincible.

Aside from the mad Syrian, there were a few others, albeit not many, who were not hypnotized by their lovable young king. One of these was Mohammed Neguib, then a major in the Frontier Corps along the Libyan border, who was temporarily in charge of the Military Museum in Cairo. In March 1938, Neguib's first son was born. Neguib wanted to name him Saleh ed-Din (Saladin) after the famous sultan, but he was overruled by his wife, who insisted the boy be called Farouk. As did many Egyptian mothers of the time, she believed the name was a good luck charm. That summer, Neguib, then thirty-seven, got to meet the revered king himself. Farouk, who was following his father's footsteps in collecting *everything*, had started his own private arms collection at Montazah. Neguib had driven down to Alexandria from the Cairo Museum with two truckloads of exhibits for Farouk. Neguib and his soldiers, all in full uniform, stood at attention in the raging heat of the palace gardens for the king to come down to inspect the treasures. Finally, Farouk arrived. He was wearing a pith helmet, slacks, and sandals with no socks. And no shirt. The emperor had almost no clothes. Neguib was shocked. How could his beloved king wear no shirt? Even Antonio Pulli, now Pulli Bey, since his friend the king had titled him, who had been swimming in the Montazah pool with Farouk "had sense enough to dress before he appeared before me and my soldiers in the garden," the ceremonious Neguib wrote in *Egypt's Destiny.*

Neguib personally presented the king with two special treasures, a brass cannon and a whale gun that had belonged to Farouk's grandfather, the khedive Ismail. The guns were huge and heavy, yet Neguib was able to lift them without any assistance. The other soldiers were so nervous, they felt they might drop them.

"Oh, Major," Farouk flattered Neguib, who one day would become the strong man of Egypt. "You're so strong. What do you eat, beans?" Neguib was not amused.

Farouk then picked up the guns himself. The sensitive Neguib was insulted by what he saw as royal one-upmanship. "I was struck by the flabbiness of his muscles and the rolls of fat on his chest. I was twice his age, but my body was in far better condition," Neguib wrote.

Perhaps Farouk had had a few banquets too many, but at this time he was hardly the porker that he later became. Now he was six feet tall, 180 pounds. He normally did wear shirts—from Jermyn Street, along with the most elegant bespoke pinstripe suits that would meet the approval of the fastidious Lampson. *Dashing* was the word, and *debonair,* and *altogether sure of himself.* But his very carefree self-possession rubbed the stolid, circumspect Neguib completely the wrong way. Neguib expected a pharaoh; when he got merely a charming teenager, he couldn't help but be disappointed.

After Neguib had stayed at Montazah for six days installing the weapons, Farouk put him to further tasks. He wanted some of the arms of Krupp, particularly an 1871 cannon that was in Giza, as well as several of Mohammed Ali's original guns and shells. Neguib called all over the country, locating the weapons. When he delivered them, Neguib observed that "Farouk, on receiving the loot, was as happy as a little boy with a new collection of toys."

When Captain Osman, who was assisting Neguib, began to disarm one of the shells incorrectly by twisting its core in the wrong direction, Farouk took over the task, did it the right way, then asked the officer where he had been trained as a soldier.

"At military school in England, just like Your Majesty," the captain replied.

Farouk told Captain Osman he would have been better off having attended the Royal Military Academy. Again, Neguib was not amused by Farouk's sense of humor. The captain, Neguib noted in his memoirs, went on to be promoted to lieutenant colonel, decorated with the Order of the Nile, and was one of those responsible for purchasing the defective Italian hand grenades that blew up in the faces of the Egyptian Army in the 1948 war against Israel. In 1952, with Farouk in exile and Neguib as commander in chief of Egypt, the Tribunal of the Revolution stripped Osman of his rank, his "illegal" fortune, and sentenced him to fifteen years in prison. Perhaps Farouk should have put his shirt on.

Neguib never let go of his grudge over the king's indecorous behavior. Later that year, when Neguib graduated first in his class from the Egyptian Staff Officers' School, whose instructors were largely British, King Farouk arrived to present the class with their diplomas. The commandant ordered the officers to kiss the king's hand.

I told my classmates that I would not kiss anybody's hand in any circumstances and urged them to follow my example. None of them did. As for myself, I disguised my refusal by pretending to be confused. After saluting the King, I shook his hand instead of kissing it. I shook it so hard, in fact, that he winced, as was revealed in a picture that appeared that evening in one of the newspapers.

Neguib's animus against King Farouk in 1938 was no doubt magnified by his revolutionary fervor at the time he wrote his memoirs in 1952. The Farouk of 1938 was a hard king to hate. He was probably the most popular head of state on the globe. Although youth and beauty were undoubtedly cornerstones of his appeal, another, certainly among Egyptians, was the grand illusion that Britain was on her way out of their country. Notwithstanding Farida's sundry modernities, the Arabic-speaking, mosque-attending "pious" Farouk was seen as the break in a long chain of khedival-Anglo puppets, a return to the off-with-their-British-heads glories of Mohammed Ali. The English in Egypt still maintained a "boy! balls" patronizing, clubby colonial arrogance that infuriated people like Neguib. They treated Egypt as if it were part of the empire, but the Egyptians, because of their momentous past and more recent taste of glory under Mohammed Ali and Ismail, believed that *they* should have an empire, that they should be victor rather than spoils. In these nationalistic ambitions, the eighteen-year-old Farouk was their stalwart. But it was a ludicrous burden to expect him to assume, given his inexperience and given that a world war was thundering closer every day.

Farouk would never be Lampson's puppet. The circumstances of the times forced the two into an essentially adversary relationship. Farouk had to stand up to and against "the headmaster" or Egypt would lose face. If there were a puppeteer in the picture, though, it was Chief of Cabinet Ali Maher. The eloquent Hassanein may have composed the speeches, but the crafty Ali Maher called the shots. Ali Maher was descended from a long tradition of Brit-baiting. His father, a prominent adviser to the khedive Abbas Hilmi, had been denounced by the great imperialist Lord Cromer as "a bad adviser, a cause of strife, and an obstacle to harmonious cooperation" between the khedive and the British. Ali Maher's brother Ahmed Maher had carried on his father's intransigence. In 1924 he went on trial for the broad-daylight murder in Cairo of Sir Lee Stack, sirdar of the Egyptian Army and governor general of the Sudan. He was defended by none other than Moustapha Nahas, his brother Ali's former law partner, and acquitted. Ahmed, like Ali Maher, eventually fell out with Nahas but never fell in with the British.

In his memoirs, *Bright Levant,* Sir Lawrence Grafftey-Smith, then the first Oriental secretary at the British embassy, recalled the Maher brothers as coming "from a narrowly British point of view . . . of bad stock." Ali Maher "was always at hand to place the worst interpretation on any British gesture or remark." Grafftey-Smith wrote of Ali Maher:

> I have never met a more compulsive ambition. When I was far down in Residency hierarchy Aly Maher invited me to dine alone with his wife and himself, and the evening was uncomfortable. Their longing for the accident of politics which might pave the way to his premiership was nakedly advertised: I was assumed to be able to pull the essential string.
> Both brothers were short and stocky. Ahmed was fleshy and had fat chops; Aly Pasha paid annual visits to Tring, where he lived on orange juice, and returned fever-eyed and wrinkled; a small ravenous wolf driven by furnace heats of ambition. I can hardly believe that his normal temperature was normal.

From the beginning of Farouk's reign, Ali Maher was behind him, advising him in his never-ending chess games with his two chief opponents, Nahas and Lampson. Some of the moves against Nahas were petty, like Farouk's refusal to wear a crown on the grounds that it would be too expensive. Nahas had encouraged him to wear one, but only as entrapment into making Farouk the object of a Wafd campaign against palace extravagance. Ali Maher dissuaded Farouk from going for Nahas's gambit, as well as from having Abdine Palace centrally air-conditioned, which would have cost two million dollars and may have left the fellaheen fuming, as well as sweating, in the heat. On a more substantive note, legal wizard Ali Maher taught Farouk how to manipulate the Egyptian Constitution to his own ends, specifically in convening and dissolving Parliaments and dismissing prime ministers, regardless of the size of their majorities. That was how Farouk got rid of Nahas in 1937, to Lampson's consternation.

Ali Maher, having vanquished Nahas, then turned to Lampson himself. He wanted to fight empire with empire. To that end, he concocted a program of strategic conjugality. Farouk's four princess sisters were the most beautiful and eligible women in all Islam, if not elsewhere. Fawzia, which in Arabic meant "the successful one," was the oldest at seventeen. She was stunning in a Hollywood-movie-star way and bore a distinct resemblance to Gene Tierney. The second sister, Faiza, which meant "winner," was the cleverest and most vivacious, a born hostess and party-giver even as a teen. The third, Faika, which meant "extraordinary," was the kindest and most thoughtful, while Fathia, only six in 1938, was sweet and shy. Ali Maher came up with the brainstorm of uniting the Sunni Muslims of Egypt with the Shiite Muslims of Iran by betrothing the gorgeous Fawzia to the handsome, Le Rosey–educated Crown Prince Reza Mohammed. Ali Maher naturally saw cosmopolitan Egypt as being the dominant partner in the transaction with relatively primitive Iran.

The crown prince's father, Reza Shah, was not the imperial sort, living on a simple diet of meat and rice and sleeping on a mattress on the floor. Although the shah was a fiercely towering illiterate, an autocratic military man with a Mongol visage who assassinated his rivals and whipped peasants in the street who failed to salute him properly, he was anything but a palace monarch like Fuad or Farouk. His court was so uncourtly that visitors joked that only the servants knew how to behave. No problem for Ali Maher. The Iranians could learn at the feet of the Egyptians. The diplomatic overtures were made, the proposition accepted. The marriage contract would be concluded between Prince Reza and King Farouk, acting in loco parentis, in March 1939. After Fawzia, Faiza would be next. Ali Maher was already investigating a union with the son of King Abdullah of Jordan. And in Iraq, the five-year-old King Faisal II had just succeeded to the throne after his father [the Harrow-trained, sports car enthusiast] King Ghazi had been killed in an automobile wreck. Faisal and Fathia could be a match made in heaven, or at least in Cairo.

All this potential marital Arab unity gave Ali Maher still another grand idea for King Farouk and for his own relentless aspirations. The title Caliph of Islam had not been occupied since 1924, when the last Ottoman sultan, Mehmet VI, had been deposed and Mustafa Kemal (Ataturk) founded the Turkish Republic. Kemal had his own ax to grind. In 1918 Kemal, a brilliant military hero and the sultan's aide-de-camp, had asked the sultan if he could marry his daughter. The sultan said no, on account of either Kemal's medical record of venereal disease or his overweaning ambition, or both. Kemal was also in line to become Turkish minister of war. The sultan took him out of line. Four years later Kemal returned the favor. The sultan went into exile first in Malta and then in San Remo (deposed sultans and khedives seemed to gravitate to Italy), and for a short while the sultan's cousin became the caliph. Caliph was the companion spiritual title to the secular one of sultan, both having resided in the same Turkish sovereign until Kemal severed the two and abolished the secular part in favor of himself. In "modernizing" Turkey, Kemal soon felt hamstrung by this imperial religious anachronism and eventually abolished it as well, putting the last caliph on the Orient Express to Europe, never to return to the Bosphorus.

Ali Maher adored the title of caliph and the notion of a spiritual leader of an Islamic world of over 300 million faithful followers. Ali Maher thus began to lobby for Farouk's ascension to the caliphate. He increased the king's Koran lessons with Sheikh el Maraghi. He publicized the folklore that Farouk's Koran had saved his life from the Syrian student assassin. He had Farouk develop a more prophet-like appearance, growing a pointed goatee and donning clerical robes for his Friday visits to the mosques of Cairo. At one of these mosques, after Farouk had led prayers as imam, the congregation, which included five hundred Egyptian military officers, actually rose and proclaimed His Majesty as caliph and Commander of the Faithful. Whether the outburst was spontaneous or orchestrated by Ali Maher, the ultimate political press agent, is a subject of conjecture. It is known that Ali Maher was in close touch with Hassan el Banna, who hated the British and their morally impure foreign influence even more than Ali Maher did, if that was possible.

As for the British, Ali Maher did everything in his fervid imagination to be sure that Farouk's encounters with Sir Miles Lampson would be interpreted in the least favorable light. The ambassador's condescensions to "the boy" were rubbed in constantly by this chief of Cabinet. As Sir Lawrence Grafftey-Smith recalled: "No sensitive young man cares to be reminded, even by his own memory, of the day a visitor knows that he has wet his trousers; but this was the sort of emotion Maher Pasha was able to evoke in his veneomous persuasions."

Lampson could not help but be amused by the irony of a major address Farouk gave on February 20, 1939, to commemorate the Muslim New Year. "It is my self-confidence and reliance on Allah which inspires my actions, although this does not prevent me from seeking the views of experienced men." He stressed the importance of a united Egypt "to impose respect for her on anyone attempting to interfere with her dignity." And he made a major demonstration of posthumous filial piety, invoking King Fuad and conceding that while he had not been heir to all of his father's praiseworthy attributes, he believed that he had indeed inherited the most outstanding of all: "Like him, no one can influence me."

All in all, 1938 was Farouk's most triumphant year. He was a king, he was a husband, he was potentially a caliph, and everyone loved him. The end of the year did bring him his first major disappointment. In November, he and Antonio Pulli had gone to a beach outside of Alexandria to pursue the king's current passion—the one in which he had enlisted Major Neguib—for old weapons. A cannon dating back to Napoleon's invasion of Egypt in 1798 had been found buried in the sand, and Farouk wanted it for his collection. He and Pulli were in the process of digging the weapon up, when a messenger from Montazah arrived with the news that Queen Farida had gone into labor. Farouk and Pulli rushed back to the palace. Farouk was praying for an heir. Otherwise, if anything were to happen to him, the throne would be taken by his sixty-four-year-old uncle and former regent prince, Mohammed Ali, a close friend of Lampson's. The prince believed that as a younger son rather than nephew (as was Farouk) of the khedive Tewfik and brother of the khedive Abbas Hilmi, he had a more valid claim to the throne than the boy-king. The prince's ambitions to see Farouk fail or die or be deposed so that he might thereby succeed him were scarcely veiled. The king was, therefore, deeply depressed when the palace guard's salvo stopped at forty-one guns rather than the 101 that would have signified a boy.

Farouk put on his normally happy front. Sticking to the F's, he named the girl Ferial, after his grandmother, the wife of the khedive Ismail. The Turkish F-word meant "light." Celebrations began again in the cities and villages, as Farouk decreed that every child born in Egypt that day would receive a gift of two dollars from him. There were fireworks and concerts, meat for the poor, and sweets for the children. The country was gay, but Farouk was not. He knew that he would have to try again, but that, unknown to anyone except the king and his queen, was another problem altogether.

VIII

WAR GAMES

The year 1939 was incredible. The Spanish Civil War ended with Franco in control, and World War II began with Hitler in control. America sat on the sidelines, seeing its Depression-ravaged economy resurrect itself on the spoils of the European war, supplying the demand for arms and other equipment. While America sat, it distracted itself with one of the vintage years in the short history of cinema, in which *Ninotchka; Stagecoach; Goodbye, Mr. Chips; The Wizard of Oz;* and *Gone with the Wind* were all nominated for the Academy Award for Best Picture. Steinbeck's *The Grapes of Wrath* won the Pulitzer Prize, Kaufman and Hart's *The Man Who Came to Dinner* was the toast of Broadway, Hitler's *Mein Kampf* was published in an English edition, and Americans reassured themselves by making Kate Smith's "God Bless America" the song of the year. Sex suffered a double blow in the deaths of Sigmund Freud and Havelock Ellis. Nylon stockings created a revolution of their own at Macy's and Gimbels, Harrods and Selfridges, Au Printemps and Galeries Lafayette. In London they danced the Lambeth walk, while in Berlin they sang "Lili Marlene." Pan Am, seemingly oblivious to the clouds of war, began regular transatlantic service on the Dixie Clipper. And the Yankees swept the Reds in the World Series, four games to none. If only the real world were so simple.

In Egypt, King Farouk saw all those memorable films in the huge screening room of Abdine Palace, but was otherwise blissfully unaffected by the big events in the world outside his palaces. His big event was marrying off Princess Fawzia to the crown prince of the Iranian Pahlevis. Again, party time was descending on Cairo, one of the great party cities and soon to become even greater. On September 1, Hitler invaded Poland. On September 3, Britain declared war on Germany and then invoked the "in event of war" loophole in the

1936 Anglo-Egyptian "independence" Treaty to send masses of troops back into the country. Cairo would be, in reality, what Casablanca would become mythologized as in the eponymous Humphrey Bogart film—a romantic desert crossroads of the world, of spies and soldiers and cafés and casbahs and women with pasts and men with futures, except Cairo threw in a king and a palatial high society gloss and grandeur that Casablanca, both on and off screen, never even tried to evoke.

Until the actual outbreak of war, Cairo was just glamorous Cairo, without the spies and the soldiers. Sir Miles Lampson would have disagreed about the spies. He was deeply convinced that Farouk's largely Italian palace staff was up to no good. Farouk responded to Lampson's apprehensions by granting all seventeen of them, from Pulli to Pietro della Valle, the barber, to Eduardo Kavatis, the keeper of the royal kennels, full Egyptian nationality by royal decree. Now stop calling them Italians, Farouk's gesture razzed Lampson. Farouk could not resist pulling a joke on his own men either. While the Italians were celebrating their new protective cover, a cross to vampire Lampson, Farouk deflated them by announcing that as Egyptians, they would also have to convert to Islam. Conversion was less of a problem than its corollary. Muslims had to be circumcised. The Italians all went deathly white. Maybe it was better to be deported, they hemmed and hawed as Farouk insisted they become "full-blooded" Egyptians. It's a royal decree, he averred. Off with it. The king even went so far as to have reserved a surgeon and a floor in the hospital for the group clipping, but at the last moment he called back the knife. Winning the World Cup in soccer couldn't have made any Italian happier.

The one Italian Lampson distrusted above the rest was Ernesto Verrucci (Fuad had titled him Bey), the royal architect, whom Lampson knew was capable of other designs. Lampson leaned on Prime Minister Mohammed Mahmoud to enlighten the king about Verrucci's checkered royal past. Lampson wrote:

> The man's appointment was a disgrace . . . he was disreputable and dishonest. Mahmoud had also told the king that there were several unsavoury reports about Verrucci's past; that it was even said that he had acted as a pimp. To which Farouk had said—"A pimp to whom?" This had rather embarrassed the Pasha, for as he said to me with a laugh, he could

hardly tell the boy that Verrucci had been the pimp used by his
own father, King Fuad!

At this stage of his young life, Farouk the Pious was not thinking
about pimps. He was a good boy, going to mosques, collecting antique weapons, driving sports cars, trying to be a good father and a
good husband. The sexual obsessions which were to become his
leitmotif had not yet kicked in. For now he was undersexed. Neither
the size nor the drive was there. This equipment failure was terribly
frustrating for his modern teen-queen, Farida. His giving her a gift a
day every morning was compensation for what he wasn't giving her
every night. He felt guilt and he felt shame and the fact that his
daughter was not a son was, in the Egyptian folklore, a blot on his
virility, his manhood. Farouk consulted his doctors about love potions and aphrodisiacs from the time of the pharaohs. What did
Antony use with Cleopatra? What about Alexander the Great? He
found the answer in food. Pigeons, since the birds reproduced like
rabbits, were considered a great cure for impotence. So were volup-
tuous-tasting mangoes. And so was mutton, for some unfathomable
reason. Thus Farouk devoured mutton by the meadow, pigeons by
the treeload, and mangoes by the grove, washing it all down with
the fresh orangeade he had a special servant squeezing and drowning in sugar. Hashish, too, was considered a sexual stimulant, but it
also spurred hunger. In Farouk's case, everything went to his stomach. By March 1939, when Prince Mohammed Reza arrived to
conclude the wedding contract for Fawzia with Farouk, the boy-
king was beginning to look less boyish and more blimpish. Since
Ferial's birth he had gained over thirty pounds and had to get a
whole new closet of uniforms made by his royal tailors to be able to
greet his prospective brother-in-law.

March 15 was both Egypt's Independence Day and the birthday
of Prince Reza's father, the shah. At Abdine, Al Azhar's Sheikh el
Maraghi threw the green silk cloth over the pressed thumbs of Farouk and the shah-to-be. Later, at the El Rifaii Mosque, where the
shah was to be buried, Farouk led the prayers and Sheikh el
Maraghi delivered an address urging the permanent reconciliation
of the two sects of Islam that were symbolically being joined in this
hopefully perfect union. A twenty-course full-regalia banquet was
held back in the Abdine Grand Buffet, a huge arabesque hall with
Koran verses written in gold in Arabic on the soaring ceiling. Fa-

rouk in full dress uniform escorted a shimmering flapperlike Lady Lampson, in a low-cut, clingy white satin evening gown and a white mink stole, while Mohammed Reza, also in full dress, followed respectfully behind. At the dinner table, photos of Farouk show him glazed with boredom while Sir Miles, his chest bursting with medals and decorations, was blustering animatedly and dominating the table.

The dinner, as were all Abdine state dinners, was stiflingly formal. The *Abdine Protocols,* a thick volume codifying who sat where, who toasted whom, who was invited to what, and so on, was a fusion of the most pompous features of the Ottoman and French courts, the kinds of things that brought Marie Antoinette to the guillotine. During Farouk's reign, the protocols were enforced by his grand chamberlain, the ancient Said Zulficar, no relation to Queen Farida's clan. Zulficar had served not only King Fuad, but the three rulers of Egypt before him, and would brook no deviation from the rule book. In 1942, when Zulficar was dying, his final words were the dictation of a revision of the order of precedence at a state banquet. Even the pouring of coffee by the Sudanese waiters was an elaborate ritual involving velvet cloths studded with diamonds over the arms of the servers, solid gold coffee cup holders, and endless bowing and scraping. Small wonder Farouk started haunting nightclubs.

After the marriage, Queen Nazli personally escorted Fawzia to Teheran, a trip that made the queen and princess feel like they were camping out. On the train to Persia via Baghdad, the electricity broke down and the water supply was depleted. They found the palace food more like prison fare and the etiquette to match, less like the *Abdine Protocols* than *Zero for Conduct.* Instead of a grand chamberlain, army officers did the seating. Still, this was a dynastic alliance, not *Romeo and Juliet.* What love—and comfort—had to do with it was irrelevant. Keeping things in the family, Farouk appointed Queen Farida's father, Judge Zulficar, as his ambassador to Iran. The first tentacle of Ali Maher's grand design had been fastened.

In April 1939, Dr. Josef Goebbels visited Cairo, ostensibly to see the pyramids. Lampson believed this about as much as he believed Mussolini's declarations of nonaggression as he built up his troop count on the Libyan border to over 200,000, and on the Ethiopian one to a quarter of a million. Mussolini had described Italy and

Egypt as "two peoples united by the same sea," and Lampson knew what *that* meant. The ambassador believed the only way to Farouk's heart was through his ego and, accordingly, arranged for the king of England to invite Farouk and Farida to London for a state visit. Between grouse shoots while on his annual English summer leave, Lampson "told H.M. that he [Farouk] was showing signs of being a much better boy" and hence was worthy of the royal invite that, despite the unfortunate wedding gift of the golf clubs, would carry more weight than the blandishments of Hitler and Mussolini combined. Kings, at least English kings, always trumped dictators.

Until September, the most dramatic event in Farouk's life after Fawzia's marriage was his having contracted chicken pox while on a spring cruise with Farida and daughter Ferial on the *Mahroussa*. Confined to his Abdine Palace bedroom, with its football field of a bed, gold leaf walls, its full kitchen for midnight suppers, and its swimming pool bathroom whose every wall was decorated with life-size reliefs of naked nymphs, Farouk commented to Prime Minister Mohammed Mahmoud, "You don't really appreciate your wife until you are ill." Shortly thereafter, Queen Farida was pregnant once more.

With the outbreak of war, Lampson cut his English sojourn short and returned to Egypt by Imperial Airways' "flying boat." In Alexandria on September 1, Lampson learned that Prime Minister Mahmoud had resigned on account of failing health. His replacement involved no guesswork. Ali Maher no longer had to scheme within the Cabinet. He had accomplished his life's dream. As prime minister he was front and center. He was a star.

Lampson went straight to Montazah and found Farouk "in excellent form and most friendly." He presented Farouk with King George's invitation for a state visit to England. "I suggested that he should open and read the letter, which he did. In doing so, he exclaimed, 'Very good of him, very good of him,' and commented that of course nothing would give him and Queen Farida greater pleasure." As for the imminent declaration of war by England, the thing that seemed to bother Farouk the most was whether to cancel the tea party at his date garden near Aboukir that he was planning for Farida's birthday on September 5. Lampson wrote that Farouk, imbued with all his father's superstitions, thought "it seemed hard luck to give it up. I said not only did it seem hard luck but quite uncalled for." Relieved that the party would go on, Farouk praised his new prime minister, assuring Lampson that he would "find him good to deal with, direct, and to the point."

Ali Maher was, naturally, none of the above. In his speech opening the Egyptian Parliament, he infuriated Lampson by the following masterpiece of indirection: "While war is raging around us, it is a pleasure for me to repeat to you that collaboration with our ally will be in the future, as it has always been in the past, our best guide in the accomplishment of our task. Our ally will therefore receive from us every possible assistance." Ali Maher never once mentioned Britain by name, and the word that stuck in Lampson's gut was *collaboration.*

Egypt did break off all diplomatic and commercial relations with Germany, sequestrated German property, marking German houses and shops with a red cross, and interned the thousand German nationals living in Egypt. Most of the Germans in Egypt were members of the Nazi party, but several hundred were not, most of whom were Jews. The authorities didn't bother to notice this distinction, herding all Cairo's Germans, Jews, and Nazis alike into the German school there, while in Alexandria the subjects of the Third Reich were locked up in the Italian school, as no German academy existed there. Terrible fighting understandably erupted between the Jews and their persecutors, but it was nearly three years before the Jews were separated from the Nazis. These logistics were all the more insensitive in view of the fact that the official sequestrator of German property in Egypt, Ahmed Sadik, had a Jewish wife.

Egypt declared martial law and an *"état de siège,"* placing all Egyptian ports in control of the British Navy. But Egypt pointedly refused to declare war against Germany. (Italy would not enter the war until the following year.) Egypt's nonbelligerence became a serious issue with Lampson and the chief British military men, General Sir Henry Maitland "Jumbo" Wilson, the general officer of command in Egypt, and General Sir Archibald Wavell, commander in chief of the Middle East. Wavell had served in Palestine in World War I and had marched with Lawrence and Allenby into Jerusalem. He was later to become Lampson's holy of holies, viceroy of India. The generals had little patience with Ali Maher's evasions. They put pressure on Lampson for results, the niceties of diplomacy notwithstanding, pressure that would later have disastrous consequences for all parties involved.

Whatever the Egyptians did to hedge their bets toward the Germans, they could not avoid or evade the hard reality that the British were coming, not that they had ever left in the first place. But now the khaki uniforms of soldiers arriving from across the empire—from Australia, New Zealand, India, and England itself—began to compete for space on the streets with the flowing white robes of the bedouins and the red tarbooshes of the bourgeoisie. Eventually two to three million British troops would pass some wartime in "Gyppo," as they called it, but outside of a very intense square mile in the center of Cairo, the worlds of England and Egypt never intersected. Then again, the worlds of Farouk's inner circle and that of the rest of Egypt never really intersected either. Yet it was the heady mixture of the Farouk elite and the English elite that gave wartime Cairo a glamour, a mystery, and a cachet that put the city in the pantheon of urban legends, with fin de siècle Paris and jazz age Manhattan and swinging sixties London.

What was this exclusive preserve and who populated it? The center of Cairo's magic mile was Ismail Pasha Square near the banks of the Nile. Around the square, or *midan*, were the Egyptian Museum, home of King Tut and today the same, the Kasr El Nil Barracks, home of the British Army and today the Nile Hilton, and the Cathedral of All Saints, the Westminster Abbey of British society and today an empty right of way for the terminally gridlocked corniche road along the Nile. A block away was Suleiman Pasha Square, named for Queen Nazli's French general grandfather, the center of Cairo's commercial glamour. Here was Groppi's, the high temple of chocolate and sugar, founded by a family of Alexandrian Swiss. In the front was a confectionery and outdoor café; in the back was a rotunda with a stained glass ceiling where *thés dansants* were held from five to eight and *soirées dansants* began at ten. Even the British who came here found themselves speaking French. Groppi's was a superb oasis for ladies who lunch to recuperate from shopping sprees at Circurel's and Le Salon Vert, the two deluxe department stores situated nearby, as were the major banks, airline offices, and specialty shops offering specialties not only from darkest Africa but from Fifth Avenue, Bond Street, the Rue St. Honoré, and the Via Condotti.

The area was not for women only. Within a few blocks of Suleiman Pasha Square were the exclusive men's clubs, the St. James's–like Turf, which allowed only British members, the fin de siède Mohammed Ali, which allowed none, and the art deco Royal Auto-

mobile Club, which was the least stuffy, the most fun, and where
Farouk loved to gamble. On an institutional level, the Parliament
was a few blocks away, as was the American University, and the
palace of Princess Shivekiar, where the city's greatest parties were
held. A few blocks in the opposite direction toward the Ramses
Station, down the *grands boulevards* that Khedive Ismail had built
in homage to Paris, was Opera Square and the Royal Opera House
that saw the premiere of *Aida* in 1871 and was the cultural gem of
the Middle East, and Ezbekiah Gardens, Cairo's Tuileries, with
Abdine Palace on the other side. Facing the gardens was hotel row,
the grandest of which was Shepheard's, with its wicker terrace and
Moorish Hall and Karnak Ballroom. And, of course, its Long Bar,
with its long drinks and its long waits for service. When Rommel
was pounding at the gates of Egypt at El Alamein and threatening
to sweep across to the Red Sea, the British soldiers would joke,
"Wait until he gets to Shepheard's; that'll hold him up."

Other grand lodgings were the Continental, the Savoy, and the
Eden Palace, where people always wore evening clothes to dine.
The low-life highlight of this posh garden district was the brothel
quarter known as the Fish Market. This area was like Amsterdam's
red light canals, minus the water, where elaborately painted and
veiled harlots beckoned the crush of soldiers from behind the iron
grilles of ground floor cribs. Near Shepheard's there were also fancier brothels for higher rollers, with European madams and beauties
of all nations housed in stately mansions whose perfumed gardens
had to compete with the Chanel No. 5 and Joy of the *filles de joies*.
Many of the call girls were moonlighting European showgirls on the
touring circuit from the Moulin Rouge or the London Palladium,
who earlier in the evening may have been in the floor show at the
Kit Kat, in a houseboat on the Nile, where the Hungarian hostesses
were all supposed to be Nazi spies, or at the Fleurent, the Petit Coin
de France, the Scarabee, Madame Badia's, or, the queen of clubs,
the Auberge des Pyramides, on the Giza road to the sphinx.

All these establishments had rather tony clienteles. Only officers
were allowed in. This left the enlisted men out in the cold heat of
the Fish Market. The discount red light district north of the
Ezbekiah Gardens was in the quarter of Cairo known as Clot Bey,
named after a Frenchman, Antoine Clot, who helped Mohammed
Ali bring the concepts of Western hygiene to the Oriental squalor of
nineteenth-century Egypt. Poor Clot would not have been pleased

at his honorary area's reversion to Orientalism, with its donkey shows and branding irons and preteen virgins, although Paris's Pigalle and Hamburg's Herbertstrasse were not any further advanced. Murders of both soldiers and whores were not uncommon. The Australians, considered the most animalistic of all the fighters, were known to toss the professionals out of the second-story windows of the curtain-partitioned sex houses when their five minutes of pleasure were up. Venereal diseases were rampant, so much so that it was often suggested that the British adopt the Italian practice of officially supplying their garrisons with prostitutes, à la Union General Joseph Hooker during the American Civil War. In any case, no one in Cairo, whether general or private, had to be lonely during the war. No city was ever naughtier.

This square mile of pomp and pleasure was Cairo's West End, or Times Square (of better days). But right outside its perimeter, where the *mouski,* or bazaar area, began, Rolls and Bentley gave way to camel and donkey, linen suits yielded to cotton djellabas, and French and English to Arabic. Here were the ancient mosques of Al Azhar, and Sultan Hassan, the medieval gates of Bab Zuwayla, the Coptic churches that dated back to Christ, the Ben Ezra Synagogue, the City of the Dead. That was the Cairo of history, just as the pyramids were the Cairo of antiquity, but the magic mile was the Cairo of pleasure, of the moment, and in war momentary pleasure was of the essence. History and sight-seeing would have to wait for peace.

Other foreign venues were down the Nile in the aptly named Garden City area, where the embassies and the mansions of the rich Cairenes were located; across the Nile in Zamalek, where foreigners lived to have polo mallet–proximity to the Gezira Sporting Club; even farther away in Heliopolis, for those who liked big estates and riding in the desert; and at the Mena House across from the pyramids, where Winston Churchill and Lord Mountbatten and other visiting dignitaries would stay. Otherwise, ancient and modern Cairo did not mix, a fact that was ultimately resented by men in the street, like General Neguib, who wrote:

> Of no country did the British demand more than they did of Egypt during the war, and of no country's interests were they less considerate. They expected Egyptians to behave as loyal allies while being treated as conquered subjects. Their troops

marched through the streets of Cairo singing obscene songs about our King . . . who was as much of a national symbol as our flag. Farouk was never so popular as when he was being insulted in public by British troops.

The troops may have been singing drunken ditties about "Farouk, the Dirty Old Crook" and "wog" bashing *(wog* stood for an employment term for the local clerical, or effendi, class, Working on Government Service, but most took it to mean "Wily Oriental Gentleman"). No one could have been further from wogdom than the inhabitants of upper class Cairo, the Farouk class. The generals knew what the troops could not understand. Brahmin Cairo was subdivided into several distinct aristocracies, all of whom mingled freely and graciously in the gilded melting pot of the magic mile.

First among equals in this upper stratum was the "Turkish" aristocracy that included King Farouk and all the descendants of the Mohammed Ali dynasty and their assorted wives. These people were in Egyptian eyes probably the most attractive in the city, because their bloodlines traced back to the blue-eyed, blond Circassian slave girls the Ottoman sultan's armies would capture and bring to the royal harems. The Turkish princes who had turned this master race into one of slaves bred their children with them. A Circassian woman could thus go from being a harem slave to a palace princess in one admiring glance, and many did. Because the Turkish elite was Muslim, few of the beautiful wives of these princes and *nabils* (a rank below prince) ever went on display, staying home in their various palaces. Their husbands, however, were more in the Farouk mode, European educated, continentally inclined bon vivants who were constantly out on the town, gambling at the clubs, gamboling at the nightclubs, and notoriously unfaithful to their princesses, which was an accepted fact of this high-toned life.

Some of these playboy princes had German ties in addition to their Turkish ones; Turkey had fought on the German side in World War I. That conflict was not a question of eugenics but merely of empire. In those days, Germany was not the Hitlerian *übermensch* monster, but actually looked on more favorably than the Triple Entente of the British, French, and Russian colonial powers that had eaten up a great portion of what was once the Ottoman Empire. In Turkey, Kaiser Wilhelm was considered a more benevolent monarch than the king of England or the czar of Russia, and a far better friend of Islam. Hence the Turks joined with the Germans in hopes of overthrowing the colonial yokes of the entente and recapturing, if not the Balkans, at least some of their former glories. The Turkish cause naturally appealed to nationalistic young Turko-Egyptians such as Farouk's rakish cousin Prince Abbas Halim, who was a Red Baron–style flying ace for the Germans in World War I, and General Aziz el Masri, who was a military hero for the Turks before becoming the young Farouk's military tutor in England. These World War I German affiliations naturally did not sit well with Lampson and the British, who were quick to spring to the worst conclusions in World War II's early days of mistrust.

If the British had their anxieties over Cairo's aristocratic Turks, they had their most loyal friends in Cairo's aristocratic Jews. Although Madame Joseph Cattawi was Queen Nazli's chief lady-in-waiting and Sir Robert Rolo was King Fuad's personal banker who transferred a considerable fortune to Italy for the king, the Jews of Cairo were not about to bite the British hand that knighted them. Victor Harari was typical of the group. He was both a "sir" and a "pasha" and saw no conflict in serving two kings. Baron Georges de Menasce was another highborn Egyptian Jew with a foreign title, this one granted by the emperor of the Austro-Hungarian Empire, but there was no question of any German sympathies. Most of the Cairo Jews had come to Egypt as Sephardim fleeing the Spanish Inquisition and made their fortunes in finance, cotton, and retailing. Their imposing temple in the heart of the Groppi-Shepheard's magic mile between the Banc du Caire and Cicurel's looked like it belonged in the Valley of the Kings. These Jews suffered no discrimination or liabilities; they were the arbiters of society. Most of them were opposed to the partition of Palestine and creation of a separate Jewish state. Why be separate from society when you were on top of it was their attitude.

The other sub-society that styled itself the true aristocracy of Egypt were the Copts, who were brought to the Christian faith by St. Mark and held on to it after the Arab conquests of the seventh century. The Cairo Coptic elite—with names like Wahba, Wissa, and Khayyatt—claimed to be descended from the pharaohs, but none could actually trace their ancestors back before the Napoleonic invasions, given the vagaries of Mameluke record-keeping. Most of the Copts tended to be small and dark. Their roots were in the Upper Egypt capital of Assiut, where the camel caravans left for the Sudan. Their long presence in the country made the Copts the major landowners, after Farouk's family. They were also dominant in law and politics, and because the women were not restrained by Islamic conventions, the Copts produced many great party girls. The men were no slouches, either. The city's preeminent playboy, Victor Simaika, escorted Barbara Hutton, Doris Duke, and Honeychile Hohenlohe among many, played polo with maharajahs in India, and shot grouse with barons in the Tyrol, all with equal aplomb.

There was also a Greek elite that lived mainly in Alexandria, a Lebanese elite that controlled much of the press, a French elite connected to the Suez Canal Company, and an indigenous British elite of archaeologists, Egyptologists, and imperial holdovers from the Cromer-Kitchener veiled-protectorate days, like Sir Thomas Russell Pasha, who was chief of the Cairo police. Russell won fame by cracking the huge Egyptian drug ring, uncovering caches of heroin and opium secreted in the stomachs of camels by slitting open the bellies of the beasts. Like his fellow old Egyptian hands, and unlike Lampson, he was one of the people, as at home in the City of the Dead as in the embassy. (The latter's rigid functions often gave it the air of the former.)

This, then, was the society that the British, and later American, military leaders would intersect. With no bombs falling anywhere around it, Cairo in late 1939 and early 1940 was an oasis of peace and parties. Nevertheless, at every fete, intrigues went on. For instance, in January 1940, Prince Mohammed Ali gave a pro-Ally rally for the British, French, and Turks (who were on the "right" side this war) at his Manyal Palace on Roda Island, across the Nile from the Garden City area (which today houses the Cairo branch of Club Med). At the party, King Farouk chatted with Sir Miles Lampson about a rare-book auction the two men had attended, and where, Farouk told Lampson "an old friend of yours" had placed the bids for the king. The "old friend" Farouk was sarcastically referring to was "royal pimp" Verrucci.

"I then," Lampson wrote in his diaries, "appear to have said that the man was a dirty dog. Anyway I certainly only said that as a more or less slang expression and in the same chaffing vein in which we were talking." This slip between cup and lip nearly produced an

international incident. Later that day the master of protocol, Grand
Chamberlain Zulficar, telephoned Lampson at the embassy, asking
for an immediate audience. Zulficar arrived, quite abashedly, and
suggested to the ambassador that he was out of line in calling one of
Farouk's closest aides a "dirty dog." Lampson claimed he couldn't
remember if he used that particular term, but did not rule out the
possibility

> . . . seeing that I knew how excellent King Farouk's knowl-
> edge of English colloquial phraseology and figure of speech
> was. But if King Farouk thought I should not have called V a
> dirty dog, I was quite prepared to say that he was a nice dog or
> any other sort of dog H.M. preferred. . . . Poor old Zulficar,
> I think, found himself very embarrassed by this silly mission
> and by this ridiculous incident. He himself incidentally alluded
> to Verrucci as "ce sale type"; but it is only one more instance
> of what we already know, namely, that King Farouk is getting
> well above himself and becoming really almost impossible.

Not as impossible as Prime Minister Ali Maher, who continued
to frustrate the arrogant Lampson. The British needed to build up
their military infrastructure in Egypt and required the assistance of
the Egyptian authorities to do so, but Ali Maher regularly dismissed all the pro-British bureaucrats such as the head of the Egyptian state railways who had sold the British Army nearly twenty
thousand tons of coal, and replaced them with runaround artists.
Ali Maher also issued a unilateral declaration that Cairo was a
neutral "open city," which under international law would protect it
from being bombed. The proclamation required that no foreign
armed forces could be within the city limits. Lampson and the generals were livid at Ali Maher's high-handed ploy to force them to
move their headquarters out of the citadel and the Nile barracks to
a spot in the desert beyond the pyramids. In still another insult to
their Egyptian "hosts," the British refused to move, and the lines
between the Palace and the embassy became even more tightly
drawn.

When Anthony Eden, then secretary of war, came to Egypt to
welcome the arriving down-under troops from New Zealand and
Australia, Lampson felt vindicated that Eden's perception of Farouk mirrored his own: "He mistrusts the young Monarch whom he
thinks assertive and a difficult customer to handle. The Prime Min-

ister he has pretty well sized up too." Helping Eden in his assessments was Prince Mohammed Ali, who was fast becoming a fifth column where the Egyptian royal family vis-à-vis the British was concerned. The prince blamed Farouk's "uppityness" on Ali Maher, "who was thoroughly untrustworthy in every respect— 'even his own brother said so,'" Lampson quoted him. The prince tried to illumine Eden on the nature of the Egyptian populace, "how they wanted firm handling, and though he realized that we might not wish to add to our embarrassments, if we treated them too softly we should find the situation all the more out of hand when it became necessary to deal with it."

Aside from his stock plummeting in the eyes of the British, 1940 proved to be a year of terrible disappointments for Farouk, as bad as 1938 had been good. The first blow came in April, when, again, the palace rifles stopped shooting after forty-one. Another girl had been born. Once more Farouk put on a celebratory face, giving food and money to the poor and naming the baby Fawzia, after his favorite sister, now in Teheran. He missed her terribly, but not as terribly as he missed not having a son. Until he had that heir, Farouk might be a king, but he would not be a man.

The problem was that there was another man. Princess Shivekiar, King Fuad's first wife and Cairo's preeminent party-giver, had married four more times, once to Fuad's archenemy, Selfhullah Yussri, who turned a grudge match into a love match. They had a son, Wahid, who was one of the most cosmopolitan and eligible of all the Turko-Egyptian elite. Wahid had done his baccalaureate in Paris, terms at both Sandhurst and West Point, and served as a chargé in the Egyptian embassy in Washington, D.C. A natural athlete, he shot, rode, and played polo, and was a superb Fred Astaire–level dancer. Why he married a homely woman twenty years his senior was a mystery to many. The woman was the Princess Samiha, daughter of King Fuad's brother and predecessor, Sultan Hussein, as well as Wahid's cousin. The Mohammed Ali dynasty was ripe with intermarriage, hence the more-than-occasional insanity. Samiha was a princess, she was charming, and she was rich, but Wahid deserved more than an aging princess. What about a young queen?

Wahid had met Farida at his mother's annual birthday extravaganza for King Farouk at her palace across from Parliament. There were always three bands for the five hundred guests, a complement of Circassian serving girls in native dress, mountains of lobster and game birds, and party favors of Cartier evening bags for the ladies and Dunhill cigar clippers for the gentlemen. At the outset, the two were "just friends." After all, both were married to royalty. But in Cairo, marriage was never a deterrent to romance. In adultery, as well as night life, Cairo was indeed the Paris of the Middle East. The baby daughter, combined with her mother's new flirtation, caused the perpetually good-natured boy-king to snap. The daily gifts ended; the daily fights began. Farouk retreated into the reassuring male company of Antonio Pulli, who would take Farouk to the Auberge des Pyramides to ogle the European showgirls and drown his sorrows in orangeade chilled in ice buckets.

Farouk could have divorced Farida straightaway for her perceived perfidy; divorce in Islam was a simple male prerogative. But Farouk hoped Wahid Yussri would fade away and that Farida was suffering nothing more than an adolescent crush. After all, she was still a teenager. Besides, Farouk needed both an heir and an air of respectability, which Farida could and would provide. The Egyptian public adored the fairy tale he and Farida were supposed to be living. The king wasn't about to destroy this image by a divorce. He wasn't about to admit failure as a husband and give his enemies, particularly his British enemies, something to gloat about.

It was devastating to any Egyptian man, much more so to an Egyptian king, to think that his wife could prefer someone else to him. It was even more devastating to learn that not only was he not front and center in his wife's affections, but that, even as an only son, he had fallen into second place in the heart of his mother as well. The very idea that his sacred, idolized Queen Nazli could have taken a lover was traumatic to Farouk. That the lover she had taken was his sacred, idolized tutor Hassanein was cataclysmic.

The attraction of the queen to the scholar-aviator-explorer had long been there even when the insanely jealous Fuad was alive. But Fuad was an autocrat, capable of terminating both wife and liege with extreme prejudice. The romance had begun in earnest on the royal family's 1937 spring grand tour. The affair was extremely discreet. Hassanein was the soul of tact, Nazli slightly less so. She had made Hassanein her chamberlain, to put an official gloss on the frequency of their encounters.

The encounters, however, were too close for Farouk's comfort, and he set his palace spies to work. One night, a report came to the

Royal Wedding • Farouk flanked by his two queens, Nazli and Farida, who hated each other.

UPI/Bettmann

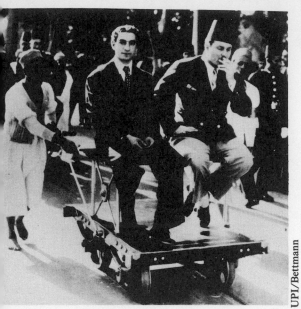

Entangling Alliance • Farouk and the shah of Iran, to whom Farouk wed his sister, Fawzia, in 1939.

UPI/Bettmann

Popperfoto

Caravaranserai • Shepheard's Hotel, the crossroads of Cairo's international set.

king that his mother and tutor were at it in the queen's chamber of the Koubbeh Palace harem. Only fools rushed in where eunuchs were to tread, and Farouk was incensed. Seizing one of his many pistols, he ran down the endless green-carpeted hallways filled with busts and portraits of his revered ancestors, who, he was sure, were spinning in their graves at the shame he would soon encounter. *O tempora! O mores!* Farouk burst into his mother's bedroom, but instead of catching her in flagrante delicto, she was fully dressed. Hassanein was sitting and reading to her, not erotic chapters from the Kama Sutra or love verses from Omar Khayyam, but rather extracts from the Koran. Farouk had missed this time, though he still issued the pair a warning, which he recounted in his post-exile memoirs:

> Unless this ceases, one of you shall die. You are disgracing the memory of my father, and if I end it by killing one of you, then God will forgive me, for it is according to our Holy Law, as you both know.

Another galling aspect of the affair was that Hassanein had been already married into the royal family. His wife was Latifa Yussri, sister of the despised Wahid Yussri. All roads seemed to lead to their mother, Princess Shivekiar, who Farouk nonetheless believed was his best friend. In fact, Farouk had restored the princess to full palace standing, prompting numerous Cairenes to question the king's good judgment. Was Shivekiar trying to destroy Farouk with her black widow's web of dangerous matchmaking? Was she trying to complete the revenge on King Farouk that her crazy brother, Ahmed, had wanted in shooting her loathed husband, King Fuad? Mohammed Ali's was a dynasty of antipathies. The princes and *nabils* of the realm begrudged the throne to Fuad, whom they felt the British had crowned out of line, and they begrudged it in turn to his son. If they were out to get Farouk, 1940 was giving them their wish. He was getting it at all ends, from two queens and an (flying) ace. And worse was yet to come.

While Americans continued to sit it out, getting no closer to the war than watching Charlie Chaplin in *The Great Dictator* at the movie palaces, listening to "The Last Time I Saw Paris" on their Victrolas, or reading Hemingway's new book *For Whom the Bell Tolls,* in Europe Hitler invaded Scandinavia, made the Low Coun-

tries even lower, routed the British troops at Dunkirk, and celebrated it all with foie gras and champagne when he took Paris.
Despite Sir Miles Lampson's continued dialogue with the House of
Savoy through the big duke of Aosta, whom he believed was pro-
Ally and simply "being dragged at Germany's chariot wheel," Italy
formally declared war on Britain on June 10. The Italian ambassador to Egypt, Count Mazzolini, was asked to close the embassy and
leave Cairo. He obliged, but he promised his servants he would be
back in a few weeks. Alexandria was ordered blacked out at night.
The air raids were expected to begin at any moment. All this
prompted an immediate British crisis of confidence in Farouk and
his government. On June 17 Lampson rushed to Alexandria, where
Farouk was summering at Montazah and put it straight to the king.
Prime Minister Ali Maher had to go. General el Masri, now chief of
staff of the Egyptian Army, had to go. Otherwise, Farouk himself
might have to go.

Lampson presented Farouk with damning evidence of palace
complicity, a report from the British admiral Elliott, senior naval
officer at Alexandria, that during the blackouts lights were being
observed onshore that could be useful as signals to Italian subma-
rines or for getting bearings to lay Italian mines. "Admiral Elliott
had given me a photograph showing the house from which the
lights came," Lampson wrote. "I handed the Monarch a copy of
Elliott's report and the photography, and was much amused when
H.M. spotted, as I had been sure he would, the house in question
was his own Palace in which we were at the moment sitting!"

The "singularly good and pleasant form" in which the ambassador initially found the monarch gradually vanished over the course
of the meeting, especially with Lampson's suggestion that Ali
Maher be replaced with Farouk's enemy, Nahas.

> He jibbed at consulting Nahas who had actually insulted
> H.M. from the very chair in which I sat. . . . At one time he
> argued that as King of Egypt it was his duty to keep his people
> out of war on the losing side; to which I rejoined that with us
> Egypt swam or sank: so better swim and make the best of it.

Lampson chided Farouk for fiddling in Alexandria when the
world was burning and urged him ("while carefully avoiding direct
threats"), to hie himself back to Cairo and follow Lampson's in-

structions, most specific of which was not even to consider "the dangerous advice" of Ali Maher. Lampson closed the audience with this: "I repeated I hoped that he realized we were in deadly earnest. He said he knew that full well, and, cryptically, that so was he."

On June 25, General Wavell rushed into the British embassy in Cairo with rumors that King Farouk was intending to flee the country by air, and that Lampson had wanted to either shoot him down or at least capture him before he left. Wavell wanted to let Farouk go, "showing that he was a poltroon and was deserting his country." Lampson stood firm. He was following Foreign Office orders not to let Farouk get to Italy, where he would become pretender to the Egyptian throne. Even though Wavell got "peppery," Lampson insisted that "the boy should not be allowed to leave the country" and accepted full responsibility for holding the king.

The "boy" had no such intentions. On June 28, he was back in Cairo at Abdine Palace. He called Lampson for an audience and couldn't have been more gracious to the man who was out to depose and imprison him, specifically assuring Lampson that he was pro-British. He had dismissed Ali Maher but stopped short of appointing Nahas, who, he told Lampson, was full of "Bolshevik schemes." Instead, the new prime minister was a cousin of Queen Nazli's, Hassan Sabry, formerly minister to the Court of St. James's, and very much an anglophile.

General el Masri was placed on "indefinite leave" and, despite his affair with Nazli, Hassanein was made chief of Cabinet, not the least of the reasons for which being that Hassanein was an Oxford man. Farouk's new Cabinet was packed with pro-British ministers. Lampson was pleased. He had "won." In his telegram to the Foreign Office, he wrote: "King was in chastened mood; and Hassanein assures me he knows he has had a narrow squeak and will have henceforth to behave himself." Farouk had the last word, though not to Lampson's face. Referring to the Italian origins of Lady Lampson and the fact that her father was now serving Mussolini as chief physician to Il Duce's armies, Farouk said, "I'll get rid of my Italians if he gets rid of his."

Despite Farouk's giving in, Lampson now had an idée fixe that "the only thing to do is kick the boy out," an idea he sold to Foreign Secretary Anthony Eden on his numerous visits through Cairo. To assist his case against the boy, Lampson created an entire negative mythology about Farouk that achieved credence because of its source. His favorite story was that Farouk had been having nightmares in which lions figured prominently, pursuing the king. With Freud dead, Farouk consulted Ali Maher for the interpretation of his dreams. Ali Maher's politico-psychoanalysis of the nightmares was that the savage beast, which takes prominence on the English coat of arms, was a symbol of Farouk's British persecutors. According to Lampson, Farouk went to the Cairo zoo at night and shot all the lions in captivity there to exorcise his nocturnal demons.

Another tale in the Lampson apocrypha involved the sequestration of Italian property once Mussolini had declared war. The main safe of a large Italian bank was ordered to the basement of Koubbeh Palace by the avaricious Farouk, seeing this as an opportunity to get money for nothing. Six large Nubian servants lugged the huge safe down the halls and stairs. A locksmith opened it, revealing a cache of cash and gold. Farouk, delighted at his windfall, wanted to thank his servants for their toil. He set up a bucket of water in the basement and threw handfuls of gold into it. Then he told the Nubians to go fishing. They would compete among themselves in a gold rush. The Nubians made for the bucket, desperately jostling one another to grab the largest handful. But then they stood up screaming—and emptyhanded. The liquid in the bucket wasn't water at all. It was acid. The skin of the Nubians' hands was burned off. Farouk allegedly lay back, roaring with laughter at his servants' wages of sin. Greed was not good.

Lampson bad-mouthed Farouk to everyone passing through Cairo. Many of the passers-through were quite interesting, from royals like Lord Mountbatten and Lord Astor to Generals Catroux and de Gaulle of the Free French to Haile Selassie to Noël Coward to Evelyn Waugh to Kermit Roosevelt. That Roosevelt was to become one of the architects of Farouk's demise, and thus accomplish what Lampson always wanted to do but never could, would have seemed unfathomable to Lampson at the time. Lampson found him pleasant but "curiously lethargic." Roosevelt, impatient with his cousin Franklin's "undue caution" in getting America into the war, had joined the British Army as a major in the Middlesex Regiment, "pretty stout work for a man of his age and position in America," Lampson conceded.

For all his lobbying to oust Farouk, Lampson still could not sell the idea to General Wavell, the commander in chief of the Middle East, who refused "to budge from his attitude. He feared this, that, and the other; he wasn't sure the country would submit; he wondered how the anti-British GreenShirts youth movement would react, and so on." Lampson's thesis that Farouk was a disloyal Nazi-Fascist puppet simply didn't play to those above him. Lampson was only theorizing. He had no hard proof. Farouk had always, sooner or later, gone along with him. He would have to wait until the right opportunity arose to bounce the boy.

The new pro-British government of Prime Minister Hassan Sabry was short-lived. In November 1940, Sabry ascended the dais on the opening of Parliament to read the king's speech. Farouk, as was the custom, sat behind him and listened. Sabry began the speech, then stopped short. He turned around to face his king, gasped, and collapsed. As the ministers of state gathered around him, a page arrived with a burning taper and put it in front of Sabry's nose. This wasn't like smelling salts to revive him but rather to see if he had any breath left that would cause the candle to flicker or go out. He had none. As several ministers carried him off, another minister finished the king's address: the show went on. The doctors' report was that the prime minister had died of a heart attack. Farouk replaced him with the uncle of Farida, Hussein Sirry, a British-trained engineer whose previous public service had been as minister of public works and commerce. Despite his English education, Sirry was hardly Lampson's first choice; Nahas was. But Farouk as usual vetoed Nahas and proposed the return of Ali Maher. That infuriated Lampson and made Sirry seem appetizing by comparison.

The speed with which everything in Farouk's life was coming apart had to have been desperately rattling to the twenty-year-old ruler. A year before it had all been perfect. Now he was losing his hair, losing his figure, losing his looks, losing his wife, losing his mother, losing his throne. The only thing he wasn't losing were his friends, because he didn't really have any. Only Antonio Pulli, but he was a man Friday, twenty years older, not a buddy. Ali Maher was even older and was like a Greek oracle, and Hassanein a wise man, not guys to hang around with. Farouk had absolutely no one his own very young age to share his incredible problems with. His cloistered royal life had isolated him completely from any adolescent realities, pleasures, and pains, and here he was, just out of his

teens, faced with a midlife crisis of mythic proportions. Tom Sawyer
meets King Lear. The best of times had become the worst of times.

The year 1941 was enormously eventful for almost everyone except Farouk. In February General Wavell won a major victory at
Benghazi, Libya, bringing relief to the Egyptians of the western
deserts, who were being bombarded by Italian aircraft. The relief
was vast but short. General Rommel soon entered the North African campaign on behalf of the Axis. The Germans were blitzing
Britain, marching on Moscow, and coveting Cairo. The sinking of
the *Bismarck* notwithstanding, they seemed unstoppable on every
front, and even more so after Japan bombed Pearl Harbor on December 7, finally bringing the United States into the conflict.

If the German war machine seemed superior to that of the Allies,
the difference in propaganda machines was a matter of comparing a
Mercedes with an Austin. As British embassy Oriental Secretary
Grafftey-Smith wrote in his memoirs:

> The Germans had two simple lines of propaganda in Egypt
> during the war: that Hitler was a Moslem, born in Egypt (I
> was shown his mother's house in Tantah) and that, when he
> won the war, the poor man would get the rich man's land.
> These were most effective talking points; the victory of "Mo-
> hammed Haidar," as he was locally known, was prayed for in
> every village.

After General Wavell's Benghazi victory, and before Field Marshal Rommel's main offensive, Grafftey-Smith, who was active in
the embassy's publicity section, came up with a ploy that would
show the Germans as something less than the master race. That was
to march the first German prisoners of war openly through Cairo
rather than transporting them, as was the normal procedure, in
covered lorries. Unfortunately, the German image was so strong
that most Cairenes believed their ears and not their eyes. As
Grafftey-Smith wrote:

> It seemed important to me that Cairo should see these ex-
> hausted youths in defeat, and abandon its belief in a race of
> supermen. We all agreed, and the march took place. One of my
> agents came to me the same evening and begged me never to
> allow such a thing again. He had been having his weekly shave,
> at the hands of an eighty year old barber on a mat on the

pavement, and the old man had asked him in a whisper if he knew that Mohammed Haidar was now in Egypt. Yes, he had continued, it was blessedly true; he had been among the Germans who crossed the city that morning! My agent protested that this was impossible, and asked: "What about those British soldiers, with rifles, who marched by the side of the Germans?" "They were showing him the way!" said the old man, finger on nose; and that was that!

The longing for Mohammed Haidar as a sort of messiah had no less to do with economic redistribution than with the galling presence of over one hundred thousand British troops in Cairo. Hooligan soldiers from Birmingham to Brisbane turned peaceful, gentle Cairo into an endless soccer match. "They molested our women, assaulted our men, and committed acts of vandalism in public places," wrote General Neguib. But in the Cairene mind, insult was worse than injury. When Prime Minister Winston Churchill, having succeeded Neville Chamberlain, who died in 1940, gave a speech saying that Egypt "was under British protection," the P-word did much more damage than any mob of Aussie drunks. Although Cairo was blissfully spared of Axis air raids and any destruction, Britain's patronizing treatment of king and country made a mockery of the notion of Egypt's independence and caused deep psychic wounds at all levels of society.

Nowhere did these wounds sting as much as among the young officers of the Egyptian Army, which was not allowed any significant role in defending Egypt. Most of what Egyptian soldiers did was stand sentry around the Suez Canal, man antiaircraft guns against raids that never materialized, and do desolate desert border patrol duty. Even the last was withheld from them when Rommel began his advance. In April 1941, the British ordered the Egyptian Army units back from the frontier and replaced them with Allied troops. Whether the British doubted the Egyptians' competence or their loyalty was irrelevant; the native soldiers were completely insulted.

These bonfires of animosity were fanned by Ali Maher, still smarting himself from being muscled out as prime minister. Maher joined with muscled-out Chief of Staff General Aziz el Masri to sponsor a secret officers' association known as the "Ring of Iron" that included Gamel Abdel Nasser and Anwar Sadat, who at the time maintained a very Afrika Korps look—close-cropped hair, a monocle, and a swagger stick—to express an attitude that was as much anti-British as pro-German. At one point Sadat was implicated in an attempt to aid his mentor el Masri in an alleged secret flight out of Egypt to join forces with the Germans in Iraq. The plane crashed on takeoff. The men survived but were arrested. Before the court-martial, it was revealed that a high-placed British secret operations officer had met with el Masri about an *anti*-Nazi mission to Iraq to *strengthen* British ties there. This proved terribly embarrassing to Lampson and company. Caught between Iraq and a hard place, the British dropped treason charges against el Masri and Sadat, only to pick them up again several years later.

Meanwhile, that other anglophobe, Hassan el Banna, who had made the introduction between el Masri and Sadat, had been exiled to a farm in Upper Egypt when the Muslim Brotherhood was suspected of planning to sabotage British communications lines during Rommel's upcoming offensive. This left Ali Maher as the chief cheerleader for anglophobia. In April 1941, Prime Minister Sirry offered Ali Maher the post of Egyptian ambassador in Washington, D.C., just to get him out of the country. Ali Maher, ambitious though he was, would not be swayed by this bold-faced bribe. When Sirry admitted to Maher that the British had put him up to it, King Farouk was incensed. He saw exactly where the loyalties of his uncle by marriage lay, and knew that he would have to look for a new prime minister.

Meanwhile, Farouk's family problems continued. His two queens had not only turned on him but had also turned on each other. The docile, obedient, grateful commoner that Nazli had hand picked for her own self-aggrandizement was now none of the above. When the royal family made its annual winter trip to the Cataract Hotel in Aswan, Nazli and Farida declared a war of avoidance on each other. Nazli would come later and later to lunches. Farida saw this as an insult, and rather than be first for lunch and be kept waiting, Farida wouldn't come down at all. Farida also had her room moved to directly above the hotel dining salon. When Nazli finally arrived, Farida, who had pleaded indisposition and illness, suddenly recovered. She and her post-adolescent ladies-in-waiting turned up their phonograph full volume and began singing and stomping to the latest records—"Chattanooga Choo-Choo" and "Deep in the Heart of Texas." The earthquakelike din made it impossible for Nazli to speak, be heard, or digest her food. Farouk couldn't take it. He left the queens in Aswan and made for his own bachelor holiday with Pulli on the Red Sea.

In 1941 Farouk had met Irene Guinle and begun his largely asexual affair with her. He was trying to make himself forget Farida, but his heart didn't seem to be that into the affair, nor, apparently was the other organ. He was only twenty, and his long palace isolation had provided little experience with women, or girls, or any real people, for that matter. His totally skewed upbringing was based on things, not people. That was why he liked collecting everything from Napoleonic cannon to Coke bottles. Because his honeymoon with Farida was over so quickly, Farouk's first taste of romance was sweet and sour, and he seemed to have no idea how to enjoy an affair other than splashing in the palace pool with his newfound friend. Farouk and Irene weren't Antony and Cleopatra. They were Dick and Jane.

Farouk had more distracting concerns than love, specifically holding on to his throne. He knew the British wanted to depose him. He saw what they had done to the shah of Iran in the summer of 1941. Allies Britain and Russia, who were taking a shellacking by Hitler, didn't like the presence of several thousand Germans in Iran, nor did they like the shah's proclamation of Iranian neutrality, not while the Nazis were on the outskirts of Moscow. The British sent an invading army in from India to take over the country, forcing the shah to sign an instrument of abdication "for reasons of health." Then they packed him off on a slow boat to Mauritius. The British allowed Farouk's brother-in-law, Mohammed Reza, to succeed his father, but Farouk knew his enhanced imperial tie was a grand illusion. The British ran the show in Iran, just as they were intent on running it in Egypt.

To describe Farouk as a Nazi sympathizer couldn't have been farther from the (Deutsche) mark. Farouk was for Egypt, not Germany, not England. If "Mohammed Haidar" won the war, Farouk was in even greater danger of being deposed, especially by the intervention of his own family. His cousin Abbas Halim was as pro-German as his uncle Mohammed Ali was pro-British. The World War I German flying hero Halim believed in national socialism, and was an architect of a September 1941 rail and transport strike that threatened to cripple Egypt, not to mention the British war effort. Farouk intervened to stop the strike and steal the thunder that would have made Halim the darling of the Third Reich. The king didn't trust Hitler any more than he did Lampson.

Another German candidate for Farouk's throne was former khedive Abbas Hilmi. Deposed by the British in 1914 while he was on his summer holiday on the Bosphorus, Abbas Hilmi remained in Istanbul as the "pretender" to the monarchy of Egypt, vowing to get back. In 1941, he was still alive in Turkey and pretending, bolstered by a substantial following among Egypt's royal family who, from the outset, resented Farouk for his youth, his looks, and his popularity. In many ways, the Mohammed Ali dynasty was as petty, competitive, and vindictive as *The Little Foxes.* Consequently, Farouk was not willing to throw his country into chaos and into the arms of Hitler. His political "education" under Sir Miles Lampson taught him to know an autocrat when he saw one.

Even without a transport strike, Egypt was in trouble enough. The British presence in the country had caused terrible inflation. The wages of the fellaheen stayed the same; they could not afford the skyrocketing prices of basic goods like food and medicine and kerosene. Ambassador Lampson, who was pathologically cheap, cashed in on the price boom by selling "embassy mangoes" straight from his garden and game birds he had shot on social outings in the Fayoum to luxury purveyors for top pound. Let them eat grouse. But the peasants couldn't afford beans. The bakeries were mixing sawdust in with flour, and "meatless" days were instituted. The public was hungry and angry, but they still loved their boy-king. Farouk's family troubles were under deep cover. He continued his visits to the mosques. He continued his gifts to the poor. He continued his inspiring speeches. If anyone was to be blamed, it was the British, and if anyone Egyptian had to be the scapegoat for the country's hunger pains, it was the British puppet, Prime Minister Hussein Sirry.

With Britain teetering on the brink in the desert and Sirry teetering on the brink in Cairo, Farouk found a way to give Sirry the coup de grâce and reappoint Ali Maher as prime minister. Ambassador Lampson had been pushing Egypt to sever all ties with Vichy France and expel its legation from Cairo since October, but Farouk refused, concerned for the safety of the three hundred Egyptian students still in Paris. In January 1942, while Farouk was on holiday in Aswan, Lampson pressured Sirry to cut with Vichy. This

Dragon Lady • Princess Chevekiar, ex-wife of King Fuad and Farouk's "fairy godmother," who sowed the seeds of dissent within the royal family.

AKHBAR EL YOM Publishing House (Cairo)

Happy Hunting • Farouk and Sir Miles Lampson on a duck shoot in one of their more cordial interludes.

The Great Pretender • Anglophile Prince Mohammed Ali, who waited in vain for the British to depose Farouk and make him king of Egypt. Ali (center) stands between Aga Khan (left) and King Farouk (right).

gave Farouk the chance to cut with Sirry, who had gone over his head and thereby violated all royal protocol.

By January 28, Rommel had captured Benghazi and was making murderous air raids on Alexandria. Allied reinforcements that had been sent to Egypt were now being moved to the Far East in the aftermath of Pearl Harbor. Britain had recently lost Greece. It seemed that it might lose Egypt as well. Ali Maher had advised Farouk that he had gotten wind of Britain's "scorched earth" policy in the Nile delta in the likely event that they lost to Rommel in the desert. The British would retreat, burning, flooding, and ruining the most fertile land on earth. Since Egypt was not a belligerent and could see absolutely no benefit from the British presence, replacing it with a German one did not seem an unpalatable alternative, and certainly less so than having the precious delta destroyed. Farouk knew Nahas was Lampson's man, and Nahas would destroy anything if the price was right. Sirry was more patriotic, but Farouk wasn't sure how much. Ali Maher was the only politician Farouk could trust, and the one most likely to hold Egypt's own against the prospectively conquering Germans.

Students from Al Azhar University and the Muslim Brotherhood took to the streets, rioting and celebrating their prospective "liberation" by Rommel. "Down with the British" and "Long live Farouk" were their rallying cries. When Hussein Sirry asked the king for militia to quell the students, Farouk simply shrugged, treating his prime minister as a nonperson. The same day, Sirry submitted his resignation. Lampson received the Sirry news on a chill and damp crack-of-dawn duck shoot in the Fayoum on February 1. Lampson packed in his Purdeys and made for Cairo. Farouk may have finally "gotten" Sirry. Now Lampson was going to finally "get" Farouk.

Hussein Sirry had told Lampson that "the boy is an absolute coward: he has to be frightened from time to time—and saved from himself." But Lampson had had enough of games. *"Must* we go on having to frighten the boy at periodic intervals?" Lampson wrote. "If so, I felt myself that our patience might very easily give out. Persia should surely serve as a reminder to King Farouk of what happened if it was overstrained." When Lampson asked Sirry whom he thought should succeed him, Sirry replied, "Send for the Wafd." Lampson lit up. He wrote: "I said this was an instance of great minds thinking alike, for before coming in to see him I had come to precisely the same conclusion but it gained in force through having been volunteered by His Excellency." Lampson's ardor for the task ahead was further inflamed when Sirry reported what Farouk had told him at the outset of this game of musical parliamentary chairs. "Sir Miles has won the first round but I am going to down him on the second." Lampson wrote one word in his diary: "Cheek!"

General Wavell, who had been a restraining force in keeping Lampson from deposing Farouk, had left the Middle East to become commander in chief of the British forces in India. Trading places with Wavell was his successor as Middle East commander in chief, General Sir Claude Auchinleck, a tall, handsome officer who had spent his entire military career in India. Auchinleck, too, "showed considerable hesitation and grumpiness," Lampson wrote, at the notion of ordering around the boy-king. Auchinleck was concerned the country might rise up in revolt against such imperialistic behavior. Lampson's line was that he *knew* Egypt and not to worry. Because "the Auk," as Lampson called him, was new in Egypt, the ambassador was able to push his ultimatum past the general. Farouk would have to accept Nahas as prime minister, or accept the consequences.

On February 2, Lampson went to call on Farouk, "who was even more cordial than usual," basically agreeing with Lampson on all his points and agreeing to "see" Nahas for a "consultation." Farouk would consider appointing Nahas as prime minister to form a coalition government. But Lampson didn't want any coalitions that involved "Palace" parties. He wanted the Wafd and only the Wafd. It was ironic that the Wafd, which had come into being as an anti-British nationalist party, had now gotten into bed with its old enemy. But Nahas was nothing if not flexible. Lampson took a break from the negotiations that evening to attend a Red Crescent Society benefit screening at the Misr Cinema, "a great affair with the two queens and all their ladies present" and then went back to bathe a painful sty ("this of all moments") for half an hour before going to bed.

The next day a round of meetings with Hassanein, representing Farouk, and Nahas, representing the Wafd, revealed the impasse. Farouk wanted a coalition government; Lampson wanted a government, period, which meant a Wafd government. "Hassanein as usual tried to wriggle," Lampson wrote, "but I made it clear that this was business." On February 4, Lampson met at the offices of the Middle East War Council of British Generals and Admirals at 10 Tolombat Street in the Garden City area, the 10 Downing Street of Cairo, to draft this ultimatum: "Unless I hear by 6 P.M. today that Nahas had been asked to form a government, His Majesty King Farouk must accept the consequences." Assuming King Farouk would refuse, Lampson and the officers prepared the consequences. General R.G.W.H. Stone, in command of British troops in Egypt, was called in to establish troops around Abdine Palace. Stone and Lampson "would go down suitably accompanied" to order the king to abdicate. "It was clear that we should have to take the king away with us," Lampson wrote, "either with or without his abdication in *my* pocket." Then they would take him to a warship off Alexandria that would take Farouk to his own Elba in the Seychelles.

The abdication document itself was to be drafted by Sir Walter Monckton, who had just arrived in Cairo as director-general of the British Propaganda and Information Services. Lampson was thrilled at Monckton's presence: "No better authority, for he was the man who arranged our own king's abdication!" Monckton had drafted the instrument whereby Edward VIII stepped down for Mrs. Simpson and became duke of Windsor. With Farouk sailing into the Indian Ocean, the new king would be Prince Mohammed Ali, who for so long had been waiting in the palace wings. Lampson was in close touch with the Foreign Office in London, where Anthony Eden gave his blessing to the enterprise, "saying that they would see me through and that they thought it was essential to clinch the matter this time when we were dealing direct with the king rather than have to cope with him later on through another prime minister."

The War Council adjourned. While the clock was ticking down to abdication time, Lampson had lunch with Duff and Lady Diana Cooper, who were on their way back to London from Singapore, where Duff Cooper had served as minister of state. Outside the Al Azhar students continued demonstrating. "Long live Rommel" "Long live Farouk" "Down with the British," they chanted while Lawrence Grafftey-Smith interrupted the lunch with a report that students in the town of Zagazig were smashing shop windows and beating up persons known to have distributed British propaganda there. Later that afternoon, Lampson was excited by news that Farouk was "packing his bags" and planning an escape. Although Lampson ordered a watch at all the Cairo aerodromes, he realized that it wasn't possible to put a check on all the roads in and out of the city. "We must risk the King doing a bunk," he wrote, "and if he did so, it would damage his cause and possibly no great harm be done." The main thing was to get the boy off the throne. At Manyal Palace, Prince Mohammed Ali was also packing his bags, preparing for his grand entrance into Abdine later that night.

After an endless afternoon of waiting, six o'clock came and went without a peep from the palace, or anywhere else. At six-fifteen, Hassanein arrived at the British embassy, with a reply to the ultimatum signed by seventeen prominent political leaders:

> That in their opinion the British ultimatum is a great infringement of the Anglo-Egyptian Treaty and of the independence of the country. For this reason and acting on their advice His Majesty cannot consent to an action resulting in an infringement of the Anglo-Egyptian Treaty and of the country.

Lampson scanned the signatures: Ali Maher, Ahmed Maher, the usual suspects. Then his eye nearly popped from his swollen eyelid. On the list were Hussein Sirry and—Moustapha Nahas. Nahas? Was he "wriggling out"? Lampson was livid. He told Hassanein that he would be arriving at Abdine Palace at nine sharp. Hassanein tried to dissuade him, searching for a solution that would save face for all parties concerned. Lampson wasn't interested. Dismissing Hassanein, Lampson called for Amin Osman, the Oxford-educated former minister of finance who played an important role for Lampson as intermediary between the British and the Wafd. Lampson blew up at Nahas's having signed the resolution. "Was I still safe in relying completely on Nahas if I carried on?" Lampson asked the go-between. "Amin said he would bet his bottom dollar on Nahas being firm, and that he could only suppose he had been lobbied into agreeing to the resolution."

Reassured of Nahas's loyalty by Osman, Lampson put on one of his trademark double-breasted white suits, fastened his watch chain, read and approved Sir Walter Monckton's abdication instrument, and went down for his last supper as ambassador to King Farouk. "It doesn't often come one's way to be pushing a Monarch off the Throne," he wrote, unable to conceal his excitement.

At the table with Lampson and Jacqueline were Oliver Lyttleton, Churchill's minister of state in the Middle East, and his wife, Moira. Over a hurried dinner, a new wrinkle arose which Lampson hadn't even considered until then. What if Farouk, "faced with the music, climbed down and agreed to summon Nahas, was I then justified in carrying on with the abdication?" Lampson had no real problem with it, but Lyttleton thought public reaction, both in Egypt and England, would be quite adverse toward "throwing the boy out for giving us at 9 P.M. the answer which we should have welcomed at 6 P.M." Lampson consulted with General Stone, who was accompanying him to Abdine. Stone agreed with Lyttleton. Lampson was outvoted. He decided that if Farouk caved in, he wouldn't depose him after all. On his twenty-minute trip across Cairo to Abdine, Lampson was praying that Farouk wouldn't cave in.

With a battalion of six hundred British troops, along with tanks and armored cars, surrounding the square around the palace, Lampson and Stone arrived in Lampson's Rolls-Royce followed by six burly, hand-picked officers, all over six feet tall and heavily armed. The ornamental palace gates had been locked. One of the officers shot the lock off with his revolver. "I could see by the startled expressions of the Court Chamberlains who received me at the entrance," Lampson wrote, "that this imposing arrival registered an immediate preliminary effect." Lampson delighted in the roar and rumble of the tanks taking position outside the palace, and in the anxiety among the palace staff the rumble caused.

Lampson was kept waiting for five minutes in the king's antechamber. Lampson wasn't about to wait any longer. He and General Stone got up to force their way in. The chief chamberlain, Zulficar Pasha, thought this was a terrible breach of his beloved protocol. Zulficar tried to block General Stone's path. Lampson shouldered the frail old man aside. Farouk, behind his desk, was shocked by this rude entrance. He told Lampson he wanted to keep Hassenein, standing behind him, in attendance. Lampson gave the boy his permission, then proceeded to scold him for being dilatory by fifteen minutes on the six o'clock ultimatum, and being evasive to boot. Yes or no, Lampson demanded of the king. What is it? When Farouk tried to explain, Lampson cut him off. An explanation was a no to him, and no was the answer Lampson wanted, and needed, to depose Farouk with.

Lampson immediately seguéd into reading Farouk a letter outlining his high crimes and misdemeanors against England, Egypt, and the treaty. The letter attacked the king's advisers, accused them of assisting the enemy, and blamed Farouk for "wantonly and unnecessarily" provoking a crisis by not acceding to Lampson's demand for a Nahas government. "Such recklessness and irresponsibility on the part of the Sovereign endanger the security of Egypt and of the Allied Forces. They make it clear that your Majesty is no longer fit to occupy the Throne."

Lampson shoved the letter of abdication into Farouk's face.

> We, King Farouk of Egypt, mindful as ever of the interests of our country, hereby renounce and abandon for ourselves and the heirs of our body the Throne of the Kingdom of Egypt and of all Sovereign rights, privileges and powers in and over the said Kingdom and the subjects thereof, and we release our said subjects from their allegiance to our person.

Sign this at once, Lampson said, "or I should have something else and more unpleasant with which to confront him."

Farouk looked over the document, which was typed on old British Residency foolscap. Owing to a paper shortage in Cairo, there wasn't even any British embassy notepaper to write on. Farouk sighed "You might have given me a decent piece of paper" to Lampson and prepared to dip his pen in ink. Then Hassanein intervened in Arabic that Lampson could not understand. "After a tense pause," Lampson wrote, "King Farouk, who was by this time completely cowed, looked up and asked almost pathetically if I would not give him one more chance?" Damn, Lampson thought. He isn't going to sign after all. Had General Stone not been standing by, Lampson might have forced the boy to sign. As it was, he had to listen to Farouk's proposal, which was to summon Nahas at once, in Lampson's presence if necessary, and ask him to form a government. Lampson himself paused. His own moment of glory was slipping away, and he hated losing it. He looked at General Stone and realized he had to let the boy stay on.

"King Farouk with considerable emotion said that for his own honor and for the country's good he would summon Nahas forthwith. I said I agreed," Lampson wrote with a heavy hand. "Thereafter King Farouk was at pains to make himself agreeable and indeed affable. He even thanked me personally for having always tried to help him."

Lampson and General Stone took their leave, past the court chamberlains, who Lampson described as "a crowd of scared hens," past the big British troops with their tommy guns and rifles at the ready, into the courtyard in view of the big British tanks, and into the big British Rolls-Royce that took them back to the big British embassy. Little did Lampson know that Farouk's even larger-than-British three Albanian bodyguards were hiding behind the curtains of his chamber, their own pistols drawn, to shoot Lampson and Stone if they moved to harm or abduct Farouk, and that Farouk's palace guards, also armed, were hiding behind his scared-hen chamberlains, ready to kill Lampson's men if the need arose.

Aside from having terrible morning-after misgivings about not having forced Farouk off the throne at this one golden opportunity, Lampson noted in his diary that the evening was a triumph "which I confess I could not have more enjoyed." Back at the embassy, where Duff and Diana Cooper were staying, a party was going on. "We found most of the principal actors in the hall of the Embassy discussing the evening as people discuss the first night of a play, when nobody is sure whether it has been a success or a failure," Duff Cooper wrote in his memoirs. In hers, Diana Cooper remembered some of the guests lamenting the night as another "Munich in not getting an abdication signed" but that others were pleased as punch. She also evoked the moment when "H.E. [Sir Miles] came out of his den, dressed in a pearly grey *frac,* arm in arm with Nahas Pasha, both grinning themselves in two."

The next morning Lampson's day was made with a personal telegram from Anthony Eden. "I congratulate you warmly. Result justifies your firmness and our confidence." Lampson was delighted. "Rather nice," he jotted in his diary. At sixty, Lampson was the darling of the Foreign Office. He saw himself as a hero and a near kingmaker. Could viceroy of India be that far away now?

At the same time, Lampson was aware that in not terminating Farouk, he would have a certain hell to pay. The sooner he got out of Egypt and off to India, the better.

> We are still faced with the fact that we have a rotter on the Throne and that if things go badly with us he will be liable to stab us in the back. It is of course just possible, though I admit

unlikely, that he may have had his lesson, but to me it seems more likely, knowing him as I do, that we shall have earned his increased hatred and be faced with the ardent determination to get square with us.

Although Lampson could often be a pompous boor, this time he was a prophet.

IX

DUEL

Whatever victory Sir Miles Lampson might have claimed in his bully-boy showdown with King Farouk soon appeared to be not only short-lived but Pyrrhic as well. Even though the British censors ordered a news blackout of the event, reporting instead that the change of government was an act of royal volition not contrition, enough people had seen the British tanks at Abdine to get the true story out. The result was a veritable Nile flood of support and sympathy for Farouk.

Despite the approbation of the Foreign Office in London, most British in Egypt were appalled at Lampson's high-handedness. At the top of this list was General Stone, who accompanied the ambassador to Abdine on the night of the *coup de palais,* February 4. Stone wrote a private note of apology to King Farouk and one of outrage to General Jumbo Wilson, now commanding the British effort in Syria. Sir Thomas Russell, the commandant of the Cairo police, thought Lampson had destroyed all the goodwill that he had worked for years to build up for the English cause. Likewise, Air Marshal Sir William Sholto Douglas, head of the Fighter Command in North Africa, deemed Lampson's action a major strategic error "treating King Farouk as if he were nothing but a naughty and rather silly boy. . . . Farouk was naughty, and he was still very young . . . but to my mind, and taking a hard-headed view, he was also the King of Egypt," Douglas wrote in his memoirs.

If the British in Egypt were appalled, the Egyptians themselves were horrified. Mohammed Neguib, now a lieutenant-colonel, wrote a letter to Farouk, saying that because the army was not given an opportunity to save the king, he was ashamed to wear his uniform and sought permission to resign from the service. Farouk denied Neguib's request. The king had once asked his chiefs of staff how long the Egyptian military could hold Cairo against a British attack. They gave him a generous estimate of two hours. Neguib's gesture, however patriotic, if executed, would have put him at best in a pantheon with Davy Crockett and George Armstrong Custer.

Stationed in the Sudan at the time, Gamal Abdel Nasser was also vicariously humiliated by Lampson's coup. Nasser set that February fourth as the true beginning of the Free Officers' movement that ultimately toppled Farouk and the ancien régime. When later that year Nasser became an instructor at the Royal Military Academy, he was able to choose the best and brightest of his charges and begin to inculcate them with his philosophy of revolution. Anwar Sadat himself was too busy for theoretics. He was actively intriguing with Nazi spies living on a Nile houseboat, drafting treaties with Rommel with Egyptian loyalty to the Reich as a quid pro quo for complete independence, and buying ten thousand glass bottles in the *mouski* to make Molotov cocktails with which to toast and roast the despised British.

On a nonbelligerent note, on February 11, Egypt went all-out to celebrate King Farouk's twenty-second birthday. One of the largest crowds ever thronged Abdine Square to shout felicitations to the young monarch, while from Alexandria to Abu Simbel, Egypt became a Farouk festival, with dancing, singing, and mutton barbecues. Farouk was deeply moved. His ego certainly was in need of such a boost. He made a radio address of gratitude to the country, beginning, as he always did, with the salutation "My beloved people," which was his own "Friends, Romans, and countrymen." The speech alluded to Egypt's power and glory and closed thus: "Thanks to your love for me, to your union round my person, my power is immense."

Whether this was postadolescent wishful thinking or face-saving bravado, the king's power at that moment was probably less immense than he would have liked it to be. More immense was that of Prime Minister Nahas, who broadcast his own birthday salute to the king, damning him with the faintest of praise and ending with the unkindest cut of all, a reference to Farouk's "unshakable faith in the future of the fatherland."

Everyone knew precisely which fatherland Nahas was alluding to. In May, the Allies lost the crucial battle of Tobruk, in Libya, and the forces of Field Marshal Rommel began streaming into Egypt, massing at the railway depot of El Alamein, sixty miles west of Alexandria. Not to be left out of what looked to be the Axis capture of the land of the pharaohs, Mussolini himself flew to Africa, taking with him his finest white stallion, on which he planned to ride through Cairo in imperial triumph. German radio broadcasted suggestive bulletins to the ladies of Alexandria to get out their finest dresses for the "victory ball," the ultimate Nazi party. The seaside cafés along the Alexandrian corniche began surreptitiously ordering stocks of wurst, which local butchers began converting from bangers and *saucissons.*

An underground land-office business began in photographs of Rommel and Hitler, which countless merchants bought to have at the ready to replace those of Farouk and Nahas they so patriotically displayed. Britain's worst nightmare—losing Egypt, losing Suez— was coming true at an inexorable pace.

As the Eighth Army was losing mile after mile of desert ground, Nahas was doing everything he could to prevent his British benefactors from being further undercut by native fifth columnists. Not content with having Ali Maher confined to his country estate outside Alexandria, Nahas had his rival former prime minister imprisoned along with thousands of other high-placed anglophobes whom Lampson described as "lesser undesirables." These siege procedures, inspired by the American internment of over one hundred thousand West Coast Japanese-Americans, resulted in a unexpected landslide of denunciations—wife against husband, business partners against each other, feuding families—all of whom saw this as a splendid way of getting rid of someone they didn't want around. Nahas even shuttered Farouk's favorite gambling den, the Royal Automobile Club. It was also the favorite of Prince Abbas Halim and other avowed as well as closet German sympathizers among the Cairo Turkish aristocracy.

Lest he be perceived as Lampson's puppet, Nahas did enact certain measures that were seen as solely pro-Egyptian, such as a law requiring the use of Arabic in all business transactions. Nahas made up for this rather major annoyance by enacting a law that gave every Allied soldier in Egypt an Easter gift package of a pack of cigarettes, a box of candy, and two painted Easter eggs. It was small consolation to the forces, who were in extremely low cotton, in view of world events. Following Pearl Harbor, the Japanese swept through Hong Kong, Singapore, Java, and Rangoon. The Nazis installed Quisling as premier of Norway, and were proceeding toward Stalingrad in the Afro-Caucasian pincers movement that would give the Axis the control of the entire Middle East, and its oil, not to mention the Suez Canal. With Suez went the war, and the British knew it. Yet Suez was looking increasingly like a lost cause, so much so that at that moment the chiefs of staff in London were considering a redeployment of troops from the Middle East to India and Burma.

By July 2, the situation appeared so bleak that Lampson went to Abdine Palace, without any tanks, to discuss with Farouk

> the big problem of what would become of himself and his government in the event of an enemy occupation. I believed his Prime Minister had explained to him my idea that they would be well advised to transfer lock, stock, and barrel to Khartoum, which had the advantage of being condominium territory. He could thus not be charged with having left or deserted Egypt. Furthermore, whatever was done by the occupying enemy, it would be unconstitutional and their [the Egyptians] escutcheon would be completely untarnished and unbroken against their return.

Farouk told Lampson he didn't like the idea of quitting, whether in the face of Hitler or of Lampson himself. He didn't want his country to regard him as a traitor, or a Quisling. Farouk and Lampson had, quite naturally, been estranged since February 4. All their meetings had been quite formal and icy, as at an earlier April lunch with the king of Greece, at which Lampson described Farouk as "the complete monarch, pomposity personified," having brought nine palace officials with him to the lunch to insulate himself from the British ambassador. At the lunch, Farouk didn't speak to anyone, including Lampson, except the Greek king, and left without shaking hands. Moreover, the Greek monarch complained to Lampson that when he asked to meet some of Farouk's ministers, Farouk laughed and dismissed the idea as a waste of the Greek's time, calling his ministers *ces canailles,* "these scoundrels." At a number of diplomatic balls where the Egyptian king was required to dance with Lady Lampson, the normally graceful Farouk somehow managed to step all over the lady's tiny feet. The band may have been playing "That Old Black Magic"; to Jackie Lampson, it was all black and blue.

The July day when Lampson came to Abdine to discuss exile

contingencies, Farouk at one point stood up and continued the discussion pacing along the edge of his carpet. Soon a door to the king's office opened, and one of Farouk's aides looked in. Lampson assumed the king's next appointment had arrived and he took his leave. In fact, there was no next appointment. Farouk had installed a special bell hidden under the carpet, on which he would tread when he wanted to get rid of someone, specifically Lampson. A red light would go on in the passage leading to the outer offices, which signaled the aide on duty to poke his head in in a pregnant silence. The device became known as the "Lampson button," Farouk's version of a diplomatic ejector seat.

Another Brit-baiting trick of Farouk's involved playing on the ultraformal Abdine protocol whereby any woman presented to Queen Farida must wear gloves (one off, one on) and a long black dress, must never cross her legs, must curtsy three times en route to the queen's lilac throne, must address Farida as "Majesty," and must walk out backward. To make sure such audiences would end with a bang, the joker king installed a sprawling tiger rug on a very highly waxed floor directly in the center of the exit route. Many a British diplomatic grande dame took a nasty spill on the frequently flying tiger, to the king's vast amusement at their discomfiture.

That July, however, there was little time or inclination for parlor games. So imminent was the Rommel menace that both the British embassy and military headquarters began incinerating all their secret files. A blizzard of black snow fell in the 110-degree heat. Meanwhile, the roads were gridlocked with families escaping both Alexandria, which had suffered frequent Axis bombings, and Cairo, which expected the worst before Il Duce would be galloping in on his white charger. The Cairo train station was mob bedlam with thousands queueing, bribing, shoving, and cheating to get on the one daily train to Palestine. Those who failed took the endless journey to South Africa. Foreign residents, particularly the British, made a run on the banks to get their money out while they could. Even Prime Minister Nahas made full contingency plans to remove the country's treasury and its Parliament to Khartoum, as Lampson had advised Farouk.

In fact, while much of Egypt may have been pleased to see the end of Lampson even if it meant the beginning of "Mohammed Haidar," of all those in the country with anything to lose, King Farouk remained the most firm. As captain, he was totally prepared to go with the ship, which was probably down. The new navigator was likely to be Prince Abbas Halim, whose blue fatherland eyes had gotten too bright for Lampson, who, upon hearing the prince raise a toast to Rommel at the Mohammed Ali Club, promptly had him interned by Nahas at a government rest house in a remote oasis.

The rawest deal in the July exodus from Egypt fell to local Jews. Although the reports of Nazi genocide had finally become public by early 1942 (over one thousand Polish Jews were being murdered every day in concentration camp gas chambers), the British administration in Palestine steadfastly refused to expand their immigration quotas, leaving the Egyptian Jews, as well as many other European Jews living in Egypt, stranded in Alexandria and Cairo, at Rommel's prospective lack of mercy. The situation was exacerbated by constant radio reports that Hitler was sending a blitzkrieg of two hundred German bombers to Cairo. Every day seemed to be *the* day. Nonetheless, Lampson did his very British best to maintain the stiff-upper-lip illusion that all was right with the world. Despite having a private railway car and engine at the ready in case Rommel, Il Duce, et alia did arrive, Lampson set about a business-as-usual course by ordering that the iron gates of the embassy be spiffed up and repainted.

In this cataclysmic atmosphere, it was small wonder that King Farouk adopted a fatalistic attitude. He had been humiliated politically by Lampson, maritally by Farida, filially by Nazli, and dynastically by his own inability to produce an heir. But now it seemed like the heir was an academic question. An heir to what? Oblivion? With Rommel at the gates, Farouk was faced with the prospect of losing it all at age twenty-two. The only thing Farouk could be sure of was his own pleasure, whatever that might be and however short it might last. It was at this point in his young life that he gave in to himself completely. He became an epicure, a hedonist with an attitude of self-indulgence today because tomorrow we're deposed. Above all, he went girl crazy.

Farouk's first significant extramarital fling was Princess Fatma Toussoun, the daughter-in-law of Prince Omar Toussoun, who ranked with Prince Mohammed Ali at the pinnacle of the country's royal family. An old-school devout Muslim who believed a woman's place was in the harem and that proper young men should neither smoke nor drink or even cross their legs, Prince Omar was shocked at the hard-drinking, horse-racing, fast-living Western ways of his two sons, the princes Said and Hassan Toussoun, and even more shocked at the licentious westernization of his sons' two striking wives, Mahavesh and Fatma, who became fast friends and ardent admirers of their cousin by marriage, King Farouk. In a sunbaked desert society where white was beautiful, the porcelain, slightly chubby Circassian-stock Fatma was considered one of the fairest of the fair. She was said to have had an enormous girlhood crush on the equally fair and godlike young Farouk. The fact that he never noticed her at all may have driven Fatma into the arms of her prince, who was over twenty years her senior. When Farouk finally got around to noticing Fatma, her marriage was no deterrent to reciprocity, especially where the king was concerned. One simply did not deny the attention of the monarch, and, besides, *haute* Cairo was a very sophisticated society. Farouk invited Fatma for moonlit evenings at his favorite trysting spot, the art deco mini-palace on the Nile at Helwan. The sweeping verandas, soft breezes, jasmine and oleander scents, and cosset-every-whim servants would make any man seem like a king, particularly a real one.

There was endless gossip about divorce and remarriage and that the baby Fatma was bearing was that of the king and not the prince. But when the baby turned out to be a girl, nicknamed in certain circles "Mademoiselle Roi," Farouk's interests shifted to the even blonder, more beautiful, far sleeker but impossible to marry Alexandrian Jewess, divorcee Irene Najjar. And then to the sleek, stunning, snippy darling of the British cipher office, Barbara Skelton, who was equally impossible to marry because the British feared she had become a spy for Farouk and shipped her to Greece.

And these were just the "official" mistresses. Antonio Pulli was indefatigable in combing all the Cairo nightclubs for adventurous European chorus girls who performed between the anti-Nazi vaudeville skits which were the rage of the period. Leaving no stone unturned, Pulli also explored the tonier brothels of both the Cairo Fish Market and Alexandria's Rue des Soeurs for fair-skinned demimondaines out to earn some royal respect in the form of the "diamond" bracelets and earrings Farouk always bestowed on his conquests, which invariably turned out to be costume jewelry. Farouk became as fascinated in "collecting" all sorts of women, just as he collected everything from Coca-Cola bottles and wine labels and sex-act cuckoo clocks to priceless coins and pharaonic antiques and

European fine art. He wanted to try everything—and everyone. For example, he went through a belly dancer phase, courting—for want of a better word—the stars of that lively art, Tahia Carioca, Samia Gamal, and Hekmet Fahmy.

Fahmy held a court of her own on a Nile houseboat next to that of two German spies working undercover as a pair of British and American playboys. The bon vivant Nazis pumped their good neighbor for any interesting information she might have obtained during her horizontal entertainments of not only Farouk but also of a cadre of high-ranking British officers. These spies, who sent out their dispatches in a code derived from *Rebecca,* the book by Daphne du Maurier that was the basis of the Hitchcock film, were assisted in their transmissions by radio whiz Anwar Sadat. The Germans supported their decadent life in the nightclubs, bars, and whorehouses of Cairo, ferreting out tips through a huge per diem in counterfeit British sterling, which eventually proved to be their undoing. Their funny-money trail was traced by British intelligence through the barmen of Shepheard's and Groppi's and Madame Badia's cabaret to their houseboat of ill repute, where they were arrested, along with Sadat. Normally, their punishment would have been a peremptory death on the Nile. However, the summer of '42 was too sensitive a time for the British to be executing Egyptian Army officers, no matter how treacherous. The Nazis were locked in a desert prison camp, while Sadat, having heretofore evaded arrest for his anti-British activities, was stripped of his rank and jailed for several years. The incident was the stuff of fiction, inspiring two movies and two novels, one of which was Ken Follett's best-selling *The Key to Rebecca.*

Farouk's womanizing was also the stuff of fiction, if not legend, notwithstanding his less-than-regal reputation as far as giving any pleasure to the women he loved other than that of his company. Equally legendary in this period was Farouk's gargantuan appetite. If he couldn't drink, he would make up for it in the epicurean holy trinity by eating and being merry. Farouk's favorite dish may have been macaroni and cheese washed down with orangeade, but as with women, he wanted to try everything, and his mania for food was as eclectic as those for sex and collecting. A menu for a typical buffet dinner at Abdine offered the following delicacies: consommé de volaille froid, tronçon de saumon à la Vénitienne, soupe de mer à l'Orientale, galantine de faisan d'Écosse truffée, agneau de lait à la bergère, chaud-froid de pigeon en belle-vue, aiguillettes de veau à la mode, poularde de Bresse Lamberty, yalandji dolmas, pâté de gibiers à la Mirabeau, langue de charolais à la gelée de porto, asperges en branches sauce divine, dinde de Fayoum rotie froid à la gelée d'or, salade Gauloise, baklava pyramidal, charlotte aux fruits, gateaux Marguerite, petits-fours variés, glacés assorties, petits pains au caviar, friandises, fruits. And this was wartime. People were starving not only in Russia but in France too. Nevertheless, with Rommel at El Alamein and the end in plain sight, Farouk treated every woman and every meal as if she or it might be his last.

But it wasn't. By August, the Eighth Army had brilliantly held the line at El Alamein. Rommel had extended himself too far; his supply arteries went back over a thousand miles into Libya and were constantly being severed by the bombardments of British aircraft. Alexandria seemed so near, yet the Nazis could simply not stretch any farther. Mussolini went back to Rome, along with his white horse. He also canceled his order for medals for his North African conquest, with Il Duce and the pyramids on one side and winged victory on the other, and ordered the Italian-language Baedekers he had had printed for his supposedly occupying troops to be destroyed. This time the British had earned their keep. They had saved Egypt and the throne of King Farouk.

By that time, at the end of July, Rommel was by no means defeated. He was simply held. Still dangerously close to the goal line, he remained a devastating threat. To the end of actually winning, Prime Minister Winston Churchill flew to Cairo in August to replace his Eighth Army commander, General Auchinleck, with General Bernard Montgomery. "The Auk" returned to India. Churchill had been very sensitive about the bad press his North African army had been getting, especially by non-British foreign correspondents. Clare Boothe Luce, for one, had visited Egypt and was horrified by the inefficiencies and disorganization of the British forces there. She wrote a scathing report which was confiscated by the British censors but the contents of which were nonetheless communicated to her husband, Henry, at *Time*. Among her many mals mots Mrs. Luce was said to have described the Royal Air Force as "the flying fairies."

Not that the small world of Americans in Cairo was not without representation in the effete department. The American minister (only Britain's man was called ambassador) Alexander Kirk was a total dandy who wore lavender silk tuxedos and whose normal suit buttons were covered in the same material as the suit itself. Sir Miles Lampson was deeply fond of the minister, who gave frequent parties on a Nile houseboat decorated with masses of white ostrich feathers. Kirk flaunted his Oedipal complex more than he did Old Glory. He maintained a shrine to his late mother, with candles burning night and day around her framed photograph, à la the eternal flame of the unknown soldier in Arlington. He further revered his mother by giving her name to a water buffalo which became Kirk's own sacred cow and whose milk the minister insisted on drinking every day.

If the entire situation in Egypt needed a bit of toughening up, Winston Churchill knew his man Montgomery was the man to do it in what was known as Operation Torch. A wiry, ruthlessly direct drill sergeant of a general, "Monty" announced on his arrival that "there will be no more bellyaching and no more retreats." Even before he actually defeated Rommel and sent him into retreat from El Alamein out of Egypt and back to Libya in November, Montgomery completely turned around the Egyptians' perception of the Germans as *übermenschen* and the British as cricketeers. Montgomery was not only a winner; almost as important, he *seemed* like one. As did Churchill, who took time out from visiting the troops to swim in the Mediterranean near Alexandria, where he floated on his back, making his famous "V for victory" sign with his legs. In Cairo, Churchill stayed at Beit el Azraq, a villa known as the "Blue House," which would have afforded a splendid view of the pyramids had it not been blocked by a grove of trees. It was also annoyingly infested with mosquitoes.

Although King Farouk had told Irene Najjar that he wasn't that impressed with Churchill ("another fat Englishman," Farouk had called him), the king did invite the prime minister to a dinner at the Mena House Hotel across from the pyramids. At the high table, Churchill suddenly was caught by surprise. Reaching into his waistcoat pocket, he found that his watch, which had been given to his forebear, the duke of Marlborough, by Queen Anne for having won the Battle of Blenheim, was missing.

All eyes were on Farouk, who, everyone knew, had recently taken pickpocket lessons from a master thief he had had pardoned from the Turah penitentiary to be his light-fingered tutor. The thief gave his lessons by having bells sewn into all the pockets of his suit. These served as mini-alarms. Farouk graduated summa cum laude; he could pick any pocket without jingling a single bell. As Churchill puzzled, Lampson fumed. He *knew* Farouk had lifted the watch. After watching the British squirm for a quarter-hour, Farouk left the table, ostensibly to play Sherlock Holmes. Ten minutes later, the sleuth king returned in triumph, holding the watch as a trophy and claiming to have traced it to a minor palace functionary with a major problem of kleptomania. Churchill expressed his great gratitude to Farouk, even if his sincerity was questionable.

Later on Churchill's visit, Farouk received the prime minister at Abdine Palace, at which Lampson noted that he wished "the monarch had been a little less inclined to try and assert himself and show off. He was all the time posing as the king." Farouk opened the conversation by presenting Churchill with a king-size cigar, one of the most colossal Lampson had even seen. At the audiences Churchill made a great show of how the British were going to thrash Rommel and win the war, and pointedly thanked Farouk for

> this staunchness of the Egyptian attitude and said with intentional emphasis that it was in times of trouble that one came to appreciate whether people were one's true friend or not, dynastically and nationally. This had an important bearing. This drew from King F the declaration of his own solidarity and that of his country to us. . . . The Monarch also said that on many occasions he had been greatly misunderstood and misrepresented but he did not wish to pursue that. . . . On the whole . . . it went well, but the P.M.'s general impression was that the boy was inclined to treat everything with studied cynicism and flippancy. At the same time, as he said to me afterwards, he wasn't entirely sure that something might not yet be made of the boy. He thought he might see him alone on his way back.

Churchill's desire for a tête-à-tête with Farouk, in the absence of Lampson, distressed the ambassador, who immediately contacted the Foreign Office to discourage and deter such a close encounter. It never took place. Otherwise Lampson made an excellent impression on Churchill, who in December 1942 sent him the following "personal and secret" telegram:

Would you care for me to consider your name among others
for vice-royalty of India? How do you feel towards proposition
from point of age and health as well as inclination? Please
understand I am asking a question and not at this stage making a proposal. All good wishes.

Here it was. The dream of a lifetime and a career, the highest post
open to any civilian in British public service. Lampson felt all his
efforts were being vindicated, that he was bearing the burden of the
empire the "right" way. He telegrammed back to Churchill, also
"personal and secret:"

I am greatly flattered you should even consider my name.
As regards inclination there is nothing I should like so much.
As regards age and health, I can claim to be hale and hearty
(touching wood): and I believe up to the demands of the post
on that score. I fully understand no proposal is implicit in your
question.
My warmest thanks.

While he waited anxiously for some decision on his dream vice-
royalty, Lampson was further lionized by King George VI by being
made the first Baron Killearn, after his family estate in Scotland. To
be elevated to the peerage while still in government service was an
infrequent and singular honor. Nahas feted Lampson with a huge
banquet to commemorate the event, which undoubtedly galled Farouk. Nevertheless, Lampson would soon be galled himself by an
enormously unlikely situation wherein Farouk began to warm to the
English and certain strategic English leaders in Egypt began to
warm to Farouk.

After the British proved their mettle at El Alamein and surged
westward into Libya to recapture Tobruk, King Farouk's attitudes
toward them seemed to change dramatically. In December, he
made a donation of thousands of pounds to assorted British military
charities for Christmas presents to the troops. Having been given a
Royal Air Force air marshal's uniform, Farouk began wearing it
everywhere and even grew a bushy Colonel Blimp–style mustache
to go with it. He liked the British militia look so much that he had a
doll made up of himself dressed this way and displayed it proudly in
his office at Abdine. Cynics attributed Farouk's stunning about-face
as wanting to bet on the winning horse, but many high-ranking

Allies in Egypt at the time were impressed by Farouk's genuine loyalty as well as by his wit and charm. It might have been as simple as that he wanted to be liked and that he responded well to being treated with the respect that he got from most important Englishmen other than Lampson.

British Air Marshal Douglas liked Farouk. Field Marshal Smuts found him "surprisingly intelligent," and Middle East Minister of State Oliver Lyttleton, who had convinced Lampson on the eve of Abdine to give Farouk a chance to say yes, thought the king was both likable and capable. Even Churchill refused to write him off, perhaps because of the deftness with which Farouk finessed the watch prank.

Among Americans in Egypt, the powerful Georgia senator Richard Russell sized Farouk up as "an attractive, clear-eyed young man . . . very much on the job . . . well above the ordinary run of rulers" in the Middle East. High financier and Yankee Brahmin diplomat Winthrop Aldrich was even more lavish in praise, noting that Farouk understood the complexities of the international gold market as well as any of the wizards of Wall Street. The American armed forces knew the way to Farouk's heart was through toys. Just as Hitler had cosseted Farouk with the Mercedes roadster, the Americans, not to be outdone, presented the king with a private plane, a jeep, and a "duck," an amphibious landing vehicle, which Farouk liked most of all, taking girlfriends for midnight landings on the beaches at Montazah.

With Rommel out of the way, life in Egypt returned to normal. Normal for Egypt was completely extraordinary for the rest of the world. As Noël Coward described it in his *Middle East Diary:*

> The uniforms indicated that perhaps somewhere in the vague outside world there might be a war of some sort going on. . . . This place is the last refuge of the soi-disant "International Set." All the fripperies of pre-war luxury living are still in existence here: rich people, idle people, cocktail parties, dinner parties, jewels and evening dress.

Photographer Cecil Beaton's diaries and letters also give some idea of what the mood was like, as in his description of Momo Marriott, the daughter of New York financier Otto Kahn and wife of a British brigadier, after Princess Shivekiar, Cairo's hostess with the second mostest:

> The smartest woman in Cairo . . . Momo Marriott, with her long red nails and simple, beautifully-cut clothes. To be seen at her parties, in the company of generals, commandos and celebrities, was to be at the heart of Cairo's wartime society. . . . Momo lived with her mother, Mrs. OK or Mother bird as she was known, in an absurdly luxurious house rented from a rich Egyptian. A bank of clocks, radios, telephones and lights surrounded the bed, and the enormous bath was worthy of Cleopatra. Momo had been obliged to install a modest tub in its marble depths, since the boiler had not been built on the same scale.

Beaton went on to write: "There is such a social life here that I am harassed." He described a typical evening. "A huge dinner party —as artificial and nonsensical as only that sort of gathering can be —then to a nightclub where the dance band is so good that one realized how seldom dance music is well played, and how thrilling it can be—the gaiety here was absolutely terrific—young English officers on leave doing a frenzied hop that continued for hours without any alleviation."

Glamorous wartime Cairo was like a Cole Porter musical or a Noël Coward drawing-room comedy. Coward himself, however, was upstaged by King Farouk. One night, Coward was at a party to which Farouk had been taken by his friend Air Marshal Douglas. The evening's entertainment consisted of two short propaganda films, followed by Cary Grant in *Arsenic and Old Lace.* By one-thirty in the morning, Douglas decided that Farouk still needed more entertaining, so he asked Coward if he would come to the piano and perform some of his songs, including his new song, "Don't Let's Be Beastly to the Germans" for the king. Until this evening, Coward had been impressed by Farouk, whom he had met before and

> found it almost impossible to believe that he's only twenty-three. He is a big, fine-looking man. . . . He couldn't possibly have been more courteous or charming, but I had the feeling that he was somehow nervous. The local gossip is that he doesn't care for the English very much but I can only say that

if this is the case he dissembled it as far as I was concerned with the most exquisite diplomacy.

This night with Coward and Farouk, alas, was to be different from the other. As Coward described it:

> I was told that the king was anxious to hear me sing, which proved in him a supreme capacity for taking punishment, and so I seated myself dismally at an upright and very upstanding piano and churned out three or four songs. I don't think I have ever performed so vilely in my life but I was far too weary to care.

Douglas, in his memoirs, recalls the cause and effect of the incident:

> I do not doubt that Coward was weary. He had been working hard and travelling great distances in his generous effort to entertain the troops. But what had caused him to perform so badly at our party—and it was indeed an embarrassingly poor show—was a comment that King Farouk made when I asked Coward if he would be so good as to play for us. In his high-pitched voice, which rang out so that nobody could escape hearing it, Farouk exclaimed, "Yes . . . come and sing for your supper." If looks could have killed, the one shot at Farouk by Coward, and rightly so, would have resulted in his losing his throne far quicker than he did.

Douglas liked Farouk and forgave him for putting Coward down. "He was only trying to be facetious, and act and speak in a way which he thought was English," Douglas wrote. Wishing to make it up to Coward, one night Farouk saw him and Lampson enter the Auberge des Pyramides, and despite his loathing for Lampson, invited them to share the king's table. Farouk could take the company only so long, and left early. Coward and Lampson stayed on to drink and watch the floor show, only to find that their entire bill had been picked up by the king. Lampson was taken completely unawares by this act of generosity, while Coward wrote that he regretted that all he had had was one beer and two packs of cigarettes.

Field Marshal Douglas was very sympathetic to and understanding of Farouk's position. Because he was, he was able to enlist the king in many activities designed to aid the British cause. Farouk

wanted desperately to have friends, to be liked, to belong. He was
still a boy and had a boy's need to be accepted as part of the gang.
Douglas and several other British officers whom he met through
Douglas brought him into the fold, invited him to dancing and
swimming parties in their weekend houses, teased him, and did the
thing that he loved the most—treated him like a commoner. Farouk
adored self-deprecation. When one of his new friends asked him if
he was going to a British military parade, Farouk replied, "Why
should I? They usually bring the tanks to me."

In return for his English hospitality, Farouk would invite his
buddies and their girlfriends for palace screenings of good Hollywood propaganda movies like *Casablanca,* or buy them recordings
of the latest Broadway hit, *Oklahoma!,* invite them to duck-hunting
parties in the Fayoum or ibex shoots in the Wadi Rishrash, or take
them all out to the Auberge des Pyramides, watching the *au courant
jeunesse doré* of civilian Cairo, which was packed with members of
the ever-increasing American colony wearing zoot suits and doing
the jitterbug to big band music. Farouk never got up to try the new
steps, even if it meant a lost opportunity to tread on the toes of
Lady Lampson. He just sat back, sipping orangeade, smoking huge
cigars, shooting bread balls at anyone who seemed too pompous,
dropping ice cubes down particularly inviting décolletages, and
making endless jokes and puns at everyone's expense, including his
own. The epicureanism that Farouk had adopted in face of the
German menace did not subside once the "tomorrow we die" no
longer applied. No one liked having or giving a good time better
than the king of Egypt, who seemed on his way to overcoming the
terminal inferiority complex that Lampson had done his best to
inflict on him.

All this appealed to Field Marshal Douglas, who developed a
true paternal affection for the young king, to the continual and
mounting displeasure of Sir Miles Lampson, who couldn't understand why anyone would spend any time at all with the boy if he
didn't absolutely have to. As Douglas wrote:

> After a time, and much to the annoyance and even indignation
> of quite a few of our people in Cairo, I began genuinely to like
> Farouk. There was no indication then there was anything that
> was vicious about him, although at times his flippancy became
> annoying. Another failing of his was that he appeared to be

almost fanatically keen on acquiring great wealth. He told me on one occasion he thought his personal fortune must be around six million pounds, and he revealed all too clearly his shortsightedness in stating openly that one of his main interests in life was to increase that fortune. This led him into currying favour with the rich people in Egypt, as they did with him, at the expense of the common people, in whom he had little or no interest.

Whenever Douglas would get into issues of social welfare, Farouk, who felt that he was totally in tune with the needs of "my beloved people," would silence Douglas by jokingly accusing him of being a Communist, which short of being a Nazi or a Fascist was about as bad as one could be in 1943. In all, Douglas found Farouk "an intelligent young man. He was well-informed and well-read and he was by no means the fool that he appeared to be through the stupid way in which he quite often behaved in public. He would mix our talks with seriousness and joking, which was what probably mystified the people who saw us together in the nightclubs of Cairo."

Although by 1943 the war threat to Egypt had passed, the continued British occupation became an increasing outrage. This crystalized into an intricate duel between Farouk and Lampson whose outcome would determine not only their own futures but Egypt's relationship with Britain as well. This protracted showdown, which lasted until 1946, when studied in detail illuminates how the profound incompatibility and hostility of the two men were emblematic of the irreconcilable differences between their two countries. The Farouk-Lampson war is thus more important to the modern history of Egypt than World War II; it certainly did more fundamental harm.

It was not in Lampson's best interest to have powerful fellow countrymen like Air Marshal Douglas vouching for the bad boy whom Lampson now had built a significant block of his diplomatic career in denigrating so that he would seem even more the statesman in having been able to handle Farouk in all his various and sundry autocracies and treacheries. In view of the looming possibility of his appointment as viceroy of India, Lampson had to look not good but great in Egypt, and could do so only at Farouk's expense. Douglas may have fallen under the young king's spell, but the last person Lampson could allow to succumb was Winston Churchill, who was in and out of Cairo overseeing the triumphant desert campaign several times in 1943. Lampson would never leave the two leaders alone, for fear that they might bond, as odd a couple as that might have been. But Farouk and Douglas were an odd couple, too, and one never knew. Luckily, Lampson ran interference quite well. He described one meeting of Farouk and Churchill with apparent relief:

> The conversation . . . was amicable enough, largely about the Monarch's collection of firearms and so on. At one point, Winston skillfully worked in a reference to our King's habit of having him to lunch once a week at Buckingham Palace, at which King F. made a wry face and he was somewhat embarrassed when I suggested he might . . . consider some such system himself. His answer was that if it was our Prime Minister he was inviting it would be different but unfortunately it wasn't: it was Nahas. At another point in the conversation Winston referred to Nahas as a very clever man. This comment equally did not meet with any particular acclamation. It was nearly 8 o'clock when I managed to get the Monarch to rise to his feet with a view to ending the interview. . . . I was electrified at one moment to hear the Monarch, lolling back in his chair, address the Prime Minister as follows, "You know, Churchill, etc. etc." . . . Later at dinner . . . Winston described the King to Jacqueline as "cheeky."

Churchill may have found Farouk impudent, but it was better than he found Nahas. The Egyptian prime minister droned on to the British prime minister about crop problems and fertilizers, which, as Lampson said, "was well over the head of the P.M. [Churchill] who naturally is not concerned with such details. . . . I was afraid at one moment, when Nahas was well in his stride, that Winston was going to sleep. He sat with his eyes shut and looked like it but in actual fact he was only getting bored."

If Churchill was getting bored with Nahas's details, Farouk and much of the Egyptian population were getting infuriated with Nahas's corruption, which had been cast into the spotlight by the defection of Nahas's closest henchman and friend for twenty years, Makram Obeid, Egypt's minister of finance. A brilliant Copt, Obeid was generally regarded as the brains of the Wafd party, while Nahas was its front man.

That this could eventually make Nahas fungible was not lost on the real power behind the dais, Nahas's dynamic wife, Zeinab el Wakil, who aspired to be to Egypt what Eva Peron became in Argentina and Imelda Marcos became in the Philippines. Madame Nahas was a pillar of Cairo society, famous for her strong-arm fund-raising through her controls on the purse strings of Wafd patronage and appointments. Madame Nahas turned her strong arms on her husband, who was ailing from a prostate disorder. She forced him to dismiss Makram from his ministry and expel him from the Wafd before Makram got him first.

Makram retaliated by sharing his inside information with the country. His so-called "black book," a compilation of the abuses of the Nahases which he planned to present to Farouk as a petition to dismiss the prime minister, was somehow printed in a bootleg version and became a hotter item than *Lady Chatterley's Lover.* As Egypt's leading muckraker, Makram listed 108 charges of abuse of office and privilege. Among them were the following: Nahas had closed a school in the Garden City area and rebuilt it as his own 10 Downing Street. He had ordered the Egyptian embassy in London to purchase six silver-fox furs for Madame Nahas on Bond Street. He passed a bill for the irrigation of certain desert land belonging to his cousin, vastly inflating its worth. Madame Nahas had sold offices for bribes, used secret knowledge of government land policy to make a fortune on the Alexandria cotton market, put a host of her relatives in lucrative government sinecures, sold passports and visas for extortionate sums. In short, Makram's black book made Egypt seem like a corrupt banana republic minus the humidity.

The protracted Nahas-Makram mudfest gave Farouk the ideal opportunity to do what he had been dreaming of since February 4, 1942: get rid of Nahas once and for all. The black book gave him the ammunition; his new coterie of British friends gave him the self-confidence; the prospect of the end of the war, the departure of the British soldiers, and the opportunity to be the leader of a truly independent Egypt gave him the drive to eliminate his chief rival for that leadership.

Although Lampson, now Baron Killearn, conceded that the "so-called book does seem to contain pretty damning evidence," he was dead set against Farouk using it as an occasion to dismiss Nahas.

Lampson was determined to shield the man who was if not a puppet, certainly Lampson's best friend in Egyptian politics. Lampson's instrument in keeping Farouk from precipitous action was Hassanein, who was now being dubbed in Cairo as "Chef de Cabinet of the British ambassador." Lampson noted that as a watchdog Hassanein "was having a hellishly difficult task in restraining the king," whom Lampson would suffer to rule but never to govern.

Lampson again assembled the British commanders in chief, who adamantly refused to countenance Lampson's suggestion that armed force might be necessary to keep Nahas and the Wafd in office, notwithstanding Lampson's exhortation that the Wafd was "the best guarantee of a stable military base." His military men were not impressed. They would never again bully Farouk with tanks at Abdine.

Annoyed at the generals, Lampson went over their heads to London, sending a telegram to Winston Churchill that "weakness never pays." Churchill, taken with this buzz phrase, sent a kick-ass telegram to General Jumbo Wilson:

> It seems to me very unlikely more than a demonstration in any case would be required and that you have ample force at your dispersal. H.M. Ambassador must be put in a position to tender formal "advice" to Palace. Pray therefore consult with him and strengthen his situation.

Lampson was feeling particularly bellicose that spring, pumped up from a gusto-ish visit with General Montgomery, who told him "that the fighting on the desert suited him down to the ground and that his army have never been in better physical form, despite the fact that they live entirely on tinned foods, mainly bully beef." Monty was soaring across the sands in an American Flying Fortress he had won in a bet with an American general about where he would be on his campaign trail at a certain date. The whole encounter left Lampson feeling that if Montgomery could whip Rommel, Lampson could certainly whip Farouk, and blindfolded at that.

Again, Lampson "won." Farouk once more backed down about booting Nahas. "The medicine had worked!" Lampson wrote delightedly in his diary. "I fancy it must be due to the hint I gave Hassanein." Farouk summoned Lampson to Abdine and presented him with

a long typewritten paper saying that he realised that the war
interest must dominate everything and that as he understood
we considered it would conduce best to our war aims to keep
the present Government in office, H.M. though reluctantly
would agree to do so. . . . Actually I think it's a pretty good
climb down with the advantage of saving H.M.'s face.

Lampson told Farouk straight out that while governments came
and went, and that because England wasn't interested in further
reducing the already dwindling number of kings in the world, Farouk as king could have a long reign if and only if he stuck by the
British. Lampson made it quite clear who was still the boss, so clear
that when Wendell Willkie published his book *One World,* in which
he wrote about Lampson stating that the British ambassador to
Egypt was "for all practical purposes its actual ruler," the book was
formally banned in Egypt. Closing their meeting over Nahas,
Lampson also chastised Farouk about "the deplorable impression
which all the younger members of the Royal Family inevitably created upon one. It was up to H.M. to behave well: to beget a son
when everything in the garden should be lovely."

Lampson's exhortation to beget a son was a particularly nasty
gesture, adding salt to Farouk's already festering marital wounds, of
which Lampson was well aware. In addition to her ongoing "close
friendship" with Wahid Yussri, Farida had developed another relationship with her portrait painter that was hotly rumored to be
more than one of subject and artist. The artist in question was a
consummate British ladies' man and sexual social climber named
Simon Elwes, then in his forties, while the queen of Egypt was
barely twenty. Elwes had come to Cairo to do the portraits of local
high society, and in this he succeeded to the point of doing that of
Ambassador Lampson himself. In Elwes's ambitious mind, his mission to Egypt would be a success only if he painted both the king
and queen, and he finally inveigled his way into the job through
Farida's aunt, the wife of ex-Prime Minister Hussein Sirry. In early
1943, Elwes agreed to the prestigious commission at the bargain-
basement price of a thousand Egyptian pounds per portrait, half
down.

At first, Elwes went to Abdine, where he was to paint Farida first.
Soon, he claimed, all the pomp and ceremony of Abdine was too
distracting. The queen would have to come to him, at his studio.

This suggestion was inflammatory on two counts. First, Egyptian queens under the harem code of honor did *not* leave the palace for such graven images. Secondly, Elwes had a reputation as a "method" painter; i.e., he needed to sleep with his distaff subjects to rise to the top of his art with them. Given Farouk's own multiple dalliances and Farida's own "modernity" and dedication to art, the queen went to Elwes in extreme secrecy, accompanied by a trusted personal servant. With Farouk, however, nothing was secret. His palace spies quickly found out about the extramural sittings, and Farouk eventually surprised the couple *in flagrante artis.* When Lampson heard about the incident, he arranged for Elwes to be sent to South Africa, ostensibly to do the portrait of the wife of Field Marshal Smuts but actually to prevent a scandal and the possibility of physical reprisal against the painter, although Elwes was quite fearless where romance and career were concerned. Elwes fully expected to return to Cairo after he did Mrs. Smuts. When Lampson blocked his return, Elwes was furious. At the same time, Farouk, always the prankster, needled Lampson through Hassanein, demanding that Elwes come back to complete Farida's portrait and do his as well. After all, Farouk said, he had already put down good money.

In the public sense, Farouk did accede to Lampson's advice to tend his garden and have a son. Farida became pregnant again in the spring of 1943, but in the rumor sweepstakes as to the identity of the father, few bets were placed on the king. Farouk fervently hoped it would be a boy. While he kept his fingers crossed waiting, he continued his sybaritic ways, atoning a bit by going through another quasi-religious phase, visiting the ancient and virtually inaccessible monastery of St. Catherine's in the Sinai lunar landscape and adding a new, small, Caliphian holy-man beard to his large Grenadier-Guard bushy mustache, which inspired Noël Coward to salute, sotto voce, "God shave the king."

Because Farouk had made a group of English friends and because he was now used to kowtowing to the ambassador, his having to back down in his latest *mano a mano* with Lampson over Nahas and the "Black Book" was somehow less scarring to him than tank night at Abdine. Still, the continual humiliation was there and Farouk wanted to find a way to end it. His English allies suggested that he go over the heads of Lampson's cronies Churchill and Anthony Eden to King George himself, king to king, to arrange to have Lampson removed as ambassador. They warned Farouk that such a dialogue would have to be initiated with total indirection and diamond-cutter delicacy. After much deliberation, Farouk and company concocted their Trojan horse to get into the inner sancta of Buckingham Palace: a box of chocolates. The gift would be from King Farouk's daughters, the Princesses Fawzia and Ferial, to King George's daughters, the Princesses Elizabeth and Margaret. But the sweetest surprise would be in the hands of the gift bearer; this was a letter from King Farouk to be hand delivered to King George at the same time the chocolates were presented to the princesses. The letter would state Farouk's interest in talking to George, at which time the troubles with Miles could be breached.

The messenger for all this sugar diplomacy was a young British officer named Patrick Telfer-Smollett, who was summoned to Abdine to collect the gift. When he arrived, he found Farouk literally wading through a sea of chocolate, over two hundred pounds of Groppi's finest. The king himself was tasting all the different configurations, picking the best and sweetest flavors for this ultimate Care package, a giant lacquer box decorated with the coats of arms of both England and Egypt. To get to England during this stage of the war, Telfer-Smollett had to go via neutral Lisbon, which entailed crossing the continent by way of Khartoum, Nairobi, Entebbe, and Dakar, during which trek the fine chocolates melted more than a few times, in between Telfer-Smollett's often hapless efforts to keep them on ice, when ice was at hand. By the time he finally got to Buckingham Palace to present the chocolates and the letter, the king and queen and their daughters were away in the country. The weary chocolates were whisked away by a palace functionary. The letter, which was under strictest orders to be hand delivered face-to-face to King George remained in the exhausted Telfer-Smollett's hands. It never reached the English king.

Farouk had a far worse piece of bad timing in November with the British. With Antonio Pulli at his side, he was going over one hundred miles an hour in his red Cadillac convertible on the way to Ismalia on the Red Sea to see a new royal yacht that was being fitted out for him. As he pulled out to pass a British Army lorry, he saw another car coming head-on at him. He floored the Cadillac, thinking he could make it. He did, but as he swerved back into his lane his bumper caught against the lorry, spinning the Cadillac out of control. The car crashed into a grove of trees along the highway.

The lorry stopped to help and found Farouk conscious, wedged between the seat and the crumpled steering wheel. When he told a British soldier he was the king of Egypt, the soldier thought the man was delirious and asided to his friends that if this was the king of Egypt he, the soldier, was the emperor of Afghanistan. Further injury was added to insult when the stretcher on which Farouk was placed, when the British ambulance arrived, collapsed under Farouk's now-considerable weight (well over two hundred pounds, but one hundred less than what was to come). Farouk hit the ground hard, which exacerbated his auto injuries, diagnosed at the British Field Hospital at nearby Kassasin as a cracked pelvic bone and two fractured ribs.

A host of top physicians were summoned to the military hospital. They wanted to move the king back to Cairo, but Farouk, who was in pain but wide-awake, insisted on being treated like an ordinary British soldier. He liked having a "war injury." It made him feel like a regular guy, normal, even a bit like a hero. He did have a telephone by his bed and special food cooked by chefs transported from Abdine, long lines of worshipful fellaheen at the hospital gates with gifts of sweets that they had made, but, otherwise, he played the role of wounded soldier to the hilt. He told military schoolboy stories to the other soldiers about his cold-shower days in England at the "Shop" and proved that he was more than mere hot air by doing impressive (for his size) pull-up exercises on a bar known as the Balkan beam that was installed over his army-issue cast iron cot. He loved the ministrations of the British nurses, their massages and physiotherapy. In fact, his unabashed heavy flirtations with these nurses gave the lie to the immediate gossip that the pelvic fracture had rendered Farouk impotent and worse.

Many second guessers on Farouk's rise and fall date the beginning of the end to this accident, with medical theories that the crash irreparably damaged Farouk's glandular and hormonal system, precipitating his obesity and all his eccentric behavior. But Farouk was already getting fat and was, in any event, on a genetic collision course with corpulence. Neither his father nor any of his Mohammed Ali antecedents were even close to slim. As for his impotence, or frequent disinclination, that, too, was already in operation, or lack thereof, as his various mistresses have attested, as were his eccentricities, which were a question of degree. None of the attending doctors' reports treated the accident as extraordinary. In fact, the doctors were ready to discharge Farouk after one week, but the king liked the hospital experience so much, he lingered on for three. He was delighted to be away from Abdine, from Lampson, from Nahas, from Farida, and from Nazli, who had gotten into such a snit over the lack of queenly attention she was getting from both Farouk and Farida that she had gone on an extended holiday to the beaches and historical shrines of Palestine and had agreed to return only if both Farouk and Nahas received her at the Cairo train station with a band and a full-dress military escort. The king and the prime minister for once agreed, and Nazli had come home, but Farouk managed to find an excuse to stand his mother up at the last minute.

Farouk was also delighted to avoid all the protocol involving the November visit of Churchill, Roosevelt, and Chiang Kai-shek to Mena House on their way to the Teheran Conference. The logistics were a comedy of errors with diplomats tripping over the international cable lines crisscrossing the hotel like spiderwebs; armies of Flit sprayers trying to make the dignitaries safe from the mosquito-borne malaria epidemic then raging in Egypt; and Chiang Kai-shek being given the code name of "Celeste," which confused everyone and made more for a French farce than a summit conference. Chiang, or Celeste, couldn't speak a word of English, and the interpreters were constantly getting lost. Much of the conversation consisted of, as Lampson described it, "inarticulate sounds of pleasure at meeting again." Still, with all these world leaders, plus the kings of Greece, Yugoslavia, and Albania, all in exile in Cairo at the time, the city by the pyramids seemed like *the* place in the world to be, except to King Farouk, who vastly preferred the Cockney nurses and infantrymen from the Midlands.

Eventually, Farouk could no longer play the invalid and had to return to reality, the harshest aspect of which was the birth by Farida on December 15 of, sadly, another girl. Farouk named her Fadia and, while admitting his disappointment to the English midwife, he assured her that "she would be loved just the same." And undoubtedly more than her mother, Farida. As one of the three bands played "People Will Say We're in Love," Farouk arrived at Princess Shivekiar's annual New Year's Eve extravaganza with Irene Najjar, which announced to Cairo and to the world exactly how badly the royal romance between king and queen had degener-

ated. In a post mortem on Shivekiar's party with Prince Mohammed Ali on January 3, 1944, Lampson wrote:

> He came to say that the young Monarch was definitely "vin-
> dictive and cracked." As proof he quoted an incident at Prin-
> cess Shivekiar's party. Prince Abdel Moneim had congratu-
> lated the Monarch on his recovery from his accident to which
> the Monarch had replied that he had disappointed many peo-
> ple, upon whom he would be revenged. It was rather odd
> Prince Mohammed Ali should tell me this as both Jac and I
> had been struck by the general boorish and unpleasant impres-
> sion made by the Monarch at the party. Jac's comment to me
> had been that the boy was "definitely bad" and I am afraid she
> is right. It is all a great pity. Indeed I often feel now that it
> would have been wiser if we had removed him . . . in Febru-
> ary, 1942 . . . I certainly wish that we had had him off once
> and for all. It is going to be much more difficult to cope with
> him a second time and certainly he and Hassanein are now
> playing a very astute game—so astute that I begin to feel that
> we should deal with the matter before things slide further.

While Lampson cogitated on how to "deal" with the increasingly
truculent boy-king and waited for any developments on the big job
in India, he distracted himself with what had become, for the British in Egypt, the resort life in a country-club country spared by the
war. He was a fixture of the party circuit, with celebrities like
Vivien Leigh, Josephine Baker, and Jack Benny, who came to entertain the troops, went hunting with international nonbelligerent bon
vivants like the Maharaja of Jaipur, who came for the wild game,
and played a lot of golf. Lampson was wild about guns. One of his
happiest days was spent in the desert firing off all the submachine-
gun varieties in the British arsenal, while he and Lady Lampson
together took a special series of lessons in revolver shooting. All the
world notables he met notwithstanding, the one man who made as
big an impression on Lampson as Roosevelt or Chiang Kai-shek
was a British major named Grant-Taylor, who was reputed to be
the best pistol shot in the world and had been hired by the Chicago
police during Prohibition to help them deal with the gangs of Al
Capone. Lampson marveled that Grant-Taylor had "no less than
fifty-seven men chalked up to his credit," the same way he would
count dead ducks at a Fayoum outing. He was also vastly in awe of

the major's death-speed record in having been let off a submarine at
a French port, killing six German airmen who were directing raids
against England, and returning to the sub, all within twenty-seven
minutes. "Certainly the war does bring one into contact with remarkable people," he wrote. Another such man was fighter pilot
Max Aitkin, son of press lord Beaverbrook, who described casually
to Sir Miles and Lady Lampson over oysters at the Union Bar in
Alexandria how "he went up for a flip round the other night and
knocked a couple of Huns out of the air over Crete. All this just in
his stride."

Sometimes Lampson would mix golfing and shooting. At the
Gezira Sporting Club course, Lampson once got so vexed at the
scavenger birds that flew off with his golf balls, mistaking them for
eggs, that he sent for his Purdey shotgun and blasted several dozen
of the birds onto the fairway. This didn't sit well with the locals, for
whom the birds maintained the balance of nature by devouring the
worms that destroyed the cotton plants, but, then again, Lampson's
treatment of Farouk didn't sit well with the locals either. Lampson
had minimal contact, far less than Farouk, whom he attacked as
elitist, with ordinary Egyptians other than his butler, Mutum, his
ball boys, and the acrobats and sword swallowers hired for embassy
dances.

Lampson was capable of compassion, especially if it was for his
patron, Winston Churchill, whom he helped nurse back to health
from a bout with pneumonia by shipping him thermoses of an
Egyptian spinach soup that supposedly had magical curative
properties, as well as tracking down the South African raisins and
calf's-foot jelly the prime minister loved.

Because of Churchill's support, Lampson had no compunction
about punishing Farouk every chance he could. Lampson resented
Farouk's new cozying attitude toward the British in Egypt and
wanted to cut the king off from any English support that could
make Lampson's now-near-pathological hatred of Farouk seem
anything less than justified. When Air Marshal Douglas was informed that he was being sent back to England in early 1944 as
commander in chief of the Coastal Command, Farouk was saddened by the prospective loss of his best English friend, the first to
show him that the British were capable of treating him like a king
and not a juvenile delinquent. As a commemoration of their friendship and as a going-away present, Farouk wanted to give Douglas

the sash and medal of the Order of Ismail, one of Egypt's highest
honors. Because military regulations required that Douglas get official British permission before any such foreign decorations be accepted, he went through the formalities. He was very surprised
when he heard from the Foreign Office that he had to turn down
Farouk's award. Although the communication of denial came from
London, there was little doubt that its impetus had come from
Cairo, and Douglas was put in a very embarrassing position. He
wrote:

> Such was his anger that King Farouk demanded to be told
> exactly why I was not accepting this decoration. I had to tell
> him that the decision was not mine. . . . Farouk immediately
> said that he detected in all that the hand of our Ambassador. I
> was inclined to think, to myself, that he might be right; but all
> I could say was to repeat that it was an official decision arrived
> at in London. Farouk then stated that he took it as a personal
> affront that I had refused this high decoration. . . . It was a
> thoroughly stupid state of affairs, and I told our Ambassador
> that, while the decoration meant nothing at all to me, my not
> being allowed to accept it was causing King Farouk gratuitous
> offense and adding to his grievances against the British. But
> Lampson was adamant about the Foreign Office ruling, and it
> was even left to me to perform the unpleasant task of having to
> write a formal refusal to King Farouk.

Thus was the ending of a beneficial friendship. Lampson was
furious that Douglas had dared to speak up about the matter, and
especially to grouse about it. "If there's any more backchat from
him I shall be moved to tell him, when I next see him, just where he
gets off," Lampson averred in his diary. For the moment, however,
Farouk turned the other cheek and in February invited Lampson to
a royal duck shoot for which Lampson had to wake up at two forty-
five in the morning. "It was quite a good shoot and for once in a
way I was hitting them nicely in the neck," wrote Lampson, who
downed 117 ducks, more than anyone else in the hunting party
except the king, "who *claimed* 437 but it emerged that he had had a
friend in the bolt shooting with him and I do not doubt that many
ghaffirs were operating in his vicinity!" Although Lampson was
annoyed at being outshot, even if not fairly or squarely, he did

concede that "H.M. was in his very best form and certainly is a most admirable host."

Farouk knew that the way to the ambassador's heart was through his shotgun. Lampson was lulled into such a false sense of security that Lampson saw it as a "bombshell" in April, when Farouk invited him to Abdine to tell him that he was dismissing Nahas once and for all and replacing him with an interim government "under a personal friend of mine (Lampson's) and a good friend of the British," namely Hassanein. Farouk then presented Lampson with a list of proposed ministers, whom Lampson viewed as a bunch of rich "nonentities," the most objectionable of whom was the millionaire Abdel Fatah Amr, whose chief qualification for office was that he was the squash champion of the world.

Farouk's immediate motivation for sacking Nahas this time was the latter's outright bid for power as the leader of the country by his relief tour of Upper Egypt, where the malaria epidemic was killing thousands at the same time Farouk was making his own relief tour. Further, Nahas founded two relief organizations, not in the name of Farouk, as was the accepted practice, but in his own—the Nahas Institutes. Nahas was doing his best to make the king seem superfluous, which is what Lampson wanted him to do. Understandably, Farouk insisted on getting rid of Nahas.

On the surface, Lampson tried to play it very, very cool. "I purposely kept the thing on a very friendly and informal basis," Lampson wrote. "When he was explaining that there really could not be two kings in Egypt, I chipped in with the observation, 'God forbid, we have found that one is quite enough.' " Lampson also joked that London's reaction to the change might be "a very decided 'lemon.' " But underneath, Lampson meant every word quite literally. He was seething. Bidding Farouk the most cordial adieu, he rushed back to the embassy and fired off to Anthony Eden and the war cabinet in London "a most personal and secret telegram . . . on the lines that I wondered whether we could afford to be faced with these perpetual embarrassments and whether we might not have to take a firmer line and assume more direct control of Egypt." Such "direct control" to the old colonialist meant finally to depose Farouk.

As usual, the trigger-happy Lampson put the issue to his commanders in chief, who again balked at the use of the military to get rid of the king. "Doubting Thomases," Lampson described them.

While Lampson was once more cabling to the war office in London to go over their heads, he learned that Farouk had already crossed the Rubicon, or the Nile, as it were, and signed the order to sack Nahas, even though he had assured Lampson he wouldn't do anything so rash without notifying him first. Not even bothering to put on the frock coat he always wore to Abdine, Lampson stormed over to the palace to confront the king, who defused the ambassador's rage by complimenting him on his snappy khaki suit and asking where he could get one just like it.

When Lampson turned the discussion from menswear back to politics, Farouk explained that he had to move quickly because Nahas was leaving for another grandstanding tour, this time of the delta, and Farouk had to establish without a doubt who was the boss in Egypt. Lampson was annoyed by the entire exercise. As Wendell Willkie and everyone else knew perfectly well, *Lampson* was the boss. Lampson whipped a telegram out of his pocket and shoved it in Farouk's face. The telegram was from Winston Churchill and ordered Farouk to take no action toward dismissing Nahas until the war cabinet considered the matter. The telegram closed:

> His Majesty's Government would almost certainly range themselves against whoever strikes first [Farouk or Nahas].
> Considering that Egypt has, through our exertions, been spared the horrors of invasion and of becoming a battlefield and remains an unravaged peaceful and prosperous land, we have a right to address you on this subject.

Lampson stamped out of the palace, only to have his ire slaked by a new telegram from Churchill, predicting that the war cabinet would meet the next day and

> will very likely support a democratic administration against a Palace clique headed by an oriental despot who on every occasion has proved himself a poor friend of England. Meanwhile however make sure C's in C have at their disposal sufficient forces to deal with any troublesome Egyptians. . . .

Lampson reassembled his commanders in chief and forced the issue on them. He relished playing supreme commander. All military plans were made for the coup, including anticipating the response of the Egyptian Army and the Cairo police, both of which, Lampson predicted, would not make any move with a change of incumbent on the throne. Once more a call was made to the Manyal Palace. Prince Mohammed Ali packed his bags for the move to Abdine.

Lampson had one final audience with Farouk before the tanks were to be rolled in and the boy locked up and sent off to an exile that had not yet been determined. Farouk told Lampson how important it was both to his own honor and to the best interest of his country to get the corrupt and power-mad Nahas out of office, to which Lampson pulled out his figurative schoolmaster's stick, rapping Farouk's knuckles for his bad syntax. "It is rather amusing that . . . he put the question of his own honour in front of the interest of his country and it was only on my suggestion that it looked a good deal better to reverse the order that he then did so," Lampson wrote. "I only mention this to show the type of childish mind with which one has to deal."

Then Lampson further castigated the boy by exhuming the ghost of his father, King Fuad, who Lampson reminded Farouk as having lamented to Lampson on multiple occasions, "The poor boy has no chance." Lampson harangued Farouk that he, Lampson, was the only chance Farouk had to stay on the throne, and that he had frittered away this golden regal opportunity to rebut his beloved father's profound pessimism about his son's prospects as a leader. Farouk remained calm. He was exceedingly polite to the raging bull confronting him, saying to Lampson that he was "absolutely detached as regards his own position. It was fate and not he that had put him on the throne of Egypt and faced him with all these problems."

Leaving Farouk, Lampson buttonholed Hassanein in the corridor. Hassanein himself was quite insulted that his dear friend Lampson had ridiculed his nomination as prime minister, but he, too, remained polite. Lampson repeated the strong-arm treatment, giving Hassanein the out of having Farouk yield to keeping Nahas on wartime emergency grounds. London was being blitzed and the top secret offensive that would emerge June 6 would justify Farouk as a "loyal ally" in preserving the status quo for the time being. Hassanein refused to endorse any such face-saving compromises. The king had been insulted, he had been insulted, and Egypt had been insulted by Lampson's perpetuation of a Nahas government that can be compared in graft, venality, and corruption only to

those of the carpetbag-scalawag regimes in the American South
during Reconstruction, or the grab-bag administration of Mayor
Jimmy Walker and Tammany Hall in New York City in the "roaring twenties."

Thus rejected, Lampson went home to the embassy to load his
Purdeys and sharpen his swords. Waiting for a letter from his commanders in chief about the next day's planned offensive, he went
into a rage when the letter never arrived. The new air marshal, who
had replaced Sholto Douglas, could not be found to sign the missive. As it turns out, he was at the Auberge des Pyramides watching
the floor show with King Farouk. The next day, making no excuses
whatsoever, Farouk sent Hassanein to Lampson with the following
simply written message:

"I am commanded by His Majesty to inform Your Excellency
that he has decided to leave the present Government in Office for
the time being."

Lampson had "backed down the boy" one more time, but he was
disappointed. He didn't want him down. He wanted him out.

As it turned out, Lampson had blown his golden opportunity.
The excitements of spring were followed by an uneventful summer
of dreary parties and drearier wartime bureaucracy. The real excitement occurred in August when a huge high-explosive Nazi mine
washed up on the beach of Montazah Palace. Farouk, who had a
fetish for weapons, felt as if he had discovered the Holy Grail of
ballistics. He ordered his Egyptian Navy officers to have the mine
defused. But the Egyptian Navy, which was barely a cut above the
Swiss navy, had absolutely no experience with mines, and therefore
turned to the British Navy for help. When Farouk found out about
this admission of incompetence, he had the mine seized from the
British experts before they could complete their task and had the
still-live mine put on a truck in Alexandria. It bounced all the way
through the delta to Cairo, where Farouk added it to his weapon
collection at Abdine. For all his loathing of Farouk, Lampson still
didn't want him to blow up and the palace with him and begged
Hassanein to let him send the British Navy back to save the king.
But Farouk steadfastly refused and figured out a way to have his
mine and his palace too. "It is just another example of how impulsive and irresponsible the young Monarch is," Lampson wrote.
When he described the incident to Nahas and some other Wafd

friends, they "somewhat cynically took the line that all in all it was probably a pity that the mine had not exploded!"

Pity, indeed. In September, Egypt was so dead that Lampson felt safe enough to take Jacqueline on a month's vacation in South Africa, visiting Field Marshal and Lady Smuts. It was his first trip out of Egypt since the war had begun. While he was away, he picked up a paper and read some very bad news. Nahas had been dismissed as prime minister and replaced by none other than Ahmed Maher, the brother of Lampson's bête noir, Ali Maher. Nahas, too, was taking his power and position for granted. He was Lampson's boy; he was Eden's boy; he was Churchill's boy. No one could touch him. But then again, no one was there to call out the tanks against Farouk either. On October 8, Nahas opened a missive from the palace and read the following letter from the king:

> My dear Mustafa el-Nahas Pasha, being anxious to see our country governed by a democratic ministry working for the fatherland, applying the spirit and letter of the Constitution, establishing equality of rights and duties between all Egyptians, and finally assuring food and clothing to everyone, we have decided to dismiss you from office.

The Egyptians didn't give Nahas as much as a going-away riot, or even a demonstration. The British gave him even less. On vacation, Lampson, who mere months before had been rolling out the tanks to keep Nahas in office, was now rolling out the rationalizations. He wrote:

> Might have been worse! And if it had to happen . . . I am really relieved that it has been during my absence. . . . Anyway I having been absent at the time cannot be charged either by Nahas or the Wafd with having let them down. . . . And anyway the crucial time of danger from the war angle is safely past. Nahas did us well then; and one must stand by one's friends. That I have done—up to the hilt; indeed many people think too much so. But if there had to be a change—and I reckon there had—better, ever so much better, whilst I was away.

In his diary Lampson lamented that he and the British would never again have anyone quite so "in our pockets" as Nahas, but such were politics and such was Egypt. Thus in the battle for control of the country, King Farouk had finally "beaten" Lampson, albeit in the same devious way he had "beaten" him in their duck shoot. But for the compulsively controlling Lampson, the ouster of Nahas was the one loose thread that unraveled the entire quilt.

A series of brutal assassinations reminded the British that Egypt was not merely a tropical resort with the fillip of antiquities, while a newly confident King Farouk fanned the campfires of nationalism into an anti-British conflagration. By 1946, Lampson's glorious career dreams had turned to ashes. At sixty-six, he was relieved as ambassador to Egypt after serving for thirteen years, and he was denied the grand prize of viceroy of India, after nearly dying of encouragement for it. Instead, he was put out to pasture, or rather to rice paddy, in Singapore as special commissioner for Southeast Asia. Privately, Farouk danced a jig on the grave of his nemesis's ambition, but to Lampson's face he was the perfect British gentleman. He gave Lampson a farewell luncheon banquet at Abdine, where Lampson noted sadly: "However pleased at heart he must be, and doubtlessly is, to see my back, he is a good actor and does not show it." Lampson spent the rest of his life ruing his own fair play. He had had three big opportunities to oust the boy; each time he gave him another chance "to be good." Lampson had hesitated and he had lost. To the victor, Farouk, belonged the spoils of the Middle East.

With Nahas gone and Lampson gone, Farouk was, for the first time in his reign, the undisputed ruler of his country. He was at last a king who could reign *and* rule. He was also the autocrat of his own personal life. Soon after Fadia was born, Queen Farida abandoned the pretense of marriage and moved with her daughters out of Abdine into their own wing in Koubbeh. His wife was out of his life. Soon his mother would be, too, as would his only father figure, when his chief adviser, Hassanein, would die in a car crash with the same kind of British lorry that had nearly killed Farouk. Queen Nazli would take a new lover and depart for America, leaving Farouk with no restraints whatsoever, political, marital, or filial. With absolute power and absolute freedom and absolute wealth, Farouk was faced with the dilemma of having an epicure's temperament and a statesman's task. He had the splendid opportunity to become *the* modern leader of the entire Middle East. Yet he was surrounded by all the temptations of an Oriental potentate and hamstrung by the inexperience that was a by-product of his political immaturity perpetuated by Lampson. Nevertheless, the occasion was there. The entire world watched Egypt and wondered if the charming, fair-haired boy-king could rise to it.

X

JIHAD

The year 1945 was arguably the most cataclysmic year of the twentieth century—the year of the dead. Following the lead of Rommel, Hitler committed suicide. Mussolini was strung up by his scrotum. Quisling, Petain, and Laval were all sentenced to death. Roosevelt was felled by a cerebral hemorrhage, Patton by a car crash, and Hiroshima and Nagasaki ended World War II. That year also marked the transformation of Egypt from wartime oasis to political charnel house, with the assassination of Prime Minister Ahmed Maher in the Egyptian Parliament kicking off a fanatical death fest that would continue up until, and beyond, the time when King Farouk was able to neither reign nor rule. The vast extremes of wealth and poverty and of power and impotence between pasha and fellah made Egypt a roiling cauldron of sociopolitical discontent that could no longer be contained by the repressions of pharaonic fealty and colonial politesse. Yet, oddly enough, when King Farouk finally bested Sir Miles Lampson and took control of his own country, the biggest problem he faced was not Egypt. It was Israel.

Farouk's troubles with Israel originated, as did so many of his troubles, in England. In 1941, Anthony Eden had given a speech at Mansion House in the City of London exhorting the countries of the Middle East to band together as a desert bulwark against the designs of not only the Nazis but also the Communists. Eden foresaw Stalin as becoming a serious threat to the global balance of power when Hitler was defeated, and in this he was prescient. What Eden envisaged was a docile league of camel kingdoms, entirely in awe of and dependent on the British, and, accordingly, Eden looked to Lampson, who looked to his man Nahas to become the prime mover in forging this alliance of the shifting sands, beneath which lay the oil that gave these countries their vital importance.

In October 1944, Nahas brought all the leaders of the major Arab states (Egypt, Syria, Lebanon, Iraq, Transjordan, Saudi Arabia, and Yemen) together in Alexandria, where they signed the Protocol of the Arab League. For Nahas it was an international diplomatic triumph, his first and his last. For Egypt it made little sense. Until then Egypt had never viewed itself as an Arab country. The only things it had in common with Arabia and Jordan and Iraq, aside from barren terrain and climate and cradles of civilization, were that most of their populations were Muslim and most of these spoke Arabic.

To describe Egypt as Arab would have caused Sultan Moham-med Ali and the khedive Ismail to turn over—and over—in their graves. Their efforts had brought Egypt out of Arabia, out of Af-rica, out of the past, and well into Europe and sophisticated modern civilization, as any of the wartime bon vivants would gladly attest. Egypt was "cosmopolitan"; Cairo was the Paris of Africa; the coun-try was a melting pot of Christians and Copts and Byzantines and Greek Orthodox and Jews. The underclass might have been squarely Muslim, but whoever thought of Egypt in terms of its underclass? And who would ever dare compare Cairo and Alexan-dria, those pinnacles of urbanity, to Amman or Damascus or Bagh-dad, unless perhaps they were talking of Baghdad on the Hudson?

On the other hand, if the choice were that of being the stepchild of Europe or the godfather of the desert, the latter choice might be viewed with considerably more favor. Standing at the helm of the Arab League in effect gave King Farouk a free and ready-made empire, one that he didn't have to conquer. Besides, Farouk, for all his self-indulgences, had always been a good and respectful Muslim, abjuring alcohol, even growing his holy-man beard. He had quite fancied the notion of assuming the title of Caliph of All Islam. Being the head of the Arab League was the secular equivalent of that holy of holies. What Farouk made the grave error of not realiz-ing was that in expropriating the fruits of Nahas's diplomatic la-bors, he was also assuming a lien of immense responsibility toward his Muslim brethren. Farouk's Arab empire wasn't anywhere as free as he thought it was. In the end it cost him his throne.

The first rumbling of disequilibrium came shortly after the Arab League Protocol was signed and Nahas was dismissed in October 1944. On November 6, while Lampson was still on his ill-fated holiday in South Africa, smarting from Farouk's *coup de Nahas,* the British minister of state running the embassy in his absence, Lord Moyne, was assassinated in the backseat of his black Humber as he was being driven to lunch at his villa across from the Gezira Sporting Club. His murderers were two members of a secret society known as the Fighters for the Freedom of Israel, otherwise called the Stern Gang, after Abraham Stern, the founder.

Lord Moyne, Walter Edward Guinness, as in Guinness stout, was from one of Ireland's grandest and richest families. The beer baron was a close friend of Winston Churchill's, whose Indian giving in regard to the establishment of a Jewish army in Palestine led to the Stern Gang's reprisal. Churchill and Anthony Eden had promised the Jews such a force, but their largess was blocked by the Palestine administration. Lord Moyne, who was then colonial secretary, had to deliver the bad news to Zionist leaders Chaim Weizmann and David Ben-Gurion. From then on, radical Zionists wanted to kill the messenger, especially given Moyne's activities in setting up the Arab League. The Stern Gang saw the league as an enemy of the Jewish people, though probably less so than Britain itself as the hypocritical evil genius behind the league and against Zionism. Lord Moyne was thus selected as a symbolic target, one that would send a message to both the Arabs and especially the British that the Zionists were not to be toyed with.

The Stern Gang sent its two hit men, both in their early twenties, to Cairo to shadow Moyne. The senior partner, Eliahu Hakim, found himself a girlfriend to go on long, hand-holding, romantic strolls around the leafy mansion—intensive thoroughfares of the Garden City area, where Moyne worked, and of Zamalek, where he lived, to reconnoiter the diplomat's every move. When they were ready, Hakim and his accomplice, another Eliahu, last name Bet-Zouri, ambushed and killed both Lord Moyne and his lance-corporal chauffeur at close range. The assassins escaped down the servants' back alleys of Zamalek on their bicycles. They were apprehended by an Egyptian policeman and might have escaped had they shot him, but they were under specific orders to shoot only British. Killing an Egyptian would have alienated the opinion of the public they wanted to convince that the British were the true enemy of Arab and Jew alike. Because of this p.r. mandate, the two terrorists were caught, tried, and quickly sentenced to be hanged.

It was the worst blow against the British in Egypt since the 1924 murder of the Egyptian Army commander Sir Lee Stack, a murder for which, incidentally, Farouk's new prime minister, Ahmed Maher, and his chief parliamentary ally (then and now), Fahmy Nokrashi, were both indicted though ultimately acquitted. Most British thought that they had clamped down sufficiently since then that such an act of terrorism would never happen again, though Cairo Chief of Police Sir Thomas Russell remained prepared for the worst, carrying in his car a revolver and a sawed-off twelve-bore shotgun. It never occurred to the British that terrorists could be Zionists.

Caught by surprise, Winston Churchill thought the Jews had betrayed him, not considering the feeling among many Jews that Churchill had betrayed *them.* "If our dreams for Zionism are to end in the smoke of an assassin's pistol, and the labors for its future produce a new set of gangsters worthy of Nazi Germany, then many like myself will have to reconsider the position we have maintained so consistently and so long in the past," Churchill warned world Jewry and its fellow travelers from the House of Commons.

Jewry, at least the pro-Zionist element, mythologized rather than denounced the two terrorists. American Jewish leaders amassed a defense fund for the two Eliahus and dispatched a team of high-powered civil liberties lawyers to Cairo to prevent the execution of the Zionist "martyrs." This incensed Churchill even further as he leaned on Lampson to make sure Moyne's killers were terminated without delay. This was Churchill's January 29, 1944, "personal and top secret" telegram:

> I hope you will realise that unless the sentences duly passed upon the assassins of Lord Moyne are executed it will cause a marked breach between Great Britain and Egypt. Such a gross interference with the course of justice will not be compatible with the friendly relations we have established. As they may be under pressure from Zionist and American Jewry, I think it right to let you have my personal views on the matter.

Lampson, in turn, leaned on Farouk and Ahmed Maher not to yield to American pressures, and warned that "any failure to confirm the sentence would have a disastrous effect." Ahmed Maher promised Lampson the hangings would proceed by the book and added "that so far as outside pressure was concerned (and he admitted there was much of it) he was deliberately refusing to read any of the shower of telegrams which were descending upon him from all sorts of quarters, especially America, urging clemency." In the end, the British prevailed in their eye-for-an-eye insistence on retribution. In March, the freedom fighters were hanged. Standing at the gallows, Eliahu Hakim, for his last words, pronounced that the red burlap prison outfit in which Egyptian criminals were customarily executed was the finest suit he ever wore. In 1975, the bodies of the two Eliahus were exhumed from their guarded graves in Heliopolis and traded for twenty live Egyptian terrorists held in Israeli jails. The Stern Gang killers were then reinterred in Jerusalem in a massive ceremony honoring them as war heroes.

Although Farouk had assured Churchill "that he had every intention . . . that they [the Jewish assassins] should be strung up in accordance with the sentence of the court," the "Jewish" issue left him in a terribly conflicted position that would be exacerbated as the question of Palestine rose to the fore as *the* burning issue of the Middle East. The crunch was that "some of Farouk's—and Egypt's —best friends were Jewish." Aside from the preeminent role of the Jewish pasha class, the "Our Crowd" of Cairo and Alexandria, in the nation's financial and political affairs, the Jews were equally indispensable to Farouk's social life. Helen Mosseri was the king's favorite matchmaker, his own Dolly Levi. Lampson described her as one of the king's "special buddies" and snidely wrote about the "special telephone by her bedside with which King F was accustomed to ring her up at any hour of the day or night—for instance at about 1 A.M. in the morning and say that he wished to have a gambling party forthwith, and so on."

Irene Najjar had been Farouk's very favorite mistress. So piqued was Farouk when she left him to marry a British soldier that, in his despair, he vowed to "make war against the Jews," among other self-destructions if he couldn't have her back. To forget Irene, Farouk had begun an affair with another gorgeous Alexandrian Jewess, Lilianne Cohen, who under the *nom de théâtre* Camelia was the star chanteuse of the Auberge des Pyramides. While at the nightclub she would perform the latest American hits, such as "Sentimental Journey" and "Accentuate the Positive;" in the palace she would beguile Farouk with Yiddish love songs and folk dances, and always wore a Star of David around her neck. Unlike Irene, who was Farouk's preferred blonde on blonde, Lillian was dark and sultrily Semitic. She had a superb figure, was all self-confidence and compelling in a way that only entertainers can be and was Farouk's favorite age for a young woman: sixteen.

Just as his father before him, Farouk loved the Jews, literally. Jews and Muslims had peacefully coexisted in Egypt for centuries, and the Jews were integral to the Mohammed Ali dynasty's ambitious progressivism. The great art deco synagogue in downtown Cairo was one of modern Egypt's most impressive monuments and a dominating symbol of the Jews' position. Before the murder of Lord Moyne, there was no racial issue. Despite the Zionists' insistence on maintaining a stance that was anti-British and never specifically anti-Arab, the insoluble question of Palestine made a pan-Semitic alliance against English colonialism a ludicrous fantasy, a pipe dream that became a pipe bomb. The Mideast became a race riot in which Jews, Arabs, and Englishmen were all at one anothers' throats.

In early 1945, in what was to be the beginning of a special friendship that helped support Farouk in his European exile, he sailed on the *Mahroussa* to Saudi Arabia to visit King Ibn Saud and his forty sons, and afterward, Mecca. It was the first step in Farouk's program as figurehead of the Arab League to "Arabize" himself. Dressed in a *kayfiya* that made him look like Yasir Arafat, Farouk exchanged traditional cheek kisses with Ibn Saud, watched tribal parades of warriors shooting rifles, sat on rare carpets and ate roasted sheep, drank gallons of Arab coffee and holy water, and received priceless jeweled swords and daggers from Ibn Saud, whom Farouk presented with the equally priceless necklace of one of Mohammed Ali's wives, ostensibly to give to one of Saud's. When Ibn Saud saw Farouk back onto his yacht anchored on the Red Sea, the Arab king gave the Egyptian one last going-away present of ten pedigreed Arab stallions and a dozen camels, declaring, "even if they had been made of gold they would have been a very small offering." In a nod to desert simplicity and austerity befitting the Arabians, Farouk humbly told the king of the Wahabis (known as the Puritans of Islam); "The most important thing is that I have met you."

Farouk soon returned the Wahabi hospitality, inviting Ibn Saud to Cairo in February to meet with him, Haile Selassie of Ethiopia, and Roosevelt and Churchill, who were stopping in Cairo on their way back from the Yalta Conference with Stalin on the Black Sea. The six-foot-five, sixty-five-year-old Saudi monarch, wearing a billowing *aba* and a gold-crowned headdress, was taken to Egypt on an American destroyer sent to Jeddah by Roosevelt. Ibn Saud arrived with his party of forty-eight retainers, including his royal coffeemaker, purse bearer, and ten bodyguards armed with swords and daggers. The ship was soon transformed into a floating magic carpet. The gray decks were covered with Oriental rugs, plush gilt chairs were arranged along the railings, and a barefoot Arab captain took command and steered the ship out into the Red Sea toward Ismailia. A herd of sheep was also brought aboard, bleating loudly, to provide the evening's shish kebab feast, after which the king slept in a silk tent constructed beside the gun turret of the front deck. After meeting with Roosevelt, Farouk, and Haile Selassie on the American President's warship anchored in the Great Bitter Lake near the Suez Canal, the party moved up the Nile to the Fayoum oasis, to the Hotel du Lac, the new hunting lodge that Farouk had recently had constructed for his duck shoots.

Because of logistical and protocol snafus as to whether the Americans or the British had the responsibility for flying Selassie back to Addis Ababa, Selassie left in a huff without seeing Churchill. Lampson did not weep at the abrupt departure of the Lion of Judah, whom he perceived as ungrateful to the British for their role in getting him back his throne. Lampson, who had a special passion for men as large as himself, was mightily impressed with King Ibn Saud.

> A magnificent man of most commanding presence. His first remark to me was that he seldom met anyone bigger than himself. I don't think anyone could help being immensely impressed by him. . . . He had with him an immense retinue and immediately behind him stood a bevy of slaves who ministered to his wants preparing his dishes for him, etc. He drank special water brought from Mecca which he insisted upon both Anthony Eden and Winston sampling. The rest of us were supplied with whiskies and sodas but served in colored glasses and described (to spare Wahabi susceptibilities) as "medicine."

Lampson was also mightily impressed by King Ibn Saud's generosity. Among the gifts the king presented to Churchill were "diamond rings, a jeweled sword and dagger, exotic scents, . . . ambergris, some curious bottles containing spices, a large case of attar of roses and a whole trunkful of magnificent robes," with which

Popperfoto

Power Elite • Farouk and his ministers, with his favorite, Aly Maher, at his far left, and his enemy, Moustapha Nahas, at his immediate right.

War Games • Lady Lampson, General "Jumbo" Wilson, and Farouk, who intentionally stepped on Lady Lampson's feet at diplomatic balls.

UPI/Bettmann

Soft Underbelly • Sir Miles Lampson's supposed bulwark against the Axis threat, Prime Minister Moustapha Nahas, a reconnaissance at one of the cabarets where bar girls might be spies.

The Good Mother • (bottom, left) Queen Farida with daughter Princess Ferial. Farida's failure to bear Farouk a son was perceived as a blot on the king's masculinity.

New World Order • (bottom, right) Farouk, as the leader of the Arab world, meets President Franklin D. Roosevelt after the Yalta Conference in 1945.

Lampson and Eden played like schoolchildren in dressing Churchill up like Lawrence of Arabia. Lampson made an appraiser's guess that all the Arabian largess totaled up to 3,500 English pounds. He was abashed that all they had to give King Ibn Saud in return were a measly hundred pounds worth of perfume that Churchill's aide had picked up in a Cairo bazaar. Not one to be shown up, they improvised a grand gesture of promising the king that a custom-built bulletproof Rolls-Royce was being prepared for him in England. Churchill ended up selling off all the king's gifts to pay for the car.

All the arabesques nearly distracted Churchill from the other king, Farouk, who had visited the soon-to-die Roosevelt on his warship in Ismailia. Churchill did belatedly invite Farouk out for a private conference at the British "Blue House" across from the pyramids. The slight was compounded when a security guard detained Farouk, proudly dressed in his favorite British air marshal uniform, for trying to go through the wrong entrance. When the king finally got in to see the prime minister, Churchill assumed Lampson's role as a stern father figure to the boy, and a politically enlightened one at that. As Lampson described it:

> Winston . . . told Farouk that he should take a definite line in regard to the improvement of the social conditions in Egypt. He ventured to affirm that nowhere in the world were the conditions of extreme wealth and extreme poverty so glaring. What an opportunity for a young Sovereign to come forward and champion the interest and living conditions of his people. Why not take from the rich Pashas some of their superabundant wealth and devote it to the improvement of the living conditions of the fellaheen? Winston kept on rubbing this in strongly.

Farouk said that he couldn't agree with Churchill more and was seriously studying the matter. Farouk was more interested in his country's external image than its internal inadequacies. He wanted very much for Egypt to be represented at the upcoming conference in San Francisco that would found the United Nations. The catch for Egypt here was that only countries that had fought in the war would qualify for attendance. If Egypt were to be considered a "founder member" of the U.N., it would have to declare war within two weeks, which smacked to Farouk of opportunism. Nonetheless,

Churchill urged Egypt on, stroking Farouk that given all Egypt's "material assistance" during the war, it would be a shame for the country to be left out of the peace action in San Francisco. The declaration was a mere technicality.

Encouraged by Churchill, who wolfed down a farewell supper of bacon, eggs, and beer and flew off to London in the new Skymaster plane Roosevelt had given him, Farouk set his new prime minister to the task of getting Egypt into the United Nations. The country had been kept out of the peace conference in Versailles in 1919. To join the upcoming one in San Francisco would signify Egypt's true independence to the entire world. Ahmed Maher's main accomplishment as prime minister thus far was having released all the so-called Axis sympathizers, including his brother, Ali Maher, from internment. Now he had the chance to play the statesman.

On February 24, having won the support of the Chamber of Deputies for the declaration of war, Ahmed Maher was proceeding through Parliament's marble halls toward the Egyptian Senate. There he encountered a young lawyer named Mahmoud Isawi, the son of an undersecretary at the Ministry of Communications. Isawi stood up to greet Ahmed Maher. Then he unsheathed a revolver and fired three bullets into Ahmed Maher point-blank. Informed of the shooting, Lampson rushed over from the British embassy, which was, in a telling juxtaposition, across the street from Parliament. By the time Lampson arrived, Ahmed Maher was dead.

Lampson learned that the assailant was a fanatical member of the pro-Axis Young Egypt Society. That morning, Ahmed Maher had actually received a threatening letter from Isawi, promising to shoot the prime minister if he proceeded with the war declaration. Ahmed Maher had brushed off the letter, handing it over to the parliamentary police whom Cairo Police Chief Russell later flayed for "a very bad case of disgraceful police work. . . . They are a fancy body of men . . . dressed in a splendid uniform of their own, carry Webley revolvers which they have never fired and which were none of them loaded at the time of the crime." The disgrace to Egyptian justice was further underscored when Isawi escaped police custody for sanctuary in Syria.

When Ahmed Maher was killed, Lampson went to pay respects to Maher's family at their house in Koubbeh, near Farouk's country palace where the estranged Farida was living. Lampson was taken aback when he arrived and found that of all people it was the wicked Aly Maher who was receiving condolences. . . . I naturally brushed aside any personal aspects and went into the house where I found Aly Maher surrounded by relatives in the deepest gloom. I shook him by the hand and told him how shocked and grieved we all were. It was rather an ordeal, for the womenfolk of the family were shrieking loudly with grief. . . . There were many elderly relatives at the entrance all sobbing and howling in the most unrestrained way.

This scene of grief would repeat itself many times in the years ahead as Egyptian politics seemed to turn into a target range. Ahmed Maher was succeeded as prime minister by his alleged former co-conspirator in the Sir Lee Stack murder, Mahmoud Fahmy Nokrashi, who himself would be assassinated in 1948. In Egypt, one was either a shooter or a shootee. Age had not stilled Nokrashi's anti-British fervor. With the war over, Farouk thought it was high time for the British to honor their promises to end their occupation and pull their troops off the city streets and back to the canal zone. The British authorities stonewalled Farouk on any departure. Accordingly, Nokrashi demanded a renegotiation of the 1936 "independence" treaty. Britain balked again, and the old rabble-rouser and new prime minister sent the nationalist students to riot in the streets.

Even though Nahas had been cast to the sidelines by both Egyptians and British, in radical nationalist eyes he was still guilty by association with Lampson. His car was bombed, but Nahas wasn't in it. The nationalists did kill Nahas's chief lieutenant and the Wafd's chief liaison to the British, Amin Osman. Oxford man Osman was probably Lampson's favorite Egyptian, but his type of Bond Street Cairene was a most endangered species. The Middle East was the new Wild West.

Gamal Abdel Nasser wrote that he and his entire generation were moved toward violence. "To my excited imagination, political assassination appeared to be the positive action we had to adopt if we were to rescue the future of our country." Nasser, his fellow alienated officers, the Muslim Brotherhood, and various student groups began scanning the pasha class for pro-British enemies of the state, or at least the state they idealized. Creating a pasha hit list, they would play not only judge and jury, but high executioner as well. The descendants of the slaves who built the great pyramids were about to cast off the psychological yokes of centuries, and the issue that galvanized them was Palestine, that emblem of colonial oppression and Zionist aggression.

Lampson might have been diagnosed as suffering from end-stage colonialism. Even as the bodies were dropping around him, he held high the banner of the white man's burden. Here was his position on the Palestine issue, expressed in April 1945, when the entire issue of partitioning the country into Jewish and Arab sectors was beginning to be debated back in England.

> It had always struck me that we should do well, seeing that we had now practically won the war, to approach the Palestine problem from the purely British angle. Indeed, given a free hand, I should have plucked up my courage to have disregarded all external factors including pressure from America, and to have come out boldly with a decision that being in Palestine we were just going to stay there indefinitely and that our future standard should be simply and solely that of our world strategy; that this war had confirmed the vital importance of certain factors, to wit, communications and oil. It so happened that Palestine covered both. Accordingly, I should tell the world perfectly straight that . . . we were determined to stay where we were regardless of the shrieks of either Arab or Jew. . . . Damn it all, were we not winning the war and was it not time that we . . . do what we damn well thought best and most expedient in our own interests?

Lampson's hard line presupposed the Britain of the Raj, of Kipling, of Queen Victoria. It ignored the reality of the toll that the war had taken on the already tottering British Empire. The glory days were over. Britain couldn't *afford* an empire anymore. Lampson, like his empire, was an anachronism. He was too much even for England. He wanted to be viceroy, but viceroy of *what?* The way things were going, India wasn't going to be there to kick around much longer, while Egypt was already kicking back. With every pronunciamento, Lampson dug one more shovel of dirt into his diplomatic grave, and when Churchill was replaced as prime minister by Clement Attlee of the Labour Party, Lampson's end was in sight.

In August 1946, the Union Jack was lowered over the citadel in the hills above the City of the Dead. Farouk kissed the green Egyptian flag before it was raised, replacing the British one. Then the British troops marched out of the Egyptian fortress, after having held it as their chief base of Cairo operations since 1882. A month later, led by General, now Lord, Montgomery, the British also evacuated their wartime barracks along the Nile in downtown Cairo, as well as their headquarters in Alexandria. Their retreat to the canal zone had begun.

The student riots that had erupted under firebrand Prime Minister Nokrashi had had their effect on a Britain too spent to fight anymore. The Labour foreign secretary, Ernest Bevin, was an antiimperialist who wanted to make peace with Farouk and Egypt and therefore agreed to the troop evacuation. Intent on working out a new Anglo-Egyptian treaty, Bevin also pulled the plug on a flabbergasted Sir Miles Lampson. Lampson was shuffled off to Singapore and replaced with a nonavuncular, nonarrogant, polite, and conciliatory career diplomat named Sir Ronald Campbell. He didn't have Lampson's stature but Britain was now a Labour country and such stature was no longer the required or even desirable hallmark of London's man in Cairo.

Lampson's last day in his post was March 9, 1946. Two hundred British employees, soldiers, and diplomats but almost no native Cairenes of the upper orders assembled at the embassy to say farewell and present Lampson with a rose bowl of Turkish silver as a token of their esteem. It was the nadir of an awful year for Lampson, who just the week before had ignominiously split his formal trousers at a fancy dress reception and was having terrible dental problems to boot. He realized the minute he got his change-of-post telegram from "Ernie" Bevin that he was being, as he put it, "kicked upstairs." He warned the Foreign Office of the error of its decision in one of his last missives before, perfect civil servant he was, heading east to accept his fate.

> Nothing could be more damaging to our prestige in Egypt, for it will be obviously regarded by the public here as a complete triumph by the palace over the Embassy and that, I think, is going to be disastrous.

Lampson was right, at least about the public perception of his transfer. Once Nahas was out of office and the British troops out of Cairo, Farouk barely thought about Lampson or his successor. The

king relished his new unfettered power and the prospects for increasing it. But Farouk's emphasis was less on the power than on
the lack of fetters. The throne was like the ultimate toy. Farouk
didn't rush off to build dams and schools and hospitals, or become a
royal Robin Hood and take from the rich and give to the poor.
What he did was dress up, the way Lampson and Eden dressed up
Churchill in Ibn Saud's robes. Farouk was like a little boy whose
parents had gone away and whose nanny was taking a long nap.
With parental restraint lifted, he did whatever he felt like. He
played king.

Before Palestine erupted into a full-scale war, Farouk went on a
new epicurean binge, but it wasn't like the fatalistic one he embarked on in 1942, after his humiliation by Lampson and in view of
the dire prospect of losing his throne to the Nazis. That was a
rampage of insecure self-indulgence. Farouk's postwar *grand bouffe*
was founded on total security, if not hubris. He was so self-confident that Louis XIV might have had to reach for sunglasses to
shield himself from the glare of Farouk's extravagances. Farouk's
newest passion was that of eminent domain. Under the guise of
developing the Palace Collections of Egypt into a monument to the
country's splendor, the already compulsive collector became a regal
kleptomaniac. Now if he pilfered Churchill's watch, he would simply keep it in the name of the state. No house or palace was safe
from the king's predatory glance. Pashas hid their best paintings,
furniture, and china if the king was coming to one of their parties.
His greatest passions were weapons, coins, and postage stamps. In
these areas his collections were among the finest in the world. But
he was not above removing an emerald brooch or a ruby necklace
from the plunging bodice of a princess or wife of a pasha and thanking her for her gift to the nation.

Nor was Farouk above expropriating the princess or the wife
herself. For example, millionaire Baron Empain, who built the Paris
metro and retired to a great Heliopolis villa in the style of a Hindu
temple, had a widowed daughter-in-law whom Farouk fancied. She
was a saucy British stripper-showgirl who had caught the baron's
late son's eye onstage at the London Palladium. The son made a
baroness out of her. Farouk wanted to make something else. When
she refused, she found that her immigration papers had been re-
voked. To avoid Egyptian red tape and further royal propositions,
the not so merry widow left Cairo for the French Riviera.

Farouk also had a very strange flirtation with Princess Peter of Greece, which gives some sense of his curious style of courtship. Lampson described the dance that Crown Prince and Princess Peter were giving, when

> one of the servants had come to her [Princess Peter] and said that King Farouk had climbed over the hedge and got in by the back door and had gone upstairs where "for safety" the servant had locked him, the Monarch, into Princess Peter's room. She had gone upstairs and found him there and explained that this was a highly unconventional proceeding on his part: he had better come down and join the rest. This he had refused to do so she went out and fetched Prince Peter and together they induced him to go into the neighboring room opening onto the same balcony. She and her husband had then gone downstairs and told the two Touson princesses, Helen Mosseri and some other lady . . . that their Monarch was upstairs and refused to come down. What about it? The four of them had then gone up and joined the Monarch. . . .

As a ladies' man, Farouk combined elements of Romeo and Buster Keaton, Don Juan and Daddy Warbucks, and Casanova and Caligula. He had a divine-right approach to the opposite sex. He saw no great difference between seducing a woman and giving an order to one of his chamberlains; he expected both to jump to attention. He also loved to tease in the most infantile way. Once on winter holiday in Upper Egypt, he took a liking to one of the beautiful Ades girls whom he saw at a ball at the New Cataract Hotel. The Adeses were, with the Rolos, the Cattawis, and the Mosseris, the gratin of Cairo Jewish society. The Ades in question was the magic age, sixteen, but she was extremely rich and extremely independent and wanted no part of Farouk, king or not. She paid no attention to his entreaties to sip orangeade with him. The Adeses' getaway was a Victorian winter palace of their own on an island in the middle of the Nile. A few days after the ball, a launch docked at the island and off came Farouk and his entourage, all armed with Purdey shotguns. They marched up to the stately home, where Antonio Pulli announced that the king was there to hunt the wild gazelles that inhabited the island. What an honor. What a horror! The Adeses, after a protracted discussion with Pulli, worked out a wildlife preservation plan. Farouk would escort their daughter to

the weekend party. Putting his gun away and returning in triumph
to his launch, Farouk, who had no intention of hunting anything
except the heiress, was thrilled that his ruse had worked. When he
saw the long-faced dream girl glaring at him through a window, this
excited him immensely. He took Mademoiselle Ades to the dance,
actually charmed her out of her antipathy into an infatuation, then
never spoke to her again.

Another of Farouk's nonconquests was Princess Ashraf, the sister
of his brother-in-law, the shah of Iran. Farouk made the first of
several proposals, not propositions, to her when she visited Cairo in
1945, accompanying her sister-in-law Fawzia home to recuperate
from an attack of malaria she caught in Teheran. Ashraf was
aghast. Farouk was married. No problem, Farouk assured her. His
marriage was one of inconvenience, a charade that needed to end.
Ashraf could provide the coup de grâce. Farouk would get a divorce
and wed her.

Or so he said. Apparently, the royal "proposal" was one of
Farouk's favorite seduction tricks, as were the royal jewels that
turned out to be fake. Furthermore, Ashraf was predisposed to be
indisposed to Farouk to begin with, as her family suspected him of
stealing the fabulous jeweled sword, belt, and medals that adorned
the body of her late father, the shah, who had died in exile from the
British in South Africa in 1944 and was buried in a great white
mausoleum on the Nile in Aswan. Although locals called Farouk's
alleged theft a funeral tax, the king denied it to the hilt and went
through a great show of an investigation, which turned up nothing.
Eight years later, when Farouk was deposed, the shah's regalia
turned up in the treasure vaults of Abdine.

After the war, Farouk began traveling. His pilgrimage to Mecca
marked his first trip out of Egypt since his demi-grand tour *cum*
skiing holiday in Europe in 1937. With the Mediterranean at peace
once again, Farouk began cruising on the *Mahroussa* or the more
intimate *Kassed Kheir,* often with his mistress of the moment
aboard on what some of them considered romantic cruises to nowhere, others voyages of the damned. Eventually, he selected Cyprus as his own Levantine Isle of Capri. He took Lilianne Cohen
there several times. On board she had to share the king's boudoir
with his new pet rabbit, also named Farouk, a virile creature who
lived up to his species' reputation. King Farouk liked to let animal
Farouk play on newspapers spread out on his bed, watching his

conquests of smitten female rabbits brought for the furry Farouk's delectation.

Farouk would take side cruises from Cyprus to the coast of Turkey to shoot the abundant game there. One of his favorite huntsman's suppers was to cook the partridge or quail that he had bagged, making a thick high-gusto gravy by mixing the animals' blood with egg and lemon, à la grecque. On the morning after, he would continue his high cholesterol orgy by topping off the Kellogg's Rice Krispies he loved for breakfast with a huge platter of eggs scrambled with the hearts and kidneys of the little game birds. Ironically, Farouk went through the fetish of being concerned about his weight by altogether eschewing bread, which was the one food he believed was fattening.

The departure of Sir Miles Lampson left Farouk without any disciplinary force in his life whatsoever. However overbearing and autocratic Lampson may have been, he did provide a perimeter to Farouk's excesses. Now the field was wide open, the horizon endless. Farouk had not taken an order from Nazli since he assumed the throne, leaving Hassanein as the only other potential authority figure in Farouk's life. But the role Hassanein took was more that of the permissive parent. Nor had Farouk really reconciled his tutor and chief of Cabinet's continuing affair with his mother; it was never discussed.

In February 1946, the sore point became a moot point. Hassanein, who had not been well, having suffered a mild heart attack at Lord Moyne's funeral, was driving home over a rain-slick bridge across the Nile when an oncoming British Army truck lost control and skidded out of its lane, slamming into Hassanein's car. The famed explorer and diplomat and the king's mentor died of internal hemorrhaging later that day at the Anglo-American hospital. He was sixty. Going through Hassanein's state and personal document file after the unexpected tragedy, Farouk found a secret morganatic marriage contract between Hassanein and Nazli, dated 1937. Father figure indeed. Once again Farouk felt betrayed. He destroyed the document and cut off all communications with his mother.

Nazli did not immolate herself on the pyre of Hassanein's memory. Soon after his death she began traveling again to Europe, ostensibly to Switzerland for medical treatment of a chronic kidney ailment. She was accompanied by her two youngest daughters, Faika and Fathia, now in their late teens but still dressed completely alike as innocent schoolgirls, with bobby sox and gray jumpers, and not a trace of makeup. Their older sister Faiza had been married in 1945, to a Turkish aristocratic distant cousin, Mohammed Bulent Raouf, a cosmopolitan charmer whom Farouk liked far better than his favorite sister Fawzia's spouse, the young shah. Romance seemed to be the furthest thing from the innocent minds of Faika and Fathia, but not so far from that of their glamorous mother, who still hadn't been able to live and love enough to compensate for King Fuad's harem repressions.

In Marseilles, Nazli met a young Egyptian consular official, a Copt named Riad Ghali. In his twenties, Ghali was tall, dark, and languid, with a pencil mustache that gave him the aura of a too-slick matinee idol in the Don Ameche/Gilbert Roland mode, or perhaps one of the suave European playboys Fred Astaire was always rescuing Ginger Rogers from by sweeping her into the continental. Nazli didn't want to be rescued, by Fred Astaire or even Clark Gable, for that matter. It was one thing for the dowager Queen Mother to have an affair with an intrepid explorer and eminent politician like Hassanein. It was quite another to dally with an unsung minor bureaucrat half her age.

Nazli's solution was to continue playing Queen Mother and pass Ghali off as Fathia's companion. Rumors began to spread, especially when photos of the trio at assorted European boîtes appeared in newsmagazines and scandal sheets. All of a sudden the demure Fathia was dressing in low-cut couture gowns, painted with makeup, dripping with diamonds. There she was, with the tuxedoed Ghali hanging on her arm, making big eyes at her, while the equally plunging, painted, and bejeweled Nazli was hanging on Ghali's arm, making big eyes at him. If the pictures told a story, here was one out of the Arabian Nights. Farouk was more appalled at his mother than ever before, but if anyone lived in a glass house, it was he. Had the great Mohammed Ali dynasty culminated in a battle of indiscretions?

Farouk managed to desecrate the late Hassanein politically even more than Nazli did romantically. In Hassanein's place, Farouk assembled a new cadre of advisers worthy of a Gilbert and Sullivan operetta. The king's favorite remained Antonio Pulli, who might best be described as the social secretary. Succeeding Hassanein as Farouk's political éminence grise was his press secretary, Karim Thabet, who quickly became the man everyone despised. Thabet came from an important Lebanese-Egyptian newspaper family that owned the influential daily *Al Mokhattam*. Thabet had won the king's favor by running a series of puff pieces about Farouk during his dark days with Lampson during the war. Thabet was a p.r. man before they even knew in Egypt what p.r. men were. He made Farouk seem like the greatest leader the country had had since Ramses. Thabet's ascent in the Farouk court was proof that flattery could get you everywhere. Thabet was a semi-hunchback, and as unctuous as his press releases. But he was capable of witty repartee, and that above all was why Farouk favored him: he amused the king.

Farouk's chief economic adviser was, like Thabet, another Egyptian of Levantine descent. Unlike Thabet, who attracted the king's attention via sycophancy, Elias Andraous did it via integrity. Andraous had been the trusted estate manager of the greatest cotton pasha in the Nile delta. When it seemed as if the Germans would be conquering Egypt, the pasha transferred titles to much of his land into Andraous's name, hoping to deceive the Nazis and thereby preserve his fortune through his straw man nominee. When the German threat passed, Andraous transferred all the land back to his master, notwithstanding his opportunities for extortion and self-dealing. His fiscal selflessness made Andraous a legend in Egypt. Here was that rarity of rarities, a Levantine with the soul of a Swiss banker. Farouk *had* to have him.

Farouk's reasons for choosing Edmond Galhan, still another Levantine, for his inner circle were far less fathomable. Galhan, who was described as "general purveyor to the Royal Palaces," was actually an arms dealer operating undercover as an importer of American fountain pens. He would make a fortune, allegedly on defective weapons, in the Palestine war in 1948. He spent much of that fortune, and much of his time, in Monte Carlo. He was also extremely superstitious and had the wherewithal to pursue all his neuroses. One of these was being close to the spirit of his late father. Galhan had his father's corpse disinterred from its Cairo cemetery, recasketed, and flown to Monaco for reburial.

There were still the barbers, valets, doctors, and kennelmen that Farouk needed around him, but Pulli, Thabet, Andraous, and Gahlan were the four horsemen of the king's apocalypse. No matter how viciously they were criticized, and they did become one of the

sorest points of the king's reign, Farouk remained completely loyal
to them.

Such loyalty was one of Farouk's most stellar character traits, but
what made the king such a wonderful friend would ultimately
brand him as a myopic politician. Although Farouk would play
high stakes poker, baccarat, and chemin de fer almost every night at
the Royal Automobile Club with his many Jewish pasha allies (and
he continued to do so, straight through the 1948 Palestine war), by
day he was making a major show of cementing his ties to the Arab
League. At first the show was all verbal. In January 1946, Farouk
and Ibn Saud met again in Cairo and issued the following proclamation:

> We associate ourselves with all Muslim Arabs in their belief
> that Palestine is an Arab country, and that it is the right of its
> people and the right of Muslim Arabs everywhere to preserve
> it as an Arab land.

It was only talk, but the talk soon began to box Farouk into a
corner he didn't really want to be in. By allying with the king of the
desert, the king of the city was making it impossible for himself to
also be king of the Jews. The urban, urbane, and altogether unpreju-
diced Farouk had Jewish friends, advisers, lovers; he even talked,
quite seriously, of making Irene Guinle his Jewish wife. If anything,
Farouk's father had inculcated in his son the notion of the Jews as
the true master race. Ibn Saud, on the other hand, took pride in
Saudi Arabia's having a *zero* Jewish population and in his never
even having *seen* a Jew in his lifetime, as he boasted to Sir Miles
Lampson. Ibn Saud's attitudes toward Jews were much more repre-
sentatively "Arab" than those of Farouk and explain how, in joining and, nominally, leading the Arab League, Farouk could not
avoid being swept up in the desert tide of anti-Zionist, anti-Jewish
revulsion.

Before he was packed off to Southeast Asia in 1946, Lampson
gave a dinner for Ibn Saud at the British embassy, at which the
Wahabi monarch uninhibitedly held forth on his various and sundry
prides and prejudices:

> Ibn Saud stressed his strong friendship for Great Britain who
> had stood by him as his friend for so long. He stated all Arabs

looked on Great Britain for protection and as their particular friend. . . . If the Arabs gave vent from time to time to anti-British sentiments, it was only like a father when cross with his son wishing him dead. But the same father would immediately strike dead whomever said "Amen" to this sentiment. He further stated that nothing could shatter Anglo-Arab friendships and understanding unless it be through an act of oppression or some act endangering Islam or the future of the Arabs. . . . He considered the Jews were at present a danger, both to Islam and Anglo-Arab relations.

Ibn Saud went on to elucidate to Lampson how the Muslims had won Palestine "by sword" from the Romans fourteen hundred years before and had taken nothing from the Jews. Accusing the British of a double standard, the Arab king asked Lampson if any European country would be expected to cede a territory it had held for fourteen centuries. Ibn Saud was also puzzled as to why the Arabs should be asked to make reparations to the Jews for the atrocities the Germans and Poles had committed during the war. Ibn Saud told Lampson he felt that Palestine was none of America's business but rather was a strictly Anglo-Arab problem. The king put it to Lampson as a "friendly warning" couched as a rhetorical question.

After Britain had sacrificed so many lives . . . in winning the war for the sake of justice and peace, were they going to sacrifice both for the sake of the Jews in Palestine? Were the Jews stronger than the Germans and Japanese?

His Majesty stated that the late President Roosevelt had told him the Jews were of no real political importance in American politics as they only controlled three million out of about fifty million votes. He, Roosevelt, did not fear Jewish opinion in America and would see the Arabs were not unjustly dealt with vis à vis the Jews. . . . He felt that all [British] soldiers disliked the Jews and this had further increased his respect and liking for them. His Majesty added, if he had a beloved friend and later he discovered this friend hated the Jews, he became even more endeared to him than before.

Such was the view of Jewry from the Arab League, of which Ibn Saud was a prime exponent. Yet at this stage of pan-Semitic affairs, Ibn Saud was not belligerent. He had never seen a Jew and would be delighted to perpetuate that state of deprivation. Ibn Saud was thus all bark, yet other Arab leaders who crossed Farouk's path were much more eager to bite. Preeminent among these was the man Farouk welcomed into Egypt in June 1946 as a "political refugee." This was Hajj Amin el-Husseini, the grand mufti of Jerusalem, undoubtedly the Arab World's most uncompromising enemy of both Zionism and English imperialism, so uncompromising that he had joined forces with the Nazis as the "fourth partner" in what he saw as a Berlin-Rome-Jerusalem-Tokyo axis during World War II in hopes of deposing his two bêtes noires—the Jews and the British—in one totalitarian swoop. When that failed, he had been held a postwar prisoner under house arrest in France, from which he escaped to Cairo and Farouk's palace hospitality with a forged Syrian passport.

Again, in granting asylum to the man the British saw as a powerful and dangerous escaped war criminal, Farouk was operating out of his Achilles' heel of loyalty. The mufti had been a close friend of Farouk's father-in-law, Farida's father, Judge Zulficar. During the post-Abdine-Palace-incident dog days of 1942, German intelligence claimed to have discovered a British plot to have Farouk assassinated. The mufti, through Judge Zulficar, who was then Farouk's ambassador to Persia, created an elaborate warning system through a code based on radio broadcasts of the Koran to alert Farouk that the attempt on his life and coup against his regime was imminent. Equally elaborate escape plans were also prepared whereby Farouk would be flown first to the safety of Field Marshal Rommel's desert headquarters and hence to the ultimate safety of the führer in Berlin. Whether the plotted coup was a red herring, an invention of the Germans to smoke Farouk out of Egypt, or a bungled but actual British operation was never known, but it was the subject of a great deal of secret German correspondence and documentation. In any event, Farouk was grateful for the solicitude and all the attention and felt that at the least he had to give shelter to the man who was dedicated to saving his life.

That same man, however, with total alacrity, would snuff out the lives of Jewish and British political enemies. Hajj Amin el-Husseini was no desert bedouin firebrand. He was an upper class, wordly man of letters, from one of the great Arab families of Jerusalem that had lived in the Holy City for centuries. Jerusalem was his birthright, and no one could have guarded it more jealously. El-Husseini, who was forty-seven when he arrived in Cairo, looked much younger. Lean, hungry, intense, he also had a revolutionary red beard that won him the appellation "Barbarossa" from British intelligence, which watched his every foxlike move. El-Husseini, who looked a bit like Alec Guinness in costume, had had a top education at Turkish schools in Jerusalem, then at Al Azhar in Cairo, from which he impatiently dropped out just before he was awarded his degree of sheikh. After his pilgrimage to Mecca, he then returned to Jerusalem, took one job as a customs official, another as a teacher, but his main avocation was tilling the fields of social upheaval.

El-Husseini had actually served as an intelligence operative for the British cause in World War I. He thought the British would "liberate" his people from the Turks, who were fighting with the Germans. They did, but only to place them under a new yoke—that of England. The Sykes-Picot Agreement of 1916 was an imperial land grab that carved up the Ottoman Middle East between the English, who got Iraq, Jordan, and Palestine as their "spheres of influence," and the French, who took Lebanon and Syria. Sykes-Picot was a supposedly secret agreement between Britain, France, and czarist Russia that came to light only when it was published by the Bolsheviks during their revolution in November 1917 as evidence of the piggishness of their *deposés*. The revelation exposed T. E. Lawrence, among other British "friends" of the Arabs, as something of an imperialist tool, a dashing and romantic tool, but a tool nonetheless. Lawrence's Hashemite allies from Mecca, Hussein, King of the Hejaz [western Arabia], his son Faisal, who became king of Iraq, and his other son, Abdullah, who became emir of Transjordan, together led the Arab revolt against the Turks. But they were viewed by el-Husseini not as Arab revolutionaries but as Anglo puppets. Indeed, the British did help Hussein's boys get their thrones and British military and fiscal intervention kept them seated.

The worst perfidy of all to el-Husseini was the letter of November 2, 1917, from the British foreign secretary, Lord Balfour, to Lord Rothschild, one of the pillars of British Jewry.

> His Majesty's Government view with favour the establishment
> in Palestine of a national Home for the Jewish people, and will
> use their best endeavours to facilitate the achievement of this
> object, it being clearly understood that nothing shall be done
> which may prejudice the civil and religious rights of existing

non-Jewish communities in Palestine, or the rights and political status enjoyed by Jews in any other country.

In 1918, the British census of Palestine listed 700,000 Arabs and 56,000 Jews. Yet the Balfour Declaration, as the above letter outlining British foreign policy for the mandated region came to be known, treated the Arab ninety-percent majority as "the existing non-Jewish communities in Palestine." Suddenly, after a thousand years of such a majority, the resident Arabs were being sloughed off as interlopers. Even that supercolonialist, Lord Curzon, the viceroy of India who succeeded Lord Balfour as foreign secretary, appreciated the now-upside-down predicament of the Palestinian Arabs, "who own the soil. . . . They will not be content either to be expropriated for Jewish immigrants, or to act merely as hewers of wood and drawers of water to the latter."

El-Husseini was definitely not content. Commencing a grass roots campaign of radical nationalism in the souks and coffeehouses of the Old City of Jerusalem, el-Husseini mobilized the vitriol that led to the Easter Sunday riots in 1920 at the Jaffa Gate that left six Jews and six Arabs dead, scores more injured, and a festering puncture wound of Semitic animosity that would never heal. El-Husseini fled to Transjordan to evade arrest. Meanwhile, he was sentenced in absentia by a British military court to fifteen years in prison for his catalytic role in what was the first act of bloodshed in the long battle over Palestine.

One negative trait el-Husseini could not accuse the British of was the capacity to bear a grudge against him. Within two years after his flight to Transjordan, he was called back to Jerusalem by the British and not only pardoned but rewarded with the powerful religio-political post of mufti, which had become vacant with the death of el-Husseini's stepbrother, who had held it for years. While Islam does not have a priesthood, if it did, mufti would be closest to bishop. The appointment of el-Husseini to the Muslim office was an act of Christian charity conceived by the Jewish high commissioner of Palestine, Sir Herbert Samuel. As a Jew in an Arab powder keg, Samuel was intent on bending over backward to demonstrate his impartiality and deep desire to keep the peace by appointing this man of war. It was a huge error of judgment. El-Husseini was not converted into a pacificist by virtue of his elevation to muftidom, nor by his subsequent appointment in 1922 by Samuel as president of the Supreme Muslim Council, which had been formed by the British as an adjunct to their mandatory government. This put him in charge of all religious funds, courts, mosques, and cemeteries. "Jerusalem, *c'est moi,*" might well have been his motto. El-Husseini, the mufti, was now *the* leader, both spiritually and temporally, of the Palestinian Arabs, and he was relentless in never giving the British or the Jews a day of rest.

By 1929, the mufti was orchestrating a new wave of bloody riots triggered by the Jewish erection of a portable screen at the Wailing Wall to separate the men from the women at prayer time. The mufti transmuted this seemingly innocuous gesture into a Jewish plot to expropriate the Dome of the Rock, adjacent to the Wailing Wall. The riots spread beyond Jerusalem throughout Palestine. Over a hundred Jews were killed. Now the mufti turned from the Jews to the rich Arabs, the men of his class, some of whom had sold their land to Palestine Jews. The *haute Mussulmanie* of Jerusalem knew the mufti from way back, and they knew a dictator when they saw one. Opposing his rise to power, the Arab elite accused the mufti of misusing religious funds in the millions of pounds for his own private purposes, belligerent and otherwise. In response, an estimated two thousand of these and other Arabs died in the mufti's assorted purges.

One might not have perceived the mufti as capable of such a reign of terror. He was elegant, polite, courtly, impeccably mannered, with the most mellifluous voice and delicate, perfectly manicured fingers. He spoke softly, yet he always carried a bodyguard of six men, wore a bulletproof vest under his holy robes, and traveled in an equally bulletproof Mercedes. He never arrived on time for his rendezvous. Sometimes he would be early, sometimes late, but he eschewed any pattern that would give an advantage to any of the countless enemies who wanted him assassinated.

The führer, with his prescription of genocide for the Jews and destruction for the British, was precisely the mufti's sort of man. Hitler felt likewise. As early as 1936 the Nazis began supplying funds to the mufti to accomplish his "good works" in Palestine, especially in view of the increasing numbers of European Jews arriving, beginning in 1933, fearful of the rise of Hitler. As World War II approached, the British in Palestine, now that the naive Zionist peacemaker, Sir Herbert Samuel, was gone, decided that the mufti should be put in mufti, if not in prison, for his fascistic behavior.

The British authorities stripped the mufti of all his offices and issued a warrant for his arrest. At first the mufti sought shelter from the police at the Dome of the Rock. That failing, he disguised himself as an Arab woman and fled to Lebanon. When the French government there tried to apprehend him, he continued his flight on to Iraq, arriving in Baghdad in October 1939.

The mufti's Holy Land bloodbath had scared the British into a massive retreat from the pro-Zionist stance of the Balfour Declaration. In May 1939, they issued their white paper calling for the creation of an independent binational state to be formed in Palestine in ten years and placing an annual cap on Zionist immigration into Palestine of 75,000. This, at a time when millions of Jews were fleeing from the Nazis, with nowhere but Palestine to go. America had closed its own immigration gates in 1924. Despite the alleged power of the American Jewish lobby, only a few thousand of the desperate Jews of Europe were allowed into the country. Their own vast prairies and wide-open spaces notwithstanding, Australia and Canada, too, hung out no-room-at-the-inn signs. The most generous country was the Dominican Republic, which offered to admit one hundred thousand Jews. Zionists thus saw Britain as stabbing them in the back; Arabs were delighted, although the mufti wasn't. He thought the white paper hadn't gone nearly far enough. He didn't want *any* Jews in Palestine. Perfidious as Albion may have seemed, it *was* fighting Hitler. The Jews needed all the help they could get. Still, this was another betrayal they would not forget, and the murder of Lord Moyne in Cairo in 1944 was the beginning of the payback.

Back in Baghdad, the mufti's crusade against the British was given an outlet in the power vacuum created by the death of the young Iraqi King Ghazi, son of Faisal. Ghazi was a Harrow-educated, charming bon vivant in the Farouk mode who perished in a sports car crash following a cocktail party. His six-year-old son, Faisal II, whom Farouk had already eyed as a potential mate for his youngest sister, Princess Fathia, or his oldest daughter, Princess Ferial, ascended a shaky throne.

Iraq was immensely valuable to the British because of huge oil deposits that had been discovered there, beginning in 1927, which made it, after Iran, the leading oil country in the Middle East. Germany was not unmindful of these petroleum assets, and the mufti became their ally in Baghdad. He was instrumental in the

1941 coup d'état of Colonel Rashid Ali, like the mufti a local aristocrat and nationalist anglophobe. The king's regent, Amir Abdul
Ilah, the fox-hunting brother of King Ghazi's widow and as an-
glophilic as Rashi Ali was phobic, escaped to Transjordan. This was
when the mufti made his bid to Farouk to "rescue" him from the
alleged British assassination plot; and also the time when Farouk's
chief of staff and former military tutor, General el-Masri, made his
aborted attempt to leave Egypt for Iraq to aid the pro-German
rebels (which el-Masri, once he had been captured by the British,
was cleverly able to twist to make it seem that he was traveling to
Mesopotamia to *aid* the British cause).

Ultimately, the Iraqi rebellion fizzled out because the Nazis never
came through with the aid, equipment, or troops they had promised. Hitler was too involved with his plans to invade Russia, and
the Middle East took a backseat in his strategies, much to the dismay of the Arabs, who had seen "Mohammed Haidar" as their
messiah of deliverance from British imperial domination. Farouk
kept his head and his throne, the peripatetic mufti fled once again,
first to Teheran, then to Berlin, and Iraq became more English than
ever before. His palaces furnished like stately homes in Oxfordshire,
little King Faisal II was given a British nanny and eventually was
sent on to public school in England. The year after the British
recoup, the royal Harithiyah Hunt was founded in Baghdad, but it,
too, might as well have been in Oxfordshire. With the Iraqi king on
the playing fields of Harrow, the Iraqi regent rode to the British
hounds on the playing fields of Mesopotamia, then drove home in
his very polished Rolls-Royce, albeit with Oom Kalthoum singing
on the car radio.

Such Arab Uncle Tomism was precisely what goaded the mufti
into never giving up the fight. In Berlin, he was set up in a lavish
villa on Goethestrasse. The Nazis gave the mufti a hero's welcome,
declaring "that the destruction of the so-called Jewish National
Home in Palestine is an immutable part of the greater German
Reich," while the mufti declared "that the Jews of Palestine should
be disposed of in exactly the same way that their problem was
resolved in the Axis-controlled countries—namely by extermination." The mufti urged the bombing of Tel Aviv and Jerusalem on
November 2, the date of the original Balfour Declaration, to "celebrate" its anniversary. Field Marshal Göring never had a large
enough task force to spare for the endeavor. On a less grandiose

scale, the mufti worked with Himmler to develop a sabotage school in Athens for pro-Nazi Arab terrorists, as well as to organize Albanian and Yugoslavian Muslims into SS units to oppose Marshal Tito. He aided Rommel's North Africa campaign effort with espionage contacts in Libya and Tunisia and worked hand in hand with Foreign Minister Ribbentrop to block the emigration to Palestine of four thousand Jewish children trapped by the Nazis in Bulgaria. Women and children were not to be spared, especially if they were Jewish.

After the German defeat in 1945, the mufti turned himself over to the French, whom he thought, correctly, would give him a better deal than the British. He was first interned at the Cherche-Midi prison, but soon transferred to a comfortable villa in the Paris suburbs. The French were themselves put out with the British for having thwarted their own colonial aspirations by driving Charles de Gaulle's Free French forces out of Lebanon and Syria to ensure those countries "independence." The mufti provided France with a potentially valuable wild card in the postwar shuffle.

Jews around the world wanted the mufti tried as a war criminal at Nuremberg, so much so that American Zionist leaders warned former French Premier Léon Blum that there would be no U.S. postwar aid to France until the mufti was served up for justice. The current French premier, Georges Bidault, evaded the issue by letting the mufti "escape." The deal for his release was supposedly the mufti's promise to endorse and support France's position over its North African colonies of Algeria, Tunisia, and Morocco as one of paternal protector, and not exploiter, like the British. The mufti shaved his red beard, donned a gray Western suit, was given a phony Syrian passport, and was placed on a Trans World Airlines flight to Cairo and the open arms of King Farouk, eager to return the favor the holy man had been so eager to do for him.

Like the Germans and the French, Farouk understood that the mufti had a certain standard of accommodation. Accordingly, the king of Egypt installed the "king" of Jerusalem in his lavish villa on the Nile at Helwan, Farouk's favorite seduction spot. Unlike Farouk, who, when he was at Helwan, partied until dawn and slept until noon with his mistress of the moment, the mufti slept never more than three hours, woke at sunrise, and knelt to the east to pray to Mecca on the little prayer rug his father had given him forty years before. Wherever he had fled, whether to Baghdad, Berlin, or

Cairo, the rug was the one possession he never left behind. After his prayers, the mufti did the calesthenics that maintained his athleticism. Then he went out in the gardens overlooking the broad green Nile and visited the chicken coop he had had constructed under Farouk's palms and bougainvillea. The mufti loved chickens. He loved scattering grain before them and watching them gobble up the feed just as much as he loved mass murder. After his morning ritual, the mufti served Arabic coffee and held court to old followers in exile as well as potential new followers in Egypt, like Captain Gamal Abdel Nasser, who came to volunteer his services in the mufti's ongoing crusade "to drive the Jews into the sea," and with them the British.

Even though the mufti had been out of Palestine for nearly seven years, the British estimated that at least ninety-five percent of all Palestinian Arabs would do whatever he bid them. The British were understandably uneasy about the mufti's presence in a Cairo where assassination was becoming endemic. In London, Winston Churchill denounced Farouk's hospitality and called on the Labour government to apprehend the war criminal. Yet Britain was unwilling to send the holy man back to Nuremberg and thereby create a new holy war in Egypt. The mufti announced that he was "at King Farouk's mercy," which gave Farouk an even greater sense of his own power by having this charismatic fanatic in his midst. However, mercy had absolutely nothing to do with it. The mufti's revolutionary presence was of some significance in the British decision to pull their troops out of Cairo and Alexandria and back to the canal zone within a few months of the mufti's arrival.

Other beneficiaries of Farouk's hospitality that summer were King Victor Emanuel and Queen Elena of Italy, who came to live in Alexandria after Victor Emanuel abdicated in May. Again Farouk was simply returning a favor, as Italy had received the khedive Ismail when he was forced to abdicate. Yet by his good manners, what Farouk ended up with was a Fascist king and a Nazi mufti. He did nothing to endear himself to Fleet Street, which would use his hospitality to kick off a campaign of vilification against Farouk that would continue through his abdication until long after his death.

Farouk's perceived alliance with the mufti also brought him closer to the man who saw himself as the mufti's counterpart in Egypt, Sheikh Hassan el Banna. Given his fellah background, compared to the noble roots of the holy man from Jerusalem, el Banna was something of a poor man's mufti. Both were ascetic fundamentalists, studied at Al Azhar, preached their messages in the souks and in the mud-hut villages, and were superb rabble-rousers. Until now, the mufti had been much quicker on the trigger than the Supreme Guide, who had been essentially a vociferous man of peace, not a mellifluous man of war. Furthermore, el Banna's targets were not so much the Jews as the infidel British and the decadent pasha class. Farouk's position at the pinnacle of the latter had to have been the cause of some discomfort in the face of el Banna's puritan ire and may explain Farouk's abstinence from liquor, Friday mosque attendance, occasional pious beards, and other displays of religious circumspection. Notwithstanding the women and the gambling and the nightclubs and the big spending, Farouk was, in essence, a good and devout Muslim. With a stickler like el Banna as the religious gadfly of the state, Farouk had to be. After all, for many years he aspired to be Caliph of All Islam, Protector of the Faith. Piety had to begin at home.

The Palestine issue, and the volatile presence of the mufti in Egypt, served to refocus el Banna's sacred wrath. The Muslim Brotherhood now numbered over a million Egyptians, and the movement had become as political as it was religious. These people, almost all poor and disenfranchised peasants who had moved off the land into the cities, wanted their piece of Egypt's postwar pie. Basically unscathed by the war, Egypt was the richest country in the Middle East, but the wealth was even more maldistributed. Now there were five hundred millionaires in the country instead of the fifty antebellum plutocrats. These pashas, representing less than half of one percent of all landowners, owned a third of all cultivated land in the country. Yet Egypt was past the "let them eat cake" point, where Farouk could distract the fellaheen from their deprivations by flying in one of his planes over the mud-hut villages along the Nile and dropping colored Ping-Pong balls for the peasants to redeem for boxes of candy at the royal military depots.

Great Britain owed Egypt a stunning sterling balance for war debts of over four hundred million pounds, but little of that was likely to trickle down from the felt tables of the Royal Automobile Club to the fellaheen, over eighty percent of whom suffered from ophthalmia and bilharzia. This was one case where religion could not stand alone as the opiate of the masses. Following the mufti's example, Supreme Guide el Banna called his brotherhood to arms, forming paramilitary cells and swearing in new adherents with a Koran in one hand and a revolver in the other.

As menacing as the mufti and the Supreme Guide were to the established state of things in Egypt, Farouk and his pasha class were in many ways relieved that peasant fundamentalists had, with the advent of the Palestine question as the burning symbolic issue of the Middle East, been distracted away from the pashas by the new villains, the Jews. Farouk and the pashas knew Egypt was too entrenched for any immediate social change that would be anything other than a mere token. The pinnacle of Egypt may have outshined the French or British aristocracies in its level of "civilization," but the discontents at the base of the social pyramid came from a desperate standard of living that rivaled the untouchables of India. Farouk proved quite adept at deflecting this boiling rage over Egypt's inequities away from himself over the slap in the face to Arab nationalism and amour propre by that old enemy of the people, the British, for their putative alliance with the Zionists of Palestine.

Not that the British were that much fonder of the Jews than the mufti. Witness the following letter to the troops from the British commanding officer in Palestine, Lieutenant General E. H. Barker, following the Jewish terrorist bombing of the British headquarters at the King David Hotel in Jerusalem in June 1946, in which the general was lightning quick to blame *all* Jews for the act of a handful:

> "If the Jewish public really wanted to stop these crimes they could do so by active co-operation with us.
>
> Consequently, I have decided that . . . you will put out of bounds to all ranks all Jewish places of entertainment, cafés, restaurants, shops, and private dwellings.
>
> I appreciate that these measures . . . will be punishing the Jews in a way the race dislikes more than any, by striking at their pockets and showing our contempt for them.

The one and only area where Jew and Arab could agree was in their hatred for the English. Regardless of what happened in Palestine, Farouk wanted the British out of Egypt. That was a platform that couldn't miss. It seemed that they were going. In June 1946, Field Marshal Montgomery was sent to Egypt by Labour Foreign

Secretary Bevin as window dressing for British troop evacuation of delta cities to the canal zone. Bevin was frank about Montgomery's presence to "ginger up" the retreat. While Montgomery was there, Farouk made a public point of politely needling the war hero that all Egypt was really suffering from was "forty years of British misrule."

Averse to any conflict, Montgomery spent most of his diplomatic time with the new prime minister, Ismail Sidky, an ailing seventy-one-year-old elder statesman who had served King Fuad as prime minister in 1930, and whom Farouk chose to replace the inflammatory Mahmoud Fahmy Nokrashi. Nokrashi had served his purpose in whipping up the flames of nationalism and scaring the British into believing that Egypt could become a revolutionary battlefield with King David Hotel–like bombings a regular occurrence. Sidky, the consummate diplomat, was called in to close the deal, that is, to conclude a new Anglo-Egyptian treaty whereby Egypt would be, once and for all, truly independent.

It almost happened. After long talks with Bevin in London, in October 1946, Sidky returned to Cairo in apparent triumph. The British move out of Egypt was under way; the only big issue that remained was who would control the Sudan, which had been an Anglo-Egyptian "condominium" ever since Lord Kitchener had vanquished the forces of the Mahdi at Omdurman, with Winston Churchill there riding with the Twenty-first Lancers. Although the Egyptian crescent flew alongside the Union Jack, all policy was sent down from London and the civil service was dominated by English foreign service officers.

Yet Egypt held on to the fiction that the Sudan was hers, and by the laws of nature had to be. As Herodotus had written, "Egypt is the gift of the Nile." Since the headwaters of the upper Nile were in the Sudan, whoever controlled that country thereby controlled the lifeblood of Egypt. Egypt could not be in a position where its water could be shut off no more than Britain could be in one where its imperial honor could be besmirched, its colonial grandeur sullied. The result was one of the most forked-tongued, internally contradictory diplomatic accords ever concluded—the Sudan Protocol. Under it, Egypt was promised that all future policy in the Sudan would be formulated "within the framework of the unity between the Sudan and Egypt under the common crown of Egypt." Based on that, Sidky returned triumphant to Cairo, assuring King Farouk that the Sudan was his, and that the Nile would never go dry.

But the second section of the protocol guaranteed that the Sudanese, not the Egyptians, had the right to choose the future status of their country. This point thus gave the Sudan the right of self-determination. Until one read the third part of the protocol which stated that the British would continue to select the governor-general of the Sudan. This was the most powerful position in the country and its control guaranteed that when all was said and done the British still were the big boss of the Sudan and of the Nile. In short, all the double-talk canceled each point out and perpetuated the status quo. The *British* status quo. As Labour Prime Minister Clement Attlee dryly stated: "No change in the existing status and administration of the Sudan is contemplated."

The Egyptians were incensed. Britain had once again outmaneuvered them. Hassan el Banna's Muslim Brotherhood newspaper exhorted "every Egyptian and every Oriental to teach his children from the tenderest age to detest and anathematize the British Empire." The treaty talks collapsed completely, Sidky pleaded ill health and resigned from office in December 1946, and Farouk brought back the belligerent Nokrashi as prime minister. Nokrashi formally terminated all negotiations with the British, repudiated the protocol signed by Sidky, and brought the Sudan issue to the Security Council of the United Nations, which considered the matter to death and never made any decision. Meanwhile, the British continued their removal to the canal zone. Under the still-in-force 1936 Anglo-Egyptian Treaty, their peacetime forces there were to be limited to ten thousand. In flagrant violation of these terms, the British now kept eighty thousand men, at the ready, at the canal. The lines were drawn.

Where Britain was concerned, the year 1947 gave Egypt a great deal to gloat about. The only nice thing that happened to the country was the royal wedding of Princess Elizabeth to the dashing Philip Mountbatten, Duke of Edinburgh. Otherwise, Britain suffered its most bitter winter since 1894. The resulting coal shortage saw Britain forced to nationalize its coal industry. Railroads and gas would soon follow, as London was seeming more and more like Moscow. While socialism gained, imperialism lost. The British gave up India. They also decided to give up Palestine. Tired of trying to flog the Jews into submission and boycott them into starvation and hang them into fear, the British decided they simply couldn't take it anymore and dumped the entire Palestine question into the lap of the U.N. Security Council, which recommended partition. In the pubs and music halls, the song of the year was "Almost Like Being in Love."

With the Middle East time bomb ticking down to the General Assembly's partition vote at the U.N.'s temporary headquarters in a converted former World's Fair skating rink in Flushing Meadow, Queens, New York, Palestine became the big story of the year, with many spinoffs. One was that anti-Semitism came out of the closet. *Gentleman's Agreement,* with Gregory Peck playing a Christian muckraker disguising himself as a Jew to be turned away from tony resort hotels, won the Academy Award for Best Picture of the Year. Because of the atrocities of World War II, the Jews had the sympathy of the Western world. What was this patch of desert? Why couldn't the Jews have it? Hadn't they suffered enough? To the lay Westerner, it all seemed fair and just and easy.

With all the attention on Palestine, Egypt was ominously silent. The country was being devastated by a cholera epidemic that had originated when an Egyptian pilgrim returning from Mecca poured a bottle of what he thought was holy water into a desert well near Assiut. The water was infected. Thirty-five thousand people died within six months. Economically, the British withdrawal to Suez had been a mixed blessing. With the British went their pounds. Unemployment reached all-time highs. King Farouk stayed out of public view, continuing his romance with Lilianne Cohen and continuing his gambling nights with his Jewish pasha friends at the Royal Automobile Club, jokingly calling out, "Bring me my Zionist enemies so I can take their money." His pro-Jewish deeds notwithstanding, his words were all pro-Arab. In June, Farouk gave sanctuary to another muftiesque political refugee. Abd el Krim, who had led the Riff rebellion against the French and Spanish in Morocco in 1925 and had been kept by the French in exile on the island of Réunion in the Indian Ocean for over twenty-one years, jumped ship at the Suez Canal on his way back to France for a sort of retirement-home house arrest there.

Krim debarked with his two wives, six sons, five daughters, sixty pieces of luggage, and his mother's coffin. Thanking Farouk for giving him sanctuary at his Inchass country palace, the sixty-seven-year-old rebel said, "I depend on Allah and I have decided to land with my family to be under the protection of Farouk, the great defender of Arabism and Islam." Such encomia, combined with occasional Muslim Brotherhood bombings of downtown Cairo movie houses that were showing American films from "Jewish-controlled" Hollywood, kept Farouk on the Arab straight and narrow.

The high road to Jerusalem had a crucial way station in Cairo in December 1947, when the prime ministers of the seven Arab League nations met at the palace that housed the league across from the mummies of the Egyptian Museum to determine how their forty-five million subjects would crush the six hundred thousand Jews of Palestine. The septet had differing approaches. Prince Faisal of Saudi Arabia, who constantly sipped fresh asses' milk to soothe his stomach ulcer, wanted to punish the West with an oil blockade. Nuri Said of Iraq, who had ridden with Lawrence and was accused of being a British pawn, dressed like an English gent in Savile Row suits and Pall Mall club ties and urged his Arab brethren to play cautiously and play for time. More impulsive was Lebanon's Riad Solh, a nationalist agitator whom the French had unsuccessfully sentenced to death six times. He wanted immediate guerrilla attacks, as did his Syrian counterpart, Jamil Mardam, a founding member of the Al Fatat secret society that had helped overthrow the Ottoman sultan from control of Syria. Then there was Faisal of Arabia's uncle, Abdullah of Transjordan, who wanted to annex Jerusalem to his own country. At the same time, he wanted to seek an accommodation with the Jews and had his own secret meetings with Golda Meir to that end. Abdullah had a black slave mistress, wrote poetry, detested the mufti, and scorned the decadent Western ways of King Farouk and the Mohammed Ali dynasty. "You do not make a gentleman of a Balkan farmer's son simply by making him a king," Abdullah said.

Eventually, these strange bedfellows had to face the inevitability of war. The Arabs' honor guard was to be the Egyptian Army, which was publicly estimated at nearly 200,000 strong. Privately, the largest force that Egypt could actually field was barely 35,000. Although 180,000 recruits were called up each year, 50,000 were exempted for various reasons, 60,000 declared unfit, and another 50,000 evaded service by not responding to the draft. Of the remaining 20,000, only about 5,000 would actually serve their full term. The remainder managed to desert, or simply vanish. Rommel's Africa Korps this was not.

And Prime Minister Nokrashi knew it. Even this reputedly trigger-happy warmonger was aware of his country's military limitations. On May 15, 1948, the British mandate over Palestine ended. British troops immediately pulled out. The State of Israel was declared and immediately recognized by the United States and the Soviet Union. And the Arabs wanted to go to war. Yet Nokrashi demurred. He met with his Cabinet and concluded that Egyptian troops were woefully unprepared. Farouk overruled him. The combined Arab armies had forty-to-one odds over Israel. The Muslim Brotherhood was armed, dangerous, and champing at the bit to surge into Palestine, goaded on by the war drums being pounded by both the Supreme Guide and the mufti. Better that they unleash their divine rage in Palestine on the Jews than in Egypt upon himself, Farouk concluded. As the king of kings in the Arab world, Farouk couldn't *not* fight. Here was his jihad and he had to lead it.

The jihad turned into a fiasco. As first King Farouk was like a boy playing war games. He dressed in his desert khaki field marshal uniform, inspected his troops on a stallion, handed out thousands of miniature Korans, awarded military rank to his sisters, and even ordered a new triumphal avenue built from the suburb of Heliopolis, adjacent to Cairo's main airport, to Mohammed Ali Square, an Egyptian equivalent of the Champs-Elysées for the expected parade of the conquering heroes. The parade never occurred.

The only Egyptians who benefited at all from the war, by which Israel decisively established itself as a nation, were Major General Mohammed Neguib, who was wounded three times, once left for dead, and became a great hero; Captain Gamal Abdel Nasser, who became a minor war hero for his never-say-die defense of his brigade that had been pinned down by the Israelis in a pocket on the Gaza Strip; and Farouk's kitchen cabinet of Pulli, Galhan, Andraous, and Thabet, who allegedly all made fortunes on deals for old Italian armaments that often turned out to shoot backward at the moment of truth. The humiliated Egyptians found these arms and the men of Farouk convenient scapegoats for their ignominious defeat.

For the first time in his reign, Farouk began to lose the support of "my beloved people." The Egyptian masses had stood by Farouk through the Lampson era and all its repeated indignities, through starvation and inflation and malaria and cholera, through all the mistresses and the cars and the food and the nightclubs. The Egyptians were the most tolerant people on earth, the most understanding, the most forgiving, especially when their king, their pharaoh, was concerned. But they couldn't bear losing a war to this little nation of upstart Jews, especially in the light of Karim Thabet's barrage of press releases and radio broadcasts of Egyptian victories that never occurred. Once the reality of being vanquished overtook the propaganda of being invincible, the Egyptian public felt more betrayed than they ever had by the British, because this time they sensed they were being betrayed by their own ruler. The unkindest cut of all was when the *Emir Farouk,* the flagship of the Egyptian Navy, was sunk by a makeshift Israeli gunboat. That said everything. The rest was silence.

Farouk's once-soaring stock crashed in a largely pro-Zionist America. Nor did his past Nazi associations, actually flirtations unearthed by his ties to the mufti, burnish Farouk's image. The Nation Associates, a group of intellectuals that included Marc Connelly, Erskine Caldwell, Lillian Hellman, Thomas Mann, Reinhold Niebuhr, Eugene O'Neill, and Rabbi Stephen L. Wise compiled an elaborate booklet outlining Farouk's Axis connections (all were rather tenuous stretches) and presented it to the United Nations as part of its condemnation of Egypt's war on Israel. The stature of the group got Farouk terrible press around the country, out of all proportion to the nature of his alleged "crimes." Such would become the leitmotif of Farouk's treatment by the media.

The Arab-Israeli war was a protracted affair of cease-fires and new offensives until the fighting finally ended in January 1949. But it was clear early on who the losers were. With his popularity plummeting in Egypt as well as abroad, with each military reversal, it is particularly curious why Farouk chose November 17, 1948, to terminate what had become strictly a marriage of convenience to Queen Farida, who was still a figure of great public appeal, Egypt's dream girl. The king and queen had slept in separate bedrooms of separate palaces for the last four years, and Farouk's mistresses were anything but private affairs, but there was no reason to obliterate the myth of the royal marriage at a time when Egypt needed every myth it could cling to. Perhaps the death of his beloved and manipulative stepmother, Princess Shivekiar, the year before had deprived Farouk of his last bit of sage counsel. Perhaps Farida's continuing involvement with Shivekiar's son, Wahid Yussri, had pushed *her,* not Farouk, to force the divorce. Perhaps neither Farouk nor Farida could endure the charade of marriage any longer, war or no war.

Farouk's last tangle with Farida had been at Princess Shivekiar's birthday party for the king on February 11, 1947. Shivekiar invited both Farouk and Farida, which was rare, hoping for a rapprochement, which was unrealistic. At Shivekiar's urging, Farouk approached his wife in Shivekiar's palace library with a huge box of jewels. As American Ambassador Stanton Griffis (after the war, America's chief diplomat was accorded ambassadorial rather than ministerial status) noted in a "confidential" airgram to the secretary of state in Washington, the queen "reproached the King for his mode of life and . . . said, 'If the jewels are the price for my return to you, you may take them away.' The King left the Queen in high anger." The aborted peace talks ruined Shivekiar's party, which turned out to be her last. She left the gala, took to her bed, and died a week later. Farouk gave his doting stepmother, who had recently installed a giant statue of Farouk at the end of her palace's hall of ancestors, an enormous state funeral. He led the mourners for her.

Ambassador Griffis also noted that Farouk had "made several efforts during the past year to bring about a reconciliation but that the terms demanded by the queen were too high." He did not specify what the terms were. After Shivekiar's death, Farouk made the difficult decision about the divorce that he had long avoided. Farouk took some comfort in the fact that his action was not without precedent in the Mohammed Ali dynasty. Farouk's father, Fuad, had divorced and remarried, as had his forebears Sultan Hussein and Khedive Abbas. At first Farouk had vowed to "punish" the intransigent Farida by depriving her of all the jewels he had given her, having the Muslim court forbid her to remarry and reduce her to the unqueenly living allowance of two hundred pounds per month. Eventually, he relented, not wanting to seem vindictive.

Farouk turned his divorce into an international daily double by linking it with the simultaneous divorce by the shah of Farouk's empress-sister Fawzia in Teheran, another arranged romance that produced no male heir and little love lost. After having been treated for depression by an American psychiatrist in Teheran, Fawzia had returned to Egypt in 1946 to recover from a severe bout of malaria. Under Farouk's doctors' orders, she had been forbidden to return to "the climate and elevation of Teheran" and never did. She and the shah had one daughter, Shahnaz, which means "pet of the shah."

Everyone had had great expectations that the dynastic union would be a perfect one. Fawzia had come to Teheran with a trousseau of nearly a half million dollars worth of jewels, a hundred evening dresses, and seven fur coats. She left with nothing but disappointment. Cecil Beaton, who photographed Fawzia in Teheran, gave a brief but incisive account of the Persian royal family. The shah and shahbanou [Fawzia], wrote Beaton, lived in a

> modern and perfectly hideous palace and garden of such bad style and expensive ugliness as would not be found in Hollywood today . . . They looked like a gang of South Americans, not of very high standing. The King in an old grey suit looking very young, Jewish and untidy long hair, not much of a shave, jagged frayed collar and dirty black and white shoes. The Queen in a Shaftesbury Avenue dress, very short skirt, very tight-waisted, bright poison green. She was very painted, very common, very pretty, almost very beautiful, but of film star quality, coarsely *photogénique,* a real treat for the afternoon. There were also present a tough-looking sister of the Shah [Princess Ashraf], a real virago . . . a boy of three that looked like a girl, a daughter of the Shah, a pretty little hoof-nosed doll. . . .

The coordinated divorces by the Egyptian and Persian monarchs was a global public relations ploy of the "two wrongs *do* make a right" school to dilate the unpopularity each divorce might have had separately. In both cases, the missing heir to the throne was stressed as the reason for sundering the otherwise blessed pairing. By acting in concert, the two rulers cloaked their personal motives in dignity as acts of state and not of whim. They made divorce seem as royal as coronation.

On November 17, Farouk and the shah, in Cairo and Teheran respectively, each proceeded through the simple Muslim ceremony of repudiating his wife. Karim Thabet's press release from Abdine Palace read:

> God has willed, in his supreme wisdom, that the sacred ties uniting his Majesty King Farouk I and her Majesty Queen Farida be dissolved. He has permitted a regretful desire to separate to grow in the hearts of the noble couple. To realize this desire, his Majesty on November 17 issued the official document of divorce. In announcing this event, the royal cabi-

net prays that divine Providence will gladden the country by
granting his Majesty happiness.

Queen Farida now became Madame Safinaz Zulficar, but she always insisted on everyone, including her mother, addressing her as
"Majesty." She continued to live like royalty. Farouk let Farida
keep her crown jewels, gave her a huge country estate at Zagazig as
well as a lavish villa across from the pyramids, where she took her
youngest daughter, Fadia. The older two princesses, Ferial and
Fawzia, continued to live in Koubbeh Palace under Farouk's care
and were allowed to visit their mother once a week.

If the public were shocked and saddened by the divorce, they
were quickly distracted by an even more shocking and saddening
event less than a month later. Frustrated by their thrashing in the
war in Palestine, the Muslim Brotherhood had responded by doing
exactly what Farouk worried they would do if he hadn't sent them
to Palestine to work out their aggressions: they turned inward, on
his government. First, in October 1948, they assassinated the commandant of the Cairo police. Weeks later they assassinated the governor of the Cairo province. And in December, a brotherhood terrorist disguised as a police officer assassinated Prime Minister
Nokrashi as he was entering an elevator at the Ministry of the
Interior. Nokrashi had always joked that he was living on borrowed
time in that he was lucky not to have been convicted and hanged for
his role in the murder of Sir Lee Stack in 1924. Now his borrowed
time ran out. Ahmed Maher and Nokrashi, the two alleged nationalist assassins, had both become prime minister and both died at the
hands of nationalist assassins.

The bloodbath would not end. Six weeks later, in February 1949,
Hassan el Banna, who was waging an open campaign to unseat
Farouk and establish himself as the president of a new Egyptian
republic, was leaving the Young Men's Muslim Association in
downtown Cairo when he was shot in the back. The assassin escaped into the crowds. The Supreme Guide was taken to a hospital,
but emergency care was unusually slow in coming, perhaps deliberately so. El Banna bled to death. All Egypt looked to King Farouk
as having ordered the retaliatory killing. Whether he did or not, the
Muslim Brotherhood had lost its leader and its fire. That other
gadfly, the mufti, had left Egypt to go to live in Lebanon and inspire
Holy Land assassinations in retribution for the Palestine debacle,

most notably the emir, now king, Abdullah for his greed in annex-
ing Jerusalem into his kingdom. Abdullah was shot down by an
assassin as he was entering a mosque in Jerusalem for his Friday
prayers.

Farouk emerged from the war, his first and only war, a changed
man. His enemies were gone. But so were his friends, especially the
Jews, whose privileged niche in Egyptian society was irrevocably
altered. And so was his family. He had a clean house, yet it was also
an empty house. Farouk's isolation was underscored by the bitter
experience of having truly failed, for the first time. Lampson's endless colonial bullying had made Farouk a sympathetic victim. This
time, though, he had to accept responsibility for his decision, and it
was an unfamiliarly chastening experience. At twenty-eight, Farouk
suddenly stopped being the boy-king. Losing his hair and his vision,
gaining weight in unsightly amounts, Farouk looked twenty years
older than he was. The golden boy had turned into an old man, and
a fat, bald, blind, and dirty old man at that, presiding over a nation
of cotton pashas and fellaheen whose shocking disparities were reminiscent of those of the American plantation South before the Civil
War.

Farouk's Egypt had much less to do with civilization than its
discontents. Nevertheless, the discontents, massive as they were,
were unfocused and, with Lampson, Nahas, the Supreme Guide,
and the mufti all out of his life, Farouk had no serious organized
opposition, loyal or otherwise. Despite his military disaster, Farouk
in early 1949 was, more than ever before, an absolute monarch. He
could divorce his wife by fiat. He could, and would, excommunicate
his mother by fiat. He could, and did, eliminate his enemies by fiat.
Not only was he above considerations of petty popularity, he was
above the law. He *was* the law. He was the king.

XI

CHILD BRIDE

King Farouk was extremely superstitious, understandably so from having a father who had a fixation on the letter F and from having grown up in the harem with a mother who kept her own soothsayer down the marble hall and was a passionate believer in the ability to learn the future from crystal balls, tea leaves, tarot cards, and pigeon entrails. At the beginning of Farouk's marriage to Farida, the young queen would wake up to find in her royal bed bloody bones and shanks of hair that the king had placed there as talismans to bring him a son and heir to his throne. To bring his daughters the luck that had been denied to them for having not been born male, Farouk would rub incense on their heads and have them jump up and down a strictly prescribed number of times.

Given these antecedents, when Farouk's royal fortune-teller in the fall of 1949 augured to him that "you will meet a blond young woman in a jewelry shop who will give you a son," the king of Egypt saw every reason to believe the prophecy that he wanted to come true above all others. What Farouk didn't know was that the prophecy came not from the stars, or the runes, or a pigeon gut, but rather from the pocket of his royal jeweler who had bribed the fortune-teller to put in the magic word for the sixteen-year-old daughter of the woman with whom the jeweler was having a romance.

The year 1949 had been terribly lonely for Farouk. The volatile aftermath of the war with Israel had prevented the king from taking a long-desired trip abroad. He whiled away evenings with Lilianne Cohen at the Auberge des Pyramides, or watching the abdominal gyrations of Samia Gamal at the Helmia Palace or pursuing his newest flame, a voluptuous twenty-year-old French chanteuse named Annie Berrier, who performed at the piano bar of Cairo's chic boîte of boîtes, the Scarabee. Berrier always seemed to be singing the same song in her deep, throaty bedroom voice. *"Je me sens bien . . . bien . . . bien . . . bien, bien, bien,"* she crooned, linking eyes across the smoky room with the monarch, who toasted her with the endless orangeades that were adding more and more unwanted inches to his royal carriage.

Bar girls and belly dancers and boring songbirds did not a happy king make. Farouk, for all his dalliances, was quite old-fashioned. What he had were mistresses. He wanted a wife, so much so that Harry Truman's new ambassador, Jefferson Caffery, the Louisiana gentleman who had just arrived in Cairo after serving as ambassador to France, reported to Secretary of State Dean Acheson that Farouk had tried to effect one more reconciliation with Farida. She turned him down flat. She refused to even begin a dialogue with Farouk unless he got rid of Pulli, Thabet, Galhan, and Andraous first. Preferring loneliness to disloyalty, Farouk began an earnest search for someone else.

Caffery noted that the king had actually promulgated a set of requirements for his prospective new queen:

1. She must be an only child of parents who are too old to have any other children.
2. She must not have any Syrian, Lebanese, Turkish, or other foreign blood in her veins.
3. She must be of the upper middle class and not of the pasha class.
4. She must be at least sixteen years of age and physically able to bear children.

The genesis of these exigencies was Karim Thabet, Farouk's royal p.r. man whom Caffery described as a "jackal." Thabet's prescription of a commoner, a girl of the people, was a bold popularity bid to disentangle the king from his own class and create a smoke screen of democracy, the panacea of fantasy that any Egyptian girl could become a queen. What ensued was a sweepstakes to find the Cinderella of the Nile.

No action of Farouk's was a greater insult to the Egyptian upper class than investing his jeweler, Ahmed Naguib, as a pasha. Naguib, who was no relation to Mohammed Neguib, was the man from whom Farouk bought all the baubles, mostly costume but occasionally real, for his many mistresses. Naguib Pasha was a genuine operator. Working an inside deal with Karim Thabet, Naguib sold the same costly jewel box hundreds of times as a gift vessel for chocolates for the king. Once Farouk had eaten the chocolates, back from the palace came the jewel box, and Naguib Pasha would sell it once more to an unsuspecting donor looking for the ideal receptacle to curry the king's favor.

Naguib Pasha's relationship with Assila Sadek enabled him to discover Farouk's ideal marital candidate quite literally in his own backyard, or at least back room. Narriman Sadek was sixteen, an only child, bourgeoise, a full-blooded Egyptian Muslim, virginal, and ostensibly fertile. She had a striking blond streak in her light brown hair, pure white skin, and lush red lips. Once she lost the baby fat that made her seem like a dumpy schoolgirl, she could be viewed as rather pretty, especially by Egyptians, who weighed blondness and fairness above all other attributes on the scale of beauty. Narriman seemed perfect. There was, however, one small catch. She was formally engaged to Zaki Hachem, a Harvard Ph.D. candidate and economist for the United Nations who had bought Narriman's ring from Naguib Pasha. The owlish, dapper, twenty-seven-year-old Hachem was the kind of fiancé that would have been the pride and joy of any Egyptian family. But Hachem wasn't King Farouk, and the Sadeks weren't a typical Egyptian family.

A secret report from the British ambassador, Sir Ronald Campbell, described the Sadeks with the Arabic term *baladi,* which meant "of the country" and denoted low social standing. Narriman's father, Hussein Fahmy Sadek, was an upper level bureaucrat, the secretary-general of the Ministry of Communication who, according to Campbell, did "not enjoy a good reputation for integrity and is said to owe his advancement in the government service partly to the fact that his wife was on very intimate terms with Ibrahim Dessouki Abaza Pasha, who was minister of communications under the late Nokrashi Pasha." Campbell further noted that both Narriman's father and mother, who lived in the upscale Cairo suburb of Heliopolis, had "an unsavoury reputation for graft."

Naguib Pasha was not above making the young girl pay for the sins of her parents, especially if some of those sins had been committed with him. Playing matchmaker to the hilt, he arranged the bribe of Farouk's fortune-teller and then arranged for Narriman to "happen" to drop by his shop in downtown Cairo on Queen Farida

Street (the street was in the process of being renamed) when King
Farouk was scheduled to be there.

Narriman, who, with a ghostwriter, serialized her memoirs in the
Ladies' Home Journal after the Free Officers' coup d'état of 1952,
described her first encounter with the king in the "treasure room"
of Naguib's emporium through the rosiest-colored glasses:

> I found myself speaking to the King as if I had known him
> all my life. . . . He has his own way of listening to what you
> have to say to him, as if it were prodigiously witty or wise.
> . . . King Farouk encouraged me to talk and made me feel
> that everything I was saying seemed to him bright and intelli-
> gent. . . . His shoulders fascinated me, and his arms and his
> powerful wrists covered with dark virile hair. He was very
> massively built, with a heavy bone structure such as many men
> in the Middle East have, a type which is attractive to all of us.
> I could not help thinking of Zaki Hachem, who compared
> with the King seemed like a little absent-minded, insignificant
> schoolteacher. Perhaps every woman—especially in the Orient
> —hopes for a husband at whose side she will feel frail, and
> whom she has to learn to manage by little artifices and affec-
> tionate wiles which every woman likes so much to use. In the
> Islamic world our husbands are so much our lords and masters
> that it is pleasant when his very physical appearance shows
> indisputably who is the master and it is not only his words
> which remind us of our duty.

Narriman, who could not be accused of latent feminism, was
herself barely five feet tall. She was attracted to opposites, and the
biggest problem she seemed to have with the man to whom her
father had promised her was that he wasn't big enough. She constantly referred to him in her memoirs as "little Zaki Hachem," and
she was less impressed by his Harvard and United Nations creden-
tials than depressed by the fact that "he was so thin and so small,
for he was only slightly taller than myself. . . . It would have been
beyond his strength . . . for him ever to be able to lift me off my
feet."

Naguib Pasha proved as adept at gauging the king's taste in
women as well as he could in jewel boxes. Although Farouk had
been involved with so many genuinely ravishing women, not to
mention the delicately beautiful Farida, he was somehow smitten by
the unformed innocence of this chubby teenager from the Princess

Ferial School for Girls. At the jeweler's, Farouk shocked Narriman
by holding her tiny hand and shocked her even more by calling her
father and inviting himself for tea two weeks later. Succumbing to a
desperate schoolgirl crush, Narriman went out and clipped every
photograph she could of the king to create a scrapbook. She was
most impressed by those of the king in his field marshal uniform, by
one of him holding a fencing mask and rapier, and by one with his
caliph beard which, Narriman admitted, she "found very romantic."

The day of the king's visit, Narriman and her mother went to
Groppi's pastry counter to buy a lavish assortment of sweets. They
festooned their house with plants and flowers. Narriman got a new
dress and her mother even permitted her to wear a touch of lipstick.
But Farouk, who was expected at three, never showed up. Narriman went to her bedroom in tears.

Finally, at ten, a long red Cadillac pulled up to the house, and
out came King Farouk, accompanied by Karim and Touta Thabet,
who gave the red-eyed Narriman "an encouraging smile." Farouk,
who wore a black tuxedo, put Narriman to the ultimate domestic
test, sending her to the kitchen to see if she could make good coffee.
She passed. Farouk and the Thabets stayed only twenty minutes,
but those twenty minutes shook the world for the Sadeks. Narriman
tried to take the Havana cigar Farouk had stubbed out in an ashtray
as a souvenir, a trophy to flaunt to her girlfriends the next day at
the Princess Ferial School, but her father beat her to it.

Farouk kept calling. When Zaki Hachem found out from Narriman's father that his marriage plans had been canceled, he cried
foul play to the press in December 1949, saying that he had had to
inform the five hundred guests that had been invited to his wedding
to Narriman in December that the whole thing had been called off.
Hachem also complained that he had been followed by Farouk's
secret police and that his apartment had been broken into and
stripped of all of Narriman's photographs. The world's newspapers
responded to Hachem's lament with "stolen sweetheart" headlines,
quoting the little diplomat's affirmation of his love for the little
teenager. "I will marry no one else," Hachem said. "I still love
Narriman, and I know she still loves me."

Zaki Hachem may have spoken too soon. Within weeks he had
resigned from his six-thousand-dollar-a-year job at the U.N. and
was reported being sent to Moscow to work in the Egyptian em-

bassy there. Later, the Russian story proved untrue. Instead of being exiled to Siberia, Hachem was going back to Harvard to complete his doctorate. Meanwhile, Narriman's father was made a bey, and, although Abdine Palace discounted all rumors of King Farouk's new romance as "without foundation," Farouk and *Père* Sadek Bey had agreed that Narriman would be taken from the Princess Ferial School and sent to Rome for a year to prepare her to become not only a cultured European lady but the next queen of Egypt. Farouk had decided to play Pygmalion, albeit by long distance. When, according to Narriman's memoirs, a friend asked Farouk why he chose Narriman out of all the women in Egypt, demanding what she had that the others did not, Farouk smiled and said, sphinxlike, "I don't know what she's got—but she's certainly got *something.*" And then the king broke out laughing.

Narriman's Roman holiday/tutorial was cloaked in secrecy. As Farouk assured her, "Don't be afraid, *chérie.* Wherever you are, you will be surrounded by an impenetrable protecting wall." In Rome, Narriman lived at the Egyptian embassy, the Villa Savoia, former home of the Italian royal family who were now in Alexandria. Narriman was given a new identity, as "niece" of the Egyptian ambassador, Abdel Aziz Badr. Excited by her prospects, Narriman lived in the bedroom of a former queen of Italy and imagined future antiques dealers touting that "two queens, one European, one Oriental, slept in this bed." Countess Lily Martellini, "one of the most cultured and experienced ladies of Europe," was hired as Narriman's lady-in-waiting, to teach her history, general deportment, and court etiquette. The countess would give Narriman daily quizzes as to who was seated where at state dinners, for example, who took precedence between a titled second secretary of one embassy and an untitled ambassador of another. (Answer: the diplomat who had been in residence longer in that particular city.) Narriman had a Russian gym instructress to drill her in "self-discipline and physical culture," an Italian opera diva music teacher, and the wife of an Egyptian diplomat to work with her on the arcana of the *Abdine Protocols.*

Following Farouk's linguistic dictum that Italian was used for songs, German for philosophy, English for evasion, and French "for love, for children, and for play," Narriman studied the four languages. Narriman was studying so hard that she had no time for anything else, though the vicious rumor mill in Egypt had it that the real purpose of her incognito stay in Italy was to bear Farouk's child. If it were a boy, Farouk would marry her, the baby would be secreted in Italy for another nine months, then rolled out in triumph as heir to the throne of Egypt, the crowning glory of the Mohammed Ali dynasty. If the baby were a girl, then it would be *Arrivederci,* Narriman. But these were just rumors.

The English were keeping a close eye on the future queen of the Nile. One of the English spies was a woman who had been hired to give a series of twenty English lessons to Narriman. The English teacher noted how Narriman addressed the Egyptian ambassador as "Your Excellency" but the ambassadress as "Aunt." Her impressions of her student were as follows:

> She is conventionally patriotic and nationalist in her views. She expresses strong dislike of the Jews, of Communist ideology, and of Soviet Russia. She considers that the well-to-do Egyptians should in Egypt speak Arabic rather than the customary mixture of French and Arabic. She is aware of the great gulf between rich and poor in Egypt, but considers that the poor and illiterate peasants are nonetheless content[!]. She is anxious to travel but not to live abroad, as she might have done had her previous marriage plans gone through. She professes interest in music and history; she paints and likes the cinema, clothes, jewelry and walking. She shows considerable interest in the British Royal Family, seeking out magazines and newspaper articles about them. She is evidently a devout Moslem and deplores the fact that many people in Egyptian high society neglect their religion; she says that she herself prays every day. Miss Sadek professes admiration for King Farouk, describing him as a lover of his people, who has done much for the country by building many schools and a fine university.

The English teacher also noted that Narriman had no political understanding, had "regal notions" about jewelry and clothes, and looked to Paris as her ideal capital rather than to London or Rome. She also had "little knowledge" of Farouk and seemed "reconciled to have been put into cold storage until he sees fit to bring her out again." The teacher remarked that Narriman was being kept in haremlike seclusion in Rome. More than in any other area of her makeover, the greatest attention was being focused on her weight. The goal was to prevent her from weighing more than one hundred ten pounds. She was given a regimen of Turkish baths to bring her down to Farouk's avoirdupois ideal.

While Narriman's cold storage and steam baths continued in Rome, Farouk was extremely busy in Cairo, trying to extinguish the blaze that had ignited in his own family. Ever since Queen Nazli had begun her affair with Hassanein, Farouk had been on the outs with his mother. After Farouk's marriage to Farida, Nazli had moved out of Abdine Palace to her own small palazzo in the verdant Cairo suburb of Dokki, where many foreign diplomats lived. Nazli had a vast garden surrounded by a high wall. There she would read Proust and discuss it with Hassanein. She would also have all-night parties almost every week, with jazz orchestras that came back to Cairo with the most salacious gossip about the bacchanalian goings-on. Nazli's ladies-in-waiting warned her that some of her jazzmen were on Farouk's informers' payroll; Nazli didn't care. She was still the queen. Parties were her birthright, her privilege. Eventually, even the wildest Cairo party couldn't sate Nazli's thirst for adventure. She started traveling in Europe, where she met Riad Ghali. Then she decided that she would conquer the New World.

Farouk, who had always wanted to visit the United States, was very disturbed when his mother, against his orders, preempted him with her own royal visit. Big plans had been made as early as 1945 for Farouk's trip, with a chartered TWA plane at his disposal, minimal diplomatic time in Washington, which Farouk wanted to avoid, and maximal free time in New York, Hollywood, and the Grand Canyon, which were the places he most wanted to see. The American minister in Cairo, Pinkney Tuck, also prescribed tours of airplane plants and navy yards because, as he noted in planning the itinerary with the State Department, "the king loves mechanical objects and is fascinated by gadgets." A weekend duck shoot was also planned, as were many casual home visits for hamburgers and Cokes, which was the Yankee fare the king was hungry for. Tuck did stress that Farouk "has an eye for the ladies and this should be constantly borne in mind. It would be best if a departmental representative could be with him for the entire trip to avoid any possible incidents of this nature."

Once Queen Nazli violated Farouk's order to her that he be the first of his family to visit America, Farouk had to scrap all the plans. He didn't want to be on the same continent as his mother, not in view of the way she was cavorting with the matinee-idol Copt, Riad Ghali. Although Nazli, who had her younger daughters, Faika and Fathia, with her, had ostensibly gone to America for a kidney disorder treatment at the Mayo Clinic in Minnesota, the queen, who was now a glamorous fifty-five and looked a decade younger, was not acting like a woman who was ill. She had remained in America for several years and showed no signs of homesickness.

The last straw in the mother-son drama came in April 1950, in San Francisco, which had become the American base for the Egyptian Queen Mother and her entourage. Just the month before, Princess Faika, twenty-one, had married Fuad Sadek (no relation to Narriman), like Ghali one of Nazli's personal chamberlains, whom Nazli had gotten a position at the Egyptian consulate in San Francisco. Sadek was from a good and social family in Cairo and while not particularly a catch, he was also not a disgrace.

Farouk had been more pleased with his sister Fawzia's remarriage in March to Ismail Sherine, thirty-one, a Cambridge graduate and a rising ministerial official in Cairo. Sherine was from a fine Alexandrian family that had already married into the Mohammed Ali dynasty. His sister was the wife of Prince Said Toussoun, whose brother Prince Hassan Toussoun's wife, Fatma, was the former flame of Farouk's. Ismail Sherene was, thus, almost family to begin with. Fuad Sadek was different, but Farouk was prepared to accept him.

No sooner had Sadek and Faika returned to San Francisco from their honeymoon in Hawaii than the real scandal erupted. Nazli announced that Fathia, now nineteen, would wed Ghali, thirty-one, who was converting to Islam for the event. Even though Ghali was a Coptic commoner, Nazli told the press: "I have studied him for four years and know he will be a good husband for her."

Farouk, who had given his mother and sisters over a million dollars' expense money for their American grand tour, ordered his family home to Cairo and forbade the marriage. Nazli refused, constantly and futilely phoning Farouk "to reach his heart. I am trying to stir his sympathies so he will understand this means his sister's happiness." But Farouk had seen all the press pictures of Nazli, Ghali, and Fathia *ensemble* and he knew precisely whose happiness was at stake. Farouk responded by revoking Ghali's diplomatic passport, denouncing Ghali as a manipulative fortune hunter, and forbidding the Muslim imam of Sacramento, where California's only mosque was located, from performing any marriage ceremony between Fathia and Ghali. Nazli was not disturbed. From the Fairmont Hotel on Nob Hill, where she lived in a $100-a-day suite, and where the wedding would be held, she told the press that "an imam will come down from heaven."

The imam actually came from Pakistan. Farouk's imprecations went unheeded, and the wedding took place, as planned, in one of the Fairmont ballrooms, while at another party in the adjacent ballroom the band kept playing, "I'm in Love with a Wonderful Guy," from the Broadway hit, *South Pacific,* so loud that it nearly drowned out the Egyptians' eternal vows. Most of Nazli's fifty guests were California socialites, including the daughter of Governor Earl Warren, and Ed Pauley, the millionaire oilman with strong ties to President Truman as well as to the Middle East. There seemed to be an equal number of reporters, press agents, and private eyes. The last locked the celebrants into the ballroom, which was a jungle of hundreds of white gardenias with a twelve-foot magnolia tree at the end, where the wedding ceremony was held. Nazli wore an off-the-shoulder gown in a spectrum of the gray-to-rose colors of the dawn, with a million-dollar diamond tiara and a veritable Cartier's of diamond bracelets from her wrists to her elbows. Fathia wore a Paris-made ivory satin wedding gown studded with sequins, a filmy veil, and a plumage of white bird-of-paradise feathers around the bodice. She had a twenty-foot train and carried a spray of orange blossoms and white orchids. Ghali wore a morning coat and a white carnation. The press reported him as "quite nervous," as was the State Department, which had received reports from Ambassador Caffery in Cairo that a contract may have been taken out by the Palace on Ghali, whom Caffery described as "a first class rogue."

At the magnolia tree, the Pakistani imam gave a long marriage lecture that included at least one barb at Farouk. "A man who wants to marry anybody has the right to do so," the imam said. "It is against the Muslim religion for another man to put obstacles in his way." Then the imam looked at Ghali and at Nazli and said, "A man can find paradise at his mother's feet."

After the vows were exchanged, Ghali, following Muslim custom, refrained from kissing his new bride. Everybody else did, including the headwaiter. Nazli, floating on air and sighing, "I am so happy," over and over, danced with nearly the entire press corps. When a British reporter twirled her around the floor to "C'est Si Bon," he asked her what she thought would happen next.

"Allah will show us," the queen replied. "I have been a queen a long time. I am tough—a queen has to be."

What happened next was that Farouk signed a royal decree annulling his sister's marriage and depriving her of her title of princess and all the privileges attendant to it. The decree also terminated Nazli's guardianship of Fathia and ordered the confiscation of all of Nazli's property unless she returned to Egypt within sixty days. Prince Mohammed Ali, chairman of the Crown Council that issued the decree that, in effect, excommunicated Nazli and Fathia, denounced the Queen Mother. "She has set at naught the institution of monarchy, the foundation of religion, the dignity of the country, and the pride of the Royal Family."

Nazli never returned to Egypt. Dressed in a Chanel suit with a lei around her neck, she left San Francisco on the *President Wilson* with Fathia and Riad Ghali for Honolulu and a tropical honeymoon *à trois*. Queried about being stripped of her property and her title of queen of Egypt, she answered blithely, "Maybe I should get a job. And what's in a name? I can use my maiden name. Just call me Madam—Madam Sabry." As the ship sailed for Hawaii, Nazli took one last question, which gave her the chance to deny a rumor that she was planning to open a nightclub in Paris.

While Nazli flaunted her son's fiat, Princess Faika and Fuad Sadek heeded the call of the king. They returned to Cairo, performed another marriage ceremony presided over by the grand mufti of Cairo, and were pardoned by King Farouk, who made Sadek a bey for his obedient behavior. Mr. Disobedience, Riad Ghali, deprived of his Egyptian passport and facing deportation from the United States as an alien, threw himself on the mercy of the Immigration and Naturalization Service and asked to be given permanent refuge as a displaced person.

The world press came down very hard on Farouk for his double-standard hypocrisy of punishing his mother and sister for behaving no worse than he normally did. How could Farouk, the night crawler, the high roller, the super playboy, the wife stealer, and cradle robber dare tell his mother and sister that the man they loved was just a gigolo? Who did Farouk think he was? The king of Egypt?

What no one could accuse Farouk of was falling prey to Emerson's dictum that "foolish consistency is the hobgoblin of little minds." In the aftermath of Prime Minister Nokrashi's assassination, Farouk made an unholy alliance with the most unlikely of all of his bedfellows—Moustapha Nahas, whom Farouk brought back as prime minister in 1950. Farouk had realized that the best way to involve the Egyptian public in the government and ameliorate the sense that they were the slaves of the pashas was to have free elections. But the concept of free elections was a very relative one. Since the great majority of fellaheen were illiterate, they could not read a ballot. Vote rigging was standard practice. The Wafd, still the biggest political organization in the country, was summa cum laude in election fraud. Policemen in charge of the polls were often Wafd flunkies and would "show" the poor fellaheen where and how to vote. One such policeman boasted that he was responsible for five thousand straight votes for the Wafd in one Nile village. Thus free elections meant Wafd elections and a Wafd victory meant the return of Nahas, Farouk's anathema.

Nevertheless, Karim Thabet convinced Farouk that the elections were worth it and that Nahas was a changed man. To prove it, Thabet arranged for an audience with Nahas, at which Nahas submitted a "proposal" described in a secret report to Secretary of State Dean Acheson from Ambassador Caffery:

> The proposal was that the King would receive Nahas in
> private audience prior to summoning a Wafd Government and
> that if the King were not satisfied by his conversation with
> Nahas, Nahas gave his word or honor that he would retire
> from the leadership of the Wafd Party as an "elder statesman"
> and that the King would then be free to choose any of the
> younger Wafd leaders in whom he had confidence. The King
> agreed to this proposal and was completely captivated by
> Nahas, who tactfully started the interview by swearing that his
> one desire in life was to kiss the King's hand and to remain
> always worthy in His Majesty's opinion of being allowed to
> repeat the performance. At this point Nahas went on his knees
> before the King who according to Thabet was so charmed that
> he assisted him to his feet with the words, "Rise, Mr. Prime
> Minister."

The conciliation of the two bitterest enemies in Egypt was some proof that Nahas, who had been cast in the slag heap of national affairs, was truly a masterfully sycophantic politician. Nahas was seventy and had had a recent stroke, but nothing could quench his desire for a comeback, a return to power, even if this time he had to bite his antiroyalist tongue and share that power with Farouk.

Jefferson Caffery was horrified at the return of Nahas, not on ideological grounds but because of his "completely total ignorance of the facts of life as they apply to the situation today." Caffery simply couldn't believe how completely out of it the "partially senile" Nahas could get away with being, and still be prime minister:

> Most observers are willing to concede that Nahas knows of the existence of Korea, but I have found no one who would be willing to seriously contend that he is aware of the fact that Korea borders on Red China. His ignorance is as colossal as it is appalling.

Caffery criticized Nahas's shortcomings in languages beside Arabic; he said the prime minister's French was "of dubious quality." He called him a "street politician" with no platform other than the mechanical mouthing of the "tried and true formula of "Evacuation and Unity of the Nile Valley."

> At the time of my interview with Nahas he was totally unconscious of the subject which I was discussing. The only ray of light which penetrated was the fact that I wanted something from him. This prompted the street politician's response of "aidez-nous et nous vous aiderons."

Caffery concluded that the only good thing about Nahas was that "we can get anything which we want from him if we are willing to pay for it." As for Farouk, it appeared that he was getting Nahas for nothing. The bill would arrive much later. Nahas took every opportunity he could to extol the king and never competed with him for the spotlight. No more Friday visits to mosques, no more naming hospitals after himself, no more goodwill tours of Upper Egypt. Furthermore, Nahas inculcated this royal respect throughout the entire Wafd organization. Instead of denouncing the king as a wastrel and a dilettante, the Wafd leaders, to a man, never lost an opportunity to sign paeans to Farouk as "the light of the world."

It was as if the Wafd speeches had been written by that master of unctuous hyperbolic sycophancy, Karim Thabet, now Karim Thabet Pasha, of course. They had. It was Thabet who was the architect of the Farouk-Nahas rapprochement. Once Nahas was back in office, one of the fringe benefits of his restoration and his forbearance in letting the king "rule and reign" at the same time was that Nahas, his wife, and his cronies could get back to their old tricks, the first of which was rigging the Alexandria cotton market, which was enjoying a windfall boom because of the demand created by the Korean War and the shortfall of the American cotton crop. The boom was a powerful incentive for the pashas to devote their acreage to cotton for export rather than to wheat, barley, and rice for the fellaheen to eat. The result was rising food prices. The Nahases and their allies got even fatter, while the masses of Egypt ate *foul* and cried foul, but there were no real leaders to articulate the fellaheen dissent. Nahas did so well by his peers that Parliament voted him a remarkable thirty-thousand-pound stipend for his summer holiday and "rest cure" in Europe. The new British ambassador in Cairo, Sir Ralph Stevenson, was inspired to write a note to the Foreign Office:

> Probably only in Egypt would it be the thing for a grateful country to vote £30,000 for the holiday of a Prime Minister who has only been in office on this occasion so briefly and whose wife . . . has already made a great deal of financial hay while the sun of her husband's premiership has been shining.

Although the Nahases returned from their European idyll with eighty suitcases and trunks of acquisitions, the British ambassador later noted, dryly, that they paid "the princely sum" of five Egyptian pounds in customs duty.

Another example of the exercise of the power of the purse was reported by the British ambassador when "the Palace," which meant the King's kitchen cabinet, invested in establishing a Pepsi-Cola plant in Egypt. When Pepsi fared far less well against Coke than had been expected, the Coca-Cola delivery vans suddenly began receiving summonses for various traffic offenses, summonses that soon numbered over three thousand per month. To get the "Pepsi treatment" and keep their vans rolling, Coke was forced to bribe Karim Thabet with a seat on the Coca-Cola–Egypt board of directors and a payment to Thabet and the director of the Royal Treasury of twenty-five thousand pounds for them to donate, at their discretion, to King Farouk's favorite charity. Ambassador Campbell observed, again dryly, that "charity in the Palace begins at home."

Whether Farouk, whose fortune was then estimated at over fifty million pounds sterling (then over one hundred forty million dollars) and one hundred thousand acres, received any of the spoils of the Nahas-Thabet pork barrel is not at all clear. What is clear is that he did receive the lion's share of the blame. The press in Egypt had been muffled by a 1950 law passed by the Wafd Parliament in the wake of the Riad Ghali affair making local editors liable to up to six months in prison for publishing anything at all about the royal family without explicit written permission from the Palace. When one of Farouk's consular officials in Khartoum clipped out the part of a newsreel shown in a local cinema reporting Farouk's family troubles, British Ambassador Stevenson complained to Farouk that such censorship was not allowed in the Sudan. Farouk retorted, according to Stevenson, "that this might be so but he very much doubted whether the Sudan government would allow a film to be shown which, for instance, brought out the imperialist tendencies of the British." If the Sudan thereafter remained silent on the Egyptian royal family's internecine stresses, the rest of the world press took up the slack and pilloried Farouk for the monumental graft that was taking place in his country.

So what did Farouk do? Did he deny the allegations? Did he donate millions to the poor? Did he tax the pashas into the Nile? Did he go on an austerity binge? Not at all. In his most insensitive gesture to the collective opprobrium of nations, Farouk went on the most excessively lavish, self-indulgent bachelor party in the annals of sybaritism. Taking his Cairo act on the road to Europe, Farouk, whom the Continent had so fondly remembered from his last visit in 1937 as Prince Charming, returned in 1950 as Daddy Warbucks. This grand tour made King Farouk the synonym for high living beyond anybody's wildest imagination and kicked off what would become the dolce vita decade of shameless revelry and conspicuous consumption.

Knowing that he would probably be marrying Narriman Sadek at some point after she completed her Pygmalionization in Rome, Farouk, who had just turned thirty, realized that he had only one last summer to sow any wild oats he had left. Exhausted from his battle with his mother, yet exhilarated at having silenced the Muslim Brotherhood and transformed his archenemy Nahas into his yes-man, Farouk believed that he had earned a real vacation. Now he was seasoned enough to really appreciate what Europe had to offer, and he wasn't thinking about art museums and Gothic cathedrals.

Sailing from Alexandria on the *Fakr el Bihar* ("pride of the seas") with an Egyptian destroyer as an escort, Farouk disembarked at Marseilles in early August, traveling incognito under the assumed name of Fuad Masri Pasha. Wearing a natty gray flannel double-breasted suit, an open shirt and ascot, a panama hat, and dark glasses, Farouk looked, for all his excess poundage, fit and dapper. He might have passed as just another *grand boulevardier* except for his thirty-man entourage of Albanian bodyguards, Nubian food tasters, Egyptian doctors and secretaries, plus Antonio Pulli, Karim Thabet, and innumerable distaff camp followers. This foreign legion traveled north to the casino of Deauville in a caravan of seven black Cadillacs with motorcycle outriders, with one of the king's private planes tracking the procession in case Farouk wanted to make a quick getaway. The first evening, the entourage arrived in Lyon in the middle of the night, waking up a hotel desk clerk and demanding twenty-two rooms and then complaining that the beds were too small. Because the king's many trunks had been sent on to Deauville, Farouk found himself without a clean shirt. The plane was dispatched to the Atlantic coast and returned with fresh clothing. Farouk's disguise fooled no one. Europe knew the king had arrived. A crowd of three thousand surrounded Farouk as he left Lyon. He ordered fifty pounds of chocolate to be passed out among the admirers. It was as if he were in Egypt.

Deauville might have rechristened itself Doughville when Farouk hit the resort. The royal party took twenty-five rooms at the Hotel du Golf. There *tout le haut monde* that was reemerging as the casinos of the Continent dug out from the rubble of the war could be seen in the lobby, people like the Aga Khan and his wife, the begum, the Aga's son, Aly Khan, and his wife, Rita Hayworth, French playboy-playwright Sacha Guitry, and an infinity of other glamorous high rollers and Thoroughbred owners out in Deauville for the high season of gambling and racing.

Farouk gorged himself on the French haute cuisine. He ate enough cream sauces to warrant his own dairy as well as coronary unit. One of his menus at the hotel featured sole à la crème, côte de veau à la crème, champignons à la crème, and framboises à la crème. After the grand *bouffe,* with each dish tasted in advance by nine of Farouk's staff, the king put on his white dinner jacket and went to amuse himself in the lavish nightclub of the lavish casino with entertainment he had brought with him from Egypt. Samia Gamal, billed as "the national dancer of Egypt," performed for the king's delectation a seven-veils number called "The Bride of the Nile."

The real and future bride of the Nile, Narriman Sadek, was safely stowed away at her etiquette lessons in Rome. Despite a buzz of gossip that she would be joining the king in Deauville, she didn't show up. Nor did Lilianne Cohen, for whom a suite had been reserved adjacent to Farouk's. Her plane to Paris had crashed in the desert shortly after takeoff from Cairo's Farouk Airport, killing fifty-five passengers. Lilianne was only twenty when she died. Farouk wept, but tried to conceal his deep grief because Lilianne's being a Jew was the one issue that he was now careful to sidestep.

Lilianne Cohen's place as royal songbird was taken by Annie Berrier. Farouk came up with what he thought was a brilliant idea to slake Annie's career ambitions and create a popular theme song that would do for Egypt what "The Sidewalks of New York" or "Hooray for Hollywood" or "I Left My Heart in San Francisco" did for those American cities. He hired a French composer, who came up with a signature piece for Annie's show, "Chanson du Nil." Despite all of the king's high society song plugging, "Chanson du Nil," backed by a twelve-piece orchestra, sank like a stone, and Annie Berrier was later reputed to have left Farouk for a torrid romance with French heartthrob, actor Jean-Pierre Aumont, later the flame of Grace Kelly.

Women appeared to be a lower priority for the king than gambling. He never left the casino tables before five in the morning. The first night, he won twenty million francs (then about $57,000) at no-limit baccarat, fifteen million the next. The royal coffeemaker was installed on the casino balcony to make industrial strength Turkish coffee to keep Farouk and his numerous distaff good luck charms awake. When the king wasn't sipping the jolting brew, he sipped ice

Imperial War Museum

UPI/Bettmann

Menage • (top, left) Queen Nazli, her swain, Riad Ghali, and her daughter, Princess Fathia, who would marry Ghali. The trio would be disinherited and banned from Egypt by Farouk.

Marriage of Inconvenience • (top, right) Cecil Beaton photo of Shahbanou Fawzia, the Shah, and their daughter Shahnaz in Tehran, before their Farouk-orchestrated divorce in 1948.

Cinderella of the Nile • Narriman Ladek, who filled all the criteria to become Farouk's new queen, her own fiancé notwithstanding.

AKHBAR EL YOM Publishing House (Cairo)

Royal Family • Colonel Ismail Sherine, his wife, Princess Ferial Farouk, Princess Fawzia (Farouk's daughter), Princess Faika, her husband, Fuad Ladek, Princess Faiza, her husband, Mohammed Bulent Raouf. Note the conspicuous absence of Queen Nazli, whom Farouk had banished, and Queen Farida, whom he had divorced.   Associated Press

Bachelor Party • Farouk does Deauville in his 1950 continental fling.

water and chain-smoked cigarettes, and always let out a huge belly laugh at the end of each hand, win or lose. While he played, the casino was ringed with hundreds of French police, protecting Farouk from thousands of curiosity seekers. Liberty, equality, and fraternity aside, royalty was an irresistible siren call to the French, and there hadn't been a king that lived up to his throne this way since before the revolution.

While Farouk was in Deauville, he became an unknowing and innocent pawn in a publicity scam that is a case study in the making —and unmaking—of a reputation. The preeminent press agent in the world in the postwar era was a charmingly unscrupulous Italian named Guido Orlando, who represented everyone from deposed monarchs to Hollywood moguls. As recounted in his memoirs, *Confessions of a Scoundrel,* Orlando was always looking for new, rich clients. When he saw the sensationally bad press Farouk's high stakes and high living were getting him in Deauville, Orlando hied himself there to offer his services to the king. Through a powerful Franco-Egyptian film producer named Rafael Hakim, Orlando got to meet Antonio Pulli. Bonding through their Italian heritage, Orlando persuaded Pulli to introduce him to Karim Thabet. Orlando pitched Thabet his brainstorm that would let Farouk play his cards and have them too. Orlando would recrown Farouk as the "gambling king," a Robin Hood of the chemin de fer tables who gave all his winnings to the fellaheen of Egypt. "That way," said Orlando, "we'd have children, mothers, poor people, all over the world, praying for His Majesty to win."

Thabet liked the idea and put Orlando on a week's trial retainer, at $125 a day. But it wasn't an exclusive. Orlando had picked up another client at Deauville, William Medart, a St. Louis "hamburger king" who owned a successful chain of restaurants. Medart's wife, Blossom, had been a Twentieth Century Fox starlet in the films of Cecil B. De Mille, for whom Orlando had done publicity. The Medarts were traveling with their sixteen-year-old daughter, Mimi, who was struck with her mother's almost stardom. Orlando promised the Medarts to get Mimi a Hollywood contract.

Orlando decided to give Mimi the Garbo approach. She would be a woman of mystery. He ordered her not to talk, just to smile, show her teeth, and not utter a word. What Orlando thought was his big coup was his having Mimi stand directly in front of the Hotel du

Golf elevator as Farouk was coming down to go to the casino. When Farouk exited, everyone in the hotel, including the Aga Khan, got down on one knee to show respect. But as the king crossed her path, Mimi, on Orlando's cue, got up and extended her hand. Always gallant and vulnerable to a pretty teenager, Farouk bent and kissed it, and hundreds of flashbulbs went off from the press corps. Alas, Karim Thabet screamed out, "Destroy plates!" and the armed Albanian bodyguards and French police jumped in and seized every camera in the room.

Never one to give up, Orlando on the next night draped Mimi in a sash of Egyptian Nile green bunting he had stolen from one of Farouk's Cadillacs and planted Mimi once more in one of the king's egresses. Again Farouk went for the bait, stopping to compliment Mimi on her untrue colors. Again the flashbulbs went off. Again the bodyguards leapt forward and seized the cameras. But this time Thabet discovered Orlando was serving two masters and fired him for conflict of interest with three days' severance pay. Orlando, declared persona non grata, was barred from Farouk's daily lobster lunch at the William the Conqueror restaurant. In a pique, Orlando went back to Paris.

Orlando was still on the Medart payroll, and he would direct Mimi's Hollywood campaign by phone. Because he had Farouk's complete itinerary, he would have the Medarts shadow him in every hotel from Deauville to Biarritz to San Sebastian to Cannes. Orlando made it seem to the press as if Farouk were chasing Mimi, not vice versa. Over forty newspapers around the world picked up the story about the playboy king pursuing the heartland teenager. Was Mimi going to be the next queen of Egypt, the American Cleopatra? Pretending to spurn Farouk's attentions, Mimi expressed dismay at his hot pursuit. "I thought all kings were as dignified and remote as the king of Britain," she said. Her mother "forbade" her to see Farouk anymore, lamenting: "It was all so difficult, because little Mimi knows nothing of the ugly side of life."

At Biarritz, Orlando had Mimi pose with a group of knockout Jacques Fath mannequins who were asking her for pointers on how to win Farouk's favor. When Mimi was refused entrance to the casino at Biarritz for being under age, Orlando called in a favor from professional party-giver Elsa Maxwell, who had the duke and duchess of Windsor bring Mimi in. The more Karim Thabet denied the whole affair, the more the public believed it. In Rome, Narriman Sadek read the daily blow by blow and couldn't stop crying at her true love's philandering. Eventually, a Hollywood producer, Gregory Ratoff, on location in Spain, went for the bait, or actually *was* the bait. Mimi's father promised to bankroll Ratoff's next feature. Ratoff signed Mimi to be in it. Guido Orlando received a fee of $18,000. "Not bad pay for five weeks' intensive work," he wrote. The career in films never panned out, but in 1955 Mimi married the earl of Coventry and became a Lady.

Farouk was indifferent to the bad press. He called his old *amour* Barbara Skelton, who left her soon-to-be husband, Cyril Connolly, in London and flew to Le Touquet to be Farouk's *belle de la semaine* for his road trip to Biarritz. Barbara, misidentified as an American, became Farouk's "mystery woman." In Biarritz they stayed, as did the duke and duchess of Windsor, at the Hotel du Palais, which Napoleon III had built for Empress Eugénie. While the Windsors had one room, Farouk had fifty; while the Windsors dressed in beach whites and espadrilles and walked on the sand, Farouk slept all day, woke up to lobster breakfasts, bought a cache of jewelry to console Narriman for all the amorous horror stories she was reading, and made and lost fortunes at the gambling tables. Farouk liked theme outings; one day he bought four dozen Basque berets, outfitted his entire entourage in them, and took them in the Cadillac flotilla for an al fresco lunch in the Pyrenees. The king and the duke of Windsor, who had been boyhood acquaintances in England fourteen years before, did go pigeon hunting together.

Farouk's next stop was across the Spanish border at the resort of San Sebastian, where a film festival was taking place. He slept through the Carol Reed thriller, *The Fallen Idol,* even though its star, Michele Morgan, was sitting next to him. Barbara Skelton had been let go back to her fiancé, Connolly, who had followed the Farouk fleet from a jealous distance, hoping, in futility, that Farouk would give Barbara a priceless jewel that they could hock to pay for their honeymoon.

Even with Barbara's departure, Farouk's extended family had grown to fifty-one, including fourteen Egyptian secret police, eleven brand-new black Cadillacs, and four "of his ladies of the moment," as the British ambassador to Spain reported to London, adding that the late king of Spain traveled with a suite of only six. The ambassador described how the secret police would arrive in advance at the Hotel Reina Cristina to choose the king's bedroom and that on his right for "the principal lady and the bedroom on the left for her understudy. . . . The whole of the king's suite were frightened to death of him, and as a local paper remarked, they had never seen a king laugh so much with an entourage so grave and gloomy."

From Spain, Farouk motored on to the Riviera, where he bought everyone frogmen's goggles, flippers, and harpoons for an en masse afternoon of undersea fishing. At Cannes, where he took over several floors of the Carlton Hotel, Farouk's gambling *bakara,* or luck, ran out, but not as badly as that of the man who beat Farouk, Italy's Gianni Agnelli, Hollywood's Jack Warner, and India's Nawab of Palanpur at an $80,000 game of chemin de fer at the Palm Beach casino. "Lucky Mickie" Hyman, an English textile manufacturer, had broken the bank at the Cannes casino in 1948, winning $200,000 in one week. Now Hyman won a very tense three-bet showdown with Farouk. When he reached over to rake in the chips, he clutched his chest and keeled over dead of a heart attack. The headlines read: "Lucky Mickie Beats Farouk—and Dies."

Decamping for better luck in Italy, Farouk made his final stop in San Remo, where he went antique shopping, then caught the *Fakr el Bihar* back to Alexandria, where he arrived at the end of October. It was perhaps the most expensive summer vacation ever taken. Back in Egypt, Farouk was greeted by a crowd of ten thousand subjects who had been lured to the docks with free meals. Then his bubble was burst when he was presented with a book of press clippings that denounced everything about him, from his spending to his governing. A piece in *The Economist* upset even the British, who had tried to make peace with Farouk by sending the duke of Gloucester to Egypt to make Farouk an honorary general in the British Army. (In return, Farouk gave the duke a signed photograph.) The *Economist* piece accused Farouk of diverting municipal funds to heighten the six mile wall around Koubbeh Palace, ridiculed his "unholy alliance" with Nahas, and closed by stating that "in thirty years he has done almost everything except make his horse prime minister."

London began seeking ways to "plant" favorable articles about Farouk in the Fleet Street tabloids of Lord Beaverbrook, while Cairo took a more direct approach. The richest nonroyal in Egypt, the landowner-manufacturer Mohammed Abboud, who had married a Scottish woman and had major connections in Britain, came to England with several hundred thousand dollars to "correct" Beaverbrook's impressions of Farouk and his court. The press proved uneducable. British Ambassador Stevenson wrote: "Abboud Pasha seems fairly resigned to this publicity but remarked regretfully that it was a pity that the British Press, unlike the Egyptian, did not seem much interested in bribes."

Perhaps they should have hired Guido Orlando. But he was on the wrong side. His next client was Princess Bayan Djavidan, seventy-four, widow of Khedive Abbas Hilmi II, whom the British had desposed for his Turkish ties in World War I. The Philadelphia-born ex-khediva was charming but broke, and thought that Orlando could help her get a pension from her fellow dynast, King Farouk. Shame was Orlando's prescription. He brought the princess from Innsbruck, Austria, where she was living, to Paris and had her "collapse of malnutrition" outside the very mansion she used to own in the sixteenth arrondissement. "A former queen of Egypt starving to death—it was sensational," Orlando trilled. He staged a picture of the princess preparing fried eggs over a hot stove and the newspapers jumped at it, imploring someone to give this riches-to-rags saga a happy ending by hiring the princess as a cook. The Egyptian embassy in Paris offered the princess five hundred dollars to go back to Austria; she referred the offer to "her manager," Orlando. When the Egyptians found out he was harassing Farouk again, they drew the line and offered her nothing. Nevertheless, Orlando sold the princess's memoirs in thirty-eight countries and finally got her a job in Ethiopia, not as a cook but as Emperor Haile Selassie's wardrobe mistress.

The only press damage control that seems to have been accomplished was the suppression in England of the publication of a biography of ex-Queen Farida with the title *The Name Was Paradise but the Life Was Hell.* Otherwise, the Farouk attack continued, culminating in the first "open letter" Farouk had ever publicly received from the united parties constituting the "opposition" to the Palace and the Wafd. The letter declared that the patience of the public was exhausted and that a "revolt was near: that would "not only destroy those who are unjust but would leave the country in a state of financial, moral and political bankruptcy." The "unjust" were, of

course, Farouk's kitchen cabinet. The petition was polite in that it
did not name names but said:

> Circumstances have placed in the palace certain officials
> who do not deserve that honor. These ill-advise and mishandle
> matters. Some of them have even come under suspicion that
> they are implicated in the arms scandal effecting our valiant
> army.
>
> The belief prevails that justice will be incapable of touching
> these officials, just as the belief has prevailed . . . that Parlia-
> mentary government has become mere ink on paper. . . .
>
> The world Press describes us as a public that bears injustice
> silently and says we do not know that we are being maltreated
> and driven like animals. God knows that our breasts are boil-
> ing with anger, and that only a little hope restrains us.

That little hope was King Farouk, whom the opposition challenged again to become the country's golden boy they had known
and loved and to sever himself from his venal cronies.

> The country remembers the happy days when your Majesty
> was the honest good shepherd. All the hopes of the country
> were concentrated on your Majesty. No occasion passed when
> the country did not demonstrate its loyalty and sincerity.

The yellow press may not have mattered to Farouk. But this
opposition petition hit hard. Farouk responded in the one way he
knew to silence this sort of criticism. He went on the political offensive and remounted that most surefire of platforms: Get the British
out of Egypt! This he did soon after his return from Europe. Nahas
read Farouk's Opening of Parliament speech on November 16,
1950, calling for the union of Egypt and the Sudan under Farouk as
king and the abrogation of the 1936 Anglo-Egyptian Treaty, plus a
nod to Palestine that "the untold sufferings of displaced Arab refu-
gees will ever remain a blot upon civilization and be removed only
by their return to their homes and by their being indemnified for
their losses." No sooner had Nahas finished reading the speech than
anti-British, anti-Zionist riots began in the Cairo streets outside the
Parliament. The riots eventually ended, with the British on the extreme defensive and Farouk again high in the saddle in the dual role

of peacemaker and Brit-sweeper. The prodigal vacation was forgotten in the melee.

Farouk's next move was intended as the deal closer that would guarantee him the hearts and minds of the Egyptian masses. On his thirty-first birthday, February 11, 1951, he finally declared his engagement to "the commoner," Narriman Sadek, who, nonetheless, was described as "an exquisite flower of Egyptian society, the descendant of an illustrious and noble family," by Karim Thabet in his usual baroque style as he made the announcement:

> Giving thanks to God, the Cabinet of his Majesty is pleased to announce to the noble Egyptian people the good tidings of the engagement of its King, who has given them his heart and his love.

Nahas praised the event, stating that "the king's forthcoming marriage will strengthen the ties between the throne and the Egyptian people." Cynics derided the engagement, speculating that the only reason it happened was that Narriman had finally given birth to an heir, who would be unveiled in due course. What about Rome? What about royal etiquette? The cynics laughed. The only etiquette that mattered was that the child be a boy. Anything else would have gotten the "flower of society" the rudest bum's rush. The betrothal photograph showed no hint that Narriman was great with child. In fact, she looked like an Egyptian Scarlett O'Hara, with a tiny, cinched waist, a dramatic, tiered lace gown, sophisticated makeup, and luxuriantly coiffed, honey-colored hair. She was well under Farouk's goal of one hundred ten pounds. The schoolgirl pudge was gone. Rome had agreed with Narriman. Farouk had worked some sort of magic. He had turned her into queen material.

Now Farouk, or, rather, Karim Thabet, went on an all-out, old-fashioned publicity offensive. Triumphal arches were built, monuments floodlit, the army sent on parades, the air force on display. Free meals were dished out to thousands in Cairo and Alexandria soup kitchens. Three thousand acres of royal land in the Nile delta were distributed in parcels to landless peasants, together with small huts and annual supplies of seed. Sweets and clothes were given to mothers in maternity clinics, more sweets to hospital patients and inmates of orphanages. Special services were held in every mosque.

The king, who admitted that he had been "a lonely man in my heart," was in love.

Ambassador Jefferson Caffery wrote to Secretary of State Dean Acheson about the upcoming nuptials:

> The political significance of this occasion arises largely from the kudos the King and the palace are reported to hope to derive from the emergence of King Farouk in the public eye as a "settled down," happily married, highly domesticated man. . . . It is a natural part of Muslim practice in Egypt to accept somewhat unorthodox personal behavior from an unmarried man. This does not carry over into the behavior expected of a married man, and if the King should revert to his present rather conspicuous nocturnal existence in Cairo nightclubs, the constructive propaganda derived from his marriage, if any, may well boomerang. From a standpoint of power and influence the King's position in Egypt today is surprisingly great. From a standpoint of respect and admiration it is pretty close to its *Nadir.* He is undoubtedly faced with an opportunity to improve this situation, but whether he will have the strength to take full advantage of it remains to be seen.

Initial plans for Farouk's second wedding, which was delayed by Narriman's unexpected appendectomy in March, to be a small, low-key private affair, gave way to Karim Thabet's plans for an extravaganza. On May 6, 1951, exactly fifteen years from the day he became king of Egypt, Farouk entered the khedive Ismail room of Abdine Palace and clasped hands under a silk cloth to conclude the marriage contract with Narriman's uncle, Mohammed Ali Sadek. Her father had died of a heart attack several months before. Farouk had made the uncle a bey and Egypt's ambassador to the Netherlands. Now he was making him family. While the two men were plighting her troth, Narriman, aided by Princess Fawzia, was across the city, at Narriman's modest two-story home in Heliopolis, getting into her white satin wedding gown studded with twenty thousand diamonds. The gown had been constructed over a period of four thousand hours by a team of twenty dressmakers at the Paris couture house of Germaine Lecomte. Narriman covered her face with an ancient veil of Venetian lace and donned the diamond diadem that Farouk had given her. He had also given her a trousseau valued at $250,000. It included fifty handmade nightgowns of lace, a hundred pairs of hand-embroidered bras and panties, bed linen in every pastel shade, five mink coats, and one hundred pairs of shoes, several fitted with solid gold heels. Until Imelda Marcos, no first lady was ever as well heeled. The new queen and the princess then got into the red Rolls-Royce that would lead a procession of red Cadillacs under suspended emerald crowns and through heart-shaped triumphal arches, with the initials F and N emblazoned on them, to meet her new husband at the foot of the grand stairway of Abdine.

Following regal decorum and without a kiss, Farouk led his queen up the stairs, through the Hall of Mirrors, and into the gilded Throne Room, where Madame Nahas presented the wives of the Cabinet ministry and Mrs. Jefferson Caffery presented the wives of the Diplomatic Corps. A tea party in the Abdine gardens was followed by a banquet at which Farouk cut the first slice from the seven-foot-tall, seven-tier wedding cake with a gleaming saber and presented it to Narriman on a gold plate. Telegrams and gifts arrived from around the world. President Truman sent four Steuben crystal vases; King George VI of England an oversize silver inkstand; and Premier Stalin a writing desk made of rare Ural stone for Farouk, who never lifted a pen, and a full-length sable coat for Narriman, who couldn't wait to find a cold climate to wear it in. From Switzerland came a gold watch, Turkey three rare carpets, India three silk bedcovers, Czechoslovakia a china tea service, Holland a crystal goblet. Haile Selassie sent the couple a gold vase with a jeweled inscription. Abdullah of Jordan presented a twelve-piece gold toilette set studded with precious stones. The king of Morocco's gifts were a jewel-encrusted sword for the king and a pearl necklace for the queen, while that of the British governor general of the Sudan was a dining room gong on an ebony stand supported by two elephant tusks. The rector of Al Azhar University gave Farouk still another inkstand, this one in gold in the shape of the Al Azhar Mosque. All the gifts that were in gold were later secretly melted down to ingots, a practical if not sentimental idea that originated, as did most of these ideas, with Karim Thabet.

In the streets, a hundred-and-one-gun salute went off, the army paraded, fireworks exploded, and fatted calves were slaughtered in accordance with tradition. A new popular song, "Glory for King Farouk's Reign," blared from radios and the Royal Egyptian Air Force swooped overhead, dropping a snowstorm of leaflets congrat-

ulating the royal couple. At night, feluccas and dahabeah and
steamers on the Nile strung up lights on their decks and sails. On
land there were torchlight parades, dancing in the floodlit squares
and, best of all, that hallmark of Farouk's party-giving, for the poor
an enormous amount of free food. Even the British in the canal
zone paid their respect with a full-dress parade. The day after, in
her first official appearance as queen, Narriman, dressed completely
in black, traveled by red Cadillac through the Old City of Cairo to
the El Rifaii Mosque to pay her respects at the marble sarcophagus
of King Fuad. While her entourage stood behind her, she proceeded
alone to the tomb and bowed. It was a powerful symbol. She was
now a member of the dynasty.

The wedding was followed by a royal honeymoon that immediately eradicated whatever goodwill had been achieved by marrying
a "commoner." That the king departed on his yacht for three
months in Europe of gluttony, gambling, and self-indulgence just as
the sacred and austere holy month of Ramadan was beginning did
nothing to endear him to his more devout subjects. Moreover, as a
European grand tour on an even more gargantuan scale than
Farouk's bachelor party of the previous summer, the honeymoon
made the teenage queen from the Cairo bourgeoisie seem like an
atomic age mutation of the stereotype of a Jewish princess on a
Miami Beach shopping spree. The enduring image of the trip was
that of Farouk, Narriman, and their entire entourage of yes-men
and ladies-in-waiting disembarking at Capri from the *Fakr el Bihar,*
identically dressed in peaked white yachting caps, navy blue blazers
with an Egyptian crown-pharaonic barge crest, white shirts, and red
ties. It was all unisex except that the men wore gray flannel pants,
the women gray flannel skirts.

The outrage of the yellow—and other—press was very confusing
to the seventeen-year-old Narriman. In her memoirs, she tried to
justify the honeymoon, but managed only to jam her tiny foot
deeper into her royal mouth.

> People hated us who had never met us, never known us, and
> Communists who wanted not love, but power, were probably
> already whispering in the bazaars of Egypt that the King and
> Queen were spending for a honeymoon money that might have
> been used to buy bread for the poor.
>
> Had our honeymoon cost three hundred thousand dollars,

this would have been only half a piaster each for the population of Egypt. And this, indeed, was exactly how much they paid the royal family of Egypt: one half a piaster per head of population—the cost of one cigarette—per year!

Yet it was enough to start the weapons of hatred and reviling!

If the fact that the President of the United States received a salary less than a third as much as that of the king of Egypt made the entire world cock a collective eyebrow, the way Farouk threw that salary—and much more—away on this honeymoon made the world's collective jaw drop. For thirteen weeks the royal party of sixty traveled by yacht and Cadillac from Sicily to Capri to Cannes to Paris to Geneva to Milan, dogged by reporters every inch of the journey. The press had little interest in the "human" aspects of the trip, such as Farouk and Narriman's pilgrimage ascent by ropewalk to a Roman Catholic shrine outside of Rapallo dedicated to the Madonna who was credited with helping mothers bear male children. What sold papers was Farouk's loss of $150,000 in a seven-hour marathon of baccarat with Darryl F. Zanuck at Cannes's Palm Beach casino, the biggest setback ever recorded there. Or Narriman's Paris whirlwind through the ateliers of the top couturiers, ordering a dozen of every style, all adapted for maternity wear. Narriman even hired the Polish-born Hollywood dress designer, Marusia, who was summering on the Riviera, to create a wardrobe for her. Marusia told the press that Narriman's figure was identical to that of another famous and statuesque client, Jane Russell, except that Narriman's waist was one inch smaller. Aside from dressing herself, Narriman also purchased in Paris two hundred sets of baby clothes in pink, white, and blue.

Or Farouk and Narriman's excursion to Turin for an eighty-mile-per-hour test ride on his Fiat-built, two-million-dollar private train, which was being shipped to Egypt. The engine and two coaches were streamlined in silver and Nile green. Equipped with television and air-conditioning, the train had alligator-trimmed upholstery, fourteen telephones, and a royal suite with twin beds, twin baths, and twin showers. Or the recitation of a typical Farouk lunch menu: Dover sole, Charolais beef, Bresse chicken, à la crème of course, Baltic lobster, mashed potatoes, rice, peas, artichokes, peaches, pomegranates, mangoes flown from Egypt, and orangeade. And be-

cause the royal couple were so diet conscious, and because Narriman thought she could preserve that wasp waist, no bread.

Despite a Muslim Brotherhood death threat in Paris over all the
unholy extravagance, Farouk maintained his good humor, except
for several episodes when the leechlike paparazzi photographed
Narriman in a bathing suit, which would be seen as sacrilegious by
the conservative Muslims back home. Farouk also lost his patience
with photos of him beside a champagne bucket with a bottle of
Vichy water. This could be, and was, easily misconstrued and exploited by "the Zionist papers," who Narriman feared would also
plant pork chops and wine bottles on the royal table for a quick
snapshot that would shake the world.

Although Farouk refused to alter his spending habits, he did
mend his ways in one very significant respect. At no time during the
three-month trip was he seen with any woman other than his wife.
He eschewed all nightclubs. And every morning of the honeymoon
he woke Narriman up with a different gift—a pearl necklace, a ruby
ring, Belgian chocolates, her favorite orchids. When Narriman began to show signs of morning sickness, he jettisoned the royal yacht
and chartered an entire passenger ship, the *Malek Fuad,* to give his
bride the smoothest possible sailing back to Egypt.

Once again Farouk found himself returning home to very hot and
choppy water. The Aga Khan, who saw Farouk just before he left
Europe, found the king very depressed over his "unnatural" alliance
with the terminally corrupt Nahas and the Wafd. Farouk had done
it to keep Egypt from exploding, but he knew he was only masking
the symptoms of a disease that could not be cured. The "sad and
shoulder-shrugging pessimism" that the Aga Khan observed explained in part Farouk's unabashed self-indulgence. As the Aga
Khan wrote: "He was enveloped in a mood of depressed fatalism,
an atmosphere of 'I cannot do what I wish—very well, let them do
what they want,' which in the long run was bound to contribute to
his defeat and downfall. He had tried in his own way to help his
people and improve their lot, and now he felt that he had failed."

In early 1951, the Wafd inaugurated the Arab world's first social
security plan, allocating $20 million a year to benefit the poor and
elderly fellaheen. Six months later, the minister of social affairs, in
charge of administering the plan, threw up his hands and quit in
disgust at the impossibility of his task. Nahas announced an ambitious Five Year Plan for roads, drinking water, literacy, and the

like, but most of the promised infrastructural work was never done, and many of the allocated funds ended up not in the public coffers but in the private accounts of the Wafd leaders. The average wage of a fellah held the line of bare subsistence at a world-shocking ten cents a day. When the Korean War cotton bubble burst, the Wafd leaders kept cotton prices artificially inflated until they could sell off their own stocks. They also prevented a shift from using land for cotton to growing wheat, which might have lowered soaring food prices and aided the masses.

Madame Nahas, whom everyone in Egypt saw as the evil brains behind her husband's rhetoric, acquired nearly one thousand new acres of prime delta farmland in 1951 alone. The Wafd were running a spoils system. Farouk was well aware how rotten his country had become because of it. He was not blind to the self-dealing treacheries of Wafd accounting practices. As he once joked to Jefferson Caffery: "Don't think I know nothing of business matters. Don't forget that the founder of my dynasty was a tobacco merchant."

In the face of this corruption, the only thing Farouk could do was to dismiss Nahas as prime minister, the act that had precipitated all his troubles with the British when he had done so at the height of his power as the perfect boy-king in 1938. Before Farouk could act, Nahas used the British once more to keep his office—this time by turning on them and making them the scapegoats for all the problems actually brought on the country by the Wafd. In an adept stroke of rabble-rousing, Nahas, in early October 1951, unilaterally abrogated the Anglo-Egyptian Treaty of 1936, the very treaty Nahas had led his delegation to London to negotiate, the treaty Nahas had rammed through the Egyptian Parliament, the treaty Nahas had called one of "honor and independence," even though it had left the door to Egypt wide open to British "emergency" occupation and had made Nahas the darling of Whitehall. Nahas knew how short the Egyptian memory could be. All he said to Parliament was "It was for Egypt that I signed the 1936 treaty and it is for Egypt that I call on you to abrogate it." The legislators shouted "Agreed!" and gave a standing ovation to Nahas, who threw a sop to the palace by simultaneously annulling all Anglo-Egyptian agreements on the Sudan condominium and declaring Farouk "King of Egypt, Sovereign of Nubia, of the Sudan, of Kordofan and of Darfur." Nahas called Great Britain "the enemy and usurper" and

promised Egypt that not only was this the end of foreign domination but also that the usurper would be brought "to severe account."

Even before the British could react, Egyptian guerrilla raids on
the canal zone began, fresh food was cut off to the zone, and all the
Egyptian laborers who worked for the British in the zone were
called home. The Muslim Brotherhood came out of its hibernation
since Hassan el Banna's death, and fanatic terrorism was given a
shot in the arm. In addition to the sabotage and the night raids,
Egyptian nationalist extremists called for a total boycott against
England and the English in Egypt. Nahas had been heartened by
the recent coup in Iran of populist leader Dr. Mohammed Mos-
sadegh, who had nationalized the Anglo-Iranian Oil Company, a
colossal colonial intrusive presence that was to Persia something of
what the Suez Canal was to Egypt. If the Iranians could rout the
British, why couldn't the Egyptians? When the crowds took to the
street shouting "Down with the British! Long live Nahas!" Farouk
saw history repeating itself. For all his obsequiousness, Nahas was
coming back out of the closet for one more power grab. The prime
minister had seized the football of nationalist revolt and was heading in open field straight for the end zone, which just happened to
be the canal zone.

Nahas's offensive put King Farouk in the completely anomalous
position of taking sides with the British. "The enemy of my enemy
is my friend," that great double negative of Egyptian political life
that had caused such trouble by linking the country with the Nazis,
was now at work again. If Farouk hated anything worse than
Nahas, it was the British, whose puppet Nahas used to be. But that
was the Lampson British. And those British seemed to belong to
another era. The Labour British who were in colonial retreat had
done everything in their power to make reparations with Farouk for
Lampson's arrogant behavior, from giving him a luxurious Avro-
Anson airplane to making him an honorary general to entertaining
him with such imperial heavyweights as Lord Mountbatten and the
duke of Edinburgh.

If Farouk hated anything worse than Nahas *and* the British, it
was communism, the enemy of czars, the enemy of kings. Although
there was no active Communist party in Egypt, there was an increasingly active underground Communist press, and if any country
on earth seemed ripe for communism, it was Egypt. Farouk knew it.

Farouk was also well aware of Lenin's three necessary components for revolution. One was popular discontent, which Egypt surely had. Another was the deterioration of governmental authority, which was definitely occurring. Only the third was missing, which was the leadership for the revolution.

With Hassan el Banna dead, there was no obvious leader for the underclass. Farouk remained the most charismatic man in Egypt. Nevertheless, if the anti-British discord Nahas was fomenting did succeed and politicians didn't have the British to kick around anymore, the masses would then realize that their real problem was not the British at all but the maldistribution of wealth. Then Nahas would go. The Wafd, which was no longer the party of the people but of the pashas, would go. And Farouk would go. Even though Narriman was pregnant with what the royal establishment was praying would be a boy who would perpetuate the throne, Ambassador Caffery wrote to Washington: "The birth of a son and heir would only postpone that inevitable day when we will realize that we can get along very well without a King." While the Americans had a basic problem with the notion of kings, Farouk saw the British as fellow travelers en route to becoming anachronisms. He wanted to delay his day of reckoning as long as possible, and assumed the British did as well, if only for the sake of tradition. Given this haunted house of evils, Farouk decided that the British were the least of a menacing lot.

Nostalgia aside, the British had warned Farouk of an imminent Communist menace, both to his throne and their own crumbling position in the Middle East. The previous year, Field Marshal Sir William Slim, chief of the imperial general staff, had come to Cairo with a very alarmist message. He told Egyptian leaders that Britain believed war was nearer now than it had been in 1936, that the Russians were planning to invade Egypt by air and by land via Persia and Turkey to take the Suez Canal, not only as the gateway to the East but also to Africa, which Russia saw as ripe for communism. Slim reminded the Egyptians that if they couldn't defeat Israel, they were totally defenseless against Russia. Unless, of course, Britain stood behind them. If Britain were to leave Suez, Slim warned, the Cold War would quickly become a hot one.

In face of these dire predictions, Farouk gave the British what their ambassador described as "a horrid moment" when Farouk asked the question that since he was now a British general, whether "we should now have the inestimable advantage of his commanding a British Division or Army" if war with Russia broke out. There was a long, dead silence, punctuated only by Farouk's wild laughter. "I had you," he said, as he always did whenever he pulled one of these trademark deadpan tricks.

While Nahas dismissed Field Marshal Slim's warnings as self-serving British scare tactics, Farouk took them to heart. Convinced that he had a better chance of keeping his throne by an alliance with the likes of Slim than with those of Nahas, Farouk inaugurated his pro-British stance by appointing to two important Palace positions two former Egyptian ambassadors to England who were also known anglophiles. The first ambassador was Hafez Afifi, who became head of the royal Cabinet. The other, who became Farouk's adviser on foreign affairs, was Adbel Fatah Amr, the millionaire world squash champion. Through the exit door went the man who put together Farouk's ill-fated marriage to the Wafd, Royal Press Councilor Karim Thabet. Ambassador Caffery wrote: "There is no man in Egypt as universally hated . . . nor . . . as universally dreaded and obeyed. There will be few mourners at his loss of power. The politicians, the people, and, incidentally, the British, will all be delighted."

Thabet himself blamed his demise on the "numerous and ambitious" relatives of Queen Narriman, who had launched a "whispering campaign" with King Farouk to get Thabet out of the palace so they could take his place. While the king was in Europe on his honeymoon, Ambassador Caffery had had a brief anxiety attack that the king might not come back at all, especially in view of the embassy's estimate that Farouk's holdings abroad were in the neighborhood of $75 million. "There are many who feel that the King would be well advised to return at an early date if he expects to find very much left," Caffery wrote, worrying that if Farouk decided to call it quits and keep the "sure" European money and jettison the "doubtful" Egyptian wealth, "one would indeed have a precarious situation. However, there is one encouraging fact. All sources agree the King still likes being King."

Indeed he did. And he liked it even more on January 16, 1952, when at six-twenty in the morning 101 guns went off, announcing the birth, a month premature, of Farouk's first son, Crown Prince Ahmed Fuad. The future king weighed over seven and a quarter pounds and urinated in the face of the pediatrician, Dr. Magdi, whom Farouk made a pasha immediately upon delivery of the heir. "I have had two honors at the same moment!" the doctor-pasha said with aplomb, reaching for a towel. Farouk, tears of joy streaming down his cheeks, took Narriman's hand and kissed it. "Well done, Nunny," he said, calling his queen by her special pet name.

Across town at Manyal Palace, the former heir presumptive, Prince Mohammed Ali, who was now seventy-five but kept his youthful jaunty appearance by rubbing lemons on his skin, heard the 101 guns and wept also, for himself. He knew once and for all that he would never be king of Egypt. Throne fantasies were also extinguished for the third in succession, Farouk's fifty-two-year-old cousin, Prince Abdel Moneim, an amateur ichthyologist who had the world's largest collection of small tropical fish. He could now devote all his time to his aquaria.

Farouk devoted all his time to his new son. He even slept on a mattress placed at the foot of Narriman's bed to be near Fuad. For all the obsessive attention, he promised Narriman not to spoil their son and quoted to her a favorite poem by Kipling that he had learned in England and taken to heart.

> If you can talk with crowds and keep your virtue
> Or walk with Kings—nor lose the common touch—
> And all men count with you, but none too much
> Yours is the Earth and everything that's in it,
> And which is more—you'll be a Man, my son!

Farouk's happiest moments lasted a grand total of nine days. Continuing their food blockade of the British troops in the canal zone, nationalist guerrillas launched a major attack on a British munitions depot during which it was discovered that the Egyptian Auxiliary Police had been secretly aiding the "unofficial" commandos. The British officer in command of the zone, General Erskine, lost all patience. On January 25, he ordered a large force of British tanks to surround the Egyptian police headquarters in Ismailia, near the canal, and gave the occupants one hour to surrender all their arms. The Egyptian commander telephoned Fuad Serag ed Din, Nahas's right-hand man and Wafd minister of the interior, who was in his bathtub smoking one of the fat Havana cigars he always had in his mouth. Fully aware of the garrison's shortage of arms and the ludicrous odds, the 240-pound Wafd strongman who liked spending his evenings at Cairo nightclubs like the Scarabee with Madame Nahas (her husband was too sick to step out), sensed a powerful martyr campaign in the making. He ordered the police to fight "to the last man and the last bullet," or else be court-martialed by a military tribunal. Then he returned to his smoky ablutions.

When it was all over, forty-three Egyptian policemen had been killed, and three English soldiers. One hundred more were wounded. The police station had been leveled. The Egyptians had surrendered, but now the country had a cause, a jihad against the British. The next day, January 26, the Egyptians struck back. The day was Black Saturday. And the crowd did not recite Kipling. Instead, they sang, "Narriman, Narriman, Why Does Your Baby Have Teeth?" To the foaming mob the birth of Crown Prince Fuad was as big a sham as everything else the Palace stood for.

The crown prince the rioters were reviling was being feted by his father at a luncheon banquet at Abdine for six hundred officers of the Egyptian Army. According to Karim Thabet's inside sources, Farouk was never made aware of the destruction of the city until he saw the billowing smoke of downtown Cairo from the windows of the palace ballroom. Narriman's relatives, who had come to domi-nate the palace staff, insisted on insulating the king for any unpleas-antries. Had Farouk been alerted two hours earlier when the vio-lence had begun, he might have saved Shepheard's, or the Opera House, or Cicurel's, or the Turf Club, or the twenty-six foreigners who were beaten or burned to death. The second Farouk saw the flames, he knew his war of survival had begun. The fairy tale that had been his life and that had been imperial Egypt had ended with the rudest jolt. Farouk was face-to-face with all the ugly realities no courtier could shield him from again. If the king still liked being the king, he now would have to step off the throne and fight for it.

XII

EXILE

The world political cliffhanger of the year 1952 was what was going to happen in Egypt. While the Communist witch hunts continued in America, the Mau Maus rose in Kenya, Elizabeth became queen in England, the bullets kept flying in Korea, and the first H-bomb exploded in the Bikini Atoll, King Farouk was doing fancier footwork than Rocky Marciano against Jersey Joe Walcott to retain the heavyweight crown of his country.

By the time Farouk finished his banquet and got his army officers out of the ballroom and into the streets on Black Saturday, every single cinema, cabaret, nightclub, and bar, in all four hundred establishments that had made Cairo the Paris of the Middle East, had been torched. Now it looked more like Pompeii. The pleasure-dome focus of the riots pointed a long finger of suspicion at the Muslim Brotherhood, which had recently been permitted by Prime Minister Nahas, as the designer of this act of rage against the foreign infidels and heathen pashas, to rearm.

The most symbolic gesture of defiance of the Old Guard was the premeditated arson of Shepheard's Hotel. Early on the morning of January 26, a truckload of men in workers' uniforms entered the hotel's lobby and identified themselves as a municipal extermination crew that had come to spray the establishment for vermin. In their minds, the impostors were telling the truth. The DDT they had come to spray was actually gasoline. In a short while, all that remained of this ultimate caravanserai was the Sakkara sphinx at the entrance and the charred lintel with three carved lotus blossoms around the hotel's motto, Quis Aquam Nili Bibit Sarum Bibit. ("Whoever drinks the water of the Nile drinks wine," bilharzia notwithstanding.) The era of the Long Bar and the "suffering bastard" was over.

During Black Saturday, Nahas was busy getting a pedicure. His only strategic move of the day was to send an armored car to bring his wife home from the hairdresser. His lieutenant Fuad Serag el Din spent the day negotiating a real estate deal in Swiss francs. By the next morning, order had finally been restored, and Farouk took the occasion to heap all the blame for the riots on the Wafd. Rising to the height of the authority that the constitution conferred upon the monarchy, Farouk dismissed Nahas with great brio. In his place as prime minister Farouk brought back his oldest ally, Ali Maher, whom Nahas had interned during the war for his alleged Axis sympathies. The consummate politician, Ali Maher, who at seventy was one of the richest men in Egypt, bore no grudges, much to Farouk's dismay.

Age and wealth had dulled Ali Maher's sting. The old firebrand had become the great compromiser. Instead of dissolving the Wafd-controlled Parliament, he tried to work out a modus vivendi with it. Ali Maher didn't want to start purging Parliament until he had worked out some sort of canal exit deal with the British, and he knew he could count on the Wafd to rally support in the smaller cities up and down the Nile. Farouk couldn't, and wouldn't, wait for a purge. On March 2, after barely a month in office, Ali Maher was forced to resign.

Farouk's new prime minister was Egypt's Mr. Clean. Neguib el Hilaly, sixty, was, like Ali Maher, one of the country's preeminent lawyers. Unlike Ali Maher, he was above reproach and expected his peers to be as pure as he was. In November 1951, he had been expelled from the Wafd for having accused Fuad Serag el Din of illegal wiretapping. Now, declaring as he took office, "There is sedition in this country and I must eradicate it," the virulently anti-Communist Hilaly suspended Parliament and sent a fifty-man police force to seize Serag el Din in his Cairo mansion, take him to his country mansion in the Nile delta, and hold him there under house arrest for his complicity and duplicity in Black Saturday. Trials began for over eight hundred of the rioters and an official campaign began to root out Wafd corruption, starting by an order to halt construction on Madame Nahas's new eighty-passenger yacht, the *Sudan.*

Then Hilaly turned to the British, but he was unable to make any inroads into their intransigence over the Sudan, which had become the efficiency showcase of their colonial administration. The British needed the Sudan as a sop to their dwindling prestige as a super-power and held the line. At the same time, Hilaly became the victim of his own purity. Jefferson Caffery reported to Washington a secret conversation with one of the prime objects of Hilaly's graft cleanup, Karim Thabet, who spoke fast and eloquently about the pitfalls of reform: What terrified Thabet most was Hilaly's new Fortunes Bill, which would require all past, present, and future ministers to declare the sources of their wealth. Thabet called this effort at full disclosure the "where-did-you-get-it" bill. He thought it could destroy Farouk.

> He (Thabet) feared that . . . by purging the Wafd a verita-ble Pandora's box would be opened and Egypt would go through a Roman holiday of charges and countercharges which could only result in the man-in-the-street becoming aware of the fact that he has been ruled by crooks of various colorations for at least the past ten years. (Thabet) said that he was deeply concerned that such an awareness could only result in a further deterioration of the King's reputation with the people for having been responsible for the naming of such men to his Cabinets. This in turn . . . meant a further disillusion-ment and a further turning toward the Communists and radi-cal Socialists in an already dangerous situation. His conclusion was that Hilali Pasha must be discharged from office immedi-ately.

Karim Thabet's solution, of course, was himself. He pressed Caf-fery to advise Farouk to get rid of Hilaly and appoint an obedient "king's man," the venerable former prime minister Hussein Sirry, who was Farida's uncle but still loyal to Farouk. In this scheme, Thabet would be brought back to the palace as Farouk's go-between with Sirry, whose first act, in Thabet's opinion, would be to "come up with a broad social and land reform scheme which could be sold to the people in such a way as to rebuild the King's presently shat-tered prestige as the 'savior of Egypt.' " Thabet recommended that the Sudan issue be back-burnered and efforts focused on reducing the cost of certain living essentials, such as bread, "so that the millions of Egyptians who are unconcerned with politics but very much concerned with keeping their stomachs filled would see im-mediately a substantial amelioration in their personal lives flowing from the wisdom and example of their king."

Self-serving as it might have been, Thabet's advice was taken. On July 1, Hilaly resigned. Hussein Sirry became the new prime minister. And Karim Thabet made his comeback. Thabet inaugurated his return with a preposterous public relations gesture. Thabet had the Egyptian Union of Sherifs, the final authority on Muslim lineage, declare Farouk a direct descendant of the Prophet on Queen Nazli's side. Now, in addition to being king of Egypt and sovereign of Nubia, the Sudan, Kordofan, and Darfour, Farouk could add the El Sayed to his titles, denoting his holy as well as royal descent. For a king who gorged on lobster and bathed in the chips of baccarat during Ramadan, this was a bit much for the now-dubious Egyptians who denounced the entire affair, making it even clearer that the masses needed tangible appeasement and not sacred hot air. As General Neguib wrote: "If there was any Arabic blood in Farouk's veins, it was so diluted that it couldn't possibly have been traced back to Mohammed, and it was a sacrilege for anyone to have tried to do so."

Before Prime Minister Sirry could address himself to any social or land reforms, he had certain priorities to attend to. His first act was to release Serag ed Din from house arrest. Both the Americans and British groaned with the agony of déjà vu. The status quo of corruption was about to be restored. It was Sirry's second act, however, that brought down the house of Mohammed Ali. This was Sirry's attempt to appoint as his minister of war none other than General Neguib. Farouk couldn't have been angrier if Sirry had somehow brought back Sir Miles Lampson. Sirry, like Ali Maher, was trying to coopt the army to keep the peace, tenuous as it was.

Farouk had throughout the entire Black Saturday aftermath assumed that if any segment of Egypt was in his royal pocket, it was the army. After the Palestine war, Farouk had boasted to Jefferson Caffery that even though his soldiers lost, they hadn't done badly for being so underequipped. "They were fighting with bare breasts against tanks and armored cars. The Egyptian Army did that for me and they will do anything I say and they won't do it for anyone else. That is why I feel so strongly about them." So strongly that he tried to push Caffery to get more Egyptians admitted to West Point and more American arms for them to be prepared with, so there would not be another Palestine rout. Farouk saw himself as the generous father of his military; his officers would not bite the hand that fed them at the January 26 banquet for Prince Fuad. They were

Teen Queen • Mimi Medart, the hamburger heiress whose parents hired a ruthless press agent to fabricate a front page tabloid romance with Farouk, to further their ambitions for Mimi's Hollywood career.

Conjugality Redux • Official photograph of Farouk's palace wedding to Narriman, 1951.

O Captain • Farouk and Narriman in identical yachting garb on their three-month royal honeymoon in Europe.

Hit Men • General Gamal Abdel Nasser, with General Mohammed Neguib, whom Nasser ousted as the figurehead of the Egyptian "revolution."

defenders of the Old Order, part of the status quo. Farouk's assumption was his fatal mistake. It was also shortsightedness of the first order, for in the army lay the missing element, leadership, that would complete the Lenin trinity that would make for a revolution.

Perhaps his preoccupation with the birth of his son caused Farouk to overlook the early warning signs, ominous though they were. In early January, Neguib had been elected president of the Officers Club in Zamalek over the king's candidate, General Sirri Amer, whom Neguib had accused of masterminding a plot to sell diesel oil, scrap metals, and munitions belonging to the Egyptian Army to a ring of Jewish smugglers living in Giza. The Jewish smugglers in turn had sold the material to Israel. Neguib felt Amer was thereby guilty of trading with the enemy and, hence, treason. The clandestine Free Officers group of Nasser and Sadat, whose propaganda was known but whose members were scrupulously anonymous, first tried to leaflet a prosecution of General Amer. That failing, they tried to assassinate him. Fourteen bullets having missed, they changed their strategy and got behind Neguib as an "alternative" candidate. They scored their first minor victory, which was minimized even further when Farouk refused to recognize the vote as a valid one.

Prime Minister Sirry, sensing the dissension in the army as Farouk's Achilles' heel, thought that by bringing front-man Neguib into the government, he could short-circuit any other anti-Farouk movements within the military. Farouk wouldn't have it. The only front Farouk would consider Neguib for was the western front, out in the desert where Neguib had led the Frontier Corps, out of Cairo, and out of the minds of the restive younger officers. The most Farouk would agree to compromise with Sirry on was that he would permanently retire the hated-by-junior-officers General Amer in return for the permanent retirement of the hated-by-Farouk General Neguib. Unwilling to get involved in such horse trading, Sirry resigned after eighteen days in office.

Farouk brought back the clean man, Hilaly, and promised to let him unleash his scruples on the Wafd and purify the country. As part of the cleansing process, Farouk had his own addenda to Hilaly's agenda. First, he appointed as minister of war the one army man he knew he could trust, Princess Fawzia's second husband, Colonel Ismail Sherine. Sherine was no MacArthur, nor even a Neguib for that matter. But he was family. And he certainly looked the part—tall, dark, as dramatically handsome as Fawzia was beautiful, an Egyptian version of Tyrone Power in *The Long Gray Line*. Besides, wasn't Farouk the British general? He could tell Sherine what to do if it came to war.

War, however, wasn't what Farouk was contemplating. This time around he would give Hilaly a mandate to root out not only corruption but subversion, subversion that could undermine his reign and lead to insurrection and, Farouk's horror of horrors, communism. Farouk knew who his enemies were. His espionage network had finally identified the Free Officers. It knew about Nasser and Sadat and their ten cohorts. He wanted them all either arrested or otherwise disposed of, the way Supreme Guide Hassan el Banna had been disposed of, by the time the Alexandria summer was over and the season resumed in Cairo in October. Farouk was convinced that after these steps, as in the step with el Banna, Hilaly would do his fall cleaning; Britain and America, which both endorsed Hilaly, would be pleased, and Egypt would go back to business as usual, with a new deal for the fellaheen and a chastened yet still dominant pasha class. On July 20, 1952, Farouk truly believed that he would have peace in his time.

If only Farouk had been less of an Egyptian when it came to time. This was a king who had two huge signs reading PATIENCE on his royal desk. He had more of a *mañana* mentality than any Latin American. This was Egypt, after all, and this was summer, when it was too hot for anything, even a revolution. It was 117 degrees in Cairo. Farouk assumed he had plenty of time to round up the Free Officers. His patience cost him his throne.

On the three-day voyage of the *Mahroussa* between Alexandria and Naples, ex-King Farouk had little to console himself with besides the ironies of departure. Here he was with his young son, Fuad, sailing off to exile on the same yacht his father had sailed on as a boy with *his* exiled father, the khedive Ismail. The two Fuads. If British action caused the fall of Ismail, it was British inaction that caused that of Farouk. Here Farouk was, a king in what was for so long, in effect, a British colony, an honorary general in the British Army, in so many ways one of *them*. Why had they forsaken him? Because they were British, that was why, and he felt all the more the fool for trusting them. And the Americans! How could these phobic anti-Communists let Egypt fall to a junta that Farouk believed with all his heart was Communist, a radical regime that would cause Red Square to rejoice. Did America simply have a hostility toward kings, whatever they stood for? Farouk had thought the Americans were his friends as much as he was theirs. Wrong again. And Ali Maher, *his* Ali Maher. Of all people, the royalists' royalist, to become the mouthpiece of the mob.

Aside from compiling an inventory of betrayal, there was nothing else to do on the *Mahroussa*. Not even eat. The Free Officers had done everything to ensure that Farouk's last voyage was anything but a pleasure cruise. Above all, they hit the king where they knew it would hurt, in the stomach. The only sustenance on board was bread, cheese, and cottonseed oil, and only enough to provide one meal of a grilled cheese sandwich each day. Farouk let his three daughters vote when they wanted the repast. They chose dinner so they could have something to look forward to. The previous summer Farouk was sailing on this same Mediterranean, the king of kings on his epic honeymoon. Now he was in exile, eating scraps.

At least he wasn't torpedoed. The first day out of Alexandria, the captain of the yacht, who was still loyal to Farouk, received information that he was being followed by a gunboat that was planning to blow up the *Mahroussa*. He zigzagged across the Mediterranean for twenty-four hours and eluded the attack. The Free Officers had ensured that none of the crew would be too loyal to Farouk by holding one family member of each crewman and officer hostage until the yacht returned to Egypt. Still, Farouk was lucky to be alive. Ali Maher admitted to Jefferson Caffery that "some young hothead officers were out to kill the king." One of the most brutal of the Free Officers, Gamal Salem, had decided to override Nasser's decision to spare the king by having Farouk shot dead on board during the farewell twenty-one-gun salute at the Ras-el-Tin quay. Only because Caffery, who had become the American sponsor of the Free Officers, was standing beside Farouk during the fusillade was the king not assassinated. Even though the Americans may have cost Farouk his throne, they left him his life, and he never once publicly expressed any bitterness or resentment toward the United States for the fall of his dynasty. For that he saved all the blame for Great Britain.

All rumors to the contrary, Farouk was not able to escape from Egypt with a king's ransom. To begin with, virtually all his great treasures were in Abdine Palace in Cairo, and he was summering at

Montazah when the coup occurred. Although the royal family brought a total of sixty-six pieces of luggage onto the yacht, when these were allocated among Farouk, Narriman, the children, the bodyguards, and the nurses and governesses who were allowed to go with them, it was not an impressive haul. Farouk himself had only two good suits and six shirts from his wardrobe of a thousand suits and a hundred uniforms, while Narriman could throw together only seven outfits in the gunpoint getaway. Prince Fuad's (now with his father's abdication, King Fuad) nurse, Anne Chermside, had made the biggest score, secreting four of the baby monarch's finest gold and jewel-encrusted ceremonial gowns under a suitcase full of diapers. The three princesses, who all elected to leave Egypt with Farouk rather than remain with Farida, left with little more than a few sundresses and their favorite dolls. Farouk had put the choice of exile not only to the princesses but also to the new queen. Farouk warned Narriman that she might never see her beloved mother again and that, at seventeen, there was no question about starting a new life. As Farouk recalled in his serialized memoirs what his words to her were: "You must not accompany me in pity, for pity does not last, and it is better to part now than to live to hate each other." He had no idea how quickly prophetic he would be.

When the *Mahroussa* reached Naples on July 29, Farouk bade a teary farewell to the crew, who lined up to kneel before their ruler, shake his hand, and shout out three times, "Long live Farouk, king of Egypt and the Sudan." Then reality set in. Dressed in a black suit and a black tie, Farouk and his family (Narriman wore a yellow dress) transferred their belongings from the royal yacht to a shabby little steamer, the *Linda*, that was normally used to ferry day-tripping tourists on excursions around the Bay of Naples, as an infinity of press cameras from around the world recorded every minute twist and turn of Farouk's fall from grace. The *Linda* took the family on to Capri. It was the height of the summer season, and Farouk easily eclipsed the Grotta Azzurra as the fabled romantic isle's chief tourist attraction. The ignominy did not let up. At the grand luxe hotel, the Cesare Augusto, where Farouk and Narriman had spent part of their honeymoon the year before, there was no room at the inn. Farouk was forced to settle for the "bad" west end of the island known as Anacapri and the entire top floor and roof garden of the Eden Paradiso Hotel to house the entourage of twenty-six. Farouk was registered as "His Royal Highness Prince Farouk Fuad of Egypt." At least the food was good. Famished after the sea rations of bread and cheese, Farouk laid out a first supper for his family of spaghetti marinara, cold lobster with mayonnaise, steak and french fries, green salad, chocolate ice cream, white peaches, and a case of orangeade. For his first breakfast Farouk ate ten eggs. Why, a reporter hounded him. "I like eggs," Farouk replied.

The next day he held a press conference on the terrace of his hotel, fielding questions in English, French, and Italian from over one hundred reporters. At his side were Narriman, his daughters, and King Fuad, suckled with a bottle by Anne Chermside. Praising the beauty of Capri, Farouk asserted that his exile was his first real holiday since he had become king. During his bachelor party and honeymoon, he said he had been preoccupied with the business of state. He introduced his son, the king, and alluded to the difficulties attendant to the throne, carefully avoiding any comment that might embarrass his host, the Italian government. Farouk stressed that he alone was in exile and that his wife and children were free to return to Egypt. Asked where he would live, Farouk said he wasn't sure except that it would not be behind the Iron Curtain. Then came the big questions, the ones about money. "My children are now all the kingdom that I possess. I am no longer a rich man," Farouk said, conceding only that "by the standards of the very poor I am still to be envied." He vowed that it was untrue that "I have brought from Egypt a fortune, just as it is untrue that I have a fortune abroad. My wife, my son, and my three daughters will live very, very simply." Not one reporter in Capri believed him.

While Farouk's Roman lawyer, Carlo d'Emilio, who also was counsel to the Italian royal family exiled in Alexandria, searched for suitable housing for Italy's most famous summer visitors, Farouk would take his daughters to swim each day at the Canzone del Mare. Between laps the princesses took their daily lessons from their French tutor, Mademoiselle Tabouret, then took turns at the grand piano in the nightclub. Princess Ferial, thirteen, was already something of a virtuoso. She would play Chopin and Liszt while Princess Fawzia, eleven, an intellectual in the making, read *Jane Eyre* in French, and Princess Fadia, eight, played with Gracie Fields's Alsatians. All the while the swarms of reporters outside the club were trying to trump each other with sensational stories. Telephoto lenses provided one of the young Muslim princesses in bathing suits, which was supposed to be scandalous. Imagination provided another when Farouk sent a hotel porter out to buy a Mother Goose lampshade to enliven Fadia's dreary hotel room. What emerged in the papers was that Farouk was going to redecorate the entire Eden Paradiso like an Arabian Nights seraglio. A request to the restaurant manager to play some cheerful music became a rooftop orgy for six hundred people.

By September the gawkers had left Capri and Carlo d'Emilio had installed Farouk and his family at the Villa Dusmet, a massive, forbidding thirty-room Etruscan red stucco rented estate in the Alban Hills outside Rome. The villa was just down the road from Castel Gandolfo, where the pope had his summer palace. The residence was guarded by a high wall, by snarling Dobermans and German shepherd attack dogs, and by a contingent of Italian police assigned to the exiled Egyptians. Here Farouk could be left in peace. Soon he was bored to death. While the three princesses spent most of their days with visiting tutors who taught them everything from dancing to fencing to Arabic, Farouk and Narriman spent theirs with their respective ghost writers, Norman Price, an ex-major of the British commandos who became a freelance writer after the war, and Klaus Bloemer, a German physician turned journalist. By December the royal couple's separate self-justifying apologia cum memoirs were being serialized throughout Europe and America. They were banned in Egypt, where they might have provided a needed counterpoint to the Alamo siege of the Egyptian Old Order that had commenced with the Free Officers' coup in July.

On July 30, Neguib abolished the titles of pasha and bey. He arrested Karim Thabet and General Sirri Amer, brought them before his military tribunal, and sentenced them to life imprisonment. That "people's" court also gave fifteen-year sentences to Wafd strongman Fuad Serag ed Din, and to Farouk's doctor and chauffeur. Farouk's cousin Prince Abbas Halim testified that Farouk posed as a playboy only to conceal his impotence, that he cheated at cards and gambled with Jews. In return, the court gave the prince a fifteen-year suspended sentence for his role in the sale of defective arms to the army during the 1948 war with Israel. It confiscated a great portion of Madame Nahas's delta farmland, but somehow let her husband, always the politician, negotiate his way out of reprisal. Not so Antonio Pulli, who was tortured until he "denounced" Farouk. And not so a number of others who were hanged for crimes against the state. All the property belonging to any heirs of the Mohammed Ali dynasty was confiscated; over four hundred members of Egypt's clan of clans found themselves suddenly dispossessed. Their hundred thousand acres was redistributed among the fellaheen. The Free Officers were heartless toward the aristocracy and anyone who had a heart toward them. When Prime Minister Ali Maher tried to enable the old and sick Prince Mohammed Ali, still the heir to the throne of little King Fuad, leave Egypt and take 100,000 Egyptian pounds of his fortune with him, the Free Officers forced Ali Maher to submit his resignation. When it came to money, the Free Officers weren't going to yield a piaster.

If Ali Maher should have balked on returning any favors, it was toward the venerable prince, who had recommended cleaning up the Cairo streets by deporting to the Sudan the first hundred families whose children were arrested for begging, and to eliminate jaywalkers by passing a law exempting chauffeurs for responsibility for any injury to pedestrians. Nor were the Free Officers amused when they inspected the prince's ledgers and discovered an expense item, Weekly Wedding and Dancers' Fees. The prince was fortunate to be able to leave the country for Switzerland. Most of his relatives were detained. Of the king's inner circle, no one escaped retribution except for Elias Andraos, who died in London soon after the coup, and Edmond Galhan, who was summering in regal style on the Riviera and never went back to Egypt. After his "confession," which did not include revealing the location of Farouk's European assets (he denied any knowledge), Antonio Pulli was released from jail. He opened a nightclub on a large houseboat on the Nile. Under the new regime, such sybaritic ventures were doomed to failure. Pulli went on to manage a small pastry shop in Heliopolis. He let them eat cake after all.

If the Free Officers were thwarted in assassinating Farouk, they more than made up for it by what they did to his character, or what was left of it. In addition to the quid pro quo denunciations of the fallen monarch that poured out of the witness box in return for the leniency of the military junta now running the country, the Neguib administration put on a campaign of Farouk defamation that was meant to justify them in their having taken his place. To begin with, they began giving "life-styles of the rich and shameless" tours of Farouk's palaces to prurient foreign journalists.

The tours started at Koubbeh Palace, with its hundreds of lavish rooms, its seventeen-million-dollar stamp collection, its royal wardrobe of two thousand silk shirts, ten thousand silk ties, and fifty gold-and-diamond-studded walking sticks, its study with huge autographed and framed photographs of Adolf Hitler over which Farouk and those who knew him protested. They claimed the Free Officers had planted the Nazi photos, which showed the stuff they were made of.

They didn't need to go that far. In the royal kennels, rare fox hounds, greyhounds, afghans, and hunting dogs lived and ate better than the fellaheen. The twenty elaborate American reducing machines in the royal gymnasium were an exercise in extravagant futility. There were Fabergé eggs which soldiers passed like footballs, and ancient Tibetan coins and suits of armor and strongboxes full of diamonds and rubies. And there was also tons of junk—aspirin bottles, paper clips, razor blades, pocket geiger counters that read "Measure nuclear energy yourself," and a wall of magic tricks.

Most titillating was the pornography. There were dirty postcards, dirty playing cards, dirty calendars, dirty cocktail glasses, dirty corkscrews, dirty fishing flies, dirty watches. And that was only at Koubbeh. There were immediate offers to buy some of Farouk's pornographic neckties. The army refused. Nothing was for sale. Yet. The Free Officers also gave the press peeks at Abdine's Baths of Caracalla–scale *salles de bain* with their life-size naked-nymph murals, or Narriman's bedroom at Ras-el-Tin with its sixty-nine pieces of Louis XV furniture, its white tulle mosquito netting, its copy of *Lady Chatterley's Lover* carefully laid out on the antique bed, or Farouk's master bedroom at Montazah with its six telephones, seventy-five pairs of binoculars, a projector filled with lesbian slides, and library of Walt Disney's *Uncle Scrooge* comics. More, much more, was to come. The Revolutionary Council had hired Sotheby's to come to Cairo in 1954 to auction off the entire contents of what became known as the Palace Collections of Egypt.

In October, when Farouk's memoirs began appearing weekly, General Neguib, who had made himself prime minister in Ali Maher's place, in addition to remaining commander in chief, stepped up the war of the words by threatening to indict Farouk for treason and bring him back to Cairo to stand trial for his many high crimes and misdemeanors, which, according to Neguib, included "treacherous assassinations." "All Egypt is now praying for its manhood," Neguib said, "which was sacrificed on the altar of his (Farouk's) lust and tyranny." What set Neguib off was Farouk's general assertion that Egypt's military revolutionary movement was dominated by Communists and heavily funded by Russia, and his specific one that the "Neguibists" had killed his daughters' pet dogs in the Montazah kennels and had killed Ferial's favorite white Arab pony by thrusting a bayonet through its eyes. "The pet dogs," Neguib riposted, "are alive, enjoying the blessings of freedom, and they bark only when they see the shadow of the past." Farouk critiqued Neguib's remarks as "a typical dictator's speech on the good Kremlin pattern" and challenged Neguib to make up his mind whether little Fuad was really going to be king of Egypt or not: "When is Egypt going to make a decision about the financial maintenance in proper dignity of its present King Fuad, my son? (Whom Farouk threatened might one day end up "living upon the charity of the Italian government like any unfortunate Neapolitan orphan.") Does this abuse and argument simply mean that Neguib cannot wait to destroy the dynasty and become dictator in full?" On June 18, 1953, the Revolutionary Council officially deposed King Fuad, age eighteen months, and brought the Mohammed Ali dynasty to its formal end. It was 148 years old. "The monarchy has decayed and is gone forever," was Nasser's terse eulogy. In October 1954, Nasser brought Neguib to his own formal end, maneuvering his avuncular figurehead out of office and stepping out into the spotlight as the real wizard of the revolution and now the undisputed ruler of the country.

Farouk could only sit on the sidelines, say "I told you so," and hope Nasser would either take one step too far that would plunge the country into civil war and force Britain to protect the Suez Canal, to restore the monarchy as the one source of stability, or that Nasser would be so foolish as to attack the canal itself. That, Farouk was sure, would also see the British come back to him and say "you weren't so bad after all, old boy. Why don't you come back and pick up where you left off?" Until that fatal move, Farouk was content to abide by his maxim, "Patience." Moreover, the sidelines where he sat were all that any man, especially a man like Farouk, could ever hope for. In the early fifties, Rome had become the urban playground of Europe. All the elements were there—beauty, antiquities, sunshine, and, above all, distress-sale prices. Because Italy was still economically ravaged by the war, the Eternal City had become the Continent's greatest bargain. And no one could smell a bargain like Hollywood, which came to Rome to shoot its epics at Cinecittà rather than at Burbank. The stars and their publicity machines created a glamorous siren call that lured the most beautiful and ambitious thespians and camp followers; the moguls of Sunset Boulevard became ersatz modern-day Caesars.

Enter Farouk, a genuine caesar, a king, a pharaoh. The fat, cigar-chomping Hollywood producers who dangled the keys of wealth and fame to the aspiring actresses who flocked to Rome from California, Texas, Scandinavia, the "starlet belt," were nothing but shoddy imitations of Farouk, who was even fatter and smoked better cigars, whose smoke became the incense of success. Here was the ultimate fat cat, and a pedigreed one at that, whom *Newsweek* estimated to have retained "only $40,000,000 of his personal fortune." Not just the starlets wanted to meet Farouk. The stars and the moguls did too. Orson Welles, for one, tried to promote Farouk into backing one of his films. Farouk couldn't have cared less about the stars; he was, however, not oblivious to the starlets. He missed the Scarabee, the Auberge des Pyramides, much more than he missed sunset over the sphinx or the Fabergé eggs he had left behind at Abdine. Farouk was the night king of Egypt; he loved going out. He felt like the prisoner of Chillon at the Villa Dusmet. Rome of the fifties was like Cairo of the forties. Although Farouk was now a mere thirty-two, he sensed his youth was fading as quickly as his throne. But Rome was there to keep him young and keep him happy, to fuel him with remembrances of Cairo past. Farouk couldn't go home again, but he could go to the Via Veneto, where he could once more reign as king—of the night.

A typical Roman evening for Farouk would begin with dinner at the Circolo Degli Scacchi (Chess Club) one of the city's most exclusive and aristocratic private preserves. (The *most* exclusive, the Circolo Degli Caccia [Hunt Club] in the Palazzo Borghese voted to deny Farouk membership.) After dinner Farouk would go to the paneled and tapestried gaming rooms, where he played, not chess, but high-stakes card games. While Farouk played baccarat, Narriman would play canasta in the ladies' lounge with Italian princesses and duchesses. Eventually Farouk would round up his wife and exit the club to their new Egyptian-green Mercedes limousine, where his Albanian bodyguards waited. Accompanied by Italian motorcycle police, Farouk and company would proceed across the city to the Via Veneto, where he would catch the floor shows at the Boîte Pigalle, the Piccolo Slam, the Gicky Club, Bricktop's, or whatever the nightclub of the moment was. Farouk would often buy drinks for the entire patronage and entertain the more talented ladies of the chorus, telling jokes, laughing, singing, tapping time with the silverware while Narriman simply sat in impassive silence. At dawn Farouk would stop at one of the Veneto foreign newsstands for a fresh supply of the latest *Uncle Scrooge*s and *Stag*s and cruise off into the dawn rising over the Alban Hills.

In time, Narriman began staying home nights, preferring daylight shopping trips in her own chauffeured red Mercedes. And in more time, Narriman stopped going out at all. In the winter of 1952, Farouk took her on a skiing holiday in the Italian and Swiss Alps, staying in the imperial suite of one mountain hotel that had been the love nest of Benito Mussolini and his mistress Claretta Petacci. Despite the roses and carnations Farouk filled her rooms with, Narriman wasn't enjoying herself. She wouldn't ski, and she wouldn't après ski either. When Farouk could coax her into a dining room, she refused to eat and refused to speak, just scowling and jangling her gold bracelets so loudly that observers weren't sure whether Farouk was holding her hand out of affection or out of restraint. She was barely nineteen, but the world didn't expect such adolescent behavior from a queen. On March 13, 1953, accompanied by her mother, her poodle, and wearing a brown suit, three inch-heeled crocodile pumps, dark glasses, and a single diamond brooch, Narriman, sans Fuad, left Farouk and Rome for Geneva. On March 23, the two Sadek women boarded an Air India flight from Geneva direct to Cairo. Farouk used to jest that Mrs. Sadek, who finally gave birth to Narriman after seven miscarriages, had raised her only child to be a queen even if he hadn't married her. Now Farouk, through his new Karem Thabet cum Antonio Pulli, a darkly handsome young third secretary of the Egyptian embassy in Rome named Amin Fahim, who had defected from his post when Neguib took power, attacked Mrs. Sadek as the homewrecking puppet of Neguib, who was using her to try to abduct King Fuad back to Cairo. Mrs. Sadek, the mother-in-law from hell, proclaimed that Narriman had left Farouk for no reason other than "she just could not go on living with him any longer. Their characters are completely incompatible."

Glad to have Narriman back in Egypt as further publicity proof of Farouk's vice and their own virtue, the Free Officers gave the ex-queen a new passport in her maiden name and allowed her to return to the palaces for a limited repossession of some of her regal belong-ings, which, a government spokesman described as "extorted by Farouk from the people." What Narriman was given as her home-coming trousseau were seven coats—three mink, a sable, a lynx, an ermine, and an astrakhan—eight Dior evening dresses, twenty-two afternoon dresses, twenty-four pairs of shoes, twelve bags, fifty pairs of slippers, forty silk nightgowns, and 130 pairs of nylons. Once General Neguib saw that Narriman could not deliver Fuad, he sim-ply abolished the monarchy and was done with it.

In September, Narriman filed for divorce in the Heliopolis Shari'a, or Moslem court, serving Farouk in Rome and demanding a huge alimony of five thousand Egyptian pounds or $15,000 monthly. Farouk sent a prominent Syrian lawyer to Egypt to repre-sent him. In February 1954, Narriman signed a divorce agreement, giving her no alimony and relinquishing her claim, under Islamic law, that a mother retain custody of her son until he was seven years old. Without King Fuad as a bargaining chip, the Egyptian justice system cared as little about the ex-queen as it did about the ex-king.

In May of that year, Narriman, who had little to show from her fairy-tale marriage except her clothes, tried once more. Her new husband was a young Cambridge-educated Alexandrian surgeon, Dr. Adham el Nakib. Ironically, the groom's father was Farouk's doctor, Ahmed el Nakib, the top floor of whose Mossat Hospital in Alexandria was converted into Farouk's "carry-on nurse" *garçon-nière*. Dr. Nakib *père* was not at the ceremony. He was in prison serving his fifteen-year sentence for Faroukian graft. Narriman told the press she was delighted to try to live on her new husband's modest income from his post at the Anglo-American Hospital in Alexandria. "Happiness," said the world-weary twenty-year-old, "does not lie in living in palaces but in love, sympathy, and good understanding between husband and wife. I have tried living in palaces, but I was miserable. I feel certain that I shall be happy with Adham el Nakib because I love him and he loves me." Narriman and el Nakib separated the next year.

The Egyptian system was no more generous with the other queens in Farouk's life. In July 1953, ex-Queen Nazli, who had moved with Princess Fathia and Riad Ghali to a mansion off Benedict Canyon in Beverly Hills, retained Cairo lawyers to lift the guardianship Farouk had imposed on all her Egyptian properties. The Egyptian government contested Nazli's petition on the grounds that she was "mentally incapacitated" and could not administer her estate, and ordered that she appear personally in Cairo to submit to a medical examination. This she balked at and instead sent sworn testimonials to her sanity from her California doctors. The Egyptian court refused to allow these statements into evidence, rejected Nazli's petition, and ordered her to pay all court costs.

In November 1953, ex-Queen Farida was forced to hand over all her crowns and jewelry, three cars, and other valuables to the "confiscation committee," which had been formed to take gestapolike action to prevent the large-scale money and jewel smuggling on the part of many Mohammed Ali dynasts such as the daughters of Prince Abbas Halim, who agreed to repay part of the smuggled capital on the condition that the charges against them be dropped. Apparently, there was a land-office business being carried on with the royal family by "professional" smugglers. As part of the embargo, royal family members were now blocked from leaving Egypt. As for Farida, while she was not evicted from the pyramid-adjacent palace Farouk had given her, the Neguibists took title to the residence and charged rent to her former majesty, who began to paint to support herself.

Farouk's princess sisters, aside from Fathia in Beverly Hills, fared no better than the queens. The revolutionaries confiscated Faiza's palace, though Faiza, through her strong connections with the American embassy (she was the most Americanized of the family), was able to escape Egypt to Paris. There she shared a small Left Bank apartment with her husband and tried—and failed—to sell the six-figure-valued jewelry she had taken with her. From there she moved to California to join her mother and sister. Fawzia actually sued the Neguibists for confiscating over 600,000 dollars worth of jewels that she said came from the shah, not Farouk, and hence were not classifiable as ill-begotten gains, at least not by the Egyptian dynasty. She lost. Fawzia did remain in Egypt, as did Faika, leading low-key family lives that would attract as little attention as possible.

Almost every day in Egypt their brother remained in the spotlight, as the enemies-of-the-people trials continued, and every defendant tried to bargain a plea by telling a can-you-top-this horror story about the deported monarch. Abbas Halim had said that Farouk was impotent *and* effeminate. Karim Thabet talked about Farouk's "abnormal glands" and accepting of "Jewish bribes." Ali Maher described Farouk as a "miser who liked to make money" and "knew nothing whatsoever," delegating all royal memoranda to be composed by his valet, whose grammar was "better than Farouk's." The valet got fifteen years of hard labor. Ali Maher went on to catalog all the books on "social problems" he had ordered for Farouk "from Oxford and Cambridge." Farouk "claimed to know everything" and never opened the books. Dr. Nakib talked about his foreign excursions to search for the world's most beautiful nurses for Farouk's Alexandria "emergency room." Witnesses at his trial testified about the international and pulchritudinous health care staff's "bad manners and neglect of their duties." The prosecutor described the medical facility as "a hospital, not for patients, but for prostitution."

Everyone had a "j'accuse" from Farouk's murdering the officer husband of one of his forced mistresses when the king was caught in flagrante delicto, to outlawing the film *Quo Vadis* in Egypt because Nero reminded Farouk too much of himself. Now *Quo Vadis* was given a belated release and was the number-one hit at the Cairo box office, held over indefinitely. Whenever Peter Ustinov, as Nero, hit the screen, the audiences would shout "To Capri! To Capri!" So successful a piece of propaganda was *Quo Vadis* that General Neguib agreed to lend Egypt's assistance to the making of another, more direct cinematic attack on Farouk, a film à clef entitled *My Kingdom for a Woman.* The producer-director of the opus, Gregory Ratoff, was same man who had given Mimi Medart, Farouk's imaginary flame of the summer of 1950, her Hollywood contract, financed in the best Hollywood tradition by her own father. In another Hollywood tradition Ratoff vehemently denied that the film was about Farouk. "If you ask me officially if it is about Farouk, I must tell you no! No!" Then he described the story about a "playboy monarch, a gambler, a money-crazy king with an enthusiasm for life and women" and added, "if the world sees Farouk in the character of the star, then we can do nothing about it."

The English comedienne Kay Kendall, later Mrs. Rex Harrison, was cast in the Barbara Skelton role as an adventurous English model. Belly dancer Samia Gamal was cast as an à clef version of herself, while Sidney Chaplin, Charlie's son, was to play a British

Army officer in a triangle with Kay Kendall and the king. For "King Abdullah," as the lead was named, Ratoff tried to cast Orson Welles. When Welles finally turned him down, Ratoff grew a beard and took the part himself, becoming a triple hyphenate—the actor-director-producer. Neguib gave Ratoff permission to film in the bedrooms and bathrooms of Abdine and Koubbeh, as well as on the *Mahroussa*. His only restrictions were no shots of the pyramids, of red fezzes, and of Neguib or any of the Free Officers or the army. Otherwise, anything could go, in what Ratoff kept insisting was "the story of a nonexistent man in a nonexistent country. It just so happens that by a coincidence there is a remarkable resemblance to an ex-king whose fabulous story everyone knows." The film was completed in early 1954. For some reason, it was never released. Anywhere. Perhaps the powerful hand of the king of lawyers, Carlo d'Emilio, was at work. D'Emilio had had no luck in trying to enjoin the upcoming Sotheby's auction of Farouk's collection, but had promised that he was waiting in the wings to sue any buyers who took any of Farouk's possessions out of Egypt. The specter of his prospective presence in a global defamation suit regarding *My Kingdom for a Woman* might well have made litigation-shy film distributors lose their nerve.

In Rome, Farouk kept his sense of humor. He could deal with anything. Except being alone. No sooner had Narriman left him than Farouk began appearing in the tabloids with assorted chorines, models, and actresses. There was the Audrey Hepburnesque red-headed Belgian model Gabrielle Wegge, and Greta Garboesque blond Danish Bluebell showgirl Margaretha Jorgenson, and the Charles Atlaseque brunette cabaret strong-girl Joan Rhodes, who bent steel bars with her teeth and tore telephone directories in half with "amazing feminine grace and coquetry," as the nightclub billed her. But these were professional beauties, "money players." What really appealed to Farouk was innocence. He genuinely missed Narriman, yet he knew he couldn't compete with the one-two combination of Mrs. Sadek and General Neguib. So he didn't even try to get her back. Instead, he tried to recreate her in the sixteen-year-old beauty he found poolside at Capri, Irma Capece Minutolo. But before he finally settled on Irma as the object of his Pygmalionization, he went through many other teenage candidates for his new queen, or at least lady-in-waiting.

One who recorded her experience of a Farouk courtship was an eighteen-year-old Swedish girl named Birgitta Stenberg, who memorialized her coming of age-of-consent in Paris, Rome, and the Riviera of the fifties in her first book, *Manplay in Europe*. She went on to write thirty other books, becoming one of Sweden's most popular authors, but in the summer of 1953 she was just another teenager eager to learn about love and life on the road. Before she met Farouk, Birgitta was having an eye-opening affair with American underworld leader Charles "Lucky" Luciano, who had been deported from Little Italy to the real one in 1946. Luciano, who was based in Naples, had met Farouk at Gracie Fields's Canzone del Mare and had struck up a friendship. They had much in common. Both were in exile. Both had known great power. Both loved beautiful women.

Luciano was later to protect Farouk's life on several occasions. Nasser had spies constantly observing Farouk and reporting back on the ex-king's every move. Nasser was paranoiacally obsessed with the notion that foreign powers might combine against him to bring back the monarchy. If Farouk were dead, and not just gone, that avenue would be foreclosed; Nasser didn't see the West restoring the throne to baby Fuad, who would be perceived as an Occidental puppet, not an Oriental potentate. The trick was how to kill Farouk. The task, which in itself was difficult, given Farouk's Albanian bodyguards and the Italian security policemen, became impossible when Luciano became the king's godfather. Luciano knew every hit man in Italy, was privy to every plot, and thwarted Nasser's every attempt to make a move on Farouk.

Luciano met Birgitta Stenberg by saving her virtue. She had met a Sicilian-American travel agent who was impressed with her language skills and offered her a job in his New York office. He gave Birgitta a free ticket to New York, with a layover in Buenos Aires, and held her passport. When Birgitta met Luciano, he told her the man was a white slaver and that the layover in South America would be a permanent one. Luciano got Birgitta her passport back. She remained grateful to him.

Farouk had seen Birgitta around with Luciano. When he spotted her with a diplomat friend from the American embassy named Donald Beeler one night at the Café Doney on the Via Veneto, Farouk called them over for a formal introduction. With the Albanians silently at his side, Farouk was otherwise alone, wearing a white suit, with a napkin around his neck to protect his clothes from the spaghetti alla Napolitana he was slurping. He stood up, and Birgitta was immediately taken with his "sweet eyes." "Royalty never forgets a face," she complimented him on remembering her, and told him about the genesis of her nexus with Luciano. Beeler left the two alone to walk down the Via Veneto to the embassy. Birgitta and Farouk talked for an hour, after which he stood up, as did the other bodyguards Birgitta hadn't noticed in the corner of the restaurant. Farouk took her to his two waiting bulletproof Mercedes, one for him, one for the guards, and dropped her off at her hotel without a kiss or the slightest pass.

Farouk made an arrangement with Luciano. The king was soon taking the young Swede out. Not exactly out, as much as to the hotel suite he maintained at the Excelsior on the Via Veneto. Farouk didn't want to make too much of a spectacle of his affair with Birgitta, so he kept out of sight, always having his guards seize the cameras of nosy paparazzi, then buying their film for more than the Fleet Street tabloids or even *Time* would pay them. Farouk told Birgitta he liked her because she reminded him of Narriman. She laughed. "Because I'm a teenage virgin?" she asked him. He laughed back.

In some ways, the voluptuous Swedish girl was more advanced than the king. In her book she described the first time they made love. "I'm doing this with the king of twenty million people. This nice fat man was one of the world's symbols of power," she wrote.

> This person lying on his back waiting for me to give him pleasure had the power over life and death.
> "Now show me what you can do, young lady," Farouk said.
> I slipped down between his legs and kissed and played with his small penis. Then I let my face slip down between his testicles. I lifted his testicles with my nose so that I could press my tongue in his anus.
> Farouk jerked with total surprise.
> I continued to twirl my tongue around him.
> "Why do you do that?" Farouk sighed in a confused whisper.
> I kept on. Then I did everything that was possible.
> An hour later, Farouk was still asking, "But why?"
> "I know it feels good," I said. "It glows, it's smooth, it's a little tight."
> "Have you experienced this yourself?" he asked me.

"Of course. How else could I do this?"

Farouk looked at me as if I, not he, was the expert on sex. Then he told me again that I looked like Narriman.

Farouk made it clear to Birgitta that he hated Narriman's mother even more than he did the Free Officers. He talked about Narriman constantly and wistfully and frequently compared Birgitta to her. According to Birgitta, Farouk was anything but impotent. They made love frequently and Farouk was not unconcerned with Birgitta's own pleasure. Possibly losing his throne had made him sexually other-directed. Aside from Birgitta's amorous surprises, the thing that discomfited Farouk the most was her incessant diary scribbling, often between acts of love. "He would always ask what I was writing," Birgitta wrote. "And I would never show him. 'Not Farouk,' was all I would say." Birgitta, like Irma, had musical ambitions at the time, and Farouk would pay for singing lessons three times a week. When she got a job performing in a small club in the Via del Umilita, near the Roman Forum, patronized largely by Scandinavian tourists, Farouk would slip in to a back table to cheer her on as she did numbers like "The Man I Love." The royal patronage was an important ego boost to Birgitta, who would have loved seeing some of the confiscated paparazzi shots of the king and herself in the papers.

At the time, Birgitta was sharing a room in a cheap hotel across from the Baths of Diocletian and the railway station with two gay American boys named Chuck and Bruce. Farouk couldn't understand the arrangement, and called the boys "perverts." Still, he paid their hotel bills as well as those for their riding lessons on the horse paths of the Villa Borghese. Wanting to keep Birgitta away from what he saw as her roommates' malign influence (they had discussed making more money by becoming male prostitutes), Farouk began having his chauffeur drive her out to the Villa Dusmet for their evenings together. He loved telling silly jokes, such as, "Have you heard what one palm tree said to the other?" "Let's make a date." Birgitta asked him if these were "Egyptian" jokes. Farouk shrugged. At the Villa Dusmet, Birgitta was confined to Farouk's wing of the house. She never saw his daughters. The servants served her but never looked at her. Sometimes Farouk would proudly bring in King Fuad, who would play under his robe. Then he would take his son back to his nurse and resume his play with Birgitta.

Afterward, Farouk would retire to his huge bathroom, where Birgitta often spied on him and found him on all fours praying on his prayer carpet. She never mentioned this or let him know she had seen him at worship.

They rarely left his bedroom. Farouk often brought Birgitta little gifts of flowers or trinkets or boxes of sugar-powdered Egyptian cookies—*loukoum,* which she was worried might be poisoned. Farouk promised her they were a gift from Greek royalty "who have nothing to gain by harming me," then scolded Birgitta for what would be considered "bad manners in Egypt" for licking his sticky fingers after he fed her the cookies. Farouk also liked to amuse Birgitta with magic tricks, making cigarette lighters disappear, and picking her pockets when she had clothes on. For all Farouk's attentions, Birgitta found the villa gloomy, spare, and claustrophobic, especially the endless barking and snarling of the attack dogs that circled the gardens.

Eventually, when Irma Capece Minutolo became Farouk's "official" mistress, the king's affair with Birgitta cooled. She had written to her mother, telling her stories that she was going to tea parties with King Farouk, and half hoped that she would be someday. Being a permanent back-street mistress held no appeal. When Farouk gave Birgitta a diamond bracelet as a sort of consolation prize and offered to take her on a business trip to Switzerland as his "secretary," she turned him down. She described their last night together at a Rome restaurant, then on the way back to Grottaferrata:

> "I'm not a secretary," I told him.
> "No one would believe you were, if you were with me," he admitted.
> In a way, it was an honor just to be his woman. He treated everyone equally, whether he was a shopkeeper or a general.
> "What about Irma?" I asked.
> "That's another question."
> "Switzerland wouldn't be like Italy," I said.
> "With me you can have fun anywhere," he said. "We could go to Davos . . ."
> "I'm going home to Sweden."
> "But you said you weren't going back. Your mother's mad at you . . . Come with me."
> "No." I took off the bracelet. There were lots of snaps on it.

"Silly, keep it," Farouk said. "It's yours." He seemed sad.

"I have to stand on my own two feet," I said. "But we can write letters."

Farouk wrote down an address. But it was a Rome address, not Grottaferrata. "It's more discreet," he said. I realized it was all about Irma. "And no newspaper articles."

"Only maybe a love poem," I replied.

"You'll never get that published." Farouk paid the bill. We left.

In the back seat of the car, I leaned against him, scared. I regretted that I had said no to Switzerland and the entire royal life.

As we neared the villa, Farouk asked me again. "You've decided?"

"I'll miss you and life with you," I said.

"Do you think it's something to miss?"

I couldn't answer. I put my hand on Farouk's knee. "Do you want the world's prettiest girl as a farewell present. Miss Universe, a Finnish girl, used to be the nanny to my aunt. Her name is Armi Kuusia. Armi and Irma," I said. "I can write her a letter and say you're interested."

"Am I really interested?" Farouk said.

The car arrived. The dogs barked. The servants serve fruit. The night is the best time.

After Birgitta Stenberg went back to Sweden, Farouk installed Irma Capece Minutolo at the Villa Dusmet. In a nod to her aristocratic Kingdom of Naples name, Farouk jokingly called her "the marchioness" and spent a small fortune on hiring singing teachers, etiquette teachers, gym teachers, just as he had when he sent Narriman to Rome, to help Irma rise to the level of her titular appellation. He soon got rid of the funereal Villa Dusmet, which cost him about fifty thousand dollars annually to rent, and took an apartment on the Via Archimede, near the Piazza Euclide in the "Greek mathematician" area of Rome's verdantly *luxo* Parioli district. He rented another large villa outside Lausanne and sent his four children there with nurse Anne Chermside, tutor Mademoiselle Tabouret, and his most trusted Albanian guard, Abdul Rostum, fifty-five, but still formidably intimidating. Rostum had protected Farouk his entire life, and Farouk could feel secure leaving his family with him. One man Farouk could not trust was his heartthrob aide Amin Fahim. After Fahim made an abortive play for the fourteen-year-old

King Without a Country • Narriman and Farouk in the gloomy first days of exile, Capri, 1952.

Mother-in-Law • Farouk in brighter times with Narriman and her mother, whom Farouk blamed for wrecking their marriage.

Brainy Bombshell • Birgitta Stenberg, Swedish novelist who got her original material as mistress of Lucky Luciano and Farouk, on the beach in Italy.

Bachelor Father • Fadia, Ferial, Farouk, Fuad, and Fawzia, with nanny and governess. Farouk lived in Rome, but kept his family in Switzerland.

Princess Ferial, Farouk fired him at once. Further investigation un-
covered that Fahim was also passing information on Farouk back to
Nasser's spies in Rome and on to Cairo. Fahim was replaced by
Lucien Gallas, another face man like Fahim, but more mature. Gallas was a French actor, a Jean Gabin type, who had befriended the
eighteen-year-old Farouk at the casino in Biarritz on his first trip to
Europe with his mother and sisters in 1938. Farouk had invited
Gallas to Cairo, and Gallas came for several visits. When Farouk
went into exile, Gallas was living in Rome, trying to cash in on the
Hollywood invasion. Good parts being hard for him to find, he
switched careers into exile diplomacy and became Farouk's press
secretary/man Friday.

With his children safely in school in Switzerland, Farouk could
once again play bachelor of the century, although he usually took
Irma with him on his jaunts by Rolls-Royce caravan or private
wagon-lit across the continent. He took her to visit his old girlfriend
Honeychile Wilder, now Princess Hohenlohe, at her husband's ancestral castle in Mittersill, Austria. The castle had become the Millionaire's Club, where the ordinary untitled super-rich could rub
shoulders and shoot grouse with the likes of Farouk for a seemingly
modest twenty dollars a night. Farouk stayed in touch with his
other mistress, Barbara Skelton, whom he invited to Rome and who
ended up "baby-sitting" with Irma while Farouk stalked the Via
Veneto for new showgirls. He sent Lucien Gallas to track down
Irene Guinle, who, after three marriages since she left Farouk during the war, had moved to Rome, by herself, to be an interior designer. Gallas arranged the bargain sale to Farouk of Guinle's
Rolls-Royce, which had belonged to her and her late Brazilian industrial magnate husband, Carlos Guinle. He couldn't arrange any
more than that. Farouk dropped by, unannounced, numerous times
at Irene's Parioli flat. She gave him orangeade but no encouragement. Farouk's Egypt was a bad memory for her. Farouk was
deeply disappointed in her lack of nostalgia.

Sometimes Farouk would go on European road trips with Lucien
Gallas, leaving Irma at home to her singing lessons. Farouk loved
Paris. He would stay at the Royal Monceau Hotel on the Avenue
Hoche, near the Arc de Triomphe, and spent his time discovering
new b-girl dives in Pigalle or visiting famous bordellos like the one
at 122 Rue de Provence, where an elaborate buffet would be laid out
and twelve of Paris's finest would typically be reserved for an eve-

ning that would never end before morning. Not that Farouk had to
pay for distaff companionship. A group of forty American million-
airesses who were staying at the Royal Monceau on the Paris leg of
a twelve-thousand-dollar round-the-world buying tour found out
that Farouk was also there and gave a cocktail party for the ex-king.
They had just similarly feted Gary Cooper on the Riviera and
wanted Farouk as their next "conquest." He stood them up.

Farouk gave equally short shrift to evangelist Billy Graham, who
was also staying at his hotel. Friends of Graham's urged him to
meet Farouk and tell him about Jesus. One of Graham's aides
knocked on the door of Farouk's suite and made a salvation pitch to
Lucien Gallas. Shortly afterward, Gallas sent Graham a note. It
read: "King Farouk cannot see Billy Graham now, tomorrow, or at
any other time." So much for proselytization.

Farouk's good friends in Paris were the Americans Jim and
Maggi Nolan. Jim Nolan was head of European public relations for
Trans World Airlines and had opened up the Cairo route for TWA.
His wife, Maggi, was also in publicity, operating Celebrity Service,
which cosseted movie stars and other famous people while they
were in the *ville lumière,* helping them get publicity in an era when
they still wanted it. Paris was very different from paparazzi—mad
Rome. Maggi Nolan remembered going on long walks with Cary
Grant down the Champs-Elysées, where no one even noticed him
much less took his picture or asked for an autograph.

Farouk would joke with Maggi about his declining importance
being measured in the kind and number of cars in his caravan that
would arrive at the Nolans' home in Passy. His last car was a Ford
station wagon. The Nolans didn't approve of all of Farouk's dates.
The nadir was a bogus and bitchy Russian "countess" he took to a
grande luxe restaurant of the period, the Auberge d'Armaille. The
dessert was a chocolate cake with delicate white spun sugar birds
decorating the icing. Farouk's lady of that evening struck a match
and set the birds on fire, one by one. Any woman would have been
an improvement. Hence the Nolans were delighted with Irma, when
Farouk brought her. They would go out to Farouk's favorite "family" nightclubs in Pigalle—the Casanova, the Monsignor, the Scheherazade, with candlelight and strolling violins and tasteful floor
shows, and where Farouk would always insist on Irma singing.
Irma did the number "Katarina" so many times that the Nolans
began calling her that. On occasion, Farouk, too, would step up to

the microphone and do *his* signature number, "The Eyes of Texas Are Upon You."

The eyes of the world focused on Farouk when the auctioneer's hammer fell to open the sale of the Palace Collections of Egypt in the spring of 1954. The sale was compared to those of the Whitehall Palace Collections of 1653, or the contents of Versailles, auctioned off after the French Revolution in 1793. BOAC offered a specially reduced round-trip air fare from London for the occasion, while the Egyptian government made the amazing (for a government) offer that anyone spending over five thousand Egyptian pounds at the sales would be allowed to visit and bid on Farouk's legendary pornography collection, which never made it into the phone-book-thick catalogues. The Sotheby's in-house firm history described the atmosphere of Koubbeh Palace, where the auctions were held:

> The Koubbeh Palace looked its best for the occasion. Outside on the neatly trimmed lawns and among the flower beds and banks of blazing bougainvillea blossoms, guests strolled around discussing their purchases or pausing to sip cool drinks from glasses tinkling with ice, served by courteous servants in the familiar white tarboosh and white galabaiya. A brass band played military music and Viennese waltzes in the gardens throughout the sales. For the Sotheby staff who had toiled to make it all possible, it was merely a more exotic country house sale with its garden party atmosphere in the old tradition. Yet no one could escape the impression that the event had a much deeper significance—the end of a dynasty.

One shouldn't have spoken so soon. One afternoon, while the Sotheby's experts were relaxing with Koubbeh Palace staff members in the vast marble entrance hall, "suddenly a portly figure in resplendent white uniform, accompanied by three uniformed officers, appeared at the top of the stairs. It could only be Farouk. The Egyptians fell on their knees, while the Englishmen gasped." The fear and tension abated only when Farouk laughed. It was Gregory Ratoff, in costume on location filming his ill-fated *My Kingdom For a Woman*. After two months, the auctions closed, having yielded a total of 750,000 Egyptian pounds, which was extremely disappointing to the Neguib-Nasser leadership, which expected many millions for the fruits of Farouk's self-indulgent labors.

In truth, the prices that were fetched were very high. Victor

Hammer, the art dealer who, with his brother, tycoon Armand
Hammer, had been Farouk's American purchasing agents, having
bought him the super-RV, Continental Clipper, that had taken Barbara Skelton across the desert and broke down, thought the prices
were "crazy," four times higher than what he had charged Farouk
for the same items a few years before. Armand Hammer described
Farouk as "the absolute monarch who treated the world as his
personal nursery and all the things in it as his toys." The Hammers,
Russian-born Americans with the very best contacts at the Kremlin, were responsible for selling Farouk his czarist treasures—the
Fabergé Swan Egg and the Romanoff jewels, as well as his copulat-
ing-watch collection, his erotic paperweights, his countless whoopee
cushions, exploding cigars, dirty joke books, and magic hats to pull
rabbits from and boxes in which to saw women in half. Farouk gave
the Hammers his royal escutcheon and title "Supplier to His Majesty the King," which the Hammers used on their letterhead to
burnish their image. Farouk's final two orders to the Hammers just
before he was deposed in 1952 were a cable BUY ME A BAKELITE
FACTORY, to which they complied, and a clipping from a movie
magazine and a handwritten note "Send me Lana Turner," whom
even the Hammers could not deliver.

Many of the treasures the Hammers did deliver were withdrawn
from the Sotheby sale, which was the real reason for its relatively
meager net. Carlo d'Emilio was making frightening legal noises,
and there were almost no Egyptian buyers at all at any of the auctions. Given the present political climate, who in the country would
have been so foolish to be acquiring former royal property for large
sums of money? The most successful auctions were those of
Farouk's stamps (an 1858 Romanian registered letter drew the highest single price) and coins (his Confederate money collection was
unique), which all went to foreign houses.

At each record price, the uniformed officers in the back of the
Koubbeh ballroom would clap and cheer gleefully, reminding the
foreign visitors where the proceeds were going. But such outbursts
of anticipatory greed dwindled when the other collections, especially the snuff boxes and Swiss automata, and other precious metal
"objects of virtue," fell terribly short of expectation. So short that
Nasser's new regime decided not to pay Sotheby's their commis-
sions at all. An international legal incident was created, with Nasser
being branded by the British press "Deadbeat of the Nile." Fleet

Street may not have liked Farouk, but no one ever accused him of stiffing his creditors. At least not until he was deposed, when Christian Dior and Harry Winston both sued him for unpaid bills for the lingerie and jewelry respectively he had bought for Narriman. Farouk defended these actions by having Carlo d'Emilio tell the purveyors to send the bills to Nasser, in that the purchases were made by the Palace and had been confiscated. All the bills, Sotheby's and the others, were lost in the shuffle in the Suez crisis.

By the time the Sotheby sales were over in 1954, so was Neguib, whom Nasser was able to maneuver into a position where he called for the restoration of political parties like the Wafd and thereby looked like a tool of the former pashas. Nasser then took on his greatest domestic challenge, the Muslim Brotherhood, which tried to assassinate him at a public speech he was giving. The bullets missed and Nasser stood tall at the podium without even flinching. "Let them kill Nasser," he declaimed. "He is one among many and whether he lives or dies, the revolution will go on." The Egyptian people admired Nasser's show of courage and condemned the brotherhood's reign-of-terror tactics. Nasser was thus able to purge the brotherhood just as he had been able to purge the Mohammed Ali dynasty. Egypt was his. Now he could take on the world.

The British took an instant hatred to Nasser, and not only for stiffing Sotheby's. Prime Minister Anthony Eden said he didn't want Nasser "neutralized," as his advisers had suggested. "I want him destroyed, can't you understand?" he railed. President Eisenhower and Secretary of State Dulles were initially much more kindly disposed to the young Egyptian mastermind of the revolution. He was a favorite of Ambassador Caffery's and the CIA's Kermit Roosevelt. He claimed loudly to be anti-Communist, which is all the Americans needed to hear. His tract *The Reality of Communism* was a vicious tirade against Marxism, which he attacked as negating the individual. What Nasser *really* had against communism, however, was that it had the potential of making Egyptians more loyal to a foreign doctrine, and to Moscow, than to *himself.*

When Dulles and Neguib met the first time in 1953, the American secretary of state presented the Egyptian general with a silver .38-caliber pistol with an inscription to Neguib from his "friend Dwight D. Eisenhower." During the early years of the Egyptian revolution, the pistol was the only piece of arms the United States supplied to Egypt. This became a sore subject for Nasser, who deeply resented and was embarrassed by the 1948 war with Israel and by Israel's successful 1955 raid into the Gaza Strip to avenge Palestinian raids and destroy Egyptian military headquarters there. Gaza showed the world how militarily deficient Nasser's Egypt was. With America refusing to supply him arms, Nasser turned to the East and bought an eighty-million-dollar stock of Soviet weapons through Czechoslovakia. America, outraged by Nasser's defection, took reprisal by withdrawing its previously promised financing for his most cherished project, the Aswan High Dam. Nasser's next move was to nationalize the Suez Canal, whose revenues would pay for the dam. He announced that if the "imperialist powers" didn't like it, they could "choke on their rage." Instead, they decided to make Nasser choke on his. In the fall of 1956, Britain and France joined forces with Israel in a plan to invade Egypt.

Farouk, in Rome, sensed that his day had finally returned. He had kept very quiet politically since his exile. In 1955 he had predicted at a press conference that "the end of (Egypt's) nightmare of terror and misery is, no doubt, very near." He called the Nasser regime a "tyrannic dictatorship" that had jailed over sixty thousand of its political opponents. To Farouk the Free Officers were "little despots," Egypt "a police state," and the Egyptians "a captive people." Whatever the shortcomings of his monarchy, Farouk took pride that "at least everyone felt free and secure," fair trials were guaranteed, and prisoners not subjected to "Nazi-like" tortures. Despite "many social inequalities and discriminations" that Farouk conceded, there was "work and bread for all." He predicted that Nasser, a chameleon who could be "anti-Communist, neutralist, and pro-Russian" all at the same time, would soon be gone. In his place would be, guess who?

Farouk was nearly right. At the height of the Suez crisis, Farouk sent a "confidential message" to Eden, Eisenhower, and President Coty of France. Farouk opened by declaring, in the still-royal "we," his continuing attention to Egypt's supreme interests:

> Although unwilling to discuss and judge the policy of our country since our departure, we must, alas, realize that we have forseen and predicted the grievous developments shown by recent events.

With the greatest compassion we are considering the dangerous march of our country and choose this moment to raise our voice to ask you, knowing the deep humanity of your country and of yourself, to try by all possible means to devise a peaceful solution of the problems which now divide your Government from the Egyptian people, who cannot be held responsible for the mistakes of their leaders and who would have, ultimately, to pay with their blood for those mistakes.

In a secret and coordinated effort with England and France, Israel made the first move and invaded the Sinai. Then Britain and France gave Israel and Egypt an ultimatum to stop fighting and to withdraw their forces ten miles from the Suez Canal. Israel, which had no troops anywhere near the canal, of course agreed. Nasser did not. On October 31, British and French planes started bombing Egypt, which blocked the canal with sunken ships and presented Western Europe with the specter of an oil shortage. International opinion was inflamed against the old colonialists who now seemed like new colonialists. Dulles, who disliked Eden almost as much as Eden disliked Nasser, threw America's weight not so much in favor of Egypt but against Britain, whom Dulles wanted to be able to outmuscle and replace as the "big white man" in the Middle East. The result was a huge net gain for Nasser, who got the Suez Canal, nationalized all British and French property in Egypt, and became an even bigger national hero for finally vanquishing the long-despised British and driving them out of Egypt, a feat which no one from Mohammed Ali to Farouk could ever accomplish. Again, Great Britain, in folding on Suez, had let Farouk down one last time. The scenario he envisioned of Nasser being destroyed and the monarchy restored as a force of stability and order for the Middle East turned out to be a daydream. Any hopes he had for ever seeing Egypt again, either as a king or even as a tourist, were now extinguished.

In a sense, Farouk as a persona was extinguished at the same time. The mystique of the last pharaoh disappeared. When Farouk went to the casino at Deauville, where he had reigned as the highest of rollers, he was turned away at the door for not wearing the appropriate evening clothes. He attended the 1956 wedding of Grace Kelly to his friend Prince Rainier of Monaco, but even there he got no respect. When Farouk signed the guest register "Farouk R.," the Egyptian ambassador to France, also a guest, objected in a huff. "Prince Rainier *knows* there is no king of Egypt." A palace functionary tried to keep the peace by suggesting that the "R" wasn't for *"roi"* but rather for René, the new French name Farouk had taken to dilute the ignominy of his own. The ambassador didn't buy it, and left in a rage.

King Ibn Saud, who had reputedly been providing his old ally Farouk with financial assistance until he could resume his throne, died in 1953. When his austere son, Crown Prince Faisal, saw that such a restoration would not occur, he was said to have cut off the royal aid, forcing Farouk to sell the yacht *Fakr el Bihar,* which had been in drydock repair in Italy at the time of the revolution, and to even make inquiries about a job in industrial relations at one of the big Italian conglomerates, all of which turned him down. The only sympathy Farouk got in his fiscal doldrums was an offer from a Danish circus to appear in top hat and tails as an elephant trainer. The forty millions Farouk allegedly had stashed in Swiss banks were nowhere in evidence. Farouk's consumption became less and less conspicuous.

The insults continued. Farouk, through Carlo d'Emilio, stood up for his honor, if no one else ever did, in several lawsuits for defamation. One was against professional party-giver, hostess-for-hire Elsa Maxwell. In her memoir, *RSVP,* she wrote the following ode to the ex-king:

> Although generations of inbreeding among the ruling houses of Europe and the Near East have produced scores of contenders for the stigma, Farouk is by all odds the most horrid specimen of so-called royalty of the last century, at least.
>
> I'm proud to say that I incurred his enmity soon after I first saw him in Deauville in 1950. My R.S.V.P. to an invitation to dine with Farouk was a telegram to his equerry which read, "I do not associate with clowns, monkeys, or corrupt gangsters." I learned that Farouk screamed like a pig—what else?—when he saw the telegram. I also like to take a bow for attacking Farouk in my column while he still was on his tottering throne and predicting on a television show that he soon would be given the boot by the Egyptians.

She went on to cite an article in the New York *Daily News* stating that there had been some talk of her being named American ambassador "to this party-loving land of the Nile. She hates ex-king Farouk like an ex-subject."

Farouk sued Miss Maxwell and her publisher in a French court. He sought a token of her lack of esteem of $15,000. Farouk won the libel action, but received only a $1,000 token. The publisher was ordered to delete the passage and excerpt the court's judgment in five newspapers of Farouk's choosing. The book went on to become an international best seller.

Art Buchwald in his fifties column, "P.S. from Rome," reported an interview with Farouk following his "victory" over Elsa Maxwell. Farouk said he knew "justice would triumph. I have always had great faith in the French and I knew they would do the right thing." All that mattered to him, he said, was the principle of the case. When asked if he and Elsa Maxwell might ever be friends, he replied, "We are living in a world where we are taught to believe the age of miracles is past."

"Are you willing to meet with her to discuss the matter?" the reporter pressed him.

"The age of miracles is past," Farouk reiterated.

Farouk went after another book in 1962, this time in a $450,000 libel suit against the New York publisher Lyle Stuart for a book entitled *Pleasure Was My Business,* ghostwritten for a "Madame Sherry," AKA Ruth Barns, a Miami, Florida, madam who claimed Farouk was one of the top clients at her tropical brothel. That Farouk had never set foot in Miami, or, for that matter, in the United States, indicates the literary license that had been taken. Stuart, who went on to publish such blockbusters as *The Happy Hooker, The Sensuous Man,* and *The Sensuous Woman,* tried to force Farouk to appear in Miami to testify. Farouk refused to come to America; the defendants refused to go to Europe. The case was never adjudicated.

Not all the defamation against Farouk was between covers. He was able to gain an injunction against Milan's Milton Chocolate Company for naming a new candy "Farouk" and showing the monarch's corpulent, smiling image over a logo of a snake charmer and a snake. An injunction was one thing, damages another. The Italian court denied Farouk's claim for $500,000, finding that he had suffered no financial harm from the libel. The judge ordered Farouk to pay $1,000 in court expenses.

Farouk's travails reflected that of his entire dispossessed dynasty.

In exile in a Lausanne, Switzerland, hotel, Prince Mohammed Ali, once among the world's richest men, wrote a series of letters to his old friend Anthony Eden, who told him British intervention to get him some of his wealth back "might do more harm than good." The prince replied to the prime minister: "I do not see how your kind intervention . . . could do me any more harm. They have already taken all that I have got, even my personal clothes. I cannot get a pair of old shoes. This is not human." The British, of whom the prince had known five generations of kings and queens and was England's staunchest supporter in the Egyptian royal family, turned him down flat. In their internal correspondence, the Foreign Office wondered how hard up the prince could be "as the Hotel Beau Rivage where he resides is reputed to be one of the more expensive caravansaries . . . in Europe." He would be considered seriously impoverished only "by his previous standards." Besides, the British saw it as a lost cause to ask the Egyptians now for anything, especially funds that would make life easier for their former rulers. The prince died alone at the hotel in 1956.

In 1959 Prince Rainier made the stateless Farouk a citizen of Monaco. There was only one drawback to the Monagasque passport; citizens of the principality were not allowed to gamble in the casino, except "in exceptional circumstances." Farouk didn't ask for an exemption. He remained in Rome, rarely visiting his new "home." He didn't have his yacht anymore to dock between Onassis's *Cristina* and Rainier's *Costa del Sol.* The *Fakr el Bihar,* which he had previously sold, had been converted to an offshore nightclub in Rimini, on Italy's Adriatic coast.

At one point in the 1950s before Princess Grace put Monaco squarely on the tourist map, Farouk was considering buying the casino in Monte Carlo. In 1955, the principality was near bankruptcy. Aristotle Onassis, who owned the Société des Bains de Mer et Cercle des Etrangers that controlled the casino, yacht club, and the Hôtel de Paris, was thinking about unloading the entire pile. Farouk, with his passion for gambling and the hidden Swiss fortune no one believed he didn't have, seemed like a prime purchaser, or mark, given Monaco's fiscal precariousness at the time. The golden Greek and the tarnished Egyptian were in negotiations. Then Onassis made a snide comment in Greek about Farouk, which he assumed no one could understand. However, Farouk's barber/butler Pietro della Valle, who had escaped from Egypt to serve his old

master, was fluent in Greek and picked up Onassis's slur. Farouk
walked out of the casino and the negotiations. Onassis ordered
shiploads of sand to Hawaiianize the beaches, renovated the Hôtel
de Paris, and began a search for a wife for Prince Rainier that
would add a Hollywood gloss to the declining dowager resort. Mar-
ilyn Monroe was considered, but was *too* Hollywood, as well as
unavailable. Then Onassis fixed on the patrician Grace Kelly, and
Monaco was never again the same.

Farouk never regretted walking out on the deal. He was fatalistic
and accepted both triumph and tragedy as the will of Allah. He
settled into a quiet, almost conjugal life with Irma Capece
Minutolo, though he did keep her in a separate apartment and continued to haunt the Roman nightclubs, both on the Via Veneto and
less soigné venues such as the Flying Dutchman all-night buffet at
the Stazioni Termini. He still gambled, but only on soccer pools. He
would travel to Switzerland every other month to visit his children
and go to a clinic for a checkup. He weighed nearly three hundred
pounds, and wanted to lose it with various "sleep diets" and other
cures that didn't work.

The eldest daughter, Ferial, had wanted to become a doctor and
had been mentioned as the prospective wife of King Hussein. Instead, she enrolled in a secretarial college near home, while Farouk
took her to several royal weddings around Europe, hoping to find
her an appropriate husband. On their outings Farouk had two rules,
that she wear a discreet chiffon scarf over her neckline and that she
not dance to rock and roll records. "I always do what Papa says,"
Ferial was quoted. The next ex-princess, Fawzia, stayed at home in
the rented walled château and took maternal responsibility for her
younger sister, Fadia, and ex-King Fuad, who studied French and
Arabic in a village school in nearby Cully, where his best friend was
the son of Congo Premier Patrice Lumumba. Farouk accompanied
his son to his first day of classes and wedged himself in a desk in the
back of the schoolroom. The other students, thinking he was a
school official, doffed their caps and greeted him: "Bonjour, Mon-
sieur l'Inspecteur."

In 1955 Farouk had agreed to let Narriman visit her son for the
first time since she left him two years before, on the ironclad condition that her mother be nowhere around. Fuad, who was blond and
curly-haired and looked very much like his mother, didn't recognize

her when she approached him. Narriman presented him with a tricycle painted the same red color of Farouk's palace cars, and several stuffed rabbits. Then he called her *"Maman"* and they embraced. The bodyguard Abdul Rostum stayed by Fuad's side throughout the hour-and-a-half visitation, as did nurse Chermside, who assured Narriman that Fuad was a good boy and was eating well.

Narriman saw Fuad only one other time while Farouk was alive. After her second marriage failed, she and her mother moved to Beirut at the height of Nasser's campaign of fear against the elements of the "old society" of which the Sadeks were by definition a part. In Beirut Narriman took up painting. The other ex-queen, Farida, also moved to Beirut during this period and painted, though the two women did not meet. At his youngest daughter Fadia's request, Farouk invited Farida to visit her daughters once a year beginning in 1956. The ex-queen, who still called herself queen, refused Farouk's offer for her to stay at the château and took a room at a small hotel. When the daughters came of age, Farida, too, was concerned they find the right mates. "It's a mother's duty to find her daughters husbands who will make them happy. . . . And it is certainly not Farouk who could help them understand the ways of men." The years had not dissipated her anger toward the man who made her queen. On March 23, 1953, both Cairo and Paris newspapers reported that Farida had wed her longtime suspected flame, Wahid Yussri, in Cairo. She vehemently denied it. In 1958, she was asked if she would ever consider marrying again. "What? After being married to Farouk? Never!" she vowed.

The one woman who people thought would marry Farouk was Irma Capece Minutolo. Farouk advanced her singing career by continuing her lessons, arranging recitals in Rome and Naples, cheering her on. She actually got good reviews in spite of the snickers about her mentor. Farouk took her on trips, but they tended to be much closer in at run-down beach resorts north of Rome. Otherwise they would just drive up on the Janiculum, with the best view of Rome's seven hills, to admire the domes and rooftops and columns of the city whose melancholy in its own vanished splendors mirrored that of Farouk's. He still would play high roller with the twenty-dollar tips to newsdealers and barmen he passed around the way Rockefeller gave out dimes, or buy rounds of champagne for tables of rich widows and their Italian gigolos or for the assorted actresses and strippers who still descended on him with their own armies of parasites. Farouk always graciously picked up the tab, much to Irma's annoyance. To soothe her and remind her that she was his first lady, he gave her cute gifts, like a check made out to the "Bank of Happiness" for "365 days" signed "Farouk, Re."

The one thing Farouk never lost was his way with women, and not only women with a price tag. The American expatriate playboys who scoured the Via Veneto extolled Farouk's relentlessly ebullient magnetism and unequaled success at his favorite sport of kings. They called him "Big Jim" and kept their prospects, the ones they wanted to keep, away from him. The Ceylonese Princess Sharmini Tiruchelvam, on most of the ten-most-beautiful lists of the fifties and sixties, recalled meeting Farouk at a party on producer Sam Spiegel's yacht in Cannes. The princess, whose family helped arrange for Spiegel to shoot *The Bridge on the River Kwai* in her country, was wearing a black and gold sari when Farouk spotted her on deck. "He enveloped me immediately," she said. "I was no stranger to royalty, but Farouk was truly special. He was overwhelming, charming, funny." Farouk made a big display of insisting that the young princess sit next to him. "He was very fat. He was in a tuxedo and the fat was rolling over his cummerbund," she said, "but he made you see beyond that. All I could do was remember how gorgeous he was as a boy-king. You could still see it in his eyes. He had immense self-confidence, the self-confidence of the tall, slim, regal young king he had been."

Sam Spiegel was terrified that the princess would run off with Farouk. He didn't want to have to tell that to her parents, who had entrusted him with the care of their daughter. The day after the yacht party, Farouk sent flowers and called to see the princess, but she was nowhere to be found. Spiegel had packed her off to Nice and a room under an assumed name at the Hotel Negresco. She never saw Farouk again.

For all the women he could have, for all his affection for Irma, there would be no more queens. "He will never marry again," Lucien Gallas insisted to one of the few pesky English reporters who bothered to hound Farouk. Was Farouk happy? the newsman pressed. "Can a deposed king ever be happy?" Gallas answered, and raced to catch up with Farouk, Irma, and his bodyguards as they entered their used green Rolls-Royce with its little Egyptian flag flying from the antenna and drove off to one last club before they finished the night at the train station. All Farouk really had left was the night. The night could seem the same as when by day he ruled a nation. Then he went out to lose himself, to forget the duties and difficulties of his immense power. Now he went out to remember, until those memories of the glory days were punctured by the hard realization that only the orangeade was the same; the rest was over. In spite of it all, he kept smiling. Kings didn't whine. Nor did Farouk talk about the past, good or bad. "I'm never sad at life," he told a friend. "I'm only sad at cards."

Barbara Skelton, who Farouk never ceased to call "my little minx," recalled a visit to Farouk in exile:

> It was not a particularly gay interlude. By then I must have been considered part of the family, so that when Farouk set off on his nightly rounds, I would be left behind in the kitchen to keep his mistress Irma company. She was a buxom, simple, friendly girl, but all she wanted to talk about were her dreams of becoming a film star. Late in the afternoon I would come upon Farouk eating grilled meat in a pitch-dark alcove. He was supposed to be on a regime and ate kosher butter with his bread. No more jolly jokes and laughter. He had become a lonely, sagging figure, ostracised by Roman society, not because of his lax morals, oddly enough—according to Princess Anne-Marie Aldobrandini—but because they found him boring. When she told me this, I expressed surprise . . . For I met some aristocratic families, and although they lived in enviably beautiful apartments, they were totally devoid of conversation. And *ouf!* were they boring. Like Irma, impoverished Roman gentlemen also had their dreams, not of becoming film stars but of marrying American heiresses.
>
> In Rome, Farouk was just as quirky as he had ever been. On my departure, he did what I wish I had the courage to do when any bookworms depart; he checked on the contents of my suitcase and came upon a comb belonging to the apartment, which he quickly claimed back. I was about to descend to a taxi waiting to take me to the station, when he called me back and said, "You've forgotten something," and my last vision of him was standing in the doorway, with his familiar mocking smile, holding up my toothbrush.

In 1965, Farouk was only forty-five, but he seemed like a very old man in a world that worshiped youth more than ever before. Now the only king who mattered was Elvis Presley, and even he had been deposed by four revolutionaries from Liverpool. The advent of the Boeing 707 had created a jet set that should have installed Farouk as a founding father, but because of weight-related health problems, he wasn't allowed to fly. It wasn't a time to be sick or fat or old or to keep mistresses or smoke cigars or dance cheek to cheek. Rome was experiencing a discothèque craze, doing the frug and the Watusi at La Cabala, and its beautiful people were discovering social drugs. When Prince Dado Ruspoli, one of the pillars of the dolce vita, was arrested for possession of half a kilo of hashish, he sought to avoid a major trafficking prosecution by telling the police it was for his own personal use. The police balked. Not *that* much. "I'm a chain smoker," the prince said. In this milieu someone like King Farouk was likely to be looked on as surreal or unreal, a character out of *Dr. Strangelove* or a James Bond movie.

The "real" world was much less amusing than its amusements. John F. Kennedy, the embodiment of the youth movement and actually three years older than Farouk, had been assassinated. Malcolm X, forty, was shot to death in New York, and there were race riots in Selma and Watts. America bombed North Vietnam, and Bob Dylan and Joan Baez and Peter, Paul, and Mary all tried to stop it by singing "Blowin' in the Wind."

Through it all, King Farouk sat on the sidewalk of the Café de Paris on the Via Veneto, as immutable a fixture of Roman life as the Colosseum. Even the Via Veneto was proving mutable. The principal thing that had interested the public in *Cleopatra* was the off-screen romance between Elizabeth Taylor and Richard Burton. When that most costly of movies to date flopped, the epic cycle ended and the film people deserted the Tiber for the Thames and movies like *A Hard Day's Night, Alfie,* and *Blow-Up.* The Hollywood press agents cranked up the publicity machines once again and made "swinging London" *the* city for the sixties that Rome had been in the fifties. All that was left for Cinecittà were the low-budget spaghetti westerns of Sergio Leone. The pipeline of starlets dried up. Farouk didn't even have the night anymore.

Rome was no longer like Cairo, but neither was Cairo. The Paris of the Middle East was becoming Moscow on the Nile, and in his quest for total power and total control, Gamal Abdel Nasser was seeming less and less like George Washington and more like Joseph Stalin. After Suez, and the ousting of the British, the entire Arab world saw him as their "liberator," their Bernardo O'Higgins, their Simon Bolivar, their Giuseppe Garibaldi. Pulling off the tightrope act of accepting billions in aid from Soviet Russia and denouncing communism at the same time, Nasser sought to unite the Arab nations in a way that hadn't been done since the heyday of the Ottoman sultan. With his picture enshrined in every coffee house and barbershop from Morocco to Kuwait, it seemed as if he had a real chance.

In 1958 Nasser joined Egypt and Syria to form the United Arab Republic. That same year, inspired by the Nasser example, Iraqi military officers went Egypt's Free Officers one better by assassinating the pro-British king, crown prince, and prime minister. They declared a republic, destroying the colonial West's last great outpost in the Middle East. In Saudi Arabia the vast new wealth from the spiraling demand for oil had created a whole new class of Farouks, millionaire sheikhs and emirs who took floors at the Dorchester and danced at Annabel's and gambled at the Clermont and became as symbolic of swinging London as Farouk had been of dolce vita Rome. Such profligacy did not endear the oil princes of Mayfair to the masses back home in the desert, throwing them under the spell of the scourge of princes, Nasser.

In 1962, the spell was broken by the eruption of a civil war in Yemen. Following the revolutionary model of the region, a cadre of army officers had revolted against the ruler, Imam Badr, and declared a republic. But the imam fought back fiercely, and the officers called on Nasser to send Egyptian troops to perpetuate their coup. The war, which dragged on for seven years, was not only a financial drain on Egypt, which had over fifty thousand troops in Yemen. In its failing to ensure a quick victory for the officers, the Egyptian military was exposed for all its weaknesses (which would flower into full disgrace in the 1967 Six Day War with Israel). For once Nasser seemed less than invincible. Other cracks in the armor were an anti-Nasser military coup in Syria and the crushing of a pro-Nasser coup in Iraq, which was becoming much more Communist than Nasserist. Nasser's tirades against the Iraqi Communists for favoring that ideology over Arab nationalism finally caused a rupture between Nasser and Khrushchev. On the West African Arab front, President Bourguiba of Tunisia pulled his country out of the Arab League on the grounds of Nasser's domination of it.

Nasser also alienated Morocco by his alliance with Algeria's leftist leader, Ben Bella.

Unable to control the entire Middle East, Nasser turned back to someplace he *could* control, Egypt. The country became even more socialist, with the nationalization of banks, cotton houses, insurance companies, and nearly three hundred of the biggest industrial concerns in the country. The maximum amount of land anyone could own was reduced from two hundred to one hundred feddans. The old pasha class was completely emasculated; most who could had fled to sharply reduced lives in England and France. But the destruction of the pashas did not mollify the masses, who didn't see enough tangible benefits from all of Nasser's sound and fury. In an effort to root out the last vestiges of the land-owning elite, Nasser instituted a "Committee for the Liquidation of Feudalism." He also instituted a similar movement to extirpate militant fundamentalism. The Muslim Brotherhood was rising again as the focus for popular discontent. Nasser went all-out to stop it. A huge purge began. His military police, gestapo-style shock troops, were known as the Visitors of the Dawn. Criticism was not allowed; no one felt safe. Nasser's own paranoia was exacerbated by his health. His diabetes had been further complicated by atherosclerosis. The liberator was not a well man.

It is against this background of the unraveling of an autocrat that the accusations that the death of Farouk was caused not by the hand of God, but by the fist of Nasser, must be considered. Aside from his death, 1965 was an uneventful year for the ex-king. In February, in the Kensington Record Office in London, Farouk's youngest daughter Fadia, twenty-one, surprised him by marrying a tall, blond, blue-eyed Russian Orthodox geologist named Pierre Orloff, twenty-four. They had met at the foreign language school in Switzerland where Orloff's mother was one of Fadia's teachers. Fadia's older sister, Fawzia, had recently won a diploma from a similar school for interpreters in Geneva. Farouk was proud that his daughters had acquired the skills of a profession; he was said to be very disappointed that Fadia had married out of her Muslim religion, out of her royal class, and without her father's permission. But Farouk was used to disappointments. He distracted himself with Irma, with a blond Yugoslavian actress named Sonia Romanoff, twenty-two, and with a blond Italian hairdresser named Annamaria Gatti, also twenty-two, whom he took to a late supper at the Ile de

France *osteria* after spending the earlier part of the evening of March 17 with Irma.

The only written record of what happened in Cairo on that same evening appears in the best-selling memoirs, *A Witness to the Aberrations of Salah Nasir,* by Itmad Khorshied, the mistress of Nasir, the sinister and powerful director of Nasser's General Intelligence Bureau, the Egyptian CIA, responsible for foreign and counterespionage activities. She wrote (in translation):

> The night of the murder was very exciting. Salah Nasir came to my villa (where he "kept" her) and was very drunk—as usual. He had several drinks of whiskey—all at one go—and did not utter one single word. I didn't ask why he was so apprehensive. Suddenly he said "Don't come near the telephone. I'm expecting an important long distance call." I asked him if he'd given my number to his friends abroad, and what should I do if they called while he was out. He said, "Don't answer . . . Just hang up."
>
> As the hours passed, his worry intensified, and he became like a caged tiger. All at once he looked at me and said, "Farouk's going to die tonight."

At the Ile de France, Farouk ate like there would be no tomorrow. A dozen raw oysters drowned in Tabasco sauce, then a rich lobster thermidor, a dish that had all but vanished since the time of Diamond Jim Brady. Still hungry, Farouk had an Italian country classic, abbacchio al forno, roast baby lamb, with extra helpings of roast potatoes and a large side of french fries thrown in, plus string beans drenched in butter. The maître d' suggested a grand finale of crepes suzette, but Farouk begged off. They were flambéd in alcohol, from which the good Muslim abstained. Instead, he had a huge bowl of Monte Bianco, spooning the dessert into Annamaria Gatti's smiling mouth. He drank another bottle of Fiuggi water, made a few jokes and puns, lit up his giant Havana, and dropped dead.

> The expected call arrived. Salah Nasir was in the bathroom. I answered. The caller spoke in Italian. I handed over the receiver to S.N. and they spoke English. The caller assured S.N. that Farouk was dead. S.N. smiled and asked for another glass of whiskey to celebrate his success. A call followed from Ibrahim Bagdadhi, S.N.'s assistant and architect of the execution plan, who again assured S.N. the mission was accom-

plished. They were using a code language. Bagdadhi then asked S.N. what they ought to do with the body, to which S.N. answered, "Give me some time to think." He put down the receiver and looked at me. There was the joy of success in his eyes and I instantly knew that he was proud of me for being the first to know of their plan to murder the king. Without my asking him any details, he surprised me by saying, "It took a lot of effort to track him down. It wasn't an easy assignment." He then called Marshal Abdel Hakim Amer to break the joyful news.

Abdel Hakim Amer was one of Nasser's oldest friends from the military academy, one of the original Free Officers, and now defense minister, chief of the army general staff, and Egypt's preeminent exterminator of any and all opposition to Nasser. Amer, himself the descendant of a rich land-owning family, was an enemy of his class and that much more dangerous for it. Itmad said that President Nasser was the last of Egypt's leaders to hear about the assassination, which was conceived and executed as a "gift" to Nasser. Salah Nasir described it to her as his "noblest achievement in protecting the republican discipline that America was so keen on destroying and on returning Egypt into a Kingdom." That "American" threat to Nasser, to teach the lesson of lessons to the problem child of the Middle East by bringing back Farouk, was Salah Nasir's justification for Farouk's last supper.

Later, Itmad wrote, she found out some of the details of the killing, which she said had been accomplished with the complicity of the Italian secret service. Italian police were no longer assigned to guard Farouk; he wasn't considered important enough. He did have two Albanian bodyguards, but he usually gave them the evenings off. He liked to drive himself in his Fiat. (He had bought a two-seat Thunderbird, but he couldn't fit behind the steering wheel and returned it.) Nasir had told his mistress that Ibrahim Bagdadhi had been able to get the information on Farouk's assorted comings and goings through the Italian authorities, who in turn had gotten them through Irma. The poison that was administered to Farouk in his lobster thermidor by an Egyptian plant in the restaurant, one of Farouk's several-times-a-week haunts, was a compound called alacontin, which would cause cardiac arrest but would not show up in an autopsy. It was tasteless, but even if it weren't, the thermidor cream sauce would have masked anything. There was no autopsy, again on orders from the Italian secret service. The cause of death was listed as a cerebral hemorrhage. Farouk had hypertension pills in a gold box in his pockets when he died. He was enormously fat. It was easy to believe Farouk could die so young, a victim of his own excesses.

The first victim of Nasser's 1967 purge that followed Egypt's defeat after the Six Day War with Israel was Nasser's chief purger, Salah Nasir's boss, Marshal Abdel Hakim Amer. Nasser was convinced Amer was preparing a military coup against him and placed the general under house arrest. The man assigned to be in charge of him was his lieutenant, Salah Nasir. Three weeks later Amer was said to have committed suicide in capitivity by taking a cyanide pill. In the purges that followed, Salah Nasir himself was arrested. Among the charges against him were torture and extortion, blackmailing women through compromising photographs, and, most significantly, the poisoning of Amer by giving him the cyanide, obtained from the General Intelligence laboratories, without his knowing. Nasir was also accused of poisoning Dr. Anwar Mufti, Nasser's personal physician, for telling the president that his advancing diabetes was affecting his ability to govern. In the trials of 1968, Salah Nasir was convicted of all charges and sentenced to life imprisonment. In 1974, he was pardoned by President Anwar Sadat.

Because Rome was the air gateway to the Middle East, it had become Egypt's largest European headquarters for the elaborate intelligence apparatus headed by Salah Nasir. Assorted embassy secretaries, Vatican liaisons, and press aides were in fact General Intelligence operatives. It was well known that Nasser had numerous men in Rome spying on Israel's European activities, and spying on Farouk as well. Given this infrastructure and given the life and crimes of Salah Nasir, the "operation Farouk" described by Nasir's mistress is not implausible. Many of those who knew Farouk, including his son, Fuad, believe it. At the time, the ex-King Fuad was only thirteen and, like his sisters, too shocked by his father's sudden death to call for the investigation of assassination conspiracies. When he received the bad news from Carlo d'Emilio, he had influenza and a high fever. He got out of bed and packed his black mourning suit. Fuad and his sisters came down from Lausanne and signed the autopsy waiver. Farouk's body, which was being held at the Institute for Legal Medicine, was released to a morgue. There, in accordance with Muslim burial custom, the body was wrapped in linen and covered with the Egyptian flag that Farouk had taken with him into exile.

Farouk was laid in a walnut coffin and taken to a private chapel, where the imam of Rome said prayers in a simple ceremony that was attended only by his children, by Farida, who flew in from Beirut, and by Irma Capece Minutolo, who was included as part of the family. A tearful but dignified young Fuad then led the procession of several hundred mourners, mostly barmen, waiters, and tradespeople to whom Farouk had been kind, behind a black hearse bearing the coffin, draped in another Egyptian flag. The cortege moved slowly through the Roman streets to the municipal cemetery, where Farouk's remains were placed in a temporary crypt. The king of Egypt had always been expected to be buried in the land he ruled and loved, but no one in Rome was sure how this could be accomplished. At the ceremony, the few royals and members of the diplomatic corps who bothered to show up bowed or knelt or curtsied or kissed little Fuad's hand. He handled it like a king.

Farouk's body rested in the limbo of the Roman and Catholic public cemetery for another ten days. During that time, Carlo d'Emilio presented a will that left Farouk's estate, consisting mainly of his apartment and its furnishings and *no* Swiss bank accounts, to his children, whom his last testament exhorted to love each other and stay united. D'Emilio was continually on the phone to the Middle East, trying to find a suitable final home for his client. Only an offer from King Faisal of Saudi Arabia to let Farouk be interred in his country was sufficient to shame Nasser into relenting on his hard insistence that Egypt never see Farouk again.

Egypt still didn't see much of him. Nasser required that the entire transport of Farouk's body be done in secret. On March 27, the walnut coffin was placed on a Comet aircraft of United Arab Airlines at Fiumicino Airport. The plane arrived in Cairo at midnight, where it was met by Farouk's sisters, Fawzia and Faika, and their husbands, Ismail Sherine and Fuad Sadek, a military truck to carry the coffin, and a contingent of army troops to deter the curious. The truck, followed by several cars of Farouk's family and Salah Nasir's General Intelligence operatives, rattled through the dark, deserted streets of Cairo. When two cars that were thought to be carrying reporters seemed to be following too closely, the convoy stopped and soldiers shot out the tires of the approaching vehicles.

Not even now would Nasser allow Farouk his full dignity. Instead of letting him be buried at El Rifaii, the grand ancestral mosque of the Mohammed Ali dynasty, Nasser insisted that Farouk's remains be relegated to the tomb of Ibrahim Pasha, the son of Mohammed Ali who ruled Egypt for only months before dying of tuberculosis. Farouk, who spent his life in palaces, would spend his death in a tomb flanked by the slums of the living and by the squatters trying to survive in the City of the Dead.

At two in the morning a minor sheikh conducted a ten-minute ceremony by gaslight for Farouk's sisters and brothers-in-law. There were no others there to pay respects. The General Intelligence men and soldiers waited outside. The mausoleum of Ibrahim was dug open. Farouk was removed from his walnut coffin and laid in the tomb pointing toward Mecca. Years later, Anwar Sadat would allow Farouk to be reinterred at El Rifaii, where he belonged. But now Egypt belonged to Nasser. And Farouk belonged to history. As the grave diggers began sealing up the tomb, the sheikh finished his prayers and Farouk's four mourners filed out into the desert stillness that was the Cairo night.

XIII

LEGACY

Cairo, 1990. The Royal Automobile Club may exist as only a shell of its formerly glimmering self. Nonetheless, it is one of the very few landmarks of the King Farouk era that remain to stand testimony, sad as it may be, to that gilded age in this once-imperial city. When the club was founded, one had to be royal, or at least close to it, just to have an automobile in a country where camels and asses were the predominant means of transportation. The club was as grand as the Bugattis, Duesenbergs, and Hispano Suizas that were parked out-side. Now the club is not much more exclusive than the Omaha AAA, and Cairo's perpetual gridlock far overwhelms that of New York's or Tokyo's worst rush hour. The ten-mile trip from Tahrir Square near the Nile out to the pyramids in Giza routinely takes three hours. Cars rarely make better time than the camels and asses.

The Royal Automobile Club still has its art deco façade and its fabulous full-wall bronze roadmap of Egypt, but the club has been refurbished in garish white and red vinyl and cheap crystal that might be described as Miami Beach arabesque. There is no sense of colonial mystique or desert mystery or pharaonic legacy that was once Cairo, only the down-at-the-heels *tristesse* of one of the crumbling resort towns along the New Jersey shore. The glory days, when King Farouk lost fortunes each night to his Jewish gambling friends while Egypt waged an equally losing war against Israel, are long forgotten.

Black Sudanese suffragis in red robes pad about bringing drinks, while lighter-skinned Egyptian headwaiters in tuxedos take orders from tables of businessmen, darkly Levantine, wearing shiny off-the-rack European-cut suits and sport jackets. Few wear ties. Many wear gold chains. All talk loudly, animatedly, in Arabic, a language that in Farouk's day was rarely heard in the club, except among the dishwashers. The businessmen fondle their worry beads incessantly, then laugh as if they had nothing to worry about. Only the food is as it was: Mediterranean sea bass caught that morning off Alexandria, jewellike beans and squash and luscious melons from the fertile gardens of the Nile delta. The food is fresh because Egypt is still low tech. Microwaves and frozen food are out of reach of all except the very rich, who don't seem to patronize the Royal Automobile Club anymore.

The anachronistic shining star in the midst of this raffish decay is Prince Hassan Hassan, the last prince of the realm, the cousin of Farouk, and one of the rare torchbearers of the Mohammed Ali dynasty who still lives on in the land of his hallowed forebears. He is just the sort of pure aristocrat that Leslie Howard might have played. *Impeccable* is the word. The fair skin, blue eyes, the Savile Row double-breasted flannel blazer, the Turnbull and Asser shirt, the custom shoes, the perfect public-school mellifluity all place him squarely in St. James's, not Tahrir. Yet here he is.

The prince wears his nostalgia as elegantly as his clothes. A victim of Nasser's confiscations and purges, he went from living in palaces to subsisting on twenty-nine Egyptian pounds a week. The silver lining of this precipitous descent was that it brought the prince into contact with the fellaheen, whom he describes as "the true aristocrats, the most elegant people on earth." An accomplished painter and pianist, Prince Hassan left the country only after Nasser died in 1970. He went to France "to breathe." Yet after a year he returned to Egypt.

Hassan is very fond of his cousin Farouk. "He had no temper whatsoever. He was charming. He spoke beautifully. And he wasn't stupid at all," the prince says, underscoring that the king's geological and biological collections were vastly more impressive than his pornography or his neckties. Farouk's fatal flaw, the prince explains, is the flip side of all his charm: he was "weak." Hassan blames Queen Nazli. He describes how King Fuad had wanted his son to marry one of Hassan's beautiful blond sisters. When Fuad died, Nazli scrapped the plan and excised Hassan's family from her Abdine guest list. Nazli wasn't worried about consanguinity. She was worried about control. She wanted Farouk to marry a "commoner" like herself. Hassan goes on to describe Farouk's obsession with money, which derived from his mother, who could never keep her maids because she was so tight-fisted with them.

The unofficial social historian of his dynasty, Prince Hassan describes the "making" of the Turkish aristocracy, whereby beautiful Circassian preteen girls would be impressed into slavery by the scouts of the Ottoman sultan and bred for royalty. The Turkish elite married "for love," i.e., beauty, the prince says, hence the amazing good looks of a family rife with real-life Cinderella stories of slaves who become princesses.

The prince goes on to describe his boyhood, of summer sailings from Alexandria to Naples tucked into deck chairs and being served finger sandwiches and hot consommé by waiters in black tie, of garden parties with flute players and native dancers and differently colored porcelain and crystal to match each guest's personality, of *tableaux vivants* played out among the crocodile fountains and marble pavilions of the Shoubra Palace on the Nile. He remembers his father's feeling that his sons should become bankers and his daughters nurses. But that was work and they were royalty. "We never *dreamed* of working," the prince says with a twinge of irony.

Then he stops short because of the screams of several wives of the gold-chained businessmen that pierce the dining room. The women jump out of their chairs. The lethargic suffragis are pressed into service by the headwaiters. Is it a thief, a gunman, a terrorist raid? The screams continue. What is it? Something large darts blindingly across the dining room, under the tables. It darts again, out into the center of the room. It is a huge rodent. The prince, always cool, laughs. It is a weasel. Cairo is infested with them. They migrate to the city from the bullrushes of the Nile to sleep under the hoods of cars. They like the warmth of the engines. This weasel is the ultimate autophile. Why sleep in a battered Fiat on the street when it can bask in the luxuries, however faded, of the Royal Automobile Club? The suffragis come in with brooms. The weasel is arrogant. It does a leisurely table-hop before scampering out into the wilds of Cairo down the once-grand marble staircase where kings and princes used to tread.

Outside the RAC, Cairo is bedlam. When Farouk was deposed in 1952, the city had barely two million inhabitants. Now there are nearly fifteen million, doubling every ten years. Cairo's air pollution index is the highest in the world. The magic square mile that had been the heart of Farouk's glamorous Cairo had been devastated by Black Saturday of 1952 and never restored. Groppi's still stands, serving tired pastries to a sparse and enervated clientele. The Mohammed Ali Club also stands, like a sore thumb, in fin de siècle Parisian elegance amid a miasma of choking dust and a rubble of soot-black high-rise office buildings and broken sidewalks. Soldiers in black uniforms with machine guns are everywhere. The mood is that of Beirut under siege.

If Egyptians of the Old Order have any non-Egyptians to thank for the state of their country, it is the Americans. Prince Hassan Hassan recalled, without nostalgia, John Foster Dulles' vow "to put colonels in place of kings." He also recalled, without great affection, Ambassador Jefferson Caffery and his fondness for Nasser and the Free Officers, whom Caffery called "my boys." The prince described the Southern-plantation diplomat as being torn between his European fascination with monarchy and his American commitment to democracy. Democracy won out, but it was really tyranny in disguise. "My boys are good boys," was Jefferson Caffery's catchphrase. These were words he and America would later regret.

Today Egypt may be inching toward democracy in fits and starts, but that sine qua non of the democratic process—literacy—has actually retrogressed, a casualty of the population avalanche. Cairo schools already operate in three shifts, and to keep up with the birth rate, a new school must be built every day. It isn't.

If democracy is a cherished dream, monarchy is an obliterated and despised memory. King Farouk has been reduced practically to a nonperson, his place in Egyptian history Stalinized into little more than a contemptuous footnote. To ask about Farouk invites an unease, a suspicion akin to what might be engendered by a query in Romania about the Ceausescus. Farouk's palaces have become headquarters of various military bureaucracies and are off limits to the general public. From the outside, Abdine is a massive, dusty, and barren monument enlivened only by the Royal Crown Cola sign glinting in the sun across the square, while tenement slums look down onto the now-scraggly, desiccated gardens. On the outskirts, Koubbeh is impenetrable with its endless high perimeter wall. The legendary Shoubra Palace, with its fountains and open-air pavilions, now languishes in a forgotten corner of the campus of Ain Shams Agricultural University, hard by the fertilizer department. Armed guards patrol the crumbling monument, as if to prevent the splendors of the Mohammed Ali dynasty from turning impressionable modern heads back to the "decadent" past represented by this great nymphaeum and pleasure garden, where Mohammed Ali lay on cushions and watched his harem swim naked before him. Shoubra inspired Lord Byron to write in *Childe Harold's Pilgrimage:*

> In marble-pav'd pavilion,
> When a spring
> Of living water from the center rose
> Whose bubbling did a genial freshness bring,
> And soft, voluptuous couches breath'd repose
> Ali reclined, a man of war and woes.

In Helwan, the spa where Russian grand dukes used to come for the famous sulfur baths, Farouk's grand Frank Lloyd Wright–style rest house has been boarded up. "Marienbad-on-the-Nile" now looks like Secaucus on the turnpike, with fire-belching smokestacks crowding out the date palms. Farouk's Pyramids Rest House has been converted into the Giza Antiquities Police Station, guarded by a kennel of foaming German shepherds. Inside, lucky tomb robbers might get a glimpse of this ultimate Egyptian playboy pad in the shadow of the sphinx. Twin statues of Ramses flank the entrance to the edifice, which resembles the Temple of Philae. Inside is a grand staircase overlooked by a huge stained glass window depicting a pharaoh resembling Farouk reclining on a barge with a bevy of lyre-playing goddesses of the underworld. The goddesses are all blond, bouffant, Hollywood-starlet types dressed in incongruous breast-baring slinky, diaphanous cocktail outfits that seem more appropriate to Caesars Palace than to that of Ramses.

The one official acknowledgment of King Farouk is in a back room of Mohammed Ali's first palace, the Gawharah, atop the citadel overlooking Cairo. In what seems to be a hall of forgotten ancestors are hung portraits of all the dynastic rulers of Egypt from Mohammed Ali to Farouk and a list of their accomplishments. Farouk's curriculum vitae is the briefest of the lot:

1. He was the son of King Fuad I.
2. Under him the Arab League was erected and resided in Cairo in 1945.
3. In 1948 Egypt took part in the Palestine War.
4. He evacuated the British Armies from the Citadel, which he

gave to the Egyptian Armies with great festivities the 9 August, 1946.
5. In 1952 the Revolution occurred and banished Farouk out of Egypt.

Also in the citadel, in the Military Museum, is a display of Farouk's naval uniform. His double-breasted wool coat with gold collar, cuffs, and Egyptian crescent buttons could easily accommodate two lesser men, maybe three. With the uniform were Farouk's high black leather shoes, made in America, of the Gridiron Battle Ax brand. Across the hall if one bribes the guard with a little baksheesh, one can be admitted to a sinister room containing a dozen ominous black busts of the Free Officers, most with glasses that in life were dark under a large photo captioned "The Departure of King Farouk" on the *Mahroussa* in his admiral's whites. In the center of these twelve dark apostles is an even larger bust of a woman with breasts worthy of the cantilevered bullet brassiere Howard Hughes designed for Jane Russell. The inscription on this Egyptian Venus de Milo, with a frieze of the army in battle below her, is "Towards Glory."

Cairo's other "official" acknowledgment of, if not shrine to, Farouk is the Hunting Museum at the Manyal Palace, the Nile island estate of the late Prince Mohammed Ali, who waited in vain most of his life to succeed to Farouk's throne. Half of the palace's banyan-shaded grounds have been given over to a spartan Club Med; the other half, including the palace itself, is Cairo's nod toward the prince's banished dynasty.

The Hunting Museum is powerful evidence that the rich are different. It is a half-mile-long hall of Farouk's collection of embalmed animals and birds that he had shot, a gallery of water buffalo heads, gazelle heads, antelope heads, and many more perverse items including Queen Farida's gold necklace of tiny birds' heads and King Farouk's eagle's-claw candlestick, rhinoceros-horn cigar guillotine, and a whip made from long fish whiskers. There are *tableaux morts* of stuffed tigers devouring monkeys, cases of embalmed scorpions and rats, and an impressive display of a stuffed hermaphrodite goat complete with udders and a penis and an annotation that Farouk found this natural aberration particularly fascinating. Finally, there is a collection of traps that culminates in an "official weasel trap" manufactured by the Animal Trap Company of London, with the instructions: "Salt with part of an English sparrow or fresh bloody meat." The Royal Automobile Club should take note.

Although most Europeans in Cairo today are either wearing backpacks or being herded into tour buses for a quick day at the mosques, the pyramids, the carpet shops, and the Khan-el Khalili bazaar before embarking for their three-day package cruise up the Nile to Luxor and Aswan, there is a large and lively diplomatic community that seems to lionize the survivors of the Farouk elite. The villas where this elite used to live were built mostly in 1869, the year Khedive Ismail opened the Suez Canal. The khedive granted enormous incentives to builders of these European-style quickie palazzos so that Cairo would seem "civilized" to the international dignitaries who descended on the city for the canal's festive kickoff. Now the embassies have taken over the villas that the *nouveau pauvre* Old Guard can no longer maintain. Nevertheless, the ambassadors always invite the former occupants to their round of parties.

One night at the Swiss embassy in the Garden City area, which was originally the town house of the noble Jewish Mosseris, there are Adeses and Wissas and Wahbas and Youneses and Simaikas and Khalils and Fodas and Halims, a ghostly pantheon of the important names of prerevolutionary Cairene high society. Drinking champagne, eating caviar, gracefully waltzing and wittily flirting, this aristocratic mix of the few remaining Jews, of Copts and Muslims, of gilded youth from Harvard and Oxford and the Sorbonne returning to their roots and tarnished age unable to escape from them, is a window into the carefree past. One can almost imagine Farouk rolling up in one of his red Cadillac convertibles and calling an all-night poker game to order.

"Polo is a disease. The only cure is poverty," says Victor Simaika, now in his eighties and one of Cairo's great sportsman-playboys. Simaika, a Copt whose name means "little fish" in Arabic, divides his time between an English home in Buckinghamshire and a modern apartment in the Garden City district. Always a big fish in the Cairo social pond, he was once imprisoned by Nasser but would never dream of abandoning the city in which his family had been involved in generations of philanthropy, including the founding of the Coptic Museum. The den of Simaika's flat is a veritable trophy room with stuffed heads of gazelles and antelopes on the walls flanking a portrait of Simaika in a polo jersey and a monocle. There are photographs of Simaika on various playing fields and hunting grounds with Queen Elizabeth, Prince Charles, the maharaja of Jaipur, and Rita Hayworth, at rhino shoots in Africa, pig stickings in India, chamois chases in the Tyrol.

Linked with some of the world's most famous women (he escorted both Barbara Hutton and Doris Duke during their days in Egypt), the still lean and erect Simaika concedes his allure to women was no match for Farouk's. "Farouk would just show up in women's rooms in the middle of the night. Humble mortals have to have a line and climb the ladder, but Farouk was at the top of the ladder. He *knew* he would get them. Royalty was his aphrodisiac. I couldn't begin to compete with him."

Simaika remembers the first time he met Farouk on the beach at Sidi Bishr, in Alexandria. Farouk was striking matches and flipping them at the pretty woman Simaika was with. "He loved putting people ill at ease." Simaika, who used to have a *garçonniere* in a houseboat on the Nile at which assignations would arrive in horse-drawn gharries, has fond memories of Farouk's mistresses. "Irene Guinle was very sexy, very pretty. She had the education of an English girl, which gave her an appeal no Oriental girl could have. And of course Barbara Skelton was the real thing, the ultimate English girl." He recalls when Farouk picked up Honeychile Hohenlohe at the Scarabee bar and extols her uncensored American virtues, or lack thereof: "Whenever I see her, she asks me 'Victor, can you still get it up?' " He compares Fatma Toussoun and Irene Guinle. "Fatma was beautiful, fat, and nonparticipating; Irene was beautiful, slim, and participating."

Simaika describes Nazli as "well read and oversexed," talks about the huge fights between Farouk and Farida, says Antonio Pulli was the only member of Farouk's entourage he liked, and denounces Karim Thabet as "the lowest of the lowest yes-man." His favorite member of Farouk's family was his sister Faiza, now living in Los Angeles. "She was one of the most attractive, charming women I've ever met," Simaika says. "But she had this fantastic feeling of insecurity. Once at a cocktail party she told me, 'When I walk into a room like this, I suffer a hundred deaths.' " Farouk's oldest sister, Fawzia, who lives a quiet existence in Alexandria with her husband, Ismail Sherine, told Simaika even less. "I met her in Budapest. She was perfect, wearing an ochre lace dress and an emerald necklace that matched her green eyes. I sat next to her at a dinner for five hours, and I couldn't get more than a yes or a no."

A much more talkative beauty is Ulvia Halim, daughter of Prince Abbas Halim, who, with her Italian husband, divides her time between Positano, Italy and a 1940's high rise in the Zamalek district of Cairo. An American potholder in her kitchen bears the inscription "It's not easy being a princess." Ulvia Halim handles it effortlessly. Widely regarded as the most stunning survivor of her dynasty for the piercing blue eyes, devastating cheekbones, and regal grace that would blow an entire défilé of high fashion models off a Paris runway, she spent the worst days of the revolution, while her father was imprisoned for three years, at the Madeira School in Virginia with her horse Butterball, studying under teachers like Jean Harris, who later murdered Scarsdale Diet Dr. Herman Tarnower and going to Georgetown parties to play charades with John F. Kennedy. A descendant of Khedive Ismail on her mother's side and Mohammed Ali on her father's, she is as dynastic as one can get and would never give up the winter "season," whatever its spectrality.

Another striking face, in from Paris for the annual Cairo Film Festival, is actor Omar Sharif. Sharif, who was twenty when Farouk was deposed, reflects on his country's "pharaoh mentality" and how it translated into a blind worship of Farouk. "I was in awe of the big man," Sharif says, reflecting on how the king would come to Sharif's parents' house in the Garden City district for all-boy all-night poker and chemin de fer marathons. Sharif's father, a prosperous Lebanese-Egyptian timber dealer who made his fortune during the war manufacturing nails from British scrap barbed wire, was honored to have the king *chez lui,* for it gave him access to palace patronage for getting licenses and other business concessions. The games had their own protocol. "If Farouk would goad you to go higher, or not fold, you couldn't disagree. You couldn't leave the table until the king said the game was over," which was invariably after dawn.

In Cairo the only people who will speak openly about Farouk are these former royals and plutocrats, most of whom live well outside Egypt most of the year. There are two schools of thought, the Farouk school and the Farida school, each of which sees its stalwart as the victim of the other. The Farouk sympathizers portray Farida as a treacherous seductress who broke the king's heart, had affairs with his male relatives, and plotted Farouk's overthrow with the Free Officers in return for a hallowed position in the New Society.

They deride Farida's pretentions, her insistence that everyone, including her own mother, address her as "Your Majesty" and with the formal *"vous"* rather than *"tu,"* how, postrevolution, she had a huge row with the French ambassador when he refused to issue her a passport in the name "Queen Farida of Egypt" (Lebanon finally issued her the requested appellation), and how she wore a crown of fake gems after her own had been confiscated by the state.

The Farida-ites attack Farouk as a willful and slothful satyr and nominate Farida for sainthood for enduring him as long as she did. They ridicule Farouk's devotion to Islam as erratic and selective. No, he didn't drink alcohol, but what about the women? Farouk was able to rationalize Pulli's position as his official procurer on the grounds that Pulli was a Catholic, hence a non-Muslim and outside the strictures and standards of that faith. With God, as with man, the king made his own rules.

Both the Farouk and the Farida camps agree in their distaste for Queen Nazli, for her unqueenly licentiousness and illicit romances, and for Princess Shivekiar for being the royal temptress and troublemaker, doing her all to divide the House of Fuad, from which she had been ejected, and thereby ensuring its fall. No one has anything bad to say about the loyal Antonio Pulli, nor anything good about the sycophantic Karim Thabet, who is remembered for the signed photos of both Hitler and Mussolini on his wall of celebrities. Pulli and Thabet are both dead, as is Elias Andraous and the rest of Farouk's inner circle, all of whom used to assemble, after being released from their revolutionary penance, at Pulli's cake shop in Heliopolis to share coffee and memories of what might have been. Virtually everyone in Cairo's Old Guard believes that things were better under Farouk, and that the religious impediments to implementing enforced birth control will be the mummy's curse that spells doom for their country.

Highest on the list of mutually agreed upon hatreds is that of the British, particularly Sir Miles Lampson, an antipathy that promises to endure as long as the pyramids. The British embassy still stands in its dominating position, but its access to the banks of the Nile, where Lady Lampson held her garden parties, has been cut off by the new road, grandly known as the Nile Corniche, that runs along the river. A bleak wall has been constructed to seal off the British compound from the relentless honking of the permanent traffic jam that clogs the road. Inside, the Union Jack flies over the porticoed embassy constructed by Lord Cromer in the halcyon Empire days of the 1850s. But now the grand ballroom has become the visa section, and the stables an office complex. The famous rosebushes are forlorn and wilted, and the lawn is overgrown with weeds and crabgrass. A chargé spends his day trying to requisition new lawn mowers but admits the ultimate futility of the enterprise. "English grass just doesn't grow in Egyptian soil," he says. If only that lesson had been learned a century before.

In December 1976, Rafik Ghali, twenty-one, was worried about his mother, the former Princess Fathia, Farouk's baby sister. Separated from Riad Ghali, she had recently taken a job as a cleaning woman, scrubbing office floors to make ends meet. Fathia, now forty-five, and her mother Nazli, eighty-one, had been living in Los Angeles with Fathia's husband, Riad Ghali, fifty-six, for over twenty years. At first they had a twenty-eight-room mansion in Benedict Canyon, near where Charles Manson and his family had murdered Sharon Tate, then a small house on Sixteenth Street in Santa Monica. They had been selling their jewels to support a less and less royal life-style, which was in part underwritten by their friend Princess Shams of Iran, the sister of the shah. The princess lived on a gated estate in Beverly Hills. But the Persian supplement had been cut off, and the resulting financial pinch precipitated the separation of Riad Ghali from the ex-princess and ex-queen.

In September 1976, daughter and mother had appeared in bankruptcy court. They moved one more level down, into a spartan apartment in the flats of West Los Angeles, a low-rent area populated largely by a mix of Japanese florists, Mexican day laborers, and students from nearby UCLA. Ever superstitious, Fathia and Nazli used the money they had to consult a Hollywood astrologer named Kebrina Kinkade, whose other clients included Farrah Fawcett, Michael and Shakira Caine, Sean Connery, and Cher. Miss Kinkade warned Fathia to beware of her husband, who worked as a salesman in a Rodeo Drive jewelry shop.

On December 10, when Rafik Ghali, who lived on his own, called his mother and got no answer, he knew instantly that something was wrong. Arriving at the apartment, he found Fathia dead on the floor in a pool of blood. A bullet was in her head. Beside her was Riad Ghali, unconscious and bleeding profusely from a head wound of his own. A gun was in his hand.

Ghali recovered to stand trial. In April 1978 he pleaded nolo contendere to a charge of involuntary manslaughter and was sentenced to a year in prison for the death of the ex-princess. He himself died several years later. In June 1978 Nazli died at age eighty-three. With her daughter, she had converted to Catholicism and was buried after a simple ceremony at the Good Shepherd Church of Beverly Hills, a strange end indeed for the queen of the Nile.

Farouk's second youngest sister, Faika, died in Cairo in 1983 at fifty-five after a long illness. She remained married to Fuad Sadek, and like Fawzia in Alexandria, led an unobtrusive life. After living in Paris for a while after the revolution, the fourth sister, Faiza, separated from her husband, Bulent Raouf, and joined Nazli and Fathia in Los Angeles, where she currently resides alone in an apartment in a high rise on Wilshire Boulevard. In a city full of self-created princesses, a genuine one like Faiza could be the toast of Tinseltown. Still sleek and glamorous, she chooses not to, staying close to a small, non-show-business circle, mostly foreign diplomats and plutocrats. Scrupulously close-mouthed about her family, at a recent dinner at Le Dôme on Sunset Boulevard, with heavy metal rockers at the back tables and slippery William Morris agents at the front tables, and hard-sell call girls at the bar in a Boschian Hollywood tableau that made even the weasels of the Royal Automobile Club look upper-crust, Faiza held forth about her brother's schooldays in England at Sandhurst. The fact that Farouk did not go to Sandhurst at all, but to Woolwich, was lost on the table. With so much to want to forget in the trauma of dispossession and exile, even the most pleasant memories can get lost in the shuffle.

Bulent Raouf's story had a happy ending. After his divorce from Faiza, the ebullient Turkish aristocrat moved to London and fell on very hard times, having to take a series of cooking and waiting jobs in several Chelsea bistros, including one called Pierrot's on Sloane Square, where his insistence on top ingredients drove the restaurant out of business. Raouf's personality that had made him Farouk's favorite brother-in-law was not lost in the London of the sixties. He became the darling of the film set to whom he had served food. It was a time when the Beatles were going off to India to sit with the Maharishi. Raouf had a better idea. Why go all the way to India? He became a Sufi mystic, and an entire cult of entertainment personalities fell under his spell, setting him up in headquarters in a great castle in Scotland. He married Angela Culme-Seymour, the

Dirge • Prince Fuad leads the procession of mourners behind Farouk's casket, Rome, 1965.

Keystone/SYGMA

Jet Set • Princess Faiza with Aly Khan in Paris. Even in exile, she remained one of the world's most glamorous women.   UPI/Bettmann

very social ex-wife of both Lord Kinross and Randolph Churchill, and died a very rich and influential figure.

Farouk's daughters still remain in Switzerland. Princess Fadia, the first to be married, albeit against her father's wishes, still is, to the Russian geologist Serge Orloff. The year after Farouk died, the eldest daughter, Ferial, who had been working as a teacher of short-hand at a secretarial school in Lausanne, went to England to be married in a public registry office as Fadia had the year before. Although Ferial, who spoke six languages and had planned to attend medical school until Farouk scotched the idea as unrealistic, had been considered as the wife for the shah of Iran, King Hussein of Jordan, and Ahmed Izzet, the grandson of the former president of Syria, the man she wed was Jean Pierre Perreten, a Swiss widower with an eighteen-year-old daughter. Perreten ran a hotel in Gstaad. "All I want is to live a quiet domestic life in Switzerland," she told a nosy reporter who unearthed the secret ceremony. She got her wish. The third sister, Fawzia, lives near her other siblings in Switzerland and has never married.

The girls' mother, Queen Farida, had perhaps the saddest odyssey of the lot, except for that of the murdered Fathia. Farida had left Egypt in 1963 to move, first to Beirut, where she took up painting, then in 1967 to Paris, where she developed her own technique of hardening her paintings with a blowtorch. During the Sadat era Farida returned to Egypt and began dividing her time, on a frugal budget, between Paris and Cairo. President Sadat granted her a small pension and an apartment as recompense for the deprivations she suffered under Nasser, who had confiscated the house by the pyramids Farouk had given her when she proved less useful as a tool of the state than Nasser had thought she would be.

A Paris-based *Time* reporter was invited by Farida to her apartment on the Rue Pergolese in the sixteenth arrondissement for coffee and to see her jewel collection. The reporter, who was from a wealthy horse-breeding Maryland family, sensed a sudden coldness from Farida, whom the reporter was instructed to call "Majesty," when she told the queen how beautiful the collection was. The reporter was quickly ushered out. Later she learned that the invitation was not to satisfy the reporter's cultural and aesthetic curiosity but rather the queen's need for money. The reporter had been expected to buy something.

Farida's best friend in Paris was Princess Beris Kandaoroff, an

English painter, author of satirical etiquette books *(The Art of Living),* and a hostess of British television specials on the rich and titled, who was married to a White Russian prince who died in 1990 at age ninety-four. Prince Dimitri and Princess Beris lived in a four hundred-year-old cottage on the Rue des Martyrs, a hilly market street just below the garish neon of Pigalle. The queen and the princess met at a cocktail party in 1980 and became friends immediately through their shared royalty and art.

When Farida had to sell her apartment on the Rue Pergolese, she moved into Beris's garret maid's room, up three steep, creaky flights of stairs. The bare, tiny, cell-like room, with its steeply angled roof, peeling paint, and noisy metal heater, had more in common with the Château d'If than with Abdine Palace. The lodgings seemed like penance for any sins Farida may have committed. Still, Beris said, Farida was happy here. Farida was anything but domestic. She couldn't even make toast, and once when she broke a glass, she had no idea how to sweep up the shards. Beris took Farida on her first trip on the metro, which the queen enjoyed as high adventure. She loved dressing up in her gold lamé gowns and going out with Beris, whom she called "honey," to Russian nightclubs or the Relais Plaza at the Hotel Plaza Athenée, where the seventeen-year-old Farouk had scandalized his entourage by visiting the room of the sixteen-year-old Farida on the king's 1937 grand tour.

Nothing happened on this visit, Farida told Beris. In general, sexually nothing happened in her entire marriage to the king. She described to Beris how Farouk had to take drugs and aphrodisiacs on the occasions when he and Farida tried to have children. Farida believed Farouk had a very Oedipal relationship with Nazli, whom Farida blamed for spoiling Farouk rotten and ruining their marriage. When asked about Farida's alleged affairs, her reported marriage to Wahid Yussri, her supposed passions that even a fully functioning Farouk might have fallen short of satisfying, Beris smiled inscrutably. "She *loved* men," was all Beris would say.

In the mid-1980s, when Farida learned she had contracted a slow, "smoldering" form of leukemia, she dictated her memoirs to Beris. Farida believed that Farouk was poisoned, a victim of the Nasser police state, though she felt that the motive was not political but financial. Farida was convinced that Farouk had a fortune hidden in Swiss bank accounts. No one in Farouk's family ever received it. She wasn't sure anyone in the Nasser regime ever found it either. In

1988, the wife of Egyptian President Mubarak suggested that Farida return to Egypt for treatment of her illness. Blood transfusions were prescribed. At first, Farida, who was very apprehensive about AIDS, refused. Then she went ahead. The blood was somehow tainted. Farida fell ill with hepatitis B. Four months later she died. Among her final words were: "Beris is out shopping. Dimitri is having his tea now." She was buried in a mausoleum in Cairo's City of the Dead.

Farida spent her last days in Egypt with her mother, who was in her nineties. Mrs. Zulficar had been senile and was constantly calling out Farida's childhood name, "Fifette," but when Farida responded, her mother didn't recognize her. Farida, who had always insisted that her mother, when compos mentis, address her as "Majesty," was very distressed at the nonrecognition. "I'm your daughter, the queen of Egypt," she would assert to her mother, who would do nothing but laugh uproariously. "Ha! Ha! Ha! Ha!" Only on the morning of Farida's death did Mrs. Zulficar make the connection Farida had desired. She wandered around the house mumbling "Farida. Farida. Where is the queen?" and wanting to bring her food. But it was too late. Mrs. Zulficar died two years later. After Farida's death, her daughter Fadia asked Beris for the memoirs Farida had dictated to her. The three daughters, whom Farida saw at most only a few times each year, decided that they didn't want the memoirs published and had them burned, Beris said.

After Farouk's death, Farida befriended her stepson, Fuad, whom she met for the first time at Farouk's funeral. She took a deep interest in the boy who was so briefly king of Egypt, both while he was at the Le Rosey School and afterward. When Fuad was courting his Jewish classmate's sister, Dominique France Picard, Farida insisted on "interviewing" the young woman before Fuad asked her to marry him. Despite Farida's efforts to provoke an argument, the girl refused to go for the bait. The future Princess Fadila and the past Queen Farida eventually became friends. Farida admitted to Fadila that many of her marital missteps were attributable to her extreme youth at the time her marriage to Farouk was arranged for her by Nazli. She told Fadila how she would smash vases Farouk had given her if she didn't like the color or the style, or hurl necklaces into the palace gardens, where they would be lost, if she didn't like the jewels. Fadila profited from Farida's mistakes. She not only created a very harmonious life with Fuad, but also managed to create a relationship between Farida and Narriman, by inviting them both for dinners on the floor in front of the television in the grand flat on the Avenue Foch. There was no protocol as to who sat where, no crown jewels, no my-reign-was-better-than-your-reign. The two queens met like this several times and got along well.

Narriman, who was only forty-six in 1990, again lives in Cairo after some years in Beirut. She, too, has not been well, having suffered a cerebral hemorrhage in the early 1980s. At first, Fuad had a hard time forgiving his mother for deserting his father in his darkest hour. But the combination of her youth, her mother, and Gamal Abdel Nasser were pretty extenuating circumstances, and Fuad is a compassionate man, as an ex-king might well be.

Today Fuad and Fadila are an integral part of the European social scene, appearing regularly at grand balls, spring collections, and on best-dressed lists. Some may sneer that they have fallen prey to the press agents of the fashion establishment and are being exploited for their royalty/publicity value to dignify otherwise undignified grabs for the press spotlight. But who today, from the Bushes to the Reagans to the Kissingers to the Hanovers, *hasn't* been exploited by the press agents? Power, as well as titles, are more than aphrodisiacs; they sell dresses.

Fuad insists quite sincerely that his father took no more than a million dollars out of Egypt with him. Farouk never believed he would be, or could be, deposed and never planned accordingly. Farouk's chief asset when he died was the apartment in the Parioli district. The jewels, the art, the stamps, the coins, the pornography, and the stuffed hermaphrodite goats, all were left behind, spoils belonging to the Free Officers. If there was money in Switzerland, Fuad and his sisters never saw it. Nevertheless, Fuad lives today, if not like a king, like a rich man. Then again, even kings don't live like kings anymore, not kings like Farouk.

The Forgotten King

The former King Farouk of Egypt was the modern equivalent of Sardanapalus, the last great King of Assyria, who is reputed to have said that he wished he had thirty stomachs so as to enjoy life thirty times more than he did. To quote Byron: "Eat, drink, and love What can the rest avail us.
So said the royal sage, Sardanapalus."
When Prince Farouk assumed royal powers at the age of 18

in 1937 he was a strong-willed, impetuous youth who seemed
to have promise and, at least, a strong sense of Egyptian nationalism. His unpopularity began to pyramid when he divorced his first wife, Queen Farida, in 1948. . . .

One could pile up pejorative adjectives like sybaritic, avaricious, lustful, greedy to reach a contemptible total. Farouk
ended up in luxurious exile, caring nothing for Egypt or the
impoverished Egyptian people . . . The epitaph for King Farouk has to be bitter and contemptuous. . . .

Such was the editorial on the death of King Farouk in *The New
York Times,* which was restrained compared to other newspapers
around the world. In effect, this was a last tango on Fleet Street, for
the final salvo against Farouk was led by the British press, both
tabloid and respectable. England, naturally, had the biggest ax to
grind, the longest grudge, and the sourest grapes. They had lost
Egypt, they had lost Suez, they had lost their empire, and Sir Miles
Lampson's long and futile battle with King Farouk was as galling a
symbol as any of that decline and fall. Although *The New York
Times* had its men in the Middle East, Egypt until 1952 was in
journalistic terms as well as political largely a British sphere of
influence. Most of the non-Arabic reporting that was done on Farouk was this British reporting. While probably more objective than
the Arabic reporting, which was constrained by Palace censorship
laws, lèse majesté considerations, and general politesse, the British
portrait of Farouk was precisely that: a British portrait.

The great tragedy of Farouk's public persona was that he wasn't
British. He wasn't Arab either, but he certainly wasn't British. Yet
he was being judged by the standards of and for a British monarch,
a British gentleman, a British aristocrat, and he was none of the
above. Sir Miles Lampson wrecked his own brilliant career trying to
make Farouk into these things, but "the boy" simply wouldn't play
by Lampson's rules, British rules. The result was that the chauvinis-
tic British press rallied behind Lampson and characterized and,
later, caricatured Farouk as an uppity, disrespectful ungrateful
"wog," a barbarian, a vulgarian, and an enemy of the people, the
British people.

Not that Farouk failed to give his assailants in the Fourth Estate
plenty of ammunition. To begin with, he *was* a boy. He may have
been a king, but he was still a boy, and unless he was a British
monarch, a boy was expected to behave with a certain degree of

deference. The 1936 Anglo-Egyptian Treaty may have made nice sounds about Egyptian independence and "demoted" Miles Lampson from lordly high commissioner to the less imperial rank of ambassador; yet everyone, everyone outside of Egypt, knew the *real* story, which was that Egypt was basically nothing but a British colony, a glorified British colony, but a colony nonetheless. Farouk was expected to behave appropriately, i.e., as a kowtowing British schoolboy puppet. He wouldn't. He didn't.

How he *did* behave was another problem. At the beginning of Farouk's reign, when he was a slim and handsome cover-boy Prince Charming who had a fairy-tale arranged royal wedding, the press adored him, and the world followed suit. The minute real life intruded into the fairy tale, and Farouk and Farida's royal honeymoon was over, so was the king's honeymoon with the press. It was most unfortunate timing that Farouk came to the throne at the outset of World War II. The exigencies of that conflict abruptly terminated the colonial charade that Egypt was independent and that Farouk had any real power. Nevertheless, the Egyptians believed it and Farouk believed it, and that was the rub: Egypt took England at its word, not its subtext. Meanwhile, Farouk began behaving not as the ersatz Etonian that Lampson sent the old-boy tutor Edward Ford to convert him into, but rather according to his Franco-Ottoman family roots. Socially, he started playing the bon vivant. Politically, his role model was the Ottoman sultan, the caliph of Islam, the Oriental potentate.

To this mix was added the beau idéal of the German field marshal. This element was no notion of Farouk's, but rather of some of his leading Egyptian advisers, who were steeped in the classical Von Clausewitz tradition of German militarism. The German sympathies of such pivotal leaders as Prime Minister Ali Maher and General Aziz el Masri were a function of anglophobia and not anti-Semitism, for Egypt was a country where the Jews as slaves may have built the pyramids but were now sitting on top of them as masters of finance and society. In Egypt, the distinction between pro-German and pro-Nazi was always very carefully enunciated. Only after the war, when the Palestine question emerged as *the* issue in the Middle East, did the distinction become blurred. Farouk was branded by the press as a friend of the Reich's and an enemy of the Jews. In truth he was neither, but the accusation was hard to rebut when he sent his troops to war against Israel.

Wanderer • Queen Farida, who became an artist in Beirut, then Paris, before dying of leukemia complications in Cairo, 1988.

Terry Daum/CP/Globe Photos

UPI/Bettmann

Low Tide • Was Farouk's appearance the cause or the effect of his demise?

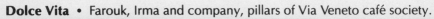
Dolce Vita • Farouk, Irma and company, pillars of Via Veneto café society.

The New Roma Press Photo

Worst of all, Farouk got fat. In a world that judged its leaders by appearances, Farouk's went almost overnight from the sublime to the ridiculous. Why Farouk got so fat is subject to long debate. Theories range from genetic propensity to depression over Lampson's humiliation of him at Abdine in 1942 to glandular disruption after his car crash to the fact that fabulous food was *there* for the eating. The whys don't matter. There is no escaping Farouk's fatness, along with his premature baldness, and the prejudice engendered by this combined gain and loss. Could John F. Kennedy, who had similar sybaritic excess, have gotten away with them if he were bald and obese? "Fat Farouk" became a cartoonish figure of such ridicule that the public forgot the slim Farouk that it had put on a pedestal as the dreamboat boy-king from the Arabian Nights scant years before. For the British, the white man's burden became that much heavier.

Once Farouk became corpulent, all the excesses that would be considered highly romantic and glamorous in a Hollywood star suddenly were seen as evil. What was revelry in the thin man became gluttony in the fat. Particularly egregious was Farouk's divorce from Farida, though it might have been less so had it not occurred in the middle of the 1948 war with Israel. His 1950 European grand tour was denounced as a mockery of conspicuous consumption, and his 1951 honeymoon with Narriman was even more outrageous, though it did get him on the cover of *Time*. His choice of Narriman was also unfortunate in terms of public relations, less because she was sixteen than because she, too, was plump. Had she been a Jacqueline Bouvier upper bourgeoise type like Farida, that might have made her much more palatable to the press. But Farouk had had his fill of Jacqueline Bouvier types. The fringes of dynasty were packed with hopeful hautes bourgeoises. Farouk couldn't stand them. He preferred whores. One of Farouk's greatest shortcomings as king of Egypt was that he wasn't concerned with appearances. All he was being was himself, which was totally unpretentious. It was a huge mistake. What he really needed was a great, subtle public relations man, not an Egyptian P. T. Barnum that he had in Karim Thabet.

Almost as damaging to his image as his girth was Farouk's having been deposed. On top of all his other flaws, he was a loser. Everyone hates a loser, especially a *fat* loser. Forget the betrayals by the British. Forget the treachery of the Americans. Forget the involvement of the CIA. The hard fact was that Farouk lost his throne, and, worse, Farouk was a two-time loser. He had also lost Palestine. There were plenty of excuses for the 1948 war with Israel, but they didn't count either. The sympathy of the world was with the victims of the Holocaust. Why shouldn't they have the right to make flowers bloom in a barren desert, to transform it into a land of milk and honey? Farouk, through the inexorable forces of Arab nationalism, was railroaded into a vastly unpopular course of action that makes sense today only if the inequities of partition and displacement of the Palestinian Arabs can be considered on a rational basis apart from the horrors of the genocide of World War II.

At the time, because Farouk, the non-Arab, was the head of the Arab League, and, by definition, the adversary of Israel, he became the symbol of the fat Arab, the rich Arab, the Jew-hating, Jew-killing Arab, the losing Arab that has persisted until the present day as a powerful image that poisons the waters of peace and prevents Jew and Arab from ever getting along. Nasser was far more an enemy of the Jews than Farouk ever was, yet Nasser was trim and Nasser was poor, and therefore the lean and hungry Nasser had to be democratic. Were Britain and America ever more wrong? But Nasser *won*. In matters of public opinion, winning was everything. To Farouk, the loser, belonged nothing but contempt.

But is such massive contempt deserved, or simply a case study in prejudice and character assassination? Given the powder keg of Palestine, could any Arab leader, even the matinee idol Farouk might have been had he kept his hair and his waistline, have had any chance at all to win the hearts and minds of the Western world? And popularity contests aside, what, if any, is Farouk's place in history other than as the end of a line?

Perhaps the best way to consider Farouk is not as an end but as a beginning, as the first popular "modern" king of Egypt. Farouk's father, King Fuad, was an autocrat of the old Ottoman school. His monarchy was entirely a creation of the British and his autocracy in Cairo existed only within perimeters defined by London. Fuad was in many ways a foreigner, having been raised and educated in Italy. He never spoke Arabic and referred to the rank and file of Egyptians as "those people." If Fuad was an outsider ruling Egypt, so was the entire Mohammed Ali dynasty, composed of essentially Turkish khedives reigning over a North African colony. While undoubtedly closer in spirit to the Egyptians than the British, they could never be accused of being "of the people."

Although Farouk had no natural empathy with the fellaheen, he at least made the effort to make a connection with "my beloved people." The people, in turn, loved Farouk back. Unlike his father, who was stuffy, aloof, and anything but a sympathetic figure, Farouk was a smiling blond god, a pharaoh whom the masses, inculcated with century after century of blind obedience, could genuinely like and *want to,* not *have to,* serve. Farouk, a natural charmer, spoke perfect Arabic, prayed at the mosques on Fridays, made a show of observing the laws of Islam. He was Egypt's native son, its favorite son.

The intolerant disrespect shown to Farouk by Sir Miles Lampson served to intensify the public's sympathy for the king and hatred for his persecutor. Even though Lampson would justify his actions on the grounds of wartime emergency, given his personality, he would have likely behaved the exact same way even if Neville Chamberlain had achieved peace in his time. Lampson's anachronistic imperialism did more than make Farouk a popular martyr. It accelerated the movement for democracy in Egypt by giving the masses a powerfully antagonistic image against which to revolt.

Even after the native son had become the prodigal son, King Farouk was still the most beloved man in Egypt. The Egyptian people were not the Fleet Street press. They didn't *care* if Farouk got fat. They didn't care if he got divorced, or bought land yachts, or collected Coke bottles, or sat in nightclubs with belly dancers and b-girls. It was to this audience of adoring fans in standing room that Farouk played to, not the British and Americans in their box seats. As long as he continued playing to these masses, he was secure that his reign would not unravel.

Unfortunately, this social contract was broken by the 1948 war. Fat may not have mattered to the Egyptians; face did. That Egypt ended up playing Goliath to Israel's David was a national disgrace. It was Farouk's Waterloo. Sir Miles Lampson's being relieved of his ambassadorship in 1946 had been considered a great triumph for Farouk, not only over the British, but also over the Wafd, which had gone from being the party of the people to the party of the pashas to the party of the puppets, British puppets, with Prime Minister Nahas Pasha as the chief imperialist tool. The people thus couldn't trust their politicians anymore. They could trust only their king as their stalwart against colonial servitude. Despite the country's profound poverty and even more profound inequities, the Egyptians had been down so long that Farouk looked like up to them. Until 1948, democracy took a distinct backseat to nationalism as Egypt's burning issue. Farouk deserves much credit for being the Peck's bad boy, the thorn in the side of British diplomacy in keeping Egypt's dreams of independence alive. In standing up to the British, he set a powerful example to the other vassal states of the Middle East, an example that would be followed by sundry military strongmen across the Arab world from Algeria to Iraq in the years ahead. Farouk was unique in declaring his independence as an incumbent ruler and not as a military revolutionary. That took a great deal of courage. As Lampson, as well as Winston Churchill, warned Farouk, he could have a long and happy reign if and only if he played cricket with the British. That Farouk elected to take his chances and be his own man marked him as a leader, and a real one.

Once Egypt lost to Israel in 1948, Farouk was stigmatized as a loser of a supposedly "unlosable" conflict and his right to be the standard bearer of Egyptian nationalism was impugned, predominantly by the radical fundamentalist Muslim Brotherhood. Again, the real focus of the Sturm und Drang was not social welfare and other democratic issues, but rather independence from the British. To the leader who could spew out the most venom belonged the spoils. Farouk was not a venomous man, nor was he trained as a statesman or otherwise equipped to deal with all the assassinations and violence and partisan power plays with which he was confronted almost daily. Nevertheless, for someone so young and so sheltered from the hard realities of life and death on the Nile, Farouk remained on top of this ziggurat of intrigue. Moving with amazing grace, Farouk was the Nijinsky of the very mad ballet of Egyptian politics. At the end he could also be seen as the quarterback who brought the football of Egyptian nationalism down to the goal line and was sacked at the last moment and replaced by an upstart benchwarmer named Nasser, who scored the winning touchdown and got all the glory.

Farouk's greatest error was his hubris in assuming Britain hated communism more than it hated him and that America hated communism more than it hated anything. Farouk saw himself as the Middle East's bulwark against Moscow, whose red claws, he suspected, were deep into the back of the Muslim Brotherhood, goad-ing it into the violent outbursts that culminated in Black Saturday of 1952. Of course Britain was so thrilled to see the end of Farouk that it would probably have stood by and let Joseph Stalin take his place. And America, which wanted control, was delighted to have Jefferson Caffery's "boys" in the palace in Cairo and in the palm of Washington. Yes, Nasser and his fellow revolutionaries were echt Egyptians, pure and poor and, yes, they destroyed the decadent pasha class and scattered its wealth across the sands. At the same time, in Nasser the British got an Egyptian despot and lost Suez, and in Nasser America got its boy and lost control. America's missionary zeal to create a world in its own 1776 image, and its glee to see the end of monarchy in Egypt and later in Iraq in 1958 when the royal family was slaughtered in front of its own palaces, completely backfired. What America wanted was democracy. What it got were military dictatorships far more autocratic and tyrannical than the royalty ever was. The name "republic" did not a democracy make. All Farouk could do was sit on the Via Veneto and say "I told you so." He didn't even bother. That was no consolation to him.

Here Farouk was, in modern terms, the father of his country whose baby had been taken away from him. Instead of being venerated as the George Washington of Egypt, the man who ended British colonialism and established a nation once and for all, Farouk was lampooned as the Diamond Jim Brady of the dolce vita, the avatar of extravagance and decadence and hot times in the Cold War era. Few remember King Farouk as a leader any more than they do King Zog, or King Tut, for that matter. To most he was an icon of excess and nothing more. Yet he *was* a leader faced with an impossible task of leadership that remains unresolved today. The tragedy of King Farouk is that he almost pulled it off.

The stories never end. Barbara Hutton used to tell her friends how she met Farouk in Paris in 1954 and felt terribly sorry for him in exile. Having spent time in Egypt in the mid-1930s, when Farouk had just ascended to the throne and remembering his sheer perfection, Hutton was shocked and saddened to see how far the mighty had fallen. Back in Manhattan, she decided to send Farouk a gift. She went to the store A la Vieille Russie on East 59th Street and purchased a jewel-encrusted antique tureen for fifty thousand dollars. She had it packed, insured, and sent to Rome. A month or so later, Hutton received at her Paris apartment a large package from

Rome. She opened it, and there was the tureen again, with no explanatory note. Taking out the tureen, it seemed much heavier than when she bought it. She opened it and was horrified. The tureen was packed with dried excrement. It is a commentary on Hutton's own perversity that she became fascinated by what kind of excrement it was. At first she assumed it was camel dung, but then she realized there were no camels in Rome. She sent a sample to a laboratory. The analysis came back. It was human dung. Further inquiry into this bizarre transaction revealed to Hutton that Farouk must have mistakenly thought the tureen was a chamber pot, which, she learned, according to etiquette (though probably not codified in the *Abdine Protocols)* was one of the most insulting offerings one could receive. She concluded that Farouk had responded in kind. The two millionaires never saw each other again.

Such was the Farouk apocrypha. Everyone has a tale; everyone swears it's true. John Brinton, the American military attaché in Egypt during World War II and son of one of the judges of the Mixed Courts, claims to be the only man to ever sleep with Farouk. It was right after the war at a house party on the beach outside Alexandria after a very late midnight supper where Farouk won a quail-eating contest. (He ate fifty to Brinton's thirty-six.) Farouk thought it would be great fun to "camp out" and dispatched Antonio Pulli back to Montazah to bring him pajamas and a shaving kit. Everyone in the house was doubling up for the slumber party, and Farouk insisted on being one of the guys. The bedmate he drew was Brinton, who had never slept with royalty. Farouk's only request was that he sleep on the outside of the bed, which was placed against the wall in case he had to make a quick getaway. The king was always alert to the possibility of an assassination in those bloody days. As it turned out, both Farouk and Brinton slept like kings.

In a small walk-up flat off Eaton Square, Gertie Wissa, a tiny woman with a regal British accent, wrapped in an ancient Egyptian silk shawl, talks about the days before the revolution. "I warned my father that there might be a coup and that maybe we should get our money out, and he laughed and said, 'We *are* Egypt. They can't take our own country away from us. It's all ours and has been for four thousand years.' That arrogance lost us everything." The Wissas were the greatest Coptic family in Egypt. Gertie Wissa grew up in a palace in Upper Egypt, where her parents entertained notables from

all over Africa and Europe. She had two pet lion cubs, countless
Nubian servants, and a French chef trained by Escoffier. Now she
supports herself as a bridge teacher. "I never thought about money
until 1952. Now it's all I think about."

Gertie Wissa is part of the pasha diaspora that occurred with the
fall of Farouk in 1952. Most of them fled to England, France, Switzerland, or Lebanon, and most of them, like the Wissas, had not
prepared for the contingency by stashing money abroad. They
owned the land, and hence the country, and couldn't imagine not
owning it. As with Farouk, it was hubris and it was fiscally fatal. A
few of them had race horses abroad they could sell, or villas on the
Riviera; most had nothing other than charm and grace, which were
not very negotiable. Unprepared to work, unprepared for anything
except balls and hunts and grand tours, the pashas of Egypt went
the way of the cotton planters of the post-bellum South, who were
similarly unprepared for survival in the real world. That way was
genteel oblivion. Today Egypt has fifty thousand millionaires, but
these rich are different from the pashas. When asked if the al
Fayeds, the Egyptian plutocrats who own Harrods and other prime
chunks of England, might have had any dealings with King Farouk,
Gertie Wissa laughs loudly. "How could they know Farouk? How
could they know that world? These people *made* their money."

Also making money today is Jackie Lampson, Lady Killearn, in
her seventies yet extremely sprightly and as vivaciously girlish as
she was when she was the queen of the diplomatic corps in Egypt.
Lord Killearn, Sir Miles, retired after two years as special commissioner in Southeast Asia. He spent the rest of his life in the House of
Lords and stalking deer in Scotland. He died at eighty-four in 1964,
a year before Farouk. Lord and Lady Killearn lived in their own
stately home, Haremere Hall, in East Sussex near Glyndebourne
and Hastings, a seventeenth-century Tudor manor house set on a
baronial estate of 140 acres. Now Lady Killearn does a booming
business renting out Haremere Hall to tourists by the night and to
corporations for weekend business retreats. In her promotional bro-
chure, she writes:

> Today I share my home with my guests because I feel it is
> much too fine a place to be shut away from the world. Also I
> love entertaining—perhaps because of the days when my late

husband, Lord Killearn, was British Ambassador in Cairo and
our homes were the setting for so many glittering occasions.

Recalling those glittering evenings, Lady Killearn describes Farouk as a clumsy dancer, an uninspired conversationalist, and very
ill at ease. "He stood around and glowered like waiters who are
anxious to get rid of the last patrons and close up for the night."
Waving her gold filigree Egyptian fan, she talked about the crack-of-
dawn duck shoots in the Fayoum, the silence of the reeds, the rustle
of the birds, the kill. The only woman at these all-boy shooting
fests, the doll-like ambassadress scoffs at being a good sport for her
giant husband, going along for the kill. On the contrary. "I *wanted*
to shoot them," she declares. Reflecting on "Monty" and "Winston" and the gay life of wartime Cairo, Lady Killearn admits she
never got to know many Egyptians, then gets in one more lick,
posthumously, for Sir Miles. "Farouk just wasn't prepared to be
king." Then she goes back to the balls, those moonlit nights on the
embassy veranda overlooking the Nile with the graceful feluccas at
full sail, dreamily drifting by. . . .

Barbara Skelton, too, can't forget the feluccas, an entire flotilla of
them, strung up with candles, a million flickering fireflies on the
water to salute the young Adonis who strode down the red-carpeted
gangplank of the *Viceroy of India,* home from England to become
king of Egypt. The crowds in Alexandria sang and danced with joy
over their new leader, and Barbara Skelton swooned.

Today Alexandria is a melancholy ghost town. The ghosts include Ptolemy and Cleopatra and the Pharos lighthouse and the
library and Justine, for even the Alexandria of the war and the early
fifties is gone today. What remains are a few boarded-up mansions
amid the many abandoned skeletal high rises that crowd the once-
fabled corniche, rotting in the salt air of the cold blue Mediterranean. Ras-el-Tin, where Farouk abdicated, is sealed off as a naval
installation, while Montazah, where Farouk played his last carefree
hours before his fall, is also closed to the public, except for the
windswept gardens dotted with grotesque bunkerlike modern resort
cottages built by the Free Officers as the holiday spoils of their coup
d'état. As with everything in post-Farouk Egypt, *spoils* is the operative word.

Cairo is a carbon monoxide pandemonium of industrialists in
Mercedes that can't move, kaftaned, water-pipe-smoking sheikhs

who know it's wiser not to even *try* to move, fundamentalist women behind the veil waiting for deliverance, anxious soldiers waiting for the apocalypse. At the Gezira Sporting Club, where Egyptians used to be excluded, anyone can join. The most sporting activity taking place is local musclemen lifting weights, and the only foreigners there are a few American embassy children, preppy types playing squash on courts that, like everything in Cairo, have seen better days. The sweeping polo fields have long been abandoned to the weasels.

Outside Gezira, fly-studded whole carcasses of lamb hang in front of butcher shops, next door to which are boutiques selling Porsche sunglasses and Armani ties. The hot seller in bookstores is a paperback whose cover features two bulging breasts under a skin-tight sweater with a Star of David dangling in between. Above it all flies the latest tourist attraction, the "King Tut" hot air balloon, boasting its own cellular phone on which to call home while soaring over the pyramids.

At the foot of the citadel, where Mohammed Ali consolidated his power in a mass massacre of his Mameluke rivals in 1811, is the mosque of his late dynasty, El Rifaii. Here amid the wails of prayer and the sweet scents of sandalwood, Khedive Ismail is buried, and his son, Sultan Hussein Kamil, and his other son, King Fuad, all in great marble sarcophagi. The shah of Iran, to whom Egypt gave sanctuary when no one else would, is also interred here, in an imposing onyx tomb with the inscription "In the name of God, be merciful and compassionate." King Farouk always hoped that he would be buried there, a wish that Nasser vindictively denied. In the 1970s Anwar Sadat relented. He allowed Farouk to sleep beside his forebears under a simple white marble slab off the women's prayer area, inscribed with his dates and the notation that he "moved into God's mercy." It was the only mercy that Farouk would receive in the country where he once reigned and ruled. The tomb is there; Farouk is not. Just as his birthright to be king had been denied, so was his deathright. For some unfathomable reason, and much in Egypt is unfathomable, Farouk's body was dug up once more and reburied among the homeless squatters in one of the countless mausolea in the City of the Dead. Again, Farouk, the king of Egypt, was not allowed to rest in peace. Perhaps he never will be.

BIBLIOGRAPHY

BIOGRAPHY:

For an overview of Farouk, there have been three biographies, none enormously reliable:

McBride, Barrie St. Clair. *Farouk of Egypt.* London: Robert Hale, 1967.

McLeave, Hugh. *The Last Pharaoh.* New York: McCall, 1970.

Stern, Mike. *Farouk.* New York: Bantam, 1965.

Adel Sabit's *A King Betrayed* (London: Quartet, 1989) is the memoir of a member of the Cairo pasha elite, while Jean Bernard-Derosne's *Farouk: La Déchéance d'un Roi* (Paris: Editions Françaises d'Amsterdam, 1953) is the memoir of a French journalist in Egypt at the time of the deluge. Farouk's own self-serving memoirs, ghostwritten for him by a British journalist, were serialized in *The Empire News,* Manchester, October 1952–April 1953. Latifa Salim's *Farouk* (Cairo: Madbouli, 1989) is the latest and largest work on Farouk in Arabic.

A nanny's-eye view of Farouk's pampered, princely boyhood can be found in the serialized diaries of his Swedish governess, Gerda Sjoberg, in *Vecko Journalen,* Stockholm, 1952, Nos. 16–19. A tutor's-eye view of Farouk as a charmingly fractious adolescent is that of Sir Edward Ford in his 1937 *Journal of a Journey up the Nile with H. M. King Farouk* and in his 1937 report to Ambassador Sir Miles Lampson of his trip to the Continent and to England with Farouk and the Egyptian royal family. Both diaries were published in part in the McBride biography and graciously furnished to me in their entire form by Sir Edward.

And a mistress's-eye view of Farouk as libidinous young king is provided in Barbara Skelton's à clef novel, *A Young Girl's Touch* (London: Weidenfeld & Nicolson, 1956). Skelton's two volumes of memoirs, *Tears Before Bedtime* and *Weep No More* (London: Hamish Hamilton, 1987 and 1989) contain evocative vignettes of Farouk at the height of his power in Egypt, at the height of his sybaritism in Biarritz, and at his lowest ebb on the Via Veneto. More Swedish diaries—these about sex in dolce vita Rome with the exiled Farouk—are in Birgitta Stenberg's *Karlek i Europa* (Stockholm: Norstedts, 1981).

By far the most valuable political portrait of Farouk, biased as it may be, is in the splendidly detailed diaries of Sir Miles Lampson, Lord Killearn, which are held in their entirety at St. Antony's College, Oxford, and published in abridged form as *The Killearn Diaries 1934–1946* (London: Sidgwick and Jackson, 1972). The most eloquent British perspective on Farouk during World War II is Lawrence Grafftey-Smith's *Bright Levant* (London: John Murray, 1970). The most sympathetic is Lord William Sholto Douglas's *Years of Command* (London: Collins, 1966).

The many folders of the British Foreign Office files, particularly Egypt File 371, at the Public Record Office in Kew, contain much scattered information on Farouk. The State Department files at the Library of Congress in Washington, consisting mostly of assorted diplomatic missives and reports from the American counsels and later ambassadors in Egypt, are much sketchier than their British counterparts at the beginning of Farouk's reign but improve with time and provide insight into Egypt's postwar chaos and reign of terror, into Farouk's sangfroid on his eve of destruction, and into America's role in Farouk's fall.

There were no available government files on Farouk in his long exile. Any published information about him during this period was found in *Life, Time,* and *Newsweek; Paris-Match;* and more frequently the London papers, the *Mirror,* the *Daily Express,* the *Daily Mail,* the *Daily Telegraph,* the *Evening Standard,* and the *News of the World.* The *Ladies' Home Journal* serialized Narriman's breathless memoirs in 1952. *The New York Times* and the London *Times* have been consulted for the entire life of Farouk but contain little about the ex-king after 1952 other than his obituary.

DYNASTY

The following books provide background on the Mohammed Ali dynasty. Special among them for an entertaining and informative overview of royalty in the Islamic world is Philip Mansel's *Sultans in Splendor* (London: Andre Deutsch, 1988). The Aga Khan's *Memoirs* (London: Cassell, 1954) affords a kingly perspective on Farouk and his father. The others are:

Al Sayid Marsot, Afaf Lufti. *Egypt in the Reign of Muhammad Ali.* Cambridge: Cambridge University Press, 1984.

Chennells, Ellen. *Recollections of an Egyptian Princess.* Edinburgh: William Blackwood, 1893.

Crabites, Pierre. *Ismail: The Maligned Khedive.* London: Rutledge, 1935.

Shaarawi, Huda. *Harem Years.* New York: The Feminist Press, 1987.

Shah, Ikbal Ali. *Fuad King of Egypt.* London: Herbert Jenkins, 1936.

Tugay, Emine Foat. *Three Centuries.* London: Oxford University Press, 1963.

HISTORY

Written in 1922, E. M. Forster's *Alexandria* (London: Michael Haas, 1982) is not only a classic guidebook; it enables the reader to comprehend the incredible sweep of Egyptian history from pharaohs to Ptolemies to Romans to Muslims to Mamelukes to khedives and realize how this could have all taken place in the same country. Afaf Lufti Al-Sayyid Marsot's *A Short History of Modern Egypt* (Cambridge: Cambridge University Press, 1985) begins with the Arab invasion and makes good sense of a dizzying succession of foreign conquests. Peter Mansfield's *The British in Egypt* (New York: Holt, Rinehart and Winston, 1972) is the history of the most hated of these conquests. The nature of the white man's burden on the banks of the Nile is described in W. S. Blunt's *Secret History of the English Occupation of Egypt* (London: Fisher, Unwin, 1907), Lord Edward Cecil's *The Leisure of an Egyptian Official* (London: Hodder and Stoughton, 1921), Evelyn Baring Cromer's *Modern Egypt* (London: Macmillan, 1908), and Cairo Police Chief Sir Thomas Russell Pasha's *Egyptian Service 1902–1946* (London: John Murray, 1949). Artemis Cooper's *Cairo in the War, 1939–1945* (London: Hamish Hamilton, 1989) is a densely detailed account of the high tide and last gasp of Anglo dominion.

Other books that depict the glamour of the Farouk era in Egypt are:

Coward, Noël. *Middle East Diary.* London: Heinemann, 1944.

Dardaud, Gabriel. *Trente Ans au Bord du Nil.* Paris: Lieu Commun, 1987.

Hughes, Pennethorne. *While Shepheard's Watched.* London: Chatto and Windus, 1949.

Nelson, Nina. *Shepheard's Hotel.* London: Barrie and Rockliff, 1960.

Samson, A.E.W. *I Spied Spies.* London: Harrap, 1965.

Vickers, Hugo. *Cecil Beaton.* London: Weidenfeld and Nicolson, 1985.

For an understanding of the morass of Egyptian party politics:

Carter, B.L. *The Copts in Egyptian Politics.* Cairo: American University in Cairo Press, 1986.

Terry, Janice. *The Wafd 1919–1952.* London: Third World Centre, 1982.

Tripp, Charles. *Ali Mahir and the Palace in Egyptian Politics.* University of London. Ph.D. thesis, 1984.

For the roots of the Egyptian revolution:

Bell, John Bowyer. *Terror Out of Zion.* Dublin: Dublin University Press, 1979.

Frank, Gerold. *The Deed.* New York: Simon and Schuster, 1963.

Little, Tom. *Egypt.* London: Ernest Benn, 1958.

Mitchell, Richard. *The Society of the Muslim Brothers.* London: Oxford University Press, 1969.

Naguib, Muhammad. *Egypt's Destiny.* New York: Doubleday, 1955.

Nasser, Gamal Abdel. *Philosophy of the Revolution.* London: National Publication, House, 1954.

Sadat, Anwar. *Revolt on the Nile.* London: Allan Wingate, 1957.

Sadat, Jehan. *A Woman of Egypt.* New York: Simon and Schuster, 1987.

St. John, Robert. *The Boss.* New York: McGraw-Hill, 1960.

Vatikiotis, P.J. *The Egyptian Army in Politics.* Bloomington: Indiana University Press, 1961.

Wynn, Wilton. *Nasser of Egypt.* New York: Arlington, 1959.

Peter Mansfield's *The Arabs* (London: Allen Lane, 1976) gives a sense of Egypt's place in the Arab world. Jon Kimche's *Seven Fallen Pillars* (London: Secker and Warburg, 1950) is an excellent study of the balance of power in the Middle East that takes into account the Americans, the British, the French, and the Russians, as well as the geopolitics of Israel and oil. Miles Copeland's *The*

Game of Nations (London: Weidenfeld and Nicolson, 1969) is the provocative account by a former CIA operative of America's complicity in the overthrow of Farouk and its subsequent hoist on its own petard by Nasser.

Major Mahmoud El Gawhary's *Ex-Royal Palaces in Egypt* (Cairo: Dar Al-Maaref, 1954) is a rare and superb picture book of all of Farouk's palaces, rest houses, and love nests, written from the disapproving perspective of the Free Officers. *The Palace Collections of Egypt* (London: Sotheby and Company, 1953) is the vast catalogue of the sale of Farouk's treasures. The pornography is not included. The singular book on dolce vita Italy is *Paparazzi. Fotografie 1953–1964* (Florence: Fratelli Alinari, 1988), an Italian coffee table volume of stunning photographs and text all about Liz and Dick and Anita and Marcello and, of course, Farouk.

Roberto Orsi's *Rome After Dark* (New York: McFadden, 1962) is a nom de plume insider's account of the high- and low-jinks on and off the Via Veneto that provided Fellini with his inspiration. Itmad Khorshied's *A Witness to the Aberrations of Salah Nasir* (Cairo: Amoon Publishing Organization, 1988) is dedicated to the proposition that Farouk, among others, was assassinated by Nasser's intelligence network.

MISCELLANY

Other books consulted for this biography:

Aldridge, James. *Cairo.* Boston: Little, Brown, 1969.

Barber, Noel. *A Woman of Cairo.* London: Hodder and Stoughton, 1984.

Beaton, Cecil. *Near East.* London: Batsford, 1973.

Berger, Monroe. *The Arab World Today.* New York: Doubleday, 1962.

Blunt, W.S. *Gordon at Khartoum.* London: Fisher, Unwin, 1911.

Collins, Larry & LaPierre, Dominique. *O Jerusalem.* New York: Pocket, 1972.

Dols, Michael. *The Black Death in the Middle East.* Princeton University Press, 1977.

Durrell, Lawrence. *The Alexandria Quartet.* London: Faber and Faber, 1962.

Eden, Anthony. *Memoirs.* London: Cassell, 1960.

Glubb, J. B. *Soldiers of Fortune: The Story of the Mamluks.* New York: Stein and Day, 1973.

Hammer, Armand. *Hammer.* New York: Putnam, 1987.

Insight Guide: Egypt. Singapore: APA Publications, 1989.

Kerr, Malcolm. *The Arab Cold War.* London: Oxford University Press, 1971.

Love, Kennett. *Suez.* New York: McGraw-Hill, 1969.

Mahfouz, Naguib. *Midaq Alley.* London: Heinemann, 1975.

Richmond, John. *Egypt 1798–1952.* New York: Columbia University Press, 1977.

Rodinson, Maxime. *Israel and the Arabs.* London: Penguin, 1968.

Runciman, S. *A History of the Crusades.* Cambridge: Cambridge University Press, 1954.

Sadat, Anwar. *In Search of Identity.* New York: Harper and Row, 1977.

Shadegg, Stephen. *Clare Boothe Luce.* London: Leslie Frewin, 1973.

Slavitt, David R. *The Killing of the King.* New York: Doubleday, 1975.

Vatikiotis, P. J. *History of Egypt.* London: Weidenfeld and Nicolson, 1980.

One final possible resource. Future students of Farouk, heavily armed with patience and persistence, might attempt to pierce the veil of secrecy of the Central Intelligence Agency, which I was led to believe had extensive records relating to Farouk and Egypt. I pursued these records under the Freedom of Information Act, to no avail. I quote from the letter denying my request of July 11, 1989, signed by one John H. Wright, Information and Privacy Coordinator:

> I must advise you that, in all requests such as yours, the CIA can neither confirm nor deny the existence or nonexistence of any CIA records responsive to your request. The fact of the existence or nonexistence of records containing such information—unless, of course, it has been officially acknowledged—would be classified for reasons of national security under Section 1.3 (a) (5) (foreign relations) of Executive Order 12356.

What this ex-king, who had been dead for twenty-six years and deposed for thirty-nine, has to do with our national security, remains a complete mystery to me. Perhaps someone else may solve it.

INTERVIEWS

I would like to thank the following people for graciously sharing their memories. They are this book's greatest resource:

Egypt: Hoda and Saad Abdelnour, Neville Baird, Tahia Carioca, Princess Ulvia Halim, Mona Abdul Hamid, Prince Hassan Hassan, Amr Khalil, Soad Rashid Khalil, Amy Matouk, Raouf Mishriki, Karima Nashkat, Omar Sharif, Victor Simaika, David Sulzberger, Mourad Wahba, Carmen Weinstein, Ambassador Frank Wisner, Dodi Younes.

England: John Brinton, Mentor Cioko, Nadia Collins, Miles Copeland, Charles Fawcett, Sir Edward Ford, Farah Gutteridge, Lady Killearn, Luigi Luraschi, Philip Mansel, Christopher Moorsom, David Pelham, Princess Charmini Tirucheulam, Gertie Wissa, Caroline and Nolly Zervudachi.

France: Alice Brinton, François Casablanca, Injay Cattawi-Dumont, Yanou Collart, Olivia de Havilland, Prince Fuad and Princess Fadila, Pierre Galante, Michael Goldman, Irene Guinle, Rene Harari, Priscilla and Simon Hodgson, Princess Beris Kandouroff, Max Karkegi, Sheikh Khalil el Khoury, Kathy Nolan, Maggi Nolan, Barbara Skelton, Samir Souki, Alexandra Tuttle, Mona Younes.

Italy: Logan Bentley, Lello Bersani, Bianca Bevaqua, Gianni Bulgari, Igor Cassini, Sally Ringling Clayton-Jones, Dr. R. Coen, Norman Cohen, Harry Cushing, Alfredo Cuomo, Carlo d'Emilio, Vanni Ferrara, Oscar Florio, Guidarino Guidi, Mickey Knox, Irma Capece Minutolo, Filippo Moroni, Carlo Palazzi, Corrado Pallenberg, Giuseppe Petochi, Beverly and Curtis Bill Pepper, Claudia Ruspoli, Tazio Secchiaroli, Dr. Frank Sylvestri, Gore Vidal, Wilton Wynne, Franco Zeffirelli.

Spain: Princess Honeychile Hohenlohe, Penn Sicre.

Sweden: Birgitta Stenberg, Gustaf Von Platen.

United States: Carlo Amato, Huguette Caland, Carl Colby, William Colby, Arthur Cooper, Princess Faiza, Alan Friedman, Beth Houston, Eddie Jaffe, Kennett Love, Dr. Afaf Lufti al-Sayyid Marsot, Earl McGrath, Luis Monreal, Rospo Pallenberg, Mahmoud Sabit, Ottavio Senoret, Iris Schirmer, David R. Slavitt, Frank Snepp, Dorothy Strelsin, William Van Patten.

Special thanks: To my researchers: Matthew Negru, Cairo; Isabella Moorsom, London; Gisele Galante, Paris; Pat Myers, Washington, D.C.; Beau Cronin, Los Angeles.

To my translators: Amira Lamey, Cairo; Gioia Acon, Rome; and Camilla Magnusson, Los Angeles. To Claudia Florio, in Rome, Isabelle and Marc Hotimsky in London, Amr Khalil in Cairo, and Suzy Patterson, in Paris, for their warm hospitality. To Beatrice Stadiem and Rosemary Torigian, for their work in preparing the manuscript. To Isaac Cronin, who steered me into this project. And to Kent Carroll and Herman Graf, with whom this book originated, for their great ideas and wholehearted support.

INDEX